MILITANT WOMEN OF A FRAGILE NATION

Middle East Studies Beyond Dominant Paradigms
Peter Gran, *Series Editor*

MILITANT WOMEN
of a
Fragile Nation

MALEK ABISAAB

SYRACUSE UNIVERSITY PRESS

Copyright © 2010 by Syracuse University Press

Syracuse, New York 13244-5290

All Rights Reserved

First Edition 2010

10   11   12   13   14   15   6   5   4   3   2   1

∞ The paper used in this publication meets the minimum requirements
of the American National Standard for Information Sciences—Permanence
of Paper for Printed Library Materials, ANSI Z39.48-1992.

All photographs courtesy of author.

Song lyrics from the musical *Mawsim al-'Izz* (Season of Glory) are quoted
with the kind permission of Rahbani Brothers.

For a listing of books published and distributed by Syracuse University Press,
visit our Web site at SyracuseUniversityPress.syr.edu.

ISBN: 978-0-8156-3212-2

Library of Congress Cataloging-in-Publication Data

Abisaab, Malek Hassan.

  Militant women of a fragile nation / Malek Abisaab. — 1st ed.

    p. cm. — (Middle East studies beyond dominant paradigms)

  Includes bibliographical references and index.

  ISBN 978-0-8156-3212-2 (cloth : alk. paper)

  1. Women tobacco workers—Lebanon—Social conditions.   2. Women tobacco
workers—Political activity—Lebanon—History.   3. Tobacco industry—Lebanon—History.
4. Tobacco workers—Labor unions—Lebanon—History.   5. Working class women—
Lebanon—Social conditions.   6. Women in the labor movement—Lebanon—History.
7. Women's rights—Lebanon—History.   I. Title.

  HD6073.T62L433 2009

    331.4'83371095692—dc22   2009039098

Manufactured in the United States of America

To the memory of Walid al-Shami and Ziad Abisaab

MALEK ABISAAB is an assistant professor of history at McGill University, Montreal, Canada. His research and teaching investigate women, gender, and labor in Middle Eastern–Islamic societies, particularly in connection to colonialism, the nation-state, and the family. His research draws upon interdisciplinary approaches and comparative frameworks of inquiry. He has written articles for *Comparative Studies of South Asia, Africa and the Middle East, Journal of Women of the Middle East and the Islamic World,* and *Journal of Women's History.* With Rula Jurdi Abisaab, he is also the coauthor of *The Shi'ites in Colonial and Sovereign Lebanon: Modernism, Islamic Militancy, and the Civil Arena* (forthcoming).

Contents

Maps and Illustrations

Maps

Illustrations

Tables

Acknowledgments

I AM INDEBTED TO several people for their professional and personal assistance during the writing of this book. When I was a graduate student at Binghamton University (State University of New York), Donald Quataert helped shape my scholarly orientation and skills. I deeply appreciate his insights and suggestions for developing this study. The extensive discussions I had with Rifaʻat Abou-El-Haj helped recast the theoretical underpinnings of this book. I benefited greatly from his ideas and critiques. Thomas Dublin offered critical assessment and feedback on the sources and conceptual framework. Beth Baron gave me significant advice on the approach and organization of various parts. Jean Quataert, Ken Straus, Safia Mohsen, Vinay Bahl, and Rula Jurdi helped me bring central aspects of this study into sharper focus.

Thanks to a research grant from Arab Aid International provided through Mansur Al-Saud and Prince Turki Bin Abdul Aziz in 1996, I obtained significant data from the French archives in Paris and Nantes. In Lebanon, Nazih Hamzi, the chair of the People's Democratic Party, and Lebanese deputies Zahir al-Khatib and Akram Shuhayyib offered me access to the management of the Régie Co-Intéressee Libanaise des Tabacs et Tombacs and its archives. ʻIsam Jurdi and Adib Abu Habib's expertise on the labor movement and our discussions clarified several points in my study. Because of them, the material of the National Confederation of Lebanese Workers and Employees was made available to me. Régie employees provided much of the quantitative data I needed for my project. I thank Nasif Siqlawi, general director; Kamal ʻAtrisi, director of personnel; Kamal Yatim; Husayn Subayti; Rafiq Subayti; ʻAbdul Aziz Harfush; and Yusuf Hariri. Research assistants Sanaʻ ʻAwada and Layla Khalil were excellent in helping me interview the workers.

I also thank my colleagues and friends at McGill and Akron Universities, who provide a collegial working atmosphere. Special thanks go to Michelle Hartman,

Laila Parsons, Robert Wisnovsky, Wael Hallaq, and Charry Karamanoukian, whose intellectual exchanges and camaraderie have enriched my thinking about gender and history. I am grateful to the staff and librarians at the Islamic Studies Library and McLennan for their help and support.

I am chiefly indebted to the women workers of the Régie who form the mainstay of this volume. A number of scholars and friends also provided me with moral and intellectual support: Nada Saab, Suheil Abdallah, Ramzi Bou Shahine, Nazih Richani, Hamid Irbouh, Mona Kaidbey, Jihad Shahif-Jurdi, Tony Haykal, Rita Hamdan, Muhammad Hashisho, Ghazi Abi Saab, Tracey Jean Boisseau, Kirk Hoppe, and Huda ʿAbd al-Baqi. Special thanks go to Karen Flynn, who graciously read and edited the manuscript.

I am also very grateful to the team at Syracuse University Press: Peter Gran, Mary Selden Evans, Marcia Hough, Annie Barva, and others.

I thank Rula Jurdi, my partner, my comrade and guiding light, and I owe much to Zeyad and Rahwie, our sons, who renew my life with their hopes. Last but not least, I am indebted to members of my family in New York and Lebanon who went to great lengths to help me complete this work. I thank my brothers Walid, Tariq, Rafiq, and Tawfiq for their kind support, and I remember Ziad, who was exceptional and died young. My mother, Zahia, and my sisters—Najat, Nawal, and Amal—evoked my early appreciation for women's work and worlds. Special thanks also go to my other family—Huda Attallah Jurdi and Anis, Fadi, Hiba, Janan, and Amer Jurdi. Adelle Jurdi (Dida) was an inspiring friend who passed away too soon.

Introduction

LITTLE HAS BEEN WRITTEN about the transformation of Arab society, its postcolonial history, and the constitution of its modern nationhood from the perspective of workingwomen. My study delineates the history of working-women in Lebanon's tobacco industry. This history is woven with strong and resilient threads of labor militancy, resistance to French colonial rule (1918–46), and opposition to the Lebanese state as a modern tribal-ethnic hegemony tied to an orbit of capitalist relations and ideas.[1] The economic system that emerged in Lebanon during the French colonial period aimed to enhance capital in the arena of commerce and entrepreneurial service rather than in industrial and agricultural production. By the 1930s, this arena of capitalist relations became the hallmark of Lebanon's liberal economy and created a new basis for sectarian divisions regulated and controlled by the national political elite. This history of tobacco workingwomen underscores their gendered and class-based resistance to Lebanon's tribal-ethnic hegemony.

Numerous women who went to work for the French tobacco monopoly, the Régie Co-Intéressée Libanaise des Tabacs et Tombacs, widely known as "the Régie," slowly experienced the social and political contradictions inherent in a transition from farm to factory, made selective adaptations to industrialization, and devised complex strategies to overcome precapitalist values. They negotiated patriarchal male authority and developed new roles in connection to the factory, urban culture, and new public spaces. Women's experiences in collective action and their leadership in labor organization during protests and strikes debunk prevalent assumptions about women's marginality in Arab societies. This focus on workingwomen in the tobacco industry brings a new dimension to the story of the "nation" even though a gendered division of labor lies at the center of the picture that the Lebanese state paints of itself. The state's acts of violence against these workingwomen stemmed from its interest in preventing an alteration in gendered power relations and divisions of labor. As such, the story of this "nation" also is ostensibly about gender and gendered authority, and, once told from the women's perspective, it takes a new turn. "Nation" becomes less homogenously omnipresent and more varied, challenged, and occasionally undermined by changing class and gendered formations. From the perspective of these workingwomen specifically, militancy against the state becomes an occasion for contesting gendered discrimination and promoting an empowered version of womanhood.

Lebanon and the Régie

The earliest entity identified as the Lebanese "nation" surfaced in the 1940s around the time that Syria and Grand Liban (Greater Lebanon) won independence from the French. Any reference to the "Lebanese" before the 1940s is a reference to a regional or colonial identity because the Lebanese were the inhabitants of Grand Liban during the French mandate (1920–43). The peoples of Ottoman Mount Lebanon also were described as "Lebanese" between 1861 and 1920, when this region enjoyed an autonomous political status.[2]

Established in 1920, Grand Liban encompassed Mount Lebanon, Tripoli, Beirut, Sidon, Tyre, Jabal 'Amil, and the Biqa', all of which form modern-day Lebanon (map 1). Some of the contradictions in the nascent Lebanese nation were reflected in the presence of a threatened peasantry and small producers, a budding industrial bourgeoisie, a converted feudalism, and an ongoing tension between Arab and Lebanese nationalisms. When the French armies landed on the coasts of Syria and Lebanon, they encountered arduous socioeconomic and living conditions because people were suffering still from the trauma of the famine that occurred in Ottoman Syria and Lebanon during World War I (1914–18). Some hoped that the French would help the economy prosper and create more jobs opportunities. These hopes did not last long because a major economic crisis unfolded in the country as an effect of the worldwide Great Depression beginning in the late 1920s.

From 1930 to 1935, tobacco planting, manufacturing, and trading expanded dramatically. Whether in the South, some parts of Mount Lebanon, or the North, every peasant family planted tobacco instead of garden vegetables. The

1. Modern-day Lebanon. © Maps.com. Reproduced with permission.

French, in the first fifteen years of their mandate over Syria and Lebanon, dismissed requests made repeatedly by Lebanese deputies (in the Chamber of Deputies) to increase the custom tariffs on imported tobacco.[3] The low custom tariffs disrupted local production and put Syrian-Lebanese tobacco growers and workers in a fierce competition with the regional and international market. They also led to overproduction, the smuggling of foreign tobacco, and a decline in state revenues. The French blamed tobacco overproduction on the brief period of autonomy in tobacco cultivation—mainly during the banderole system—as well as on the decentralization of tobacco sales and a lack of management of imported tobacco.[4]

For the nascent industrial bourgeoisie who invested in the silk industry, the demand for Lebanese silk in European markets started to decline. Several scholars attribute this decline to the intense competition coming from Asian silk, especially the Indian, Japanese, and Chinese varieties.[5] Japanese raw-silk exports in particular acquired a prominent place in the market and thrived because of their low price and rapid technological developments in Japanese sericulture and silk-reeling industries in the late nineteenth century.

During the self-rule (Mutasarrifiyya) of Mount Lebanon (1860–1918), the production of Lebanese silk sustained remarkable growth, whether in the reeling manufactures or in the cultivation of mulberry trees for silkworm nourishment. By 1909, 65 percent of the economic enterprises in the Syrian and Lebanese provinces were involved in one way or another with the silk economy.[6] Owing to serious competition with Japanese and Chinese raw-silk materials, the industry began to decline at the turn of the century; it regained strength for a short time in the 1920s, but then disappeared from the world market in the early 1930s after the world depression. Paul Saba asserts that the continuous use of more traditional methods in Lebanese silk production, cultivation, and manufacturing caused its decline in spite of growth experienced in other regions of the world where more modern techniques were employed. It was a clear example of some of "the forces at work to retard capitalist development in the Lebanese economy of this period." The economic enterprises established in Lebanon in the first half of the twentieth century reflected a declining agricultural foundation and a growing investment in service areas and tourism. Saba indicates that the majority "of small cultivators lived either in debt or in heavy reliance on remittances from émigré relatives."[7] Capital resources were invested in areas such as transit, retail trade, import-export, and real estate in Beirut—all of which fell outside the vital productive circuit of the economy, thus giving rise to a Lebanese comprador class.[8] The latter capitalized on commerce and services as the principal economic functions of the Lebanese economy and accordingly shaped the postindependence Lebanese polity.

The Régie was and still is a major Lebanese economic enterprise whose workforce reached 3,609 in 1966. Women made up a little more than 40 percent of this workforce. By 1970, more than 300,000 Lebanese relied on it for their livelihood, including 45,000 tobacco farmers.[9] Since the 1943 inception of an independent Lebanon, the Régie workers, in particular women, were renowned for their radicalism and protests against management and the Lebanese government. These women—who came from several religious, regional, and political backgrounds representing Lebanon's diverse constituencies—contributed greatly to the history of the Lebanese labor movement.

The formative capital of the tobacco monopoly was divided as follows: 30 percent was controlled by the powerful Libano-Syrian tobacco company that was formed mostly by French and European capitalists and that would administer the tobacco monopoly; 60 percent was run by the previous tobacco manufacturers in Syria and Grand Liban; and 10 percent was organized by the people of the states falling under the French mandate. This arrangement secured the hegemony of French and Western capital over Lebanese tobacco. With the independence of Syria and Lebanon, the French authorities transferred the control over the tobacco monopoly and other concessionary companies to the local governments.[10] In 1952, the united Syrian-Lebanese Régie came to an end when the Syrian government decided to take control of the Syrian branch of the Régie.[11] In 1959, the Lebanese government attempted to strengthen its role in the Régie by granting to the Ministry of Finance more power in the Régie's administration.[12] The terms of the 1935 concessionary law stipulated that the monopoly over tobacco would end in 1960, at which time the Régie's privileges and properties would be transferred to the Lebanese government. Nonetheless, the Régie continued to monopolize all tobacco production up until 1991, when the Lebanese state nationalized this important economic and financial asset.[13]

The Régie did not always conform to the rules and regulations that initially governed its production processes, nor did it fulfill its promise to contribute to the welfare of the Lebanese people. The *Cahier des charges*, which embodied the

by-laws for operating the Régie, initially decreed that the company should promote the national production of tobacco and limit to 10 percent the use of foreign
tobacco in manufacturing cigarettes. Yet for more than three decades before the
Régie became a government company, it remained free of oversight and was not
subject to any enforced national restrictions. This freedom encouraged it to delay
the production of national tobacco brands, which in turn mitigated the shift in
the consumers' preference for foreign cigarettes.[14] The change in smokers' taste
was clearly observed in an upsurge in the sale of American-blend Lebanese cigarettes from four tons in 1966 to more than thirty tons in 1968. A few years later
this taste gave way to imported foreign cigarettes, especially American ones.[15]
These transformations also could be observed in the figures offered by the Régie
itself (table 1).

It was not until 1973 that the Régie introduced two American-blend Lebanese cigarettes—Cedars and Byblos—to the local market, which for a short
period of time gained an exceptional reputation among smokers.[16] Despite
efforts to retain smokers' loyalty, and owing to the impact of the Lebanese Civil
War from 1975 to 1991, however, the manufacturing of these brands steadily
decreased, and the smoking of American cigarettes continued to rise. The Régie
essentially became an agency for importing foreign cigarettes.[17] In addition, for
decades Lebanese tobacco farmers engaged in long and bloody confrontations

TABLE 1. Sale of cigarettes in Lebanon, 1971–1973

Year	Lebanese	Foreign
1971	35%	65%
1972	25%	75%
1973	20%	80%

Sources: "RÉGIE CO-INTÉRESSÉE LIBĀNĀISE DES TĀBĀCS ET TOMBĀC. ASSEMBLÉE GÉNÉRALE ORDI-
NAIRE DES ACTIONNAIRES du 26 Mai 1972. RAPPORTS présentés par le Conseil d'Administration et par
les Commissaires de Surveillance, EXERCISE 1971"; "ASSEMBLÉE GÉNÉRALE ORDINAIRE DES ACTION-
NAIRES du 28 Mai 1973. RAPPORTS présentés par le Conseil d'Administration et par les Commissaires de Surveillance, EXERCICE 1972"; "ASSEMBLÉE GÉNÉRALE ORDINAIRE DES ACTIONNAIRES du 21 Mai 1974.
RAPPORTS présentés par le Conseil d'Administration et par les Commissaires de Surveillance. EXCERCICE
1973" (annual reports of the Régie Board of Directors and Budget Commission, Exercises 1971, 1972, 1973, presented to the General Assembly of Shareholders on May 26, 1972, May 28, 1973, and May 21, 1974), private collection of Jacques Dagher, Beirut.

with the Régie representatives and the Lebanese police over the acquisition of cultivable land, licenses for the planting of tobacco, and the fixing of fair prices for tobacco crops.[18]

Theoretical Framework

My particular position within the historiography on Arab Middle Eastern women was crystallized as I investigated, first, the connections among gender, class, and the nation-state, and, second, the relationship between anticolonial struggle and peasant culture, on the one hand, and workingwomen's radicalism, on the other. Three interconnected points emerged from this investigation as part of my overall theoretical framework. I found that the term *social process* rather than *culture* is more adequate for situating and interpreting workingwomen's history. An approach based on social process, as Ramkrishna Mukherjee describes it, takes into account economic, political, and social variables that modify and are modified by cultural values over a particular historical period.[19] An awareness of the nature and manifestation of these variables in the Lebanese context before and after French colonial rule is necessary for understanding the cultural meaning given to women's production and social roles.[20] The cultural approach that I critique was prevalent in much of the literature on the "Muslim Woman" as defined by an "Islamic" normative religious or cultural order. Advocates of this cultural approach often point to Muslim–Middle Eastern traditions as the reason why women may avoid undertaking industrial labor and collective political action.[21] Culture and, more specifically, religion are predominantly the points of reference in explaining the inferior position of women in Middle Eastern–Islamic societies, often to such an extent that one gains the impression that Arab women do not work at all. As Peter Gran notes, such a narrow-minded assumption runs counter to the basic premises of social theory, for if women workers do not exist in the Middle East, then only men are social agents and consequently the sole substance for social theory.[22] In the 1990s, Valentine M. Moghadam joined forces with a few young scholarly voices to break away from the view that the "intrinsic properties of Islam" or Islam's patriarchal character dictates the position of women in the Middle East. She considers class, the gender system, the state, and development policies operating within the greater capitalist world system as the true basis for women's status.[23]

The cultural approach gives primary weight to kinship, religion, ethnicity, and gender in determining working-class "consciousness" and action. Moving beyond this approach, I argue that workingwomen lived through multiple experiences of class, sect, and gender, and that these categories were neither constantly nor inherently in contradiction with each other. Workers utilized features of kinship, gender, family, and religion to enhance their adaptation to industrial work culture and urbanity. Workingwomen also expressed an appreciation for widely cast identities and class-based action. When Lebanese tobacco women worked with unionists and socialists, they often subordinated gender identities to class identity. At times, they rejected protective male paternalism, but at other times they manipulated it to enhance their roles as women and workers who were navigating their way strategically within the confines of a tribal-ethnic system and its wider oppressive capitalist orbit.[24] In this way, social class faced competition and "cross-breeding" with gender, sect, and religion.[25] Dipesh Chakrabarty, a major proponent of the subaltern school, accepts one version of this cultural approach. He argues that the subaltern classes carry these perceptual categories "in their own heads" and are invariably prevented by the rigidity of these categories from developing rationalized national and class identities.[26] My findings show, however, that people assign multiple cultural meanings to various aspects of sect and familialism, and as such these meanings are not reified entities that can be treated as either intrinsic or biological. The 1963 and 1965 strikes of Lebanese tobacco workingwomen and men, for instance, provide ample evidence against the subaltern emphasis on the ahistorical primacy of culture.

This study demonstrates that the formulation of workingwomen's identity is often negotiated and renegotiated within several personal, social, and political settings. As women navigate familial male control and state discrimination, they partake in communal, sectarian, and national activities—all the while aiming to improve their lives as female industrial workers. Class dynamics perpetuate and transform identity. Suad Joseph treats confessionalism or sectarianism adequately as a developmental social phenomenon instead of as a time-honored reality embedded in the nature of premodern Middle Eastern societies. She accurately argues that sects are not natural groupings, but ones that have been influenced by the institutional structure of governmental offices and organizations that allocate and mediate services and benefits on a sectarian basis, thus pressuring citizens to employ sectarianism as a political tool for resolving their daily problems and meeting their daily needs.[27]

The second theoretical point that I raise in this study is that without a close interpretation of class dynamics, we cannot gain a full understanding of the process of gender. My study questions the substitution of gender analysis for class analysis—as suggested, for example, by Joan Scott.[28] Relations of class and gender were historically intertwined in both the domicile and the workplace, as well as in processes of production and reproduction. Neither class nor gender constitutes an independent or exclusive source of group identity or group difference in the history of labor movements or in resistance to the state.[29] There is clear variability and at times contradiction between men and women in the experiences of work and culture, but not to the extent of true exclusiveness and complete disjunction. The story of radicalized tobacco workingwomen forces us to "reintegrate" class formation and gendered conflicts into Lebanese national history, thereby illuminating the place of class alliances and gender politics in the state's ideological makeup and in its actions toward its workingwomen citizens.

The third theoretical thread in this study advances a particular interpretation of patriarchy in connection to state and society. I draw upon Peter Gran's discussions of neoliberalism in the Middle East and his conceptualization of the Lebanese state as one exhibiting features of an ethnic-tribal form, otherwise referred to as "sectarian," whose constituent citizens are organized hierarchically as endogamous sectarian entities. Gran situates the debate on women's work and culture/religion in the Middle East in connection to the ideology of neoliberalism. He suggests that after 1970, many worldwide ruling classes, political leaders, and religious authorities allied together to impose liberalism and a new world order aimed at resubordinating women and forcing them to conform to the restructuring of the world economies. According to Gran, contemporary neoliberalism is an outgrowth of the type of political economy often found in historical tribal-ethnic states, a form of hegemony among many different models of modern hegemonies. This hegemonic system works vehemently against the formation of middle classes, and its proponents are "most apprehensive about the idea of development." In the late nineteenth century, liberalism was initially adopted by the leaders of the tribal-ethnic states when, after World War I, "most other countries shifted to developmentalism."[30] My study questions the alleged capacity of economic liberalism to liberate women. It also probes the foundational premises of "development" associated with the spread of capitalism worldwide. Western development models have allowed certain openings for women in the market, but they have also often left unchallenged the foundations of the tribal-ethnic hegemony that has hampered women's autonomy and empowerment.

The form of political economy based on tribal-ethnic liberalism (or neoliberalism) not only diffuses the shared experiences of exploitation between workingwomen and men, but also encourages "a collision between the man and the woman," as Gran puts it.[31] Western liberal standards have often considered women's work in "developing" countries to be associated with democracy and progress. As such, liberal standards are seen as signs of a healthy society on the path to gender equality.[32] For instance, in 1982 the United States Agency for International Development (USAID) funded two conferences on women and work in the "Third World" organized by the Center for the Study, Education, and Advancement of Women at the University of California, Berkeley. The conference participants focused on the impact of industrialization on women's work in a number of African, Asian, Latin American, and Middle Eastern countries. Some participants concluded that poor economies and cultural impediments (read *religion* in the Middle East context) were two principal factors that undermined working conditions for women and perpetuated their inferior position in their respective societies.[33] There was unfortunately no concurrent consideration given to the role of Western neoimperialism in supporting hegemonic systems in the Middle East, nor was there discussion of these systems' particular use of "culture" in manipulating socioeconomic discrepancies to prevent radical social transformations.

Patriarchal control is an expression of this tribal-ethnic hegemony and of some of the incongruent and incompatible political elements therein. One example of such incompatibility can be seen in the state's attempt to wrest patriarchal control away from "family men" and heads of households with the goal of harnessing women's labor. Workingmen benefited from forfeiting certain elements of this power, and religious leaders found themselves at times exchanging one form of patriarchy, such as confining women's work to the household, for another, such as controlling the income generated from their work in silk factories.[34] This complex picture reveals that patriarchy cannot endure for long or unchangingly, but eventually gives way to strategic female negotiation in determining both family and state authority. My position draws upon Chandra Mohanty's critique of Western feminist writings on patriarchy as an invariable notion of "'Third

World difference'—that stable, ahistorical something that oppresses most if not all the women in these countries." Indeed, as Mohanty notes, there is no universal patriarchal framework unless one assumes a worldwide male conspiracy or a "monolithic, ahistorical power structure."[35] Women and at times men have challenged the normative conduct of the tribal-ethnic hegemony and its forms of patriarchal control. Workingwomen are not "passive victims of capitalism," but rather effective strategists advancing their own forms of resistance. At critical historical junctures, a restructuring of relations among workers, capital, and the state has produced new perceptions about women's labor and social roles. In this respect, my study questions static definitions and fixed accounts of patriarchy.[36] I suggest that we take not only a closer look at the material basis of patriarchy, as other Marxist feminists have done, but at patriarchy's place in the interconnections among capitalism, the class system, and the unpredictable circumstances that are inherent to specific local histories. I do not start with the assumption that men can impose an undifferentiated and ideal patriarchal system that fully controls women's labor and sexuality. Rather, I see women as imbued with power to subvert and take away from men's dominance within that patriarchal system, particularly because it is a system riddled with contradictions and tensions. Changes in rural economies and urban labor markets under the influence of global capitalist forces have decreased the efficacy of precapitalist patriarchal and familial control over women, especially because such control is no longer always beneficial to men, in spite of their "intention" and rhetoric about wanting to continue to control women's labor and sexuality.[37] In this light, Deniz Kandiyoti's analysis of women's strategies in negotiating patriarchy is particularly insightful, and her term *patriarchal bargain,* used to describe this intentional maneuvering, is especially useful.[38]

Methodology

The scarcity of quantitative data in the form of factory records, archival reports, and primary sources such as memoirs or letters poses a major obstacle to the study of women's history, let alone of women's labor, in Middle Eastern societies.[39] The dearth of information on women is compounded by the outlook of official reporters, journalists, unionists, labor activists, and scholars alike, who in their narratives tended to unwrite women's voices, hopes, and struggles.[40] Records focused on unionized workers or socialist activists commonly leave out most of working-women's labor struggles because many of these struggles fall outside categories of "organized labor" and remain marginal to trade unions and Communist parties.[41] The Communists cast their activism predominantly in masculine terms and reinforced women's vulnerability through their hierarchies. Middle Eastern labor movements were usually tailored to men and accorded little space to women's needs and forms of leadership. Most of the existing literature on Middle Eastern workers looks mainly at organized labor movements and formal activists—that is, at only a section of workingmen.[42] In addition, the male-centered language of labor unions and Communists went unnoticed, and positions specific to women were suppressed in pursuit of a genderless class solidarity. Yet "genderless" in this context really meant a marginalization of women's styles of leadership. It also meant hampering the development of effective methods to attract working-women because of the masculinized culture of labor activism.

To pursue this study, I had to extract from these union and party records as well as from newspaper articles the ambiguous and silent spaces that pertain to women. In addition, I utilized oral history and popular culture to highlight central aspects of women's experiences at home and on the shop floor. In 1997, I also conducted a survey of 356 workers—69 men and 287 women—composing more than one-fifth of the total Régie workforce at the time. I also undertook a quantitative analysis of empirical data obtained from the Régie that covered information about the gender, age, sect, geographical origin, industrial department or unit, duration of employment, and rank of workers from the 1930s to the 1960s. There unfortunately were some gaps in the data caused by the burning of the Régie records during the Lebanese Civil War (1975–90), which forced me to recast my study on a smaller scale until such time when the full empirical data, or comparative quantitative studies covering various aspects of tobacco women's history in Lebanon, are made available. Moreover, at this time the significance of various traditions of womanhood in shaping women's militancy can only be surmised because the qualitative data are not available. We need to uncover workingwomen's lives in Arab society by using both oral histories and sociological methods for quantitative and historical analysis. I tried to compensate for the absence of workingwomen's self-portrayals, letters, and memoirs by using oral histories and by thoroughly reading newspapers, journals, and reports covering labor protests to find the silent spaces workingwomen occupied.

A handful of sociological studies by Julinda Abu al-Nasr, Janet Hyde Clark, and Irene Lorfing in the 1970s and 1980s utilized surveys and other quantitative data-collection methods as a basis for their theorizing about the gender division of labor and the experiences of factory women in comparison to their male counterparts in Lebanon. Lorfing and Abu al-Nasr furnished statistical data on gender, age, and marital composition of the labor force of ten factories in suburban Beirut in 1979.[43] Clark and Lorfing also conducted a more extensive survey of fourteen factories in Beirut in 1981.[44] They compared the types of industrial tasks carried out by women and men between 1975 and 1982 in order to determine women's potential role and level of participation in Lebanese industry. Even though these two studies were limited in scope, both provided vital information that allowed me to draw important comparisons between tobacco workingwomen and others in the textile and food industries.

By examining a wide array of activities outside the union and the party, one can attempt to redress the sexual imbalance in writing about women.[45] Women's activism and militancy were sustained by women's personal ties and informal associations ranging from social and religious congregations to the Régie Women's Fund, which supported sick, disabled, and discharged women workers. Workingwomen, more so than workingmen, appeared to define their outlook and identity within the nexus of the shop floor and the household. Women's labor was critical for support of members of their extended families in the countryside as well as of their own nuclear families in suburban Beirut. I hope that future studies will investigate facets of family and community as they pertain to workingwomen. However, this study explores features of workingwomen's collective organization and radicalism against capitalists, colonialists, and the Lebanese state, which in turn led to strategic bargaining as well as open struggle against forms of family and state patriarchy.

Organization of Chapters

The first chapter highlights the shift from the silk industry to the tobacco industry from 1830 to 1935. I discuss the emerging industrial work culture in Mount Lebanon during the late nineteenth century and the extent of its influence on Lebanese workingwomen's status and outlook. Whether in cottage industries or in modern manufacturing plants, the demand for women's labor arguably increased the contradiction between preindustrial values concerning female sexual modesty and the economic need for female labor. This contradiction, appearing during a nascent phase of capitalism in Mount Lebanon, did not achieve the kind of complexity or intensity that would transform the gender structure. The nature of capitalist enterprises, the location of silk manufacturing, and the strong interconnection between workplace and familial and village circles only partially altered women's level of autonomy and their level of integration in industrial work relations.

The second chapter focuses on the varied motives and agendas of working-class and upper-class women who led and energized the opposition to the 1935 founding of the Régie in the larger context of anticolonial struggle. The formation of the Régie's labor force marked a central development in Lebanon's industrial history and in the labor movement at large. Driven by fear of displacement and unemployment, tobacco workingwomen engaged in massive protests against industrial mechanization, which nurtured their experiences in collective organization, their adaptations to industrial life, and their forceful entry into the public arenas of strikes and mass protests. However, bourgeois women faced different challenges as they negotiated with the men of their class a feminist identity as part of a discourse of nationhood and anticolonial resistance. The feminist support for the waged work of educated elite women was framed in patriotic terms. Their constructs of womanhood tied maternalism to the image of a strong nation. In comparison, the Régie workingwomen advanced an image of women that was more militant and less committed to the nationalist ideal than the image promoted by upper- and middle-class women, the "mothers of the nation." Industrial women's participation in nationalist, anticolonial struggles against the French did, however, contribute significantly to their collective identity. Colonial struggles, in turn, became strongly tied to labor and industrial conflicts. As the tobacco women and men fought for their national independence, they became workers with a common cause. In addition, I discuss how anti-imperialism was central to the ideologies of labor unionists and socialists who were active among industrial workers and whose political culture they had tried to shape since the 1940s. I also highlight how working-class experiences became congenial to a civic-national perspective.[46]

Chapter 3 is built around my assessment of industrial women's role in the emergence of labor law that signaled a new and complex phase in the relationship between industrial workers and the state. I discuss the foundations of female radicalism, its gendered style, and the role of popular political culture in sharpening women's political consciousness during the 1946 strike. Militant women who rationalized their methods of labor organization and stood in solidarity with male strikers in pursuit of central demands for permanency were neither unionized nor members of Communist and socialist parties. After the formation of the Lebanese state under the leadership of the national bourgeoisie, the workers' approach to nationalism started to change. On the one hand, they came to see the state as an extension of colonial authority and thus as an entity that could no longer propagate a unifying nationalist ideal. On the other hand, the rise of the state also created a historical pull in the opposite direction. The very process of turning subjects into citizens, as Eric Hobsbawm notes, "tends to produce a populist consciousness which is hard to distinguish from a national, even a chauvinist patriotism."[47] I also explore an experience of citizenship that was offered by the modern state through the language of law that workingwomen and men used to address their grievances against their employers and, ultimately, to confront the state itself.

Chapter 4 focuses on the composition of the Régie workforce and shifts in gender, sectarian, and family divisions between 1950 and 1980. Government neglect, urban prosperity, overpopulation, and political instability contributed to the deterioration of the Lebanese countryside and the subsequent displacement and rural-to-urban migration of many working-class families. I explore the social processes that shaped the workers' radicalism at the Régie, particularly at the Hadath plant, and the Lebanese state's reaction to it.

Chapter 5 sheds light on the historical forces that changed the nature and social meaning of women's waged work in agriculture and industry between 1950 and 1970. I try to show how the state's patriarchal moralism and the discriminatory hiring practices in industries undergoing rigorous mechanization contributed to women's low participation in industrial labor. The number of working-class women who sought waged work was much higher than the number hired by Lebanese employers. These women were not seriously hindered from seeking industrial labor by familial or moral control, as is otherwise assumed. Instead, I argue that where patriarchal resistance existed, women devised strategies to preserve their work and seek promotion, utilizing a wide range of kinship, village, sectarian, and political ties.

During the two decades following their first major strike in 1946, tobacco women made significant shifts in labor activism and in the formulation of their short- and long-term objectives, leading to their militant clash with the Régie and the state in 1963 and 1965. In chapter 6, I delineate the historical circumstances surrounding this new phase of women's militancy, the changing nature of their demands, and the approaches they took to achieve them. The tobacco women's gender-based struggles gave class and labor radicalism a new meaning. Gender emerged as a dynamic principle in the national government's treatment of industrial conflict and in the empowerment of working-class traditions.

Abbreviations

AFU	Arab Feminist Union
GCFUWE	General Confederation of the Unions of Workers and Employees
GTUTW	General Trade Union of Tobacco Workers
IRFED	Institut International de Recherche et de Formation en Vue de Développement
PLO	Palestinian Liberation Organization
URWE	Union of the Régie Workers and Employees

MILITANT WOMEN OF A FRAGILE NATION

1

From Loom to Puff

Women and Waged Labor in Colonial Lebanon

PRIOR TO WORLD WAR I (1914–18), many of the regions that made up Lebanon today were geographically and administratively part of Greater Syria in the Ottoman Empire (1516–1918).[1] Yet one particular region, Mount Lebanon (map 2), developed a semiautonomous political character between 1861 and 1920, which paved the way for the social integration of its peoples and the distillation of a protonationalist regional identity.[2] The inhabitants of Mount Lebanon, self-defined and distinguished as the "Lebanese," continued, however, to express provincial leanings alongside protonationalist ones. By the late nineteenth century, Mount Lebanon and Beirut became the center stage for significant agricultural and industrial developments and consequently new political traditions.

The experiences of peasant women were inextricably tied to shifts in patterns of rural life, in particular the organization of agricultural production and labor, as well as to shifts in the power base of provincial leaders and large landholders from the late Ottoman to the French colonial period (1920–43). The work culture and gender relations in Ottoman Mount Lebanon were not radically transformed by the rise of the silk *karkhana* (early type of silk manufacture) during the nineteenth century. Of course, these workingwomen worked in a historically transitional socioeconomic setting. On the one hand, they remained subject to precapitalist forms of labor as long as their attachment to their families was still intact. On the other hand, with the integration of Lebanon's economy into the world market, they had entered new industrial terrain with new patterns of production and labor organization. Yet what is key here is that women workers continued to reside in the patriarchal household and within its extended kinship network.[3] Women at the silk factory experienced direct parental-religious

1

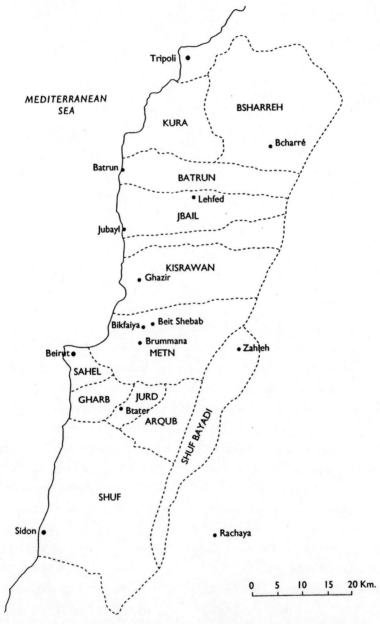

2. Mount Lebanon. From Akram Fouad Khater, *Inventing Home: Emigration, Gender, and the Middle Class in Lebanon, 1870–1920* (Berkeley and Los Angeles: Univ. of California Press, 2001), 17. © Regents of the University of California. Reproduced with permission.

supervision over their labor and personal life. Male factory owners, in their attempts to appease the religious dignitaries and the workers' families, imposed "ethical" practices such as sexual segregation at the workplace. Nevertheless, silk work also provided women with early opportunities to adapt to industrial life and work patterns, and, more important, it helped them challenge the social norms that defamed factory work as shameful.[4] At the tobacco manufacturing plants that emerged after the decline of silk factories, women obtained the least-skilled and worst-paid jobs, such as the manual sorting of raw tobacco leaves. But unlike the silk factories, these plants were located at a greater distance from the nexus of the domicile and the hometown, and they did not become the focus of religious or patriarchal discipline.

The Lebanese silk industry, which emerged in mid-nineteenth-century Ottoman Lebanon and eventually became a vital part of the broader European silk industry, started to decline in the last decades of that century owing to economic and technical developments in the international silk market. For Lebanese producers, the decreasingly profitable silk economy was replaced by a tobacco one—with its associated plantings and manufacturing—starting in the early 1900s. Tobacco work led to the rise of new societal arrangements and work patterns that decisively shaped the gender structure of society, patriarchy, and women's roles. The extension of domestic labor (with its stereotypical association with women and their "nimble hands" that were supposedly perfectly suited for the tedious and monotonous work of sorting tobacco leaves) to industrial labor contributed to manufacturers' devaluation of women's labor and justified the temporary nature of women's work. Tobacco workingwomen faced a much different world than that of the silk economy because it was one in which market forces gravitated toward a monopoly that French colonial officials, their local allies, and some members of the Lebanese elites legitimized and ruthlessly enforced.

These workingwomen's lives changed as they began to experience greater physical and social separation from home because the majority of them had to live or commute to places far away from their families. Many of these women also endured greater poverty, famine, and job loss under mechanization because, at the Régie Co-Intéressee Libanaise des Tabacs et Tombacs, the conditions were such that women dominated the least-skilled, lowest-paid, and most unstable jobs. Moreover, as these women learned of the potential support provided by the union and the Communists, they came to express greater solidarity with their male coworkers, yet they also concurrently held their own exclusively female demonstrations and formed their own delegations to articulate their particular grievances. In addition, the female-centered and cooperative nature of food production and preservation, organization of the harvest seasons, and public activities and planning that went into religious rituals also provided important opportunities for the development of workingwomen's activism before and after the French implementation of the monopoly.[5]

The French colonial authorities' creation of Grand Liban in the region of Mount Lebanon in 1920 ignited reactions ranging from ambivalence to opposition from distinct social classes and sectarian groups because it was the culmination of a political process that unfolded in 1860 during Ottoman rule following civil strife between two major sectarian groups—the Druze Muslims and the Maronite (Catholic) Christians.[6] The French, Ottoman officials, and Mount Lebanon's local leaders implemented a new political administration, known as Mutasarrifiyya. It aimed to organize and "balance" relations between the Druze and the Maronite, yet, more important, it secured the political stability necessary for the growth of French capitalist investments in the nascent silk industry of Mount Lebanon.[7] This administration also resulted in the cultivation of political and cultural ties between the French and the Maronite that laid the groundwork for the new hegemonic system that emerged in French Lebanon in 1920.[8] Herein the Maronite, in particular, became the "single most important beneficiary of the French missionary schools, hospitals, and dispensaries" and enjoyed unprecedented financial and political backing from the French government.[9]

Under this arrangement, the French aimed to integrate Lebanon within its sphere of geopolitical influence, open its markets for French economic enterprises, and eventually link them to other vital Middle Eastern cities. A mercantile-financial bourgeoisie that cut across religious sects emerged in Mount Lebanon and prospered from the Mutasarrifiyya during the mid–nineteenth century. In 1920, the French colonial government made Mount Lebanon the only region free of monopolistic regulations, allowing it to enjoy a "free enterprise system," which in turn explained why it attracted many investors.[10]

Modern industrial investments and manufacturing in Mount Lebanon were dependent on the fluctuations of the European market during the late nineteenth century and limited by the needs and interests of the local elites who were beneficiaries of the Mutasarrifiyya. For these reasons, the integration of Mount Lebanon into the world market had modest effects on the social perception of women's factory labor and on forms of patriarchal control by the family. Women's waged work, however, remained critical to the survival of parents, siblings, husbands, and children. Like other women all over the world, Mount Lebanese working-women commonly put their earnings toward better education, food, clothing, and housing for their families. Akram Fouad Khater asserts that

> Lebanese Christian peasants were caught trying to survive in the midst of those market swings. In good years, there was enough profit for the small grower to pay debts, buy more meat, and enjoy some imported luxuries. But in bad or even ordinary years the peasant became more and more indebted. Lebanese peasant men found themselves struggling not to lose their land because of their debt, while procuring sufficient funds to pay for their families' daily needs.[11]

The culture of tobacco production in the countryside and tobacco manufacturing in the city inaugurated a new phase in workingwomen's history. During this phase, peasant traditions of protesting against their landlords and political rulers found articulation at industrial sites where tobacco women worked and lived. More important, however, it was a phase in which a new level of exploitation of women's labor and domination by European capitalism emerged, and women responded through their labor and hunger protests and by merging these protests with the greater anticolonial struggle.

Producing Silk, 1880–1935

Peasant families planted mulberry trees on which silkworms fed and engaged in the manufacture of silk. The amount of profit gained by silk fabrication, along with that of cotton and wool, leads one to believe that their production was market oriented and not merely for local use.[12] The families paid Beiruti merchants interest on loans they borrowed to buy seeds, silkworms, and needed tools for the silk season. Additional household income was often derived from olive and wine production for local markets. Peasants also planted vegetables and wheat for family consumption, but regularly gave their landlords (or, more precisely, the holder of the province, the *muqati'ji*) half of the household harvest as well as additional payments for land taxes. If a peasant family did not pay the taxes in full, the landlord or his agents commonly invaded the family's residence and emptied its food stores. Peasants also were expected to perform corvée labor at the landlord's mansion and certain construction sites.

Additional demands were made of women, especially in regard to their labor and sexuality. For example, several peasant women usually served as maids in the landlord's household. Landlords also commonly expected sexual compensation, especially from destitute peasant women. For instance, a senior male peasant was often expected to "lease" or "lend" his daughter or sister to the landlord to gain exemption from a particular tax known as *rasim al-nukah,* or the landlord's "natural" right to have sexual intercourse with a bride on the first night of mar-riage.[13] Despite women's extensive labor on the land and in the rural domicile, they had no social-legal partnership with the men. Rather, they often were the object of a variety of "transactions" between their fathers and husbands, on the one hand, and their landlord, on the other. In preindustrial locales across Mount Lebanon, control of women's sexuality was maintained not merely by conserving it—that is, protecting it or keeping it "intact"—but also by spending it in a variety of semireciprocal or subservient ways with the landlord.

Given the prevalent impression that Arab Muslim women historically did not work,[14] it is crucial to understand that women of Ottoman Lebanon did indeed participate in the production of domestic work and principal handicrafts and engaged in wage labor outside the household sphere.[15]

Scholarly neglect of the nature and role of domestic manufacture, or cot-tage industries, in the lives of Ottoman peasants has been compounded by the dearth of studies on women's contribution to this manufacture.[16] Cottage industries were closely tied to land cultivation, which was central to women's work. Given the constant need for cloth and linen in the household, women's share in cottage industries was substantive. A household commonly used more than one loom to fabricate cloth for the family and sometimes for trade in the domestic market.[17] For decades before the integration of Lebanon's economy in the world economy, women's contribution to the local economy was critical to rural families' well-being.

Women prepared food provisions (*al-ma'una* or *muni,* in Lebanese dialect) on which the whole family depended in winter, in times of climatic crisis, and in market downturns. Women put extensive effort into the preparation and reser-vation of staple ingredients such as wheat, lentils, chickpeas, onion, garlic, dried figs, raisins, olive oil, olives, oregano mix, sugar, tea, tomato paste, cooked meat and fat, and other foodstuffs.[18] Hani Fahs, a Lebanese Shi'ite intellectual who came from a peasant family, recalls the extensive planting, cultivation, and conservation activities of rural southern women when he describes how "pomegranates and various trees of peach, apricot, plum, apple, cranberry, pear, orange and lemon were tended by our grandmothers who planted, nurtured, and distributed their fruits to lucky family members [and relatives]."[19]

Women also commonly exchanged different types of food items in the form of occasional "gifts." In addition to various kinds of fruits and vegetables, women often grew grapes and prunes at the margins of their lands to designate the borders of their families' property. Lentils, a main staple, were planted at the periphery of the tobacco fields by means of an intensive labor process. According to Fahs,

> Women used to ride on donkeys to fetch water from the village water spring. They soaked the tracts with water and walked behind a young man, the maestro of the cultivating band, who opened holes in the tracts. Young women poured water in the holes followed by the piercer [al-gharraz] who inserted the plant. After four hours of work, at ten in the morning, they would lie down on the grass, eat their second meal, and smoke a pipe or two. Young women then sang folk songs [mijana, 'ataba, and abul-zuluf].[20]

The work day did not end there. If the size of the landowner's land was small, then workingwomen and men would go to another field or workshop, where they pierced tobacco leaves or waited until the advent of the harvest season for tobacco and other produce. Harvest days "were mixed with light," Fahs recalls, "love with exhaustion, moist with sun robes, sleeping with awakening, dream with nightmare, love and hate of tobacco, and reverence toward parents with feelings of their oppression; especially among young women who desperately awaited a suitor against the fear of dying."[21]

Silk production—and its related tasks of planting mulberry trees and manufacturing and marketing the silk—was already drawing in large working groups during the nineteenth century.[22] The majority of farmers, both Muslims and Christians, engaged in the planting of mulberry trees to feed the growing silkworm business, which in turn accommodated the numerous traditional or "Arabic" silk-reeling manufactures. These manufactures spread out in the villages of Mount Lebanon and provided jobs, at first, for thousands of male workers and, later, for women.[23] By the 1840s, European, in particular French, demand for silk spurred technological modernization in silk manufacturing. Many aspects of silk production underwent various degrees of transformation, including the gender division of labor, which changed somewhat.[24] Before the industrialization of silk production, women's work remained auxiliary, manifest in growing the mulberry trees, raising the silkworms, and weaving the thread in the old way.[25]

Silk production started to replace wheat production as the major labor activity of the Lebanese peasantry during the mid–nineteenth century, after the incorporation of local markets into the European economy.[26] Yet the modernization of the silk industry under European domination was not the earliest phase of capitalism in Lebanon.[27] Premodern capitalist relations were evident from the late eighteenth century. Irina Smilianskaia argues that during the early nineteenth century, an increase of agricultural cash crops in Greater Syria and specialization of production in several cities and towns were clear indications of the genesis and growth of local capitalism.[28] Paul Saba suggests that quantities of wheat, wool, raw silk, and tobacco produced by peasant families, among others, before the eighteenth century went beyond the limits of the regional market and became the principal sources of cash revenue.[29] During the 1790s, handicraft production, especially that of silk and cotton textiles, developed in more than one Syrian-Lebanese town, and products were sold exclusively in regional markets in Egypt, Palestine, Syria, Anatolia, and Salonika.[30] The emerging workshops may have been owned by peasant handicraftsmen who, Saba states, "aided by members of their family, had accumulated surplus sums as a result of the widening of the market for silk and cotton cloth."[31] Many such nascent capitalist enterprises, however, were to collapse or become redirected into the world market. A Druze from Mount Lebanon explained to a British merchant that he expected his ships to arrive "loaded with fabrics and return filled with gold. A while ago we sold you [the British] tobacco and silk and we used to manufacture our own cloth by ourselves. Except for the 'Abbas (woolen wrap) nowadays we buy fabrics from you and you do not buy any of our products."[32]

The local economy did not disintegrate overnight. Rather, the old system's mode of production, labor patterns, and investment scope coexisted with the new system's. The production process and tools remained largely unchanged during the second half of the nineteenth century. The manufactures remained within rural settings in villages and peasant households, and started to witness an influx of highly competitive European goods.[33] Women's use of their physical bodies reflected these transformations. As Fawwaz Taraboulsi relates, in addition to giving birth to and nursing their children, women "used their bodies as incubators for silkworms. A poor woman used to buy a few grams of silkworms' eggs; put them in a small sack which she hanged around her neck and inserted it between her nudes. A few days would pass before the eggs hatched, facilitated by the warmth of her breasts."[34]

Industrialization of silk played a modest role in restructuring gender relations and reshaping women's work culture because of the limitations of capitalist development in Mount Lebanon, the sociological features of its industrial sites, and the level of communication between rural Mount Lebanon and urban Beirut as a major economic center. The products of the traditional manufactures, which emerged in rural settings, were used to meet local demand, whereas those produced by the modern *karkhana* were exported to foreign markets, in particular France.[35] Mahdi 'Amil suggests that unlike the process of capitalist development in metropolitan countries, the colonial economy of Lebanon tended to combine preindustrial relations and modes of production with industrial ones.[36] Thus, the conceptualization of women's material and reproductive labor, characteristic of Lebanese rural society before its integration into the capitalist system, found a partial basis in postintegration society. The silk workingwomen were transitional or seasonal.[37] Their efforts combined agrarian and industrial labor as part of the peasant household's strategy for survival. Factory and home production overlapped and continued to be sources of family income for decades. This relationship entailed a meshing of preindustrial and industrial sources of identity, social patterns, and locales. Within this context, women's labor did not undergo a modest transformation. The gendered inequalities and paternalism that sustained ethnic-tribal arrangements were simply reproduced in very different form in the emerging modern economy.

Girls and Women at the *Karkhana*

Modern silk manufacturers searched relentlessly for cheap labor and the type of laborers who could perform the "intricate" work needed for fabricating silk and operating the new steam-powered machines.[38] In the minds of male employers, there was a link between women's preindustrial craft work and the labor positions they could assume in silk manufactures. Women therefore gradually emerged as the most "suitable" workers for this work, and in most silk factories their average wage was exploitatively set at half that of men, so this shift in their status involved an improvement neither in their social condition nor in their opportunities for upward mobility.[39] During the nineteenth century, no less than twelve thousand of the fourteen thousand workers in the silkworm *karkhana*s (silk factories) were women.[40] On the production line, women occupied the lower ranks in the hierarchy of production as reelers unraveling the delicate silk threads from cocoons and as combers combing the curly thread and preparing it for spinning, weaving, and embroidery. Men had the higher-paying jobs such as supervisors, foremen, or farmers planting mulberry trees and as the generally classified "skilled" workers.[41]

The silk factories' close proximity to the workingwomen's homes and the local religious and political elites' direct involvement in the factories' business and investments allowed patriarchal control over women and gendered inequities to persist, especially within the family. The investors' need for Mount Lebanon's timber, coal, and water, as well as the poor condition of the roads, compelled silk investors to erect their factories there.[42] Factory women did not need to move out of their family's original residence and its social realm because the factories were forty minutes' to an hour's walk from their homes. As I discuss later in this chapter, factory owners accommodated the restrictions on female waged labor pronounced by spiritual and communal leaders inasmuch as doing so worked for the benefit of their investors, who needed cheap female labor.

Khater argues that modernization in the silk industry between 1843 and the 1880s and the remittances from Lebanese emigrants abroad ushered in decisive improvements in the status of middle- and lower-class women.[43] In his view, some women silk workers were no longer objectified or referred to as the "House," but rather respected as the head, home supervisor, and "Goddess of the House." The reference to the women of the household as the "House," according to Khater, pointed to women's inferior status and to the honor system and seclusion that dominated rural society of Ottoman Lebanon. For the male peasants, it was shameful to introduce their wives by their names. Rather, the women were *al-'a'ila* (family), *'ayli* in colloquial phrasing, or the "House," as Khater suggests. The shift in women's status from being the "House" to the "Goddess of the House" meant that they had achieved "control of the household" and would be called by their proper names.[44] Of course, some middle-class women may very well have experienced enhancement in their social status under these conditions, but it is doubtful whether the *karkhana* women had a similar improvement in their position as women or as workers.

Industrial work was relatively new, and so was the appearance of the factory woman on the Lebanese social landscape. Around the same time in Egypt, when women started to abandon craft and agricultural tasks to work at textile and spinning mills, many of them were called derogatory names by the bourgeois classes, including *shirkawiyya* (factory girl), and many women lived with the fear of spinsterhood.[45] The resistance that many people showed to these more "public" and independent women who moved into such uncharted spaces was a class and gendered resistance fraught with patriarchal tensions and social contradictions. It embodied the view that the rural homestead in its "idealized" features was the homestead of the landed elites, where women could afford to be secluded and the household did not depend on their waged work. In reality, the rural "lady" already often toiled in a household built around a wide array of both valued and devalued female labor.

Factory women struggled against these patriarchal values, derogatory images, and the stereotype that "gossip" and emotionality regulated female behavior. Adding to their difficulty was the fact that despite the close link between village life and industrial work in Mount Lebanon, women's daily trips to the factories, however short, often became the center of much "controversy." For example, the Maronite church insisted that family members should accompany the women workers to and from the silk factory so as to limit their contact with men along the way. Moreover, women's comingling with male workers on the shop floor came under severe attack from religious dignitaries and political leaders during the mid–nineteenth century. Between 1857 and 1869, a fierce competition among the European silk industrialists compelled the Maronite church to intervene and dictate a number of social and moral codes to regulate women's work in the factories. The Maronite archbishops Tobias ʿAwn and Jaʿjaʿ were staunchly opposed to the presence of women, most of whom were Maronite, in the silk industry and prohibited them from continuing work at the *karkhana*s side by side with male employees.[46] They objected to such intermingling of the sexes and raised concerns about the workingwomen's honor and ethical standards. Many factory owners assured the archbishops that they were hiring women exclusively, but foreign investors such as Faltakis, Portalis, and Patayel objected to the church's position because it jeopardized their interests. These entrepreneurs argued that they were forced to hire workers of both sexes because their competitors had lured many of their workingwomen away to other factories. The Maronite clergymen sympathized with the foreign investors' pleas and accepted the admission of women into factories with mixed gender composition, but only so long as they were between the age of eight and thirteen—that is, children and thus "morally" protected by the employer. They also accepted "temporarily" that male and female workers would work together in the same *karkhana,* but only as long as a physical barrier was built between them, with a separate doorway to each sex's work area.

In my opinion, when the Maronite church determined the suitable age for female industrial work to be between eight and thirteen, this act maximized the investors' interests and minimized the chances that skilled women workers older than thirteen could find alternative and better-paying jobs. In addition, this age limitation controlled wages and impeded women workers' bargaining power by giving foreign investors a tighter control of the market and by compromising the Lebanese women workers' interests. Young girls were easier to exploit and less able to defend their rights. The moral-religious objection to women's entry into the factory worked to sustain women's economic subordination and the oppressive alliance between the church, capital, and familial-patriarchal authority. Under these circumstances, it was difficult for women to improve their work conditions, wages, work hours, and health benefits between 1857 and 1869. The fact that women (girls) continued to join the *karkhana*s with their families' approval indicated that working-class families did not endorse the church's prohibitions, although they welcomed some form of sexual segregation at the workplace. It also is evident that the patriarchal disquiet and potential threat to male dominance, however strong, did not prevent women from pursuing wage labor that contributed to the family economy. Therefore, in spite of these challenges, an important dimension of their social roles as factory women was developing, which in turn expanded their household-based identity.

The Early Tobacco Manufactures

Tobacco planting and harvesting spread rapidly after the 1880s in most villages and towns of Mount Lebanon. No less than two hundred small manufactures sprang up, absorbing approximately two to four thousand workers. In 1881, the planting, manufacturing, and trading of tobacco in the Ottoman Empire became subject to the commands of the Ottoman Public Debt Administration. Only the Mutasarrifiyya of Mount Lebanon escaped the monopoly of the Ottoman Régie because of its unique political arrangement.[47] The French and the British had undermined Ottoman sovereignty among the Christian communities of Syria and expanded their activities as the "protectors" of the Maronites, thus cultivating vital political and economic interests.[48]

Lebanese silk production experienced remarkable growth in the nineteenth century, whether in the reeling manufactures or in the cultivation of mulberry trees for silkworm nourishment. The silk industry and its related tasks fell not only to Christians, but also to Muslims of various sects residing outside Mount Lebanon.[49] Cities with considerable Muslim populations, such as Latakia in the North, and Sidon, Tyre, and Bint Jubayl in the South, cultivated tobacco extensively. By 1909, 65 percent of the economic enterprises in the Syrian and Lebanese provinces were in the silk business.[50] At the onset of the twentieth century, however, the demand for Lebanese silk in European markets took a downturn. Several scholars attribute this decline to competition with Asian silk, especially Indian, Japanese, and Chinese varieties.[51] The industry regained strength for a short time in the 1920s, but eventually disappeared from the world market in the late 1930s after the Great Depression. The decline of the silk industry forced eighty-five factories to close in 1929.

Yet as the silk industry faded, other opportunities arose. During World War I, Ottoman military activities and the blockade of the coastal cities by the Allies' naval forces stifled the entry of foreign tobacco, leading to a rapid growth in local production.[52] By the mid-1930s, thousands of peasants and seasonal workers sought jobs in tobacco production and manufacturing.[53] This growth in the tobacco industry was accompanied to a lesser extent by growth in the olive oil, marble, and stone industries.[54]

In the 1930s, a number of Muslim entrepreneurs established their tobacco manufactures in Beirut, the Biqaʿ Valley, and southern Lebanon.[55] In Mount Lebanon, peasants imported Islambuli seeds to cultivate tobacco that was commercially lucrative and popular among smokers.[56] Tobacco eventually provided the raw material for two hundred manufactures in Mount Lebanon and Beirut, which employed thousands of workers, mostly women. These manufactures exported large quantities of raw tobacco to various Ottoman markets, especially Egypt.[57] With the demise of the silk industry, farmers were cutting down mulberry trees and replacing them with orange and lemon trees as well as vegetables in arable coastal fields.[58] It is interesting to note that Joseph Haykal, the mayor of Damur, a major coastal town in Mount Lebanon, asked the French high commissioner in 1935 for a high-ranking administrative post at the Régie as compensation for his financial losses in silk.[59] By 1932, Bikfaya, a major town of Mount Lebanon, had witnessed the establishment of eight tobacco factories that paid their staff total wages of seven thousand Lebanese pounds per month.[60] Chekrallah Abdallah, who owned a tobacco workshop in Shiyyah, a suburb of Beirut, highlighted the centrality of tobacco production in the lives of peasants and workers, and revealed that "in the order of the country's resources, tobacco came immediately second after silk, which was the principal resource. The ruin of that industry constituted the misery of the Lebanese peasants. . . . [O]ur efforts, supported by a sympathetic policy of the Mandate toward tobacco production, could only produce the best results."[61]

Prior to World War I, seasonal or part-time jobs in either handicraft production or manufactures were the primary types of employment in most of Lebanon.[62] Labor conditions in the old tobacco manufactures were defined primarily by the type and duration of job contracts, the division of labor, income and benefits, and relations between workers and management. The workers, mostly women, were categorized and stratified in ways that determined their specific pay in association with their skills and workload. In the silk industry, the terms of typical verbal contracts entitled workers to less than a full year of work.[63] Tobacco production, however, was contingent on the conditions of tobacco harvests that occurred twice a year.[64] The resultant shift in the "seasons" and work hours as well as the temporary nature of the tasks instilled a sense of instability and vulnerability among tobacco workingwomen.

At this time, the use of modern machines in tobacco manufacturing was still a novelty, and the prevalent method of fabrication was manual.[65] Early on, the industries demanded women workers in much greater numbers than were available for the expanding industry.[66] Many of the manual tasks were labor intensive and intricate, thus the need for "cheap and docile" female hands. For example, these workingwomen labored in tobacco workshops that typically comprised two or three rooms.[67] Destemming and then fermenting the selected tobacco leaves were the initial steps for fabricating tobacco. After the tobacco leaves were soaked in water for two hours or more, a primitive grinding instrument called *al-hawin* was generally used for chopping the tobacco *(farm al-tutun)*.[68] Workers also cut it with *al-manqala,* used initially to chop the leaves of mulberry trees.[69] Long before the importation of cigarette wrapping papers from Europe in the late nineteenth century, chewing, snuff, and pipe smoking were the prevalent patterns of tobacco consumption, and workers would chop the fermented leaves into a fine, almost powderlike mix.[70] With the advent of cigarette paper and the flourishing of the cigarette-smoking culture throughout much of the world, another step was added to the tobacco manufacturing process—namely, the making of the cigarette itself. Workers started rolling cigarettes and loading them into packs, a process performed by modern machines a few years later.[71] Another indication of the preponderance of women in tobacco production was their appearance at and input in protests and demonstrations against the introduction of modern machines in 1930. Given the work setting, production processes, and gender composition of protesters and demonstrators, it is very likely that female workers formed the core of the unskilled workforce in tobacco at this time.[72]

1. Women packing cigarettes at the Hadath factory, February 2, 1997. Photograph by the author.

TABLE 2. Average daily wage (in Lebanese pounds) in the traditional and modern weaving industry, 1937

	Traditional	Modern
Men	6	14
Women	2	8
Children	2	5

Source: République Française, Ministere des Affaires Étrangeres, "Rapport à la Société des Nations sur la situation de la Syrie et du Liban" (Conditions of Work in Syria and the Lebanon under French Mandate), *International Labour Review* 34 (Apr. 1939), 521. The report does not specify what kind of weaving industry is involved, silk or cotton. Wages have been rounded to the nearest whole number.

Other features of work for women can be discerned from data pertaining to a tobacco manufacture built by a French company at al-Muhaydithah in Mount Lebanon around 1930.[73] From the adjacent village of 'Ayn al-Kharrubah, women whose ages varied from eighteen to twenty-five commuted daily by foot for about forty-five minutes to an hour between their homes and work. Work started at 7:00 A.M. and ended at 4:00 P.M., with a short lunch break midday. Despite ventilation in the halls where the women worked, the concentrated levels of toxic fumes from chemicals used to treat the tobacco were a constant threat to their health, exposing them to lung diseases. Daily wages varied between two to five Lebanese pounds (between one to two U.S. dollars) in line with the required skill and nature of the task, one-quarter of which women commonly contributed to their families. The remaining sums were used for their own personal needs.[74] Women tobacco workers, like their counterparts in the weaving industry, experienced a discrimination, exploitation, and devaluation of their labor that translated into typical discrepancies between daily wages men received and those that women and children received.[75] Workingmen earned considerably higher wages than women in the old weaving manufactures and almost double those of women in the new weaving factories (table 2).

Mechanizing Labor

The introduction of machines in most Western countries commonly led to a reduction in the skills needed for most jobs and, in turn, promoted the entrance of greater numbers of women into factories. In colonial Lebanon in the first three decades of the twentieth century, mechanization had a mixed and ambiguous pattern, one in which unskilled women were often in demand for temporary and limited types of industrial tasks. Because they were not permanent workers, they lacked the opportunity to become more skilled. Mechanization in Lebanon, amid the particular circumstances created by the combination of colonial hegemony and immature capitalist relations, coalesced with local sectarian divisions that provided an array of culturally specific meanings. Of course, this process of localization imposed some difficulties for the hegemony; however, for the most part, the hegemony easily manipulated and was in turn manipulated by the family's patriarchal control over women in ways congenial to the former's liberal economy.

Because automation came to favor men over women, the latter organized and led the struggle against it.[76] In November 1930, hundreds of tobacco women workers gathered at the government's central office in Beirut to protest against the installation of modern machines.[77] Fuad al-Shimali, a Communist leader and the principal founder of the General Trade Union of Tobacco Workers (GTUTW, Al-Naqaba al-'Amma li 'Ummal al-Tabigh fi Lubnan) in 1924, had warned against the destructive effects of mechanization on workers in the cigarette-chopping, rolling, and packing sections, where females figured prominently. The women who feared mechanization faced an adversarial male constituency that raised arguments of a pro-natalist nature against them. Businessmen and political leaders validated women as mothers who must contribute to the family—but not to the factory. Notions of men's suitability for machines and their natural disposition toward mechanical skills also surfaced.[78]

Women showed awareness of the union and parties' support for working-class demands and thus drew from it a sense of solidarity. The GTUTW leaders and social activists' outlook and organizational strategies undermined gender variation in the labor force. Al-Shimali noted only indirectly women's grievances and aspirations as he denounced the replacement of tobacco workers by machines.[79] He asked the colonial government to provide new jobs for thousands of dismissed workers.[80] His lack of emphasis on demands particular to women forced the latter at times to take an independent course of action and march out against the government without the help of union leaders or workingmen. They used a women-and-men-united platform as well as a women's platform to announce their grievances. The unionists and socialists, on their part, did not seriously investigate the strong female-based agendas, one of which addressed domestic work and child care as a critical dimension of what women's labor entailed. They did not attempt to seek women-friendly strategies for recruitment or women-friendly schedules for labor organization meetings. Instead, male-tailored language, planning practices, and mobilization of initiatives prevailed.

For these reasons, women's early expressions of labor activism were not borne out of unionism or affiliation with socialist parties. Rather, in the 1920s and the 1930s women's labor activism derived from particular experiences of rural life, where they decided on and performed elaborate tasks for the subsistence of their households as well as organized collectively those matters related to religious rituals. Significant, too, were traditions of peasant protests and revolts against Ottoman governors and French colonialists.[81] Economic hardships and traumatic social disjunctions also impelled radicalization. Many workingwomen had vivid memories of the famine that swept Lebanon during World War I, especially between 1915 and 1918.[82] One woman noted that she lost the lease on her house after being laid off from work and becoming incapable of supporting her family. After months of debt, the nearby grocery store refused to extend her further credit. She became dependent on the mercy of friends and relatives, which also decreased as time went by.[83] The world depression of 1929 destroyed the possibility of immigrating to the New World or receiving financial aid from immigrant relatives. One might argue that all these factors pushed women to accept work under severe and inhuman conditions and to conform to the rules of the workplace under capitalists aligned to the colonial authorities.

But the loss of work meant that many workingwomen had no options but defiance and radical agitation against the Régie. For example, in February 1935 twenty tobacco workingwomen, out of thousands in Syria and Lebanon involved in factory labor, hoped that the establishment of the Régie would guarantee a decent life and stable job for them. "Since the inception of the banderole system," they said as they addressed the French governor of Lebanon,

and when you allowed the factory owners to replace modern tobacco machines with the old ones with tax exemptions . . . the factory owner started to oppress us . . . ignored our protests [to the extent] that only a few workers, out of ten thousand, are working in return for two francs daily, which is not enough to buy even a loaf of bread. As long as clause 85 of the Tobacco Monopoly Law stipulates that the Régie will provide jobs and secure the future for us and our families, we urge you not to dismiss our demands when you establish the monopoly. Herein, we repeat our trust in your majesty and also our hopes in you, the representative of the French republic.[84]

Protesters discussed not only the factory owners' tyranny, but their constant fear of losing their jobs if they did not comply with the owners' demands, particularly at a time when unfamiliar modern machinery compounded their sense of job insecurity. Living standards declined, and benefits evaporated. The workingwomen's daily wage was barely enough to pay for a loaf of bread.[85] It was only after they lost real hope of attaining jobs—in particular stable ones—that they began to consider more radical means for addressing their grievances. The abrupt shifts in the economic and, as such, personal worlds of displaced women forced them to become better organized in search for resources and means of empowerment.

From Laissez-Faire to Monopoly

Following World War I, the French tried to accelerate the pace of industrialization in their colonies through the implementation of new labor policies and decrees.[86] They allowed the tax-free importation of machinery in 1924 to modernize Syrian-Lebanese industries.[87] A turning point in these measures occurred when the French lifted restrictions on tobacco production in 1929 under a system installed known as the "banderole," which organized cultivation, manufacturing, and trading of tobacco.[88] The workers felt some respite under the banderole and tried together with the union to rationalize and stabilize their relationship to colonial officials in control of the tobacco economy. On June 18, 1930, a banderole law required factory owners to pay the government twenty Lebanese piasters for every one thousand machine-made cigarettes.[89] This money went into a special savings account to reimburse workers who became unemployed after mechanization.[90] The law also promised "fair compensation" for displaced workers.[91] For several months, tobacco workers and the union discussed and debated the definition of "fair compensation." A delegation composed mostly of workingwomen sent petitions and met with government officials to force them to specify "fair compensation," but to no avail. As a consequence, union leaders called for a nationwide conference of tobacco workers to determine their future action. As they started to organize the conference, the police attacked the union's main office in Bikfaya and arrested its leaders. Two months later the police arrested two chief unionists, Nasim Shimali and Nicolas Mishantaf, as they held a secret meeting in Bikfaya's forest. The police accused Shimali of treason and denounced him as a Bolshevik.[92] The colonial government ultimately denied the unemployed any compensation. Some of these workers then went to work at the tobacco workshops that had not yet adopted modern machinery, but they now worked more than ten hours a day and received a 60 to 70 percent reduction in their average wage.[93]

The low custom tariffs the French placed on imported tobacco products disrupted local production and put Syrian-Lebanese tobacco growers and workers in fierce competition with the regional and international markets. Most Lebanese tobacco investors supported the banderole system, which gave them significant economic freedom, and vehemently opposed the formation of the Régie.[94] French officials refused Lebanese deputies' repeated requests to increase the custom tariffs on imported tobacco.[95] In the absence of protection for local products, the banderole system led to overproduction, the smuggling of foreign tobacco, and a decline in state revenues.[96] The French colonial authorities reinstated the monopoly on all aspects of tobacco production and sales.[97] As noted in the introduction, they blamed overproduction under the banderole system on the autonomy inherent to tobacco cultivation, decentralization of tobacco sales, and lack of management of imported tobacco.[98]

More than two hundred tobacco factories sprang up in Mount Lebanon before the colonial authorities decided to enforce the monopoly. The French approved of only thirty of these factories as "principal manufactures."[99] These businesses were apparently granted favor because they were large enterprises with more than one productive department and belonged to influential families with advantageous ties to the French. The overall number of workers in these factories reached 2,710 in 1933. The top-ranking Andraous and Traboulsi factories alone contributed 16 percent of all Syrian-Lebanese production.[100] Built in Judayda (Jdaydi), a suburb of Beirut, the Traboulsi factory was expected to process one thousand kilograms of tobacco each day. Its distribution centers and warehouses were spread throughout several cities, including Damascus,

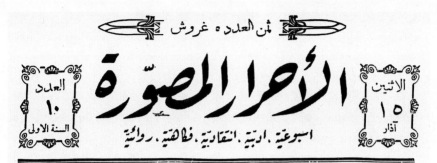

2. The Octopus Régie. *Al-Ahrar al-Musawwara*, a weekly magazine, published this caricature reflecting the apprehension that started to grow against the Régie in French Lebanon and Syria. An octopus, in this case the Régie, tightly surrounds the Syrian-Lebanese major cities (Damascus, Homs, Hama, Aleppo, Tripoli, Latakia, and Beirut), implying the stifling of their economic freedom. *Al-Ahrar al-Musawwara* 1, no. 10 (Mar. 15, 1926), 1. Reproduced by Katrin Dinkel.

Aleppo, Hama, Alexandretta, Antioch, Suwayda, Latakia, Beirut, Zahle, Tripoli, and Sidon.[101] It was from among the 340 workers of the Andraous and Traboulsi factories that major opposition emerged to the creation of the Régie-proposed tobacco monopoly.[102]

The laws governing the operation of the tobacco monopoly, the Régie Co-Intéressée Libanaise des Tabacs et Tombacs, known as "the Régie," emerged in 1935. These rules were embodied in the *Cahier des charges*.[103] Charles De Martel, the French high commissioner, granted a private company the monopoly to cultivate, manufacture, and sell tobacco in Lebanon and Syria.[104] The registered capital for the Régie was put at 1,250,000 Syrian-Lebanese pounds and divided according to the following ratios: 60 percent for former tobacco manufacturers; 30 percent for the Régie; and 10 percent to be held as "public subscription" for colonized subjects of these states.[105] Despite the large share given to former tobacco manufactures, only a few survived the competition with this new French Libano-Syrian tobacco company. The Régie received concessionary privileges from the French and nurtured business ventures with local Syrian-Lebanese capitalists within its European colonial consortium.[106] It also embodied facets of the hegemonic political system that was under way in French Lebanon.

The tobacco concession given to the Régie was twenty-five years long and expected to end in 1960; however, the Syrian and Lebanese states could repurchase concessionary privileges from the Régie in 1950 (only fifteen years later), if they so desired.[107] In addition, only a maximum amount of 10 percent of foreign tobacco could be mixed with local tobacco in the manufacture of cigarettes. And the Régie was to recruit up to 98 percent of its workforce from Syria and Lebanon, drawing from the old manufactures. Many of the employees in the banderole administration also transferred to the Régie.

Resisting the Colonial Régie

Colonial imposition of the Régie in 1935 and its integral link to the new hegemonic system set off a wave of protests in Syrian and Lebanese societies. Tobacco manufacturers, female and male peasants, and workers demanded reassurances from the French that their labor and livelihood would be protected. A group of national elites converged with both tobacco peasants and workers on the question of the monopoly and rose in revolt against the French. Rejection of the monopoly cut across religious communities and classes, and posed a serious threat to colonial objectives. To resolve the conflict, the French tried to appease a few disgruntled Libanist and Arab nationalist leaders, who opted not for a fundamental dismantling of the new hegemony, but rather for strategic positions and secure niches within it.

No single event captured more public attention across gender, class, and sect lines in colonial Syria-Lebanon than the imposition of the tobacco monopoly in 1935. The resistance to the Régie emerged primarily from the ranks of workers and peasants, but also from among national capitalists and entrepreneurs as well as from upper-class feminist organizations. Each of these groups, however, opposed the Régie from diverse class and gendered positions.

At first, the monopoly appeared to have dealt a severe blow to the Christian business elites—who aspired to protect the privileges and semiautonomy they had attained since the implementation of the Mutasarrifiyya—because the interests of the Maronite clergy and businessmen did not always converge with those of the French. The establishment of Grand Liban in 1920 had disrupted the demographic realities of Mount Lebanon—more specifically, the Maronites' numerical dominance. The latter feared that adding the regions of Tripoli, Biqa', and Jabal 'Amil to Mount Lebanon to form Grand Liban would increase Muslim Sunnite- and Shi'ite-inhabited areas to such an extent that Maronite economic privileges would be sacrificed and their interests marginalized. Thus, the Maronite Church, to negotiate its position in this new colonial formation, agitated against the French by mobilizing Christian workers and businessmen against the French-Lebanese tobacco monopoly. It directed hundreds of angry petitions to the French government in Paris, warning of the economic deterioration that the monopoly would cause.[108] In the United States, Joseph Eid, the Maronite patriarch representing immigrant Syrians and Lebanese, appealed to French paternalism, noting that from the time of Charlemagne and Saint Louis, the French had been the protectors of his people, "les français de l'Orient" (the French of the Orient).[109]

Patriarch Eid's disappointment with the French was echoed by that of yet another prominent Lebanese patriarch, Antoine 'Arida (1863–1955). For several decades, 'Arida acted as an authoritative spiritual and political leader of Maronites in the Levant. To the dismay of the French, who had considered him their supporter a few years earlier, 'Arida rose in opposition to them in the name of a united Lebanese and Syrian peoples.[110] High Commissioner De Martel sensed a resurgence of a large-scale anticolonial movement and accused 'Arida of political intrigue and disruption of public order.[111] 'Arida, whose stake in the revolt rested not on his rejection of French colonialism, but rather on the weakening of Maronite interests, was quick to reassure De Martel that his hostility toward the Régie did not diminish his deep appreciation of France and its people.[112]

The creation of Grand Liban had major implications for tobacco growers and manufacturers in Mount Lebanon, including the Maronite church over which 'Arida presided. Mount Lebanon's mostly Maronite tobacco producers and manufacturers found no tangible economic gain or political advantage in the formation of the Régie. Tobacco was the only source of income for most of the people of Mount Lebanon.[113] If the French were to proceed with the establishment of Grand Liban, the producers wanted to be consulted about its demographic and territorial composition. Yet the French had less interest in ameliorating producers' concerns than in generating tax revenues for the state—and for this purpose they viewed tobacco as an ideal commodity. They claimed that in countries with agriculturally based economies, taxes on tobacco were indispensable.[114] This justification prepared the legal ground for the formation of the Régie and the steady influx of revenues to the emerging states of the Levant.

Despite doubts, the creation of Grand Liban did eventually strengthen the economic prerogatives of the Maronite clergy and business elites. From the mid-nineteenth century, when Mount Lebanon was still an Ottoman province, the French had helped strengthen the power base of the Maronite clergy against disgruntled and rebellious peasants. In the Régie context, 'Arida and members of his class did not share the motives held by common Lebanese for the rejection of the Régie. 'Arida's agitation was an attempt to negotiate a more profitable and stable position for Maronite investors and leaders in the shadow of the new monopoly. He sent petitions to the French government, the Allies, and the League of Nations, and when he realized the plans for the Régie were moving forward anyway, he resorted to public protests that channeled the anger and disenchantment of workers, peasants, and manufacturers. Despite his motives, then, 'Arida's opposition to the Régie acquired a popular, multisectarian, multiclass character.

Two contradictory positions crystallized among Lebanese and Syrian manufacturers concerning the Régie. Owners of smaller tobacco factories, who had suffered from open competition with larger and French-protected factories under the banderole system from 1930 to 1935, welcomed the Régie.[115] Syrian manufacturers for the most part believed that the implementation of a monopoly would put an end to the dominance of Lebanese tobacco in their markets and prevent tariff increases on imported tobacco that did not suit their interests.[116] Principal Lebanese tobacco manufacturers, in contrast, rejected the Régie. Like the Andraous and Traboulsi factories in Lebanon, the large and flourishing manufactures had much at stake in the shift to a monopoly.[117] In Syria, one major tobacco factory, Salloum, that had branches in Palestine and Egypt also denounced the consolidation of the Régie and joined the opposition.[118] Lebanese parliamentarians and lawyers such as Badre Demesskie, Alfred Nasser, Joseph Gemayel, and Salah Labaki supported the opposition. They sent petitions to the French authorities and the League of Nations and dispatched deputies to Lebanese villages and towns to arrange a series of protests and visits to Bkirki, the residence of Patriarch 'Arida.[119]

Workers and Peasants Against the Monopoly

In the four Syrian states Latakia (populated by the 'Alawite, an offshoot of the Shi'ites), Jabal al-Duruz (populated by the Druze), Damascus, Aleppo, Homs, and Hama (populated by the Sunni), and Grand Liban, the reaction to the Régie varied by region and class. Most of the Syrian officials who owed their posts to French military personnel suppressed the aspirations of the peasants who opposed the Régie, as was the case in the 'Alawite region. In the remaining Syrian states, where tobacco was sparse, peasants and workers also were concerned about the establishment of the monopoly, whereas their representatives favored it.[120]

In Lebanon, the peasantry's reaction took a different course. As soon as the news circulated in 1934 about the French authorities' intention to monopolize tobacco production, industrialists halted all purchases of the tobacco harvest from peasants. The latter became divided into three groups. The first appealed to the French authorities to accelerate the formation of the Régie before the ruin of their harvest; the second rejected all French efforts to form the Régie or any kind of monopoly; and the third—represented by farmers—offered the colonial authorities a conditional consent to the formation of the Régie, demanding that the French buy the unsold quantities of tobacco piled up in their barns, establish schools to train peasants in modern methods of planting to compete with foreign

نحن غرباء في ديارنا

كيف تعامل شركة الريجي ابنا•نا !

جميل – افتحوا لي ؛ انا وعيلتي بلا اكل من خمسة ايام !

بوغوض – روخ ؛ روخ ؛ برآ ؛ هون ما بيجي الا حاييم ، بدروفسكي ؛ قيوميجيان !

3. Workers' anxiety. *Headline:* "We Are Strangers in Our Homeland." *Beneath the image:* "This is how the Régie deals with our kids." *First sentence:* "Jamil: Open the gate, my family and I have not eaten for five days!" *Second sentence:* "Boghod: Go, go away, get out. No one comes here except Haim, Bedrovsky, and Qumijian." From *Al-'Asifa* 2, no. 51 (Aug. 6, 1933), 5.

tobacco, and, most important, protect their production by limiting the importation of foreign tobacco.[121]

It is difficult to determine accurately these peasant groups' sectarian and regional character. But French records note that Shi'ite peasants favored the Régie, whereas their Maronite counterparts were against it. Yet this observation reflects the position of provincial leaders from both groups and not tobacco farmers or workers. The peasants of Jabal 'Amil, known today as South Lebanon, the majority of whom were Shi'ite, produced eight hundred thousand kilograms of tobacco in 1933, whereas the peasants of Mount Lebanon, the majority of whom were Maronite, produced only two hundred thousand kilograms. The interests of the Shi'ite peasants were in jeopardy, as were the interests of their Christian counterparts, irrespective of the position taken by their local leaders. The petitions directed from Bint Jubayl, a major town in Jabal 'Amil, to the French concerning the Régie were signed by both Christian and Shi'ite peasants. They consciously crafted an ambiguous stand toward the Régie to gain some latitude for negotiation in case the Régie was implemented by force. They addressed the French in two distinct "tongues," one opposed to the Régie and the other in favor of it.[122] These petitions show no evidence of preponderant Shi'ite support of the Régie in late 1934.[123]

Most workers of the former tobacco manufactures foresaw an unemployment crisis because they were convinced the Régie would replace them with foreign workers. Another sector of the workforce was hopeful that the Régie would offer it jobs, but continued to harbor hostility and suspicion toward the Régie's expected use of modern machinery.

In 1934, the demands made by working groups to the president of the Lebanese colonial state, the Parliament, and the French embodied the earliest formal expression of lower-class struggle against the Régie and the hegemonic political orbit it represented. Five thousand workingmen and women representing approximately thirty thousand family members protested against seeing France, "which came [originally] to help the Lebanese people," become "involved in ruining [their] most vital and important industry." The workers appealed to the French system of justice—"the most famous in the world"—to treat the Lebanese people, who had showed "their fidelity and devotion to France," with fairness. They beseeched the French authorities not to grant the monopoly to a foreign company, which would result in their living in poverty on the streets. Finally, they demanded the right to full employment at the Régie and asked that this right be guaranteed in a special article in the Régie's constitutional laws.[124]

Other factors pertaining to tobacco manufacturing complicated the picture. In February 1935, twenty tobacco workingwomen and thirty-eight workingmen from various factories in Syria and Lebanon declared their acceptance of the Régie as an alternative to the existing factories. They complained about the tyranny of the factory owners and the constant threat of being laid off. They felt that the modern machines, recently introduced into some factories, bolstered the owners' interests but compounded the workers' insecurity. The workers' standard of living and benefits suffered, and their daily wage was barely enough to "buy a loaf of bread." Finally, these workers made an outward expression of their "trust and confidence" in the French high commissioner and hoped the Régie would secure a stable and safe life for them and their families.[125] It is unclear what percentage of the workforce these fifty-eight workingwomen represented or how their concerns were viewed by other industrial workers, in particular women. In response, the *Cahier des charges* merely stated that workers of the old factories would be hired by the Régie on the condition that they meet the company's needs and demands.[126] The 2,069 workers hired in the tobacco factories under the banderole system dropped to 1,596 at the Régie by June 1935 (table 3).[127]

The monopoly anticipated the permanent unemployment of approximately 200 workers, especially of the semiskilled who received relatively good wages

TABLE 3. Number of Syrian and Lebanese tobacco workers before and after the formation of the Régie, 1934–1935

	Lebanon		Syria		Latakia		Total
Year	N	%	N	%	N	%	N
1934	1,365	66	588	28	116	6	2,069
1935	925	58	631	40	—	—	1,556
Temporary workers	60	100	—	—	—	—	60
No. workers expected to be hired after July 1935	50	—	—	—	—	—	50

Source: MAE, Paris, Syrie-Liban, 1918–40, "TELEGRAMME NO. 366," June 27, 1935, vol. 551. Figures rounded to the nearest whole number.

under the banderole.[128] In fact, *Le Jour,* a Lebanese daily, estimated that 1,500 to 3,000 tobacco workers lost their jobs in June 1935.[129] At the Zaccour cardboard factory alone, 130 to 150 workers became unemployed and thereafter demanded accountability and justice.[130] Major demonstrations against the French rose in Syrian and Lebanese cities.

Women's Labor Conditions at the Régie

When the Régie was established in 1935, 45 percent of the total labor force was women. They carried out the least-mechanized labor-intensive work, such as sorting. Table 4 offers an idea of the number of women who worked for the Régie over a period of thirty years. The table, it should be noted, does not include seasonal and part-time workingwomen, who were a substantial element of the Régie's workforce. Based on a survey done in 1970,[131] women formed no less than 40 percent of the Régie laborers, a high percentage if compared to the number of workingwomen nationwide, which was 20 percent.

The company's administrators were almost exclusively men drawn from wealthy and educated Lebanese families, and were mostly Sunnite Muslims and Maronite Christians. Women were hired as workers. Since its founding in 1935, the Régie hired laborers for a six-month period and then laid them off for the rest of the year, thus avoiding granting them permanent status. Most Régie seasonal women workers were young, single, and from various religious backgrounds who worked for less than the equivalent of three dollars per day in 1970.[132]

TABLE 4. Gender distribution of Régie workforce, 1954–1987

	1954		1969		1981		1987	
	N	%	N	%	N	%	N	%
Female	941	46.0	1,426	43	1,230	41	1,109	42.0
Male	1,121	54.0	1,855	57	1,744	58	1,499	57.0
Total	2,062	100.0	3,281	100	2,974	100	2,608	100.0
Unaccounted for	2	0.1	—	—	—	—	6	0.2

Sources: List of union membership dues paid, 1954, URWE records, Hadath; and Régie Personnel Department, "Liste nominative du personnel au 1-1-1969," "Listing du personnel par matricule, 1 octobre 1981," "Liste des rubriques de paie, 13-12-1987," Régie company records, Hadath. Figures rounded to the nearest whole number.

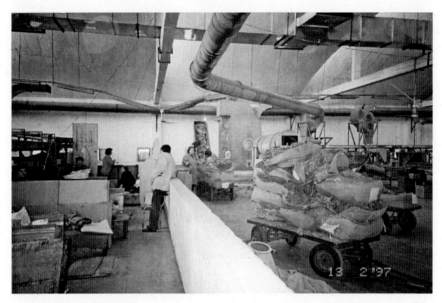

4. A heap of raw tobacco for women to sort out in the *al-farz* (sorting) department of the Hadath factory, February 2, 1997. Photograph by the author.

In the sorting *(al-farz)* department, the process of tobacco production was divided into several components. One group of women stripped off the leaves, another group sorted out the decayed ones, and then a smaller group of women processed what had been sorted by arranging the remaining leaves into bales. Men would then transport the bales for storage in a warehouse. At least four women commonly sat around one table and sorted the leaves, producing an average of twenty bales of the "medium" and thirteen bales of the "clean" grades daily. Another group of six women sifted the decayed and low-quality leaves and arranged them into ten bales daily. When asked why sorting was an "unskilled" labor task relegated to women, male Régie managers and workers alike noted that it needed "nimble fingers" and "a lot of patience."[133] In other words, the skills that men ignored but that women were assumed to have developed in private domestic circles were put to use in the public workplace of waged labor. Management thus emphasized the continuity between domestic labor and factory labor for women.[134] This idea of "continuity" unfortunately contributed to the devaluation of women's industrial labor.

5. Removing inferior leaves in the *al-farz* department at the Hadath factory, February 2, 1997. Photograph by the author.

From the time the Régie first went into production, temporary tobacco workingwomen, along with their female and male allies, fought ardently for the implementation of new and fairer labor laws. The latter were promulgated in 1946. The temporary workingwomen hoped that recourse to law would empower them to bargain for and gain certain concessions. Yet whereas these women argued that labor law stipulated that seasonal laborers had the right to become permanent after three months of uninterrupted work, the government manipulated the interpretation of these laws to deny women job permanency.[135] The government considered permanency attainable only after a six-month period of uninterrupted work and claimed that the limited quantity of raw tobacco stored at the Régie did not create work beyond six months annually, anyway.[136]

Women were reluctant to seek other types of waged work in an increasingly competitive world, but those who labored in the Régie's "poisonous departments" also worried about their health. Many of them were loathe to wear the hot and uncomfortable protective masks as they sorted and chopped tobacco leaves, but they were continuously inhaling the poisonous gases that emanated from the

6. Working without masks in the *al-farz* department, a job fraught with health hazards. Hadath factory, February 2, 1997. Photograph by the author.

chemicals that were used to protect tobacco leaves from decay. Meanwhile, the Régie stopped offering the mandatory glass of milk in the morning for additional protection. As a result of these difficult working conditions, most workingwomen suffered from tobacco-related respiratory and lung illnesses.[137]

Women suffered these conditions and even sought employment at the tobacco industries out of family need, rural poverty, unfulfilled ambitions or adventure, or a combination of these reasons. During the early phase of their experience with city life in Beirut, industrial labor became a significant vehicle for shaping their material lives, social image, and personal choices. Slighted by historians, unionists, and reporters at the time, women were perceived as acquiescent and politically conservative.[138] Throughout conflict periods with management, however, and despite patriarchal restrictions placed on their activism and the temporary nature of their work, workingwomen did not defer to men. They spearheaded the demonstrations against unemployment and displacement by machines at a time when both the labor movement and the union induced practices that marginalized their needs and prevented them from taking a central role in socialist committees and organized labor. More important, they started to push for labor laws that would protect their rights and compensate them in the event of a "capricious" discharge from work.

Conclusion

In this chapter, I highlight the work and life experiences of peasant women, showing how these experiences were inextricably tied to shifts in patterns of rural life, alterations in the power base of provincial leaders and landholders, and, most important, changes in the Lebanese economy as it became more integrated with the world market. I argued that despite the opening of new job opportunities for Lebanese women, the new work culture and gender relations in Ottoman Mount Lebanon were not radically transformed by the nineteenth-century rise of the silk *karkhanas*. Women silk workers remained subject to precapitalist forms of labor as their families, with the help of religious authorities, maintained control over their labor and their personal life. Women workers continued to live in the patriarchal household and within its extended kinship web. On their part, male factory owners imposed "ethical" and physical barriers, such as sexual segregation at the workplace, mainly to appease the patriarchal-religious system, but also to control women's work. Nonetheless, silk work provided women with early opportunities to adapt to industrial life and work patterns, and, most significant, it helped them challenge the social norms that defamed factory work as shameful.

At the turn of the twentieth century, the Lebanese silk industry started to decline owing to economic and technical developments in the international market. The imperatives of the regional and world markets gave rise to a new commodity: tobacco. Massive numbers of women's and girls' "nimble hands" found in this new industry an alternative to the failing silk one. It was a phase in which a new level of exploitation of women's labor and domination by European capitalism emerged, and women responded by waging labor and hunger protests and by combining these protests with the greater anticolonial struggle. Women tobacco workers participated and at times championed street protests against famine and against job loss due to the mechanization of tobacco factories. Most notably, they also demanded fairer labor laws and regulations that would protect their work and benefits. Their tobacco work environment put them in contact with unionists and Communists who helped to educate them on militant strategies to form their own delegations and to articulate their particular grievances. However, it should be emphasized that in the 1920s and 1930s, women's early expressions of labor activism were not the direct result of unionism or their affiliation with socialist parties. Rather, their activism was derived from their own experiences in rural and communal life and religious rituals and was related to their protests against famine. Significant, too, were traditions of peasant protests and revolts against Ottoman governors and French colonialists.

In conjunction with tobacco peasants and factory workers as well as various other social groups, women workers started a national campaign against the monopolization of tobacco production in Lebanon and the French hegemony over the country. These protests were the genesis of the political movement that followed in the 1940s, which culminated in the 1946 departure of the French and in new labor laws that I discuss in chapter 3.

2

Domesticity and Waged Labor

Gendered and Class Polemics in Colonial
and Postcolonial Times

THE VOICES of upper-class Syrian-Lebanese women pushed their way into print during the late nineteenth and early twentieth centuries to record in writing and express publicly personal thoughts at a time when workingwomen's voices in rural and urban areas remained outside written history. Domesticity, education, waged work, and patriarchal control became focal themes of discussion and debate among learned and elite women in journalistic essays, editorials, and books. The women writers emerged in part from influential and propertied families and in part from educated notable classes that flourished in the late Ottoman period, and they developed a special interest in the project of modernization, economically as well as culturally. What women journalists discussed and debated with women and men of these classes was intricately tied to questions of nationalism, French colonial rule, and modernization. What resulted was an image of "the new woman" who upheld the ideals of the national political elites at the same time as she demanded a reconfiguration of her place in the domicile, the conjugal unit, and the public arena.

By contrast, peasant and workingwomen's voices and self-portraits were invisible in print. Their experiences of modernization and nationalism, more so than of colonialism, were largely unnarrated or misnarrated in these same types of forums, which resulted in their being perceived as having no particular conceptualization of the historical changes that engulfed them or of the type of gendered and class inequalities they fought against. In all the fragments of newspaper reports, union reports, government declarations, and labor policies where workingwomen's thoughts and aspirations rarely appear, there is revealed

35

a sustained public activism against colonialism that projects little of the nationalist ideals of upper-class women. It was a public activism that was more suspicious
of modernization, particularly when mechanization was introduced to industrial
manufactures. It was less concerned with promoting women as the keepers and
promoters of the moral ideals of "the nation" against European colonialism, than
with direct rejection of colonial exploitation of their labor, its severe disruption
of peasant family life as a producing unit, and its implementation of new and
"modern" forms of patriarchal practices that, on the one hand, removed women
from direct family control and, on the other, forced them to accept half a man's
wage at the industrial plant. Workingwomen's struggle against the French and
the Lebanese colonial state and capitalists was specifically for and about women's
place in the market economy and their waged labor. Peasant and workingwomen
always have been in the public and have always worked. Seclusion and segregation were, however, what upper-class and educated women writers of this earlier
period tried to change in connection with anticolonial struggle and the discourse
of modernization.

Overall, then, there is more than one trajectory of women's history in Syria-
Lebanon, and a common gender language or culture of resistance is absent.
Beyond rallies against the Régie monopoly and French colonial rule, upper-class
feminism and working-class feminism rarely met.

In the second part of this chapter, I highlight women's contribution to the
rural economy and their involvement in domestic work and in mixed patterns of
agricultural and waged labor. By drawing on evidence from the Lebanese countryside and comparable economic systems and social arrangements in African,
Asian, and European societies, I show the centrality of lower-class women to the
labor processes outside the household unit. With a more realistic understanding
of the class-based nature of the gendered division of labor, it becomes appar-
ent that the preindustrial arrangements of female domesticity often associated
with the middle class are inadequate for interpreting the history of working-class
women.[1] Countering much of the literature on Arab women, I emphasize some
significant class variations in the perception of women's waged labor and the lifestyle it entails. I also examine a persistent discourse in the literature on workingwomen that asserts incorrectly that the cultural values of Muslim Middle Eastern
countries, the power of "tradition," and women's psychosocial traits have prohibited them from industrial labor and collective political action. I argue instead

that an accurate assessment of women's history does not start with culture, but rather with social processes that weave in economic, political, and social variables.[2] Marnia Lazreg, who studied Algerian women in the postcolonial period, accurately asserted that the culturalist conception—and the "religion paradigm" as one dimension of it—does not contribute to our knowledge about women's activities because it attempts to explain social relations ahistorically, outside their temporal moments.[3]

The Literati in Search of the New Woman

Between 1892 and 1925, women were authoring editorials and essays in magazines issued in Beirut, Damascus, and Mount Lebanon.[4] At least eleven women's magazines emerged at the time. Most of the magazine founders were upper-class female literati and the graduates of European missionary schools.[5] Except for 'Afifa Sa'b, founder of Al-Khidr (A Woman's Chamber, 1919), who was a Druze Muslim, all female founders of magazines—namely, Fasila, Angelina Abu Shaqra, Mary 'Ajami, 'Afifa Karam, Salma Abi Rashid, Mary Yani, Maryam al-Zammar, and Najla' Abi al-Lam'—were Christian. Most of the women noted that they were supported financially and socially by a male relative—father, brother, or husband—even though they themselves carried out the editorial, administrative, and printing tasks of their magazines.

Al-Hasna' (The Beauty) and Al-Mar'a al-Jadida (The New Woman), issued in 1909 and 1921, respectively, devoted special attention to questions of women's education, emancipation, reform of the patriarchal household, and work in the home. A mix of self-identified Lebanese and Syrian women thinkers and feminists contributed to the discussions and debates in these magazines. Among them were Druze women such as Amira Zayn al-Din and 'Afifa Sa'b; Sunni Muslim women such as Jamila Bitar and Salma al-Sa'igh; and Christians such as Julia Demeshkie, Lydia Birbari, and Habbuba Haddad. Others preferred to remain anonymous, using their initials or general pen names such as "a Lebanese woman," "al-'Amiriyya," or "a learned Aleppine woman."[6] These writers had traveled to European countries, but the majority learned about modern cultural and historical developments in contemporary Western societies at missionary schools or through European women living in the Middle East or by both means. A few had intimate and sustained knowledge of Western society.

These women writers appropriated elements of European colonial discourse on the "backwardness" of Islamic–Middle Eastern societies to call for changes to the institution of marriage, polygamy, the seclusion of women, and veiling. They accepted the assumptions that, first, modernization was a necessary condition for betterment of Middle Eastern women across class and, second, that the existing traditions and practices pertaining to women were not suitable for such betterment. To progress, a nation *(umma, watan)* cannot continue to seclude its women and prevent them from receiving education and taking public roles in society. This position was wedded to an anticolonial nationalism that emphasized the "cultural distinctiveness" of Arab feminist ideals.[7]

By the turn of the twentieth century, a number of Syrian and Lebanese male thinkers expressed their fears of women's increasing participation in the labor market. This view was of course extended to both elite and lower-class women, who were advised that their "sacred duty is to the home front."[8] The Syrian-Lebanese literati feared that transformation in the work culture and in working-class women's public visibility would have an indirect effect on the gender structure and place of the privileged woman in the domicile. Conveyed in articles and essays was a general upper-class male condemnation of "modernity" and its destructive impact on social life and women.[9] The controversy centered on the new roles women were assuming and their subsequent challenges to the preindustrial valorization of housework and motherhood. In 1894, Muhammad Jamil Bayhum, identified as a leading Syrian thinker from Beirut, lamented the disintegration of the family and the rise of individualism under the modern economy. Looking at European examples, he argued that the foundations of the French family were destroyed by the peasants' abandonment of their lands and their adoption of industrial labor. In addition, French society suffered from the supposed erosion of moral values and a high rate of child mortality. Worried that similar patterns might occur in Ottoman Syria, Bayhum suggested ways to dilute the negative effects of industrial and social modernization. His solutions were formulated to keep women within the confines of their patrilocal homes. Schooling fit for a "good mother" would provide her with a basic knowledge and skills in the areas of preventive medicine, nursing, child care, art, music, painting, knitting, carpet making, embroidery, and bakery. Women's acquisition of foreign languages or secondary schooling was considered unnecessary. At best, women should take elementary classes alongside craft workshops that strengthened their matrimonial lives and enabled them to become excellent housekeepers. Finally, Bayhum expressed the hope that his ideas would divert women workers from competing with men in the job market.[10]

Mitri Qindlaft, a Syrian male writer from Damascus, addressed in 1913 the pressing problems surrounding women and factory work "in the East." Qindlaft reflected that despite the role played by European civilization in liberating society from tyranny and degradation, Western ideas threatened to restore an old backward order by ruining women's "sacred and fragile temple"—that of the household. Qindlaft's statements reflected discussions among the educated sectors of the upper and newly emerging middle classes over sexual equality. One group tended to see women as responsible for their own subordination, which stemmed from their biologically based limitations. Nature had "assigned" women to housekeeping, "planting of the backyard," and raising children. Another group of thinkers blamed modernization and its embedded pressures for the changes in women's ideas and goals. Qindlaft's central thrust was the threat that factory work posed to women's health and morality. He claimed that monotony and the poisonous dust emitted by the machines were found to cause miscarriage and psychological disruptions leading to alcoholism and an "undisciplined" night life. In consequence, "Easterners" and their "nation" *(umma)* faced deterioration and decline.[11]

Curiously, both Bayhum and Qindlaft described a pristine rural haven for upper-class women, and their suspicion of industrialization exposed their fears of the involvement of peasant women in industrial work at the mills and manufactures. It seems plausible that poor women's greater scope of social and economic activities and as such their assertive public roles became at this juncture a source of jealousy and protest among secluded elite women. As the yardstick for social progress and personal status began to embody the colonial modernist perspective, elite women could no longer derive a sense of social distinction from seclusion.

Contemporary women writers espoused a number of positions ranging from an accommodation of male protest to a subtle rejection of it. Writing in 1910, Amira Zayn al-Din, a Druze woman, accepted the idea that women should carry on with the tasks of cooking, raising children, and doing embroidery work, but also should acquire a "general knowledge" of men's trades, except military skills. Like other women writers of her time, Zayn al-Din cast the benefits of women's education in collective terms that embellished women's image as the "mothers of the homeland" *(watan)*, its moral kernel, and the educators of its children. The progress of Syrian female youth enhanced national progress. She used terms such as *umma* and *watan* to point to the Arabs and the Syrian homeland respectively. She warned against a blind imitation of Western women through a superficial adoption of dress codes and fashion designs.[12] Jamila Bitar, in contrast, tried to legitimate her feminist claims by showing how prominent women were indebted to their fathers and husbands. Bitar was concerned mainly with spousal exploitation by husbands and general abuse of women within the household. The validation of modern education for women seemed a way to achieve greater physical and psychological distance from the household. Bitar, however, gauged her support for education in pronatalist terms as beneficial for a woman as a mother imparting her knowledge to her children and gaining her husband's respect.[13]

Women writers generally presented education as a means for enhancing women's role as mothers and their labor as housekeepers. In reality, they believed education would offer women more control over gender relations within the institution of marriage and in the family.[14] Education also was tied to public visibility and social assertiveness. Peasant and urban workingwomen, however, strove to improve their living conditions on the farms and their bargaining power in the labor market that helped expand their social roles beyond the home. The men of working-class households who relied on women's paid labor had accepted earlier alterations to rural patriarchal authority. In comparison, many elite women considered waged work secondary in their struggle for control over the conjugal relations and patriarchal authority at the domicile. *Al-Mar'a al-Jadida* called upon women to force men to respect and value their domestic labor "before even thinking of replacing men in the job market."[15] In other words, primacy was given to women's individual and social freedoms domestically as opposed to industrially, and such freedoms were to be gained through an adaptation of modern ideas—that is, through cultural modernization rather than industrial modernization. After 1920, away from private tutoring, upper-class girls started to enroll in 26 of the total 122 schools available to girls located in Beirut, Tripoli, northern Lebanon, Mount Lebanon, and the Biqa'.[16] By 1925, approximately 31 percent of students at the secondary-level were girls drawn from well-to-do sectors.

From 1918 to 1943, the pioneering monthly periodical *Al- Mar'a al-Jadida* directly addressed women instead of men and took major strides in articulating women's issues.[17] It stressed the importance of hired labor for women in general and for those depicted as "idle" in particular—that is, those who had a great deal of free time on their hands, "who were bored" and thus willing to earn some extra money.[18] The periodical emphasized that work outside the house empowered women to decide their future and was liberating for their minds and souls. "Honor" and "nobility," the patriarchal virtues that upper-class women were expected to uphold, were now at least in part redefined in terms of waged labor. They were no longer what a woman inherited from her parents, but what she earned when she became independent.[19] Elite women now sought to have the workingwoman's public presence and greater freedoms, yet without the type of labor real workingwomen depended on. The ideas reflected in the editorials and essays show little interest in the actual lives and experiences of poor peasant and factory women. In return, only during major anticolonial uprisings and civil disobedience did the bourgeois feminists' activism come to workingwomen's attention. One cannot ascertain the kind of exchange that might have occurred among them, but it does not seem to have been noteworthy.

At first glance, Syrian and Lebanese women authors seemed concerned with peasant and urban workingwomen and paid labor. The bourgeois feminists, however, identified schools and charity organizations as the only suitable domains for women's employment. The hard-pressed women of the countryside and factory women were represented neither by the authorship nor by the audience of *Al-Mar'a al-Jadida*. Feminist writers resisted attaching an economic value to household tasks such as baking, ironing, tailoring, and cooking, let alone child-rearing, which were normally available in the market as lower-class commodities. Instead, they aimed to reassure men of men's continued right in dominating the labor market, especially as men faced the novelty of elite women's demand for certain types of work outside the homestead. Elite men blamed the "infiltration" of European ideas into Arab society as the source of this novelty, but, in truth, women of the lower classes had already long worked in agricultural and preindustrial settings in return for wages, well before such an infiltration of European capital and ideas.[20]

The context and implications of the Tanzimat (reforms) in connection with nascent national sentiments in the Ottoman Empire, changes in landholdings and feudal relations in late Ottoman Syrian society, as well as changes in capital and business enterprises and their greater and forceful realignment with

European capital—all pushed for the social transformation of the upper class and the emergence of a bourgeoisie who would adapt to European notions of modernization and cultural progress. The women of these classes in turn went one step farther and adapted new notions of the colonial discourse on modernity and Islamic-Arab society. Elite women's seclusion, for instance, was already disintegrating and found decreasing justification among the national modernizing elites. Elite women insisted that their seclusion would prove disruptive to the male political elites' modern project. The latter, however, were divided between accommodating women's resistance to the existing patriarchal system and accepting the system's restructuring in ways that would renegotiate and reallocate patriarchal control without eliminating it. To be sure, *Al-Mar'a al-Jadida* embellished the image of the "idle bourgeois woman" that featured prominently in colonial discourses on the Islamic harem. For the female literati, home remained the stage where most of women's productive activities were performed. Men were now urged to respect and appreciate such work because it was "women's primary industrial work."[21]

Diverging Narratives

It was not until February 1935 that High Commissioner De Martel officially declared the establishment of the Régie Co-Intéresse Libanaise des Tabacs et Tombacs in Lebanon and Syria. As noted in chapter 1, Maronite patriarch Antoine 'Arida, along with political leaders, unionists, and heads of social organizations, called for a peaceful protest against the monopoly, which turned into a strike in several Syrian and Lebanese cities. The formation of the Régie became an occasion for expressing anticolonial resentment, economic grievances, and national political frustration that cut across sect, gender, and class. In Beirut, approximately half of the storeowners and merchants complied with the call to strike, and the whole city of Tripoli closed down. In Damascus, 30 percent of commercial shops closed, 50 percent in Aleppo, and 50 percent in Homs. Hama shut down completely. The strike day passed peacefully, and not a single armed confrontation was reported.[22] More than two weeks later, hundreds of Lebanese students joined efforts to protest the formation of the Régie. They were drawn from high schools and two universities in Beirut—namely, the Protestant-founded American University and the Jesuit-founded University of Saint Joseph. The students marched down the streets of Beirut shouting in French, "À bas le monopole" (Down with the monopoly) against French orders and security measures. The French-Lebanese police tried to close down the American University and the Law School of Saint Joseph University, dispersing protesters and arresting twelve students. Demonstrating students also organized a march to Bkirki three days later, where they attracted large crowds that paid homage to 'Arida. Eight students gave fiery speeches against the Régie and shouted, "À bas le monopole qui arrache d'entre les mains du peuple la derniere ressource nationale!" (Down with the monopoly that took away the last national resource from the people's hands!).[23]

Unemployed tobacco workingwomen and men reacted in their own way. For more than a week in early June 1935, hundreds of them took to the streets of Beirut, Damascus, Homs, and other cities with their families. They demanded work and indemnities for unemployment that the French had promised. For several months, the indemnities question had not been resolved, and the prospect of finding other jobs was bleak. Laid-off workers had to act quickly as economic depression was engulfing the country. In Homs, the police prevented demonstrators, mostly women presenting their grievances, from meeting with the governor of the city. The women refused to give up hope, regathered themselves, prepared a list of their demands, and elected a woman delegate to meet the governor.[24] Workingwomen, unlike all other elements of the anti-Régie resistance, denounced colonial domination as part and parcel of a new stage in the exploitation of their labor as women. Random insurgencies and mass agitations by outraged peasants, women, men, and manufacturers reflected a deep resentment against French colonial rule and its newly established hegemonic system in Lebanon.

A leading middle-class feminist group of diverse religious elements organized a nationwide campaign to boycott the Régie and the colonial designs tied to it. The group joined the Arab Feminist Union (AFU, al-Ittihad al-Nisa'i al-'Arabi), which had emerged in the early 1930s and became official in 1944. The AFU in Lebanon became an umbrella organization for several women's groups.[25] The women of the AFU, like their Egyptian counterparts, were not primarily concerned with securing support for female waged labor. Instead, they emphasized education, public volunteerism, and charity work in consonance with their class aspirations and nationalist posture.[26] The bourgeois women who joined and sympathized with the AFU aimed at negotiating the gendered power structure within the household, which at this time witnessed a greater move from the extended to the nuclear family domain. The women sought to replace gendered hierarchy with "an abstract notion of love and partnership."[27]

Led by Ibtihage Kaddura, a Muslim woman, and Secretary General Julia Demeshkie, the AFU called upon women and men to participate in a nationwide campaign against the Régie. The union declared that the Régie's establishment impeded the country's economic development at all levels. It invoked the French "spirit of fraternity," emphasizing its willingness to cooperate with the French for the betterment of their country. It demanded that De Martel fulfill promises he had made a year earlier to protect Lebanese national resources and to reform the customs policy. Finally, it stressed the Syrian and Lebanese people's national rights, arguing that a foreign monopoly over tobacco could not possibly be advantageous to industrialists from either country.[28]

The French did not respond to the numerous petitions and appeals to alter their decision vis-à-vis the Régie. Through the AFU's Committee for the Advancement of the Moral Order, the scope of the anticolonial campaign was expanded, drawing public attention to the physical, social, and moral hazards of tobacco. On April 19, 1935, the police collected nearly thirty leaflets urging women to boycott tobacco and alcohol, and traced them to the Committee for the Advancement of the Moral Order.[29] The AFU activities were suppressed. The French authorities imposed tight security measures on all types of public gatherings and group activism and declared martial law in effect. The bourgeois women, however, continued their struggle against the Régie. To reach out to their fellow women, the "guardians of morality" sent their leaflets by mail to various residences and offices. The women aimed to "enlighten the public," especially mothers, about the damage to national pride and the moral order that would result from the consumption of tobacco and alcohol:

An exhausted nation enslaved by cigarettes is a nation whose youth cannot conceive the hope of building with their own hands, a free and respected nation.

Oh women of this cherished city [Beirut], the Feminist Union calls upon you—amidst such dangerous moral disorder—to lead the way for a true life, purified of any moral disgrace for the youth.

Oh mothers, safeguard the morality of your children and prevent them from attending places of amusement, which undermine proper education.

Cultivate the flowers of the nation and support the Feminist Union's fight against alcohol and tobacco.[30]

The AFU members utilized the existing social constructs of womanhood in as far as they emphasized women's responsibility in upholding the moral order and maintaining their children's education and, by association, the "nation's morality." They accommodated male protest against their public activism and political visibility by emphasizing that they were sheltering women from the vices of tobacco smoking and alcohol. The moral-ethical motifs that ran through the AFU's campaign were somewhat similar to those advanced by the highest Shi'ite religious authority in Iran against the concessions on tobacco planting and sale given by the Qajar shah to a British company in 1890.[31] Protesters in both Lebanon and Iran, especially the bourgeoisie and the middle-class *bazaaris*, respectively, thus utilized moral and religious arguments to protect their interests.

It is noteworthy that the bourgeois feminists continued to resist the tobacco monopoly even after 'Arida and the male manufacturers had succumbed to the will of the French. The women's anti-Régie campaign was an occasion for public assertiveness and deseclusion sanctioned by nationalist crisis. The "mothers of the nation," they felt confirmed in their additional role as the keepers of the social order and cultural development. The moral discourse marked a renegotiation of feminist identity among middle and upper-middle-class women in nationalist terms and tied the welfare of the "nation" to that of women as family nurturers and vital building blocks of nationhood.

In contrast, the protesting tobacco women, first, were less conforming to this nationalist ideal and, second, aimed at elevating their status outside the domestic nexus as simultaneously workers and women. Theirs was a battle for their livelihood and job safety. Factory women were already commingling with men publicly at the workplace as they had done earlier at the rural homestead. Even though most workingwomen fiercely opposed the Régie, others appealed to the French to relocate them in the new monopoly.[32] The complex reality of bourgeois and industrial women's anticolonial struggles as well as the role of labor and capital in shaping them force one to revisit gender as an independent analytical category and to question the claim that women were "objectively united despite class stratifications."[33]

The Régie ultimately reneged on its promises and did not abide by its own constitutional provisions to protect Lebanese labor and offer employment opportunities for uprooted workers. It is possible that at this stage women workers reassessed the nature and level of their labor organization to achieve more efficacy.[34]

Overall, the colonial instigation of the Régie shaped the traditions of female labor activism in ways that brought about a sharper articulation of their grievances and an open confrontation with capital and the state.

Do Lebanese Women Work?

Much more research is needed in the area of women's labor in Lebanon and the rest of the Arab world to connect farm and factory experiences to societal changes and personal development and to change the heavily entrenched idea that Arab and Muslim women did (and do) not work outside the home.[35] The few available sources on women's labor lack sex-specific statistical data on women's particular tasks in the planting of tobacco and the circumstances surrounding their entry into the tobacco industry in suburban Beirut.[36] Moreover, there has been little research on the comparative experiences of women who were single, married, or mothers as they moved between farm and factory. To redress some of these problems, I highlight the level and form of female participation in the agricultural and industrial workforce from the 1950s to the 1970s and the connections women drew between the family economy and the world of paid labor.

Before discussing the level of women's participation in industrial work after 1950, I think it useful to step back an additional two decades to gain perspective on the modernization of major industries. It seems logical that with the introduction of industrial machinery, or the deskilling of labor, women's participation in the labor force would have increased significantly, but the opposite actually occurred. The lessons offered by the tobacco industry are noteworthy.

One of the routine reports issued by the mandatory powers to the League of Nations and published in 1934 in the *International Labour Review* states that in the early 1930s, 10,000 out of 200,000 women worked at "tobacco and cigarette making," thus indicating a majority role for women in the tobacco industry alone.[37] The 1939 report notes that the workforce in the traditional industries of weaving, raw-silk spinning, tobacco manufacturing, and handicrafts made up a total of 170,778 laborers, out of which 90,065 were men, 58,418 were women, and 22,300 were children. Although the same report notes that labor was concentrated in the silk industry (65,800 jobs), it does not delineate the ration of females to males working in each industry.[38] After 1935, the workforce of the tobacco monopoly, including females and males, was made up of 1,900 people, a little more than one percent of the total industrial workforce in Grand Liban and Syria combined. This number reflects a drastic decrease from the pre-Régie figures.[39] The 1939 report unfortunately provides neither a breakdown by gender nor the number of tobacco farmers in its figures, which makes it difficult to discern whether tobacco production remained a major sector for women's employment in the decade following the foundation of the Régie. What we do know is that during and after World War II (1939–45), when the cost of living increased tremendously, hundreds of Lebanese women joined the industrial workforce (including that of the Régie), working part- or full-time for long hours, even during night shifts, to support their families.[40] There is no way of knowing whether the Régie witnessed a decline or expansion in the number of workingwomen during the 1950s. All we know is that the earliest document at hand outlining the Régie workforce by gender notes that in 1954 women were no longer dominant participants in tobacco manufacturing (see table 4 in chapter 1).

No figures or other data are available to explain in detail the development of the Lebanese agricultural and industrial workforce during the 1940s. Occupational groups were not surveyed until 1959, when then president Fuad Shihab (1958–64) requested the help of the Institut International de Recherche et de Formation en Vue de Développement (IRFED) to evaluate Lebanon's potential for socioeconomic development.[41] IRFED's findings showed that despite the relative growth of large industrial enterprises in Lebanon during the late 1950s, family-based economic activities persisted (see table 10 in chapter 4).[42] At the time, there were approximately 366,000 employed and self-employed workers whose activities ranged from seasonal work to piecework. Independent agricultural workers made up 34 percent of this figure. Around half of those who engaged in free professions were seasonal and temporary workers.[43] The IRFED report provides no information on gender divisions or work conditions; however, a different study conducted by Charles Churchill during the 1950s does offer some of these data. Churchill shows that a considerable percentage of Christian and Muslim peasant women in the Biqa' Valley worked long hours at farms and managed to support households that averaged five to six persons. For example, in Lower Serein (Sar'in) a group of workers, 292 women and 552 men, worked as farm laborers, and around 387 women in comparison to 227 men in total acted as direct assistants to farm owners by working extensively in the fields.[44] Nonetheless, Churchill does not offer readers insight into the "invisible economy"—that is, women's additional family work or their work on their families' properties.[45]

A further example of women's significant contribution to the rural economy is reflected in the area of tobacco production. Tobacco farming and seasonal labor involved intensive tasks that drew in various family members. Except for plowing the field, which was done mostly by men, women were involved in every step of the planting process that began every February by digging in the soil small squared blocks called *masatib*. At the end of February, tobacco seeds were planted in the *masatib*. The resulting large plants are known as *mashatil*. Three weeks later, after the plants grew into large plants, women would pluck their bottom leaves, known as the *tak'iba*, and spread them on wooden hangers. At the end of September, they would collect the middle and upper leaves of the plants, called *tarwisa*, and expose them to the sun until their color turned golden. The *tak'iba* and *tarwisa* were then left in a dark room or in a water well for one or two days to be humidified. Women then sorted, piled, and pressed the leaves. They further sorted the leaves and put them in special packages to be weighed, completed the necessary paperwork, and shipped the packages to the Régie's warehouse.[46]

Up until the late 1960s, Lebanese governmental agencies and professional organizations collected little statistical data on women workers. In 1970, the government embarked on a census to document the country's workforce.[47] Women workers were found primarily in three sectors: agriculture, industry, and "other services." The largest pool of women workers (46 percent) were engaged in the latter miscellaneous services, which included seasonal and part-time work in domestic and health services, peddling, teaching, self-employment, embroidery, tailoring, and so on.[48]

Women's contribution to agricultural work also was considerable in 1970. The census classified women's agricultural labor under a number of ways, the largest of which (74 percent) included those working on their families' farms or with husbands or parents or both (see table 5).

The extent to which industrial expansion started to erode women's roles in the agricultural workforce is not clear. Many female day laborers (16 percent)—the second-largest group of agricultural workers—and non-wage-earning women evidently continued to provide critical support in rural families. This finding might mean that women farmers might have continued to rely on parental

TABLE 5. Distribution of female laborers according to occupation, 1970

	Free laborers		Business owners		Permanent laborers		Daily laborers		Family helpers		Other		Total	
	N	%	N	%	N	%	N	%	N	%	N	%	N	%
Agriculture	1,320	6	360	2	15	0	3,480	16	15,750	74	300	1	21,225	23
Industry	7,155	38	555	3	3,870	21	5,985	32	840	5	240	1	18,645	20
Utilities	—	—	—	—	60	100	—	—	—	—	—	—	60	—
Construction	15	7	15	7	165	73	60	27	—	—	—	—	255	—
Commerce and hotels	825	14	105	2	3,300	57	345	6	1,200	21	—	—	5,775	7
Transport & communication	15	0	—	—	1,635	88	180	10	30	2	—	—	1,860	2
Finance and services	30	1	15	0	2,655	94	60	2	60	2	—	—	2,820	3
Other services	1,680	4	285	0	36,150	83	3,690	9	345	0	1,035	2	43,185	46
Indefinite	15	5	—	—	195	65	30	10	30	10	30	10	300	—
Total	11,055	12	1,335	1	48,045	51	13,830	15	18,255	20	1,605	2	94,125	100

Source: République Libanaise, Ministère du Plan, *L'enquête par sondage sur la population active au Liban*, vol. 2, *Tableaux de résults, juillet 1970* (Beirut: Ministère du Plan, Direction Centrale de la Statistique, Nov. 1972), 160. "Free laborers" is a category that involves people who work on daily or seasonal terms or both and with no written contract. Permanent laborers are those people who work according to a written contract and for a long period of time. Figures have been rounded to the nearest whole number.

financial and social resources for support, yet, overall, it seems likely that more men than women tended to take up agricultural wage work.

In 1970, 38 percent of women were independent workers in the industrial sector. Women's negligible participation in permanent agricultural labor (less than 1 percent in comparison with 21 percent of permanent industrial workers) attests to the new openings for women in the industrial sector.[49] However, an equally significant percentage of women (32 percent) were temporary day workers.

Combined Work Patterns among Peasant Women

Historians Donald Quataert and Suraiya Faroqhi have researched a wide range of waged tasks among rural women in the Ottoman Empire as early as the sixteenth century.[50] They have learned, for example, that many women continued to manage their rural households and farming tasks even while they spun mohair for Ankara merchants. During the nineteenth century, states Quataert, Ottoman women around Kayseri in Turkey spun at home "for their own needs and sold the surplus."[51] Similar work patterns and mixed tasks among working-class rural women were evident in twentieth-century Lebanon. Shi'i migrants to Beirut who originated in the southern and eastern countryside embraced waged work, such as baking and temporary industrial labor at shoe and textile factories, but without abandoning their work on the seasonal harvest in the countryside.[52] It is possible that women combined rural home-based economic tasks with industrial work in areas at a distance from their homes well into the mid–twentieth century in several Middle Eastern regions. For instance, In'am A., a woman I interviewed, migrated from Ba'labak to Beirut in 1955 after working exclusively on her family's farm. Along with her mother and sisters, she took up work for a few years at a small factory before running a bakery in suburban Beirut. And while she worked both of these jobs, she continued to take part in agricultural work in Ba'labak. Even after joining the Régie in 1958, she continued to work for one to two months (June and August) at her family's farm.[53]

Combining work at the Régie with seasonal work at the family's land in Ba'labak or in South Lebanon was a common practice among many women workers. Another woman I interviewed, Latifa H., a Maronite, worked at the Régie branch in Ghaziyya beginning in 1960. In 1987, she married a man who had become a farmer during the civil war, and she thereafter spent much time helping him during the harvest.[54] Other workingwomen at the Régie shared these same types of experiences. To name only a few, Munira S., Dibi K., and Fatima Z. engaged in farm labor to assist their families during the potato harvest season and worked at the Régie during the rest of the year.[55]

Joan Scott and Louise Tilly's observations on waged female labor in nineteenth-century Europe also find resonance in the Lebanese peasant setting. They argue that peasant social organization exhibited mixed labor patterns (agricultural and industrial) in various European regions. Women's labor on the farm was an "extension of their household functions of food provisions, animal husbandry, and clothing making."[56] Tailoring, shoe making, baking, and linen and silk weaving were among the traditional, widespread ways in which peasant women worked to supplement their families' earnings. Women emerged as working partners in family enterprises and embraced sporadic or seasonal work

7. Tobacco leaves sliding down in the *al-farz* department of the Hadath factory, February 2, 1997. Photograph by the author.

in domestic industry in times of economic crisis—a fact that figured prominently among many Régie workingwomen. A number of female Régie workers whom I interviewed in 1997 attested to this reality. Nuha Ma'luf, for instance, worked on the land of her Greek Orthodox family in Hadath (Ba'labak) for years before joining the Régie in 1975. When her earnings from agricultural work declined, she decided to get an industrial job to support her family. Tamam Hashim, born in 1935 to a Maronite rural family, also worked with her parents in their field and joined the Régie in 1976 with the full support of her father and later her husband in order to contribute to the family's income. Women workers from various religious backgrounds who migrated from the countryside to Beirut told similar stories. It seems that these women's parents encouraged them to take stable jobs at the industrial companies in Beirut to supplement their low-return or diminishing farm labor.[57] Such work, along with the management of the household offered women an important measure of power in the family.[58]

Among rural Lebanese communities where women had engaged in this mixed-labor pattern for years, social support for women's waged work may not have constituted a real aberration from preindustrial peasant values. The limited social world many of these women encountered in the city continued to be inter-twined with broader village-based kin ties through the remittances these women sent to their families.[59] Many peasant families sent their daughters and wives to work temporarily in urban centers. These workers may have appeared rootless and disoriented to the more stable industrial community, but for these women, farm and factory were interlinked, making it difficult to identify males or females with either type of work exclusively. Scott and Tilly succeed in showing that pro-hibitions and restrictions on women's waged labor in nineteenth-century Europe were more of a middle-class than a working-class phenomenon.

In the case of Lebanese women, I have shown that the propagation and defense of waged labor were not on the agenda of middle- and upper-class feminists. Even later, in the 1960s and 1970s, feminists' arguments advocating women's inalienable right to pursue paid work largely ignored the longstanding mixed-work patterns of the working class, thus making working-class women seem irrelevant. Rose Ghurayyib, a leading Lebanese feminist, for instance, objected to the way Leba-nese school textbooks embellished women's image as mothers and housekeepers because they defined women's output in domestic terms. She feared that schools perpetuated the perception that a woman's desire for paid work aimed to supple-ment her family's income. It seems clear that Ghurayyib had middle- and upper-class women in mind, whose motive for taking up waged work was not primarily economic. Many middle-class rather than peasant or working-class women were told that nondomestic labor, if undertaken, should not be at the expense of their families' interests.[60] 'Adnan Muroeh, the head of the Committee for Family Plan-ning (Jam'iyyat Tanzim al-Usra), founded in 1969, also failed to recognize critical variations in the life experiences of women across class and region. He stated that part of the solution for the high birth rate in Lebanon was "enlightening the minds of thousands of women and convincing them that a woman's life transcends domes-tic work and recurring pregnancies . . . and emphasizing the virtues of waged work, which contributes to raising the family's income and welfare."[61] This statement clearly reflects a class and gender bias against industrial workingwomen, among whom waged work was already prevalent and small family sizes were favored.[62] To look more closely at male perceptions of female ability and labor, and at the chal-lenges facing workingwomen, it is helpful to explore a few case studies.

In 1979, sociologists Linda Lorfing and Julinda Abu al-Nasr studied wom-en's labor in ten factories in Beirut's suburbs and showed that for 47 percent of workingwomen, the ideal number of children was four, and for 34 percent it ranged from two to three. This preference is clearly very different from the fertility levels found among rural peasant and even middle-class women. Although working-women had little if any education on family planning or access to contraceptives, the demands of their industrial and domestic labor dictated that they actively seek ways to control their fertility. In addition, most industrial workingwomen, in con-tradiction to Muroeh's assumptions, knew from experience that their waged work did not assure their economic welfare, let alone allow them to make ends meet. For many bourgeois women, a call to engage in waged work seemed neither eco-nomical nor even socially justifiable to many of their families. Yet factory women workers readily contributed to the family economy and engaged in a wide range of temporary or seasonal waged work—and had done so for many years. By this time, 1979, working-class women also had already been for a long time in the middle of heated demonstrations against exploitation by their employers and were struggling to improve their conditions as committed workers.

Scott and Tilly further note in the case of European peasant women that full-time factory labor was an augmentation, not a complete aberration, of rural work patterns, thereby explaining why it was met with minimal resistance among the lower classes.[63] Yet in the case of Régie women, I found that industrial labor and its urban setting were more than an augmentation of peasant work culture.[64] The oral accounts Churchill collected about women's work in the Biqa' and the South during the mid–twentieth century also reveal that although mixed-labor tasks went unchallenged, full-time industrial labor was still debated in some peasant households. One might thus conclude that industrial work in Lebanon was a major structural development in the lives of Lebanese women, particularly owing to the partial or total separation of women from their families. Yet it is not surprising to find in the accounts of many Régie women that fathers and brothers expressed their objections to women's industrial work in ways that really revealed a subtext of tacit acceptance.

The range and complexity of women's labor activities are not adequately described in much of the historiography on Arab women. A major trend in this scholarship fails to account for mixed-labor patterns or waged work among rural women. It looks exclusively at documented industrial labor or at official and rig-idly defined categories of factory work. Some scholars have utilized supposed empirical indicators of Arab women's "marginal" contribution to industrial labor in order to perpetuate male biases about women's psychological fragility and their resistance to class cohesion and professionalism. Among these "indicators" is the observation that in most Arab countries women constitute only 9 percent of the economically active population.[65] In 1981, Henry 'Azzam attributed women's resistance to nondomestic work to both subjective and objective factors. On the "objective" side, he argued that Arab women lacked access to the political power necessary to shape the labor policies of their governments and reverse their scanty employment opportunities. On the "subjective" side, 'Azzam believed that Arab women suffered from a lack of self-confidence and optimism. Women's insecurity was thus exemplified in the manner in which they supposedly considered nondomestic waged labor as both temporary and irrelevant to their ultimate dreams of marriage and family. After proposing the use of "psychosocial planning" to facilitate women's entry into public economic life, 'Azzam warned that workingwomen must not neglect their domestic duties because it would be damaging to Lebanese society![66] At this same time, labor historians such as 'Ali al-Shami suggested that women's low participation in paid work was inversely correlated to the strength of local "traditions" and social customs, which placed women's proper activity in the private patrimonial home.[67] This view was part of a deep-rooted assumption in the literature that the cultural values in Muslim–Middle Eastern countries and the power of "tradition" kept women away from industrial labor.[68] Both al-Shami and 'Azzam failed to recognize, however, the types of economic systems, governmental planning, and social organizations responsible for hindering the appeal of industrial labor to women. In the same vein and also in 1981, Linda Layne placed great weight on women's views and actions almost independently of other sociopolitical factors. She argued that workingwomen could gain economic independence and overcome "traditional" forms of control by adopting new behavioral patterns that were congenial to "feminist solidarity."[69] This view assumes that change starts with an independent rational decision to change one's behavior. It also overlooks the reality of the structural basis for inequality in local legal and socioeconomic systems, in the powerful gender hierarchies in Arab societies, and in the larger hegemonic political system. In the next two chapters, I illustrate how particular social perceptions as well as state and factory policies contributed to many of the structural impediments erected in the path of working-class women, prevented an expansion of their labor tasks, and limited their ability to attain social and political empowerment.

Conclusion

The varied goals, visions, and experiences of bourgeois and workingwomen activists within the rubric of anticolonial struggle bring a much needed complexity to the story of "nation" and national history. Learned women of the elite spent much effort on communicating their protest in a language that used their male counterparts' modernist national ideal. They bargained for a different place in the domicile and emphasized the necessity of men's support for "the new woman." The question of gendered power for them was a question of deseclusion and public visibility. They insisted on public, modern education because it tended to militate against seclusion and marginalization within the conjugal unit.

Workingwomen were already in the public, however, and mixing with men in several complicated processes of production and sociability that formed the basis of lower-class family households in the countryside. They were beset by fear for the stability of their waged labor and the loss of safety in employment, and their activism was thus about power in the marketplace and empowerment against hegemonic systems defined by European colonialism but sustained locally by the national political elites. Workingwomen seemed the more reluctant citizens and lukewarm nationalists in comparison with the bourgeois women. As will become clearer in upcoming chapters, they saw state nationalism as an extension of, not a break with, oppressive colonial policies and capitalist exploitation of their labor. Workingwomen were "not fit," so to speak, for the ethical and cultural values of the "nation" that were against corruption by colonial practices and traditions. Only fleetingly were the two visions of feminism—that of middle- and upper-class learned woman and that of illiterate factory women—bridged during the anti-Régie campaign that cut across class and regions and sect.

The Lebanese nationalist narrative in both its early classical form and its later liberal version introduced the type of tribal-ethnic hegemony that provided women of all classes with a particular form of gendered inequality at the social and state levels. Up until the early 1960s, the tribal-ethnic hegemony was articulated in popular culture and legitimized by themes of the virtue of nonintegration of sectarian communities and the preservation of the communities' uniqueness and cohesiveness. Major challenges to this hegemony and the ensuing conflicts were interpreted as caused by outside factors and not by structural problems that needed to be changed from within. In this context, women's autonomy and self-actualization as producers were a threat not only to precapitalist patterns of family and village life, but also to the very system upon which the state operated: the tribal-ethnic hegemony.

This chapter also addresses the dominant denial in Western academic circles that Middle Eastern women engaged in nondomestic work. It shows that, to the contrary, these women were historically involved in various forms of income-generating activities, agriculture, and manufacturing production to subsidize their families. It demonstrates that many women workers continued to manage their rural households and farming tasks even as they produced items for the market.

3

At the Legal Frontiers

*"Unruly" Workingwomen Between Colonial Authority
and the National State, 1940–1946*

THE EMERGENCE AND DEVELOPMENT of labor laws signaled a new and complex phase in the relationship between industrial workers and the state in Lebanon. The first section of this chapter examines the social and political facets of this relationship as it was experienced and shaped by the Régie women workers from 1940 to 1946. Labor unrest and the passage of a labor law in 1946 became entangled with the ongoing national struggle for independence against colonialism begun in 1943, which led to the emergence of a tribal-ethnic Lebanese polity. Both the relationship of workers to capital and the content of their demands underwent fundamental changes during the phase when the anticolonial and capitalist national state came into being. Before independence, workingwomen and men adopted the nationalist cause, fought fervently against the French, and found the national elite's aspirations temporarily congenial to their own. Yet after this period the cross-class rationale for national unity and independence lost much of its impetus.

The second part of this chapter captures the gradual radicalization of workers in general and of workingwomen in particular against the hegemonic state and its policing apparatus in the 1946 strike. I discuss three aspects of the strike: its background and the nature of its demands; the sources of labor organization and militancy among the strikers; and the state's and Lebanese society's responses to the strike. By looking at the sources of militancy, I examine whether there was a different basis for women's labor "consciousness" than for men's. As I demonstrate, women's militancy was shaped by a number of factors, some of which were common to their male colleagues, such as their participation in the anticolonial struggle and their experience of "citizenship" in the young Lebanese tribal-ethnic nation-state that helped them transcend their provincial identity and take on a broad-based national one. Yet, unlike many workingmen, the Régie workingwomen neither were exposed to direct unionization nor affiliated with political parties during the 1940s. They were influenced instead by the popularized goals of a major labor syndicate and its leaders' diffuse socialist views. The particular labor and societal arrangements the women found themselves in also shaped their "consciousness" of their interests and their drive toward militancy.

The lack of statistical data on the rank, marital, sectarian, and regional composition of the Régie workingwomen during the 1940s unfortunately prevents me from making overarching generalizations about these arrangements. However, I believe that some ideas about them can be gleaned from the types of tasks performed by the tobacco workingwomen who went on strike in 1946, their perceptions of industrial labor, whether they were temporary or permanent workers, and whether they were able to fall back on the support of their families and draw some income from seasonal labor in their rural villages. Striking did not merely augment women's politicization and collective organization; it became an expression of a new gender identity, negotiated in a public space customarily accorded to men. The gendered dimensions of the 1946 strike are even more significant given the fact that the strike overlapped with wider national struggles against both French colonial authority and the emerging Lebanese state. The striking workers received wide popular support, igniting a sense of solidarity among female and male industrial workers, students, social organizations, parliamentary figures, and leftists.[1] In the end, however, women's contribution to the Lebanese labor movement was only faintly acknowledged. The women were unable to attain tangible outcomes for themselves, let alone direct any decision-making processes during the settlement phase between workers and the Régie.

By employing a gendered angle of analysis, I aim to illuminate aspects of industrial conflict that have been misrepresented or completely dismissed by earlier scholars. Women's activism did not make a great impression on journalists, unionists, or scholars' awareness or reports. The Régie women expressed an unwavering commitment to the 1946 strike and were on several occasions more militant than their male colleagues. Their militancy seemed unconventional when compared with the social activities of upper- and middle-class women discussed in chapters 1 and 2. Like their male coworkers, the tobacco workingwomen questioned the state-defined "national good" and challenged the foundations of their new "citizenship" as it was construed and propagated from above.

Labor Without a National Law, 1930–1946

Long before the formation of the Régie in 1935, tobacco workers had been among the forerunners in the struggle for legal protection outside the confines of the French mandatory provisions. The workers hoped labor laws would shield them from the fluctuations of the international market and the threat of unemployment posed by the growing mechanization of existing tobacco factories.[2] With the advent of the tobacco monopoly, the immediately perceived need for updated labor laws temporarily receded owing to the workers' high expectations that the Régie would be sympathetic toward their situation and protect their rights under the French mandate law. The latter, however, was suspended in 1938, leaving in its place martial law, which the colonial authorities imposed on the Levantine states as part of their defense efforts on the eve of World War II.

During World War II, demands for laws to supplement existing mandatory and martial ones steadily grew alongside increasing labor hardships and conflicts with management. Labor sporadically called upon the colonial powers to redress social imbalances and ease economic burdens. Meager and short-term remedies met these protests.[3] These tensions continued to develop and take more complex forms when on June 8, 1941, a joint British and Free French military campaign inaugurated a new colonial era by removing the pro-Axis French administration from the Levant. This move ushered in a new phase of competition and constant friction between Britain and Free France over the domination of Syria and Lebanon. The British attempted to manipulate the national aspirations for independence among the Syrian and Lebanese people to force France to evacuate the Levant. Charles de Gaulle, the leader of Free France, however, was determined to resurrect "France as a first-class world power in the postwar era," thus reinforcing the renewal of France's military and political strength in her colonies.[4]

The friction between Great Britain and Free France contributed to the relative relaxation of the French grip over Lebanon and Syria and allowed the labor movement to achieve certain goals. Numerous labor and popular demonstrations in major cities and towns attest to the workers' conscious manipulation of the British-French competition to achieve their paramount goal—full national independence. Between 1943 and the complete evacuation of the French armies from Lebanon in 1946, British-French relations oscillated between rivalry and reconciliation. When tensions eased, Lebanese and Syrian nationalists achieved modest political goals, only to face French repression and British manipulations when tensions increased. The French, despite their preliminary consent to end the occupation of Lebanon and Syria, refused to withdraw their armies before signing treaties granting them special political and economic privileges in the region. At this juncture, regional and international dynamics—including political pressures from the United Nations and the superpowers, and the French state's waning geopolitical influence—proved congenial to the Syrian and Lebanese nationalists' cause.

The mainstream narrative of Lebanon's independence omits the role of the popular social sectors in the resistance to French occupation. The political elite viewed the independence battles from above and interpreted them as the outcome of nationwide outrage at the arrest of the newly elected Lebanese president, Bishara al-Khuri, the prime minister, Riyad al-Sulh, and other government ministers.[5] Historical texts do not mention the popular demonstrations that occurred before and after the declaration of independence in 1943, mainly to cement the alliance between the Lebanese state and the political elite that came to speak for the country in the postindependence period.[6] This official narrative placed great emphasis on the intentions of the French, in particular the declaration made by Charles de Gaulle following the July 14, 1941, invasion of the Levant by the Allies and British promises of support for the national liberation of Syria and Lebanon.[7] In reality, however, independence was a culmination of several factors, only one of which was the imperial powers' international decision. On an internal level, workers rallied to the nationalist cause, which figured prominently in the declarations of the labor movement. Workers also expressed their national sentiments by participating in the parliamentary elections following independence and actively supporting their candidates.[8]

Background to the 1946 Strike

Since the inception of the Régie in 1935, job permanency and stability were focal points in the confrontation between temporary tobacco workers, both female and male, and their employers. The workers soon realized that the laws under which the company operated were the very laws governing the entire country. As noted in chapter 1, some of the workers at the old tobacco factories who initially had been suspicious of the Régie's intentions nonetheless had expected French authorities to safeguard them against unemployment and social injustice.[9] Disillusioned as these workers might have been, they believed that France "came to aid the Lebanese in recovery." The "internationally renowned" French justice system, they believed, would prevent the failure of the principles it implemented "in the name of humanity and civilization."[10] It did not take long, however, for these workers to realize that the "French justice" system served solely the interests of the Régie's owners and the newly forming tribal-ethnic hegemony.

For example, the principal mode of hiring in the Régie's largely female *al-farz* (leaf-sorting) department was based on the annual, cyclical process of recruiting a group of young women for a few months, then discharging them after the completion of their tasks. This pattern of employment also was the rule at the French Régie. In contrast, in France where the task of sorting raw tobacco attracted mostly widows and divorced or disabled women, who performed this job for a few months as a supplementary source of income. The majority of these French women never relied exclusively on their earnings from their temporary jobs in tobacco factories. They normally performed additional work in their households, such as sewing, doing embroidery, and raising chickens, all of which added to their meager tobacco income.[11] The Lebanese state's existing legal apparatus did not stipulate any rights for discharged workers, as was evident in a case presented on May 28, 1941, to a court of appeal that denied compensation for one discharged tobacco worker.[12]

In addition to this lack of job security, difficult working conditions and arbitrary company labor practices were constant sources of antagonism between temporary workers and the Régie. A prominent labor leader recounts in his memoirs that from the early days of the Régie, laborers worked daily for nine hours instead of the eight hours decreed by the Régie's administrative law. During certain times of the year, the Régie also forced its employees to work on Sundays, thereby preventing them from enjoying a weekly rest or even receiving extra money from overtime labor. The administration's "spies" attempted to implicate any worker who complained about the military-like measures that the company used against those who asserted their rights. On several occasions, tobacco workers strove to improve their conditions and overcome the capricious and oppressive measures

8. Women waiting to sort raw tobacco manually in the *al-farz* department at the Hadath factory, February 2, 1997. Photograph by the author.

of the administration, which manipulated its "spies'" reports in order to coerce and fire "unruly" workers without any compensation.[13]

The workplace was not the only platform for these struggles. The resentment against the Régie and, hence, against French capitalists and managers was translated into a growing national civic awareness. The bulk of the Régie workforce, temporary and permanent, women and men, began to take part in the Lebanese nationalists' opposition to French colonialism. Even though the nationalists' concerns overshadowed the strikes led by the Régie workers, labor grievances persisted and multiplied during World War II. The workers found themselves in yet another confrontation with their employer and colonialists. The rise in the cost of living and the devaluation of the Lebanese currency left them with less than the bare necessities for living.[14] Beginning in the early months of 1941, thousands of workers at many enterprises feared unemployment owing to serious economic setbacks in Lebanon and Syria, where major cities witnessed a number of demonstrations against the threat of famine. Their demand for the regulation of work hours started to surface repeatedly in their labor program during the World War II years.[15]

On the eve of Lebanon's independence, Régie workers hoped to fulfill four major demands: stability for temporary workers, the end of the tobacco concession granted by the Lebanese government to the Régie, regular salary increases, and the regulation of work hours. Expressing strong anti-French sentiments nationwide, the Régie workers marched out on May 5, 1943, demanding the cancellation of the tobacco concession and the transformation of the company from a foreign to a Lebanese enterprise.[16] A few months later another strike called for the same demands. The French authorities found it convenient to attribute these strikes to a British ploy to destroy the Régie alongside any economic concession given to and managed by the French.[17] They also blamed labor agitations on Communist schemes.

Owing to the lack of strong support from workers in other industries, the Régie workers did not achieve their May 1943 demands. The postindependence government that ruled during the transitional period from 1943 to 1946 also thwarted and dismissed these demands.[18] Around twenty women workers were wounded and arrested during a confrontation with the national police at a strike in mid-February 1945.[19] With the exception of the call for the formation of trade unions and the implementations of family allowances, this strike reiterated earlier demands. The recurrence of these demands pointed to the employers' indifference to the workers, who lacked a legally binding, written "text" to protect their rights. A rationalized system of job promotion, wage increases, work schedules, as well as employers and employees' duties and rights lay at the heart of a well-defined relationship between management and labor. The workers hoped the implementation of legal authority would organize and protect all the parties involved. Industrial workers nationwide became acutely aware of the need to understand and utilize the legal provisions pertaining to their livelihood against the alliance of state, sectarianism, and capital in manipulating the law.

Laborers and Legal Frontiers

Parliamentary and governmental elections were inaugurated in a relatively relaxed political atmosphere in independent Lebanon. Labor syndicates utilized this occasion to plan "peacefully" for the achievement of legal rights. On October 29, 1943, a delegation from the leading labor unions presented to the prime minister a memorandum with its chief demands, the most urgent of which was the passage of labor law. Underscoring the vague laws that governed the operation of foreign concessionary companies, the delegation further emphasized the need to attain a national labor code that applied to all workers of foreign companies.[20] The delegation's efforts unfolded at a time when the government was trying to get rid of certain clauses that limited its sovereignty in the new constitution that was submitted to the Parliament for approval in 1943. French authorities refused to discuss these clauses before the signing of a treaty and proceeded on November 11, 1943, to suspend the Constitution and arrest the president, the prime minister, and several other ministers. Expressions of civil disobedience, demonstrations, and armed clashes erupted in the country until those arrested were released and the Constitution restored.[21]

When the French persisted in prolonging the occupation, the Lebanese labor syndicates resorted to various methods of resistance ranging from petitions and mobilization of laborers to the application of greater pressure on government officials. In time, however, these measures also proved unsatisfactory and were soon replaced by intensified protests and strikes that, between 1943 and 1945, spread to almost every industry and small business in the country.[22] The most significant of these strikes, in terms of duration and frequency, were those ignited by workers at the concessionary companies. In this case, strikers made the demand for national labor laws central to their agenda.[23] A turning point in the course of these events was several unions' January 1944 decision to join forces and form a labor syndicate, the General Confederation of the Unions of Workers and Employees (GCFUWE, Al-Ittihad al-'Am li-Naqabat al-'Ummal wa al-Mustakhdamin fi Lubnan), with Mustafa al-'Aris as its president elect.[24] The main unions that joined in this syndicate were those of the bakers, carpenters, construction workers, shoe-sewing artisans, furniture upholstery workers, electricity and tramways workers, tailors, private car drivers, pharmacy workers, barbers, cooks, and tanning workers of Beirut and Mashghara in the Biqa' Valley. The workers of the concessionary companies did not participate in this meeting, perhaps because they had not yet formed their unions. A month later the GCFUWE appealed to all labor unions to join its ranks and prepared to convene a conference to discuss critical labor issues and establish future goals.[25] This appeal encouraged trade unions with large female memberships—including the textile, stocking, and match-makers unions— to join the GCFUWE.

After a half-day strike in early 1944, the government promised Régie workers salary raises.[26] The government did not fulfill its promise, however, and the workers received instead a one-month loan from the company, which they were expected to pay back. Almost a year later the GCFUWE met with the president to request a change in income tax policy to relieve working-class families. In February 1945, the Régie workers struck again, insisting on wage increases and cancellation of the one-month loan debt. They also asked for another one-month loan, which they would pay back after the end of the war.[27] Integral to the strikers' list was a new demand pertaining exclusively to women that called for the receipt of a full pension for those who left work after marriage. The government refused to negotiate with the Régie workers and sent in police to crush the strike. Using guns, the policemen attacked the workers and injured some of them, including several female workers, such as Georgette Haddad and Nadia and Mary Salih. We unfortunately know nothing about these workingwomen's jobs or background. The accounts also are vague on the outcome of this confrontation and whether any of the strike's demands were met. This strike and several others in the wool and clothing industries evidently integrated some of the GCFUWE's general goals relating to salary raises, pension for workingwomen who left their jobs after marriage, and licensing of the unions.[28] It is noteworthy that the workers at the Zumikyan Stocking Company and the National Wool Company who struck soon thereafter, in June and July 1945, also asked for full pensions for women who left work upon marriage.

It is possible to conclude on the basis of this information that many of the women who pushed for these demands in confrontations with their employers were permanent workers and eligible for a pension and, most important, were single women who anticipated leaving their jobs after marriage. In other words, a considerable number of the women who struck in 1945 perceived their stay at the Régie as transitory and temporary. Single women tended to be under less financial strain than married ones, whose families depended for survival on the workingwoman's stable job and earnings. It is difficult to know whether these single women wanted to leave work upon marriage because of disappointing or strenuous working conditions or whether they expected their future husbands to oppose their employment. One can simply suggest that the anticipation of departure from work may have allowed many single workingwomen to take greater risks and adopt more radical means to improve their work conditions. In addition, although it is unclear whether any of the women who struck belonged to the

GCFUWE, this organization was nonetheless a source of strength and solidarity for the Régie workingwomen.[29]

General de Gaulle did not conceal his suspicions of labor and popular disturbances and accused the British of instigating them. As a show of force and a warning to the nationalists, the French sent additional military troops to the Lebanese and Syrian coasts. But the nationalist uprising intensified, anyway. On May 29, 1945, the French military violently suppressed a nationalist demonstration in Damascus, using air and ground weapons that killed hundreds of civilians and destroyed scores of dwellings and businesses. The widespread condemnation of these atrocities augmented the isolation of the French and fostered the fortunes of the nationalists.[30] Meanwhile, the concessionary companies, including the Régie, sought to reap the benefits of French military control over Damascus, thus rejecting the application of any laws to their premises except the French mandate laws.

A few months later these nationalist and labor protests came to a halt. In the early days of November 1945, the government announced that the first draft of a labor law would be proposed to the Parliament for discussion. From popular defiance in the streets to deliberations in the Lebanese Parliament, the workers' grievances took a decisively polemical form. Numerous newspaper accounts and studies emphasized the strong support for the concessionary companies among members of the Chamber of Deputies, several of whom pushed to postpone the resolution of this issue until the next session. Historians Jacques Couland and Ilyas al-Buwari imply that several deputies developed vital links with foreign companies that looked unfavorably at the prospect of new labor laws. The Lebanese government justified such a postponement in its involvement in the negotiations that would decide the country's destiny. It gave utmost priority to the national question, on the one hand, and avoided a comprehensive resolution to the increasing labor unrest, on the other.[31] The postponement, however, allowed the deputies to gain an upper hand in the deliberations, probably because they were able to strengthen their position and shift the balance of power to the government's side. The Chamber of Deputies as a whole was then able to formulate a draft law favorable to the interests of foreign companies and national capitalists.[32]

The GCFUWE was aware of the perils of delay and thus convened an open meeting on May 12, 1946. It adopted several measures to reverse the Parliament's decision, central among them being the call for a general strike to be held on May 20. Following the meeting, the attendees marched out into the streets in a peaceful demonstration.[33] Meanwhile, at the national level, the United Nations asked the British and the French to determine a date for the evacuation of their troops from the region. The French had initially requested a one-year extension in Lebanon but faced strong objections from the government and the people. They departed reluctantly at the end of 1946.[34]

The United Nations resolution gave further strength to the position of the new tribal-ethnic elite and several deputies who insisted on postponing the promulgation of a labor law. In the meantime, workers prepared for a general strike to pressure the government and accelerate the issuance of a law. A few hours before the strike was to commence, the Lebanese president declared that the Parliament would promulgate a labor law in an upcoming special session, but the workers, who interpreted this announcement as a maneuver to abort the strike, insisted on carrying out a one-day strike on May 20.[35] The strike took place in Beirut, the capital city, and in a number of provinces, drawing in the workers of both major industries and commercial businesses. Only one violent incident broke out between strikers and police, when thousands of workers attempted to close the major street connecting the capital to the northern part of the country, and two workers were seriously wounded.[36]

Contemporaneous accounts of the May 20 strike do not agree on its size or scope. Remaining unanswered is the question why industrial workers outside the Régie did not participate in the strike. Observers and scholars alike were divided on the strike's efficacy and overall success in improving the workers' situation or in bringing greater visibility to their needs. The threat of the general strike, however, may have altered government deliberations in future conflicts. The day before the strike was expected to take place, the president met with several union members and said to Mustafa al-'Aris, "You know that I have sympathy toward the workers. The Chamber of Deputies will pass the labor law in a special upcoming meeting, so I ask you to cancel the strike."[37] Al-'Aris explained that even if the GCFUWE took the president at his word, it could not cancel the strike without consulting with all the union leaders, and time did not permit its doing so. With a sense of urgency, the president offered to provide al-'Aris with transportation facilities and to cover telegram expenses in order to reach the union leaders right away. Al-'Aris and his delegation refused the offer. This account clearly shows that the government was sufficiently worried by the prospect of a strike at a major concessionary company such as the Régie and tried desperately to diffuse it.

The workers' profound disappointment with the immediate outcome of the strike, at a time when decision making was transferred from the hands of French officials to Lebanese patriots, came to be understood in terms of a new historical reality—the growth in the power of the national state and its policing organs. The labor movement faced a more potent opponent and complex successor to French colonial rule—namely, a hegemonic coalition that embraced solely the rich Lebanese and their families and sects. Dismayed yet determined to achieve their goals, the Régie workingwomen and men scheduled a future strike for June 11, 1946, that would turn their resistance into a national event to rekindle the campaign for new labor laws.

Laborers Rethink the National State: Moving the Rifle from One Shoulder to the Other

The prevailing view of the circumstances leading to the passage of labor law in Lebanon can be found in the studies of Albert Hourani, Joseph Donato, and Robert Lampman. These studies tend to minimize the role of workingwomen and men in the law's birth and to emphasize the state as its primary catalyst.[38] In this chapter, I show instead that the tribal-ethnic state and industrial management were forced to formulate new labor laws by the workers' incessant and intensified protests. Moreover, labor historians in general as well as unionists and leftists have for the most part overlooked the contribution made by women workers to the passage of the first labor law. Indeed, the image of the ideal proletariat who abided by party discipline and was "conscious" of her or his class position was strongly drawn in masculine terms.[39] Even the workingmen of the Régie expressed a range of views about women's resistance to organized labor and their reluctance to commit to overt confrontation with employers.[40] Using the far from gender-blind term 'ummal (the masculine plural of 'amil, a male worker) rather than both 'ummal and 'amilat (female workers) to describe the workers collectively, many studies portray labor laws as the product of the disparate efforts of male laborers and state initiatives.[41]

To redress the gender imbalance and bias against women in the scholarship, I focus here on women's role in the 1946 strike, which unfolded during the transition from French colonial authority to Lebanese nationhood. This transition did not result from a simple military evacuation of French troops from Lebanon. Instead, it was part of a long historical process involving the development of the organs of state and of new social and legal institutions.[42] The wide popular and national support that the 1946 strike received allowed people to move beyond fears of economic setback to bravely form movements of civil disobedience among several sectors of society, revealing the fragility of the new Lebanese state.

A few months prior to the June 1946 strike, the workers and employees of the electricity company struck in pursuit of basic benefits and improved labor conditions.[43] These workers had adopted some of the labor movement's central goals, giving priority to the implementation of systematic legal procedures even though they were told that these procedures fell outside the jurisdiction of the electricity monopoly. After a series of negotiations between the electricity workers and the government, the workers cancelled the strike before realizing their demands. Perhaps to test the new Lebanese state's modern functions, the electricity workers and employees opted to solve their claims through legal means. A legal case that addressed all workers' grievances was filed under the name of one worker, Hassan al-Durzi, which was not a standard legal procedure, but nonetheless a creative and apparently successful one. On May 3, 1946, the civil court's decision surprisingly came out in favor of Hassan al-Durzi, and the electricity company was compelled to provide him with a wage increase, family allowance, and four days of paid vacation. Despite these gains, the court declined to address other major areas of contention, including the call for labor law.

Now backed by court orders, the electricity workers pressured the company to grant them the same privileges extended to al-Durzi. To counteract these demands, the company invoked the yet unsettled debate over whether French or national law should regulate the operation of the concessionary companies.[44] It considered the French mandate law as the basis for its relations with its employees, ultimately rejecting the application of Lebanese legal rulings. The company's position was, to a large extent, a preemptive step to halt the anticipated setbacks to French economic ventures in the Levant after independence. In light of the agitation and strikes by the electricity and tobacco workers, the French feared that leniency toward the electricity company workers would encourage employees of the other foreign companies to rebel against colonial privileges and challenge the very foundations of French economic concessions.

The Régie workers did indeed quickly take advantage of the partial success in al-Durzi's case, making it a point of reference for several demands they presented to the tobacco monopoly on May 19, 1946. They threatened to strike after three weeks if the Régie did not meet their demands.[45] Anticipating a long struggle with the Régie, the workers organized their ranks and unified their efforts as they circulated a leaflet urging their fellow workers in all branches to support the strike. The administration promptly reacted by transferring one of the leaders of the strike, Jean Tuwayni, to a remote branch of the company in Tripoli in northern Lebanon. This action was followed by the postindependence government's efforts to buttress the Régie's refusal to negotiate with its workers until they ended the strike and resumed their work, thus delineating the powerful and conspicuous alliance of the state and foreign capital. With the full determination and support of Interior Minister Sa'ib Salam, the Régie hardened its position and dismissed twenty-four women and men from work.[46] Some leftist news accounts noted the increased agitation against the Régie among the workers, described as "mostly women," but they failed to emphasize the significance of women's increased collective activism.[47] Efforts by the Union of the Régie Workers and Employees (URWE, Naqabat Muwazzafi wa 'Ummal Idarat Hasr al-Tabigh wa al-Tanbak) failed to get Tuwayni transferred back from Tripoli and the twenty-four fired workers reemployed.[48] A few days later, on June 15, the Régie's administration issued a memorandum calling on the workers to end the strike and promised to study their demands once they resumed work. The workers refused to comply, occupied the Régie factory and central warehouse in Mar Mikhayil (Beirut), and organized the day and night shifts to guard the warehouse and prevent the loading and shipping of cigarettes.[49] When the Régie tried to open the warehouse, the workers threatened to turn the confrontation into a bloody and costly battle.[50] They then commenced a counterplan to stifle any future attempts to undermine the strike. More than five hundred workingwomen and men organized into groups to block scabs and control company properties. At the Régie's request, the government dispatched a large police force to defeat the strikers through intimidation, threats, and arrests.

In an unprecedented move, female workers outpaced their male colleagues in forming the first strike committee. Then they called upon the men to follow suit. The two committees were soon combined into one, jointly headed by a woman, Asma Malkun, and a man, Tawfiq Subayti. They chose one of the halls of a nearby church as the command center and formed several subcommittees charged with attempting to protect workers from arrest and forced labor. The church, as strike headquarters, was soon being visited by many industrial workers, sympathizers, unionists, leftists, and students. Strong ties bonded the women workers, whose unity and assertiveness several observers vividly documented and recalled. In spite of long-established and widely taught cultural norms of deference to men in political decision making and conflict resolution, these women clearly emerged as innovators by taking labor issues into their own hands and presiding over important phases of the strike. Many observers shared their admiration for the level and quality of involvement the female workers exhibited on the strike committees.[51]

In comparison with the 1945 strike, the one a year later witnessed a forceful integration of temporary workingwomen's demands. In 1946, two groups of women stood united in their efforts to protect their labor rights: temporary or seasonal workers fought to achieve permanency, and permanent female workers aimed to win benefits and wages at levels comparable to their male counterparts.

On the one hand, most if not all of the temporary workingwomen had been hired for manual tasks such as sorting of tobacco leaves, which was central to the Régie's manufacturing process despite mechanization in other production areas. Unlike several food and clothing factories, which lost much of their female labor force after mechanization, the tobacco industry continued to rely on a substantial number of women and their "nimble fingers." The Régie was reluctant to dispense with this source of cheap labor or with its own indifference to the temporary workers' demands. The women's steadfastness in seeking job permanency may have been fueled by their temporary status, which gave them a greater margin for risk taking because, first, they had little to lose, and, second, they may have been able to rely on family or other income support during the months in which they were not sorting tobacco leaves. These women also might have felt compelled to throw themselves into these labor battles for ethical reasons—to end the Régie's exploitation of them.

On the other hand, the permanent women faced a different situation. They had a longer history at the Régie, were more skilled, and often had no source of income other than their industrial tobacco work. This group of women, as strike demands reveal, rejected the systematic bias toward men in terms of salary, promotion, and benefits. Permanent as opposed to temporary women seemed more willing to address, if not also more acutely aware of, gender inequality and the necessity of fighting for their place at the Régie not merely as workers, but as women. Despite these differences, the clear solidarity between permanent and temporary workers strengthened their overall bargaining power and possibly bolstered the militant pursuit of their aims.

It is significant that the women exhibited few if any national emblems during the strike or the confrontation with the police, avoiding the use of nationalist symbols to claim their rights as citizens. Among the noteworthy women workers who led and participated in the strike were Josephine Ashqar, Mary Baltaji, Najla Dakkash, Rose Damuri, Lur Dib, Sa'ada Hubayqa, Warda Butrus Ibrahim, Jamila Ishaq, Mary Khattar, Mary Ja'ja', Asma Malkun, Mary Mardini, Rafiqa Muja'is, Bahija Nahra, Latifa Rashdan, Jamila Shahwan, and 'Afifa Thabit.[52] These women's colleagues (of both sexes) described them as *salbin* (obstinate), *qabadayat* (courageous), and *mumayazat* (extraordinary).[53] Among them was one who reportedly carried a knife to work, another who allegedly had the physical power of a male boxer, and yet another who purportedly gave her employers little rest. Their unconventional social attitudes and protest styles earned them the laudatory titles of "daredevils" and "wild women." Yet their employers denounced them as "unruly" and "irrational." Indeed, these women upset gender conventions by outdoing men in radicalism and by appearing in the forefront of strikes and in public spaces usually accorded to men. The "transgressive" nature of their activism stirred up fears of political marginality and presumed weakness among the men, particularly among the employers and the state.

The Party and the Union

To arrive at a clearer picture of the background and motives for the Régie workingwomen's militancy, it is important to examine their political leanings and the influence of their families and colleagues on their class solidarity. I argue herein that the role of the Communist Party and the unions—namely, the URWE and the GCFUWE—were actually limited in shaping the Régie workingwomen's "consciousness" and militancy.

The Communist Party of Lebanon and Syria formed in 1924 and was joined a year later by the Lebanese People's Party and the Armenian Bolshevik Party, known as Spartacus.[54] Some of the founders of the Communist Party, such as

Fuad al-Shimali, Farid Tu'mi, and Faris Ma'tuq, were drawn from the ranks of tobacco workers in Bikfaya.[55] Two of the party's earliest cadres were formed in Hadath and Bikfaya, where the Régie later established branches.[56] Strong ties evolved early on between tobacco workers and the party, thanks to the efforts of Communists such as al-Shimali and his attempts to strengthen labor unions. He issued a booklet in 1928 titled *Naqabat al-'Ummal* (The Workers' Unions) and asked several tobacco workers in Bikfaya to offer their suggestions and feedback. It is noteworthy that the booklet urged workingwomen to join the union and become active in the Communist Party, reminding them that they were "more exploited and oppressed than their male counterparts."[57]

In 1931, the Communist Party tied working-class struggles to anticolonial resistance, calling for national independence, the abolition of the privileges of foreign companies, and the elimination of the two existing governments in Syria and Lebanon that served the French.[58] It also called for greater freedom of the press, especially with respect to the working class, and demanded unfettered rights to publish, form committees, protest, and strike. Before 1939, the Lebanese Communist Party benefited from the open support of its counterpart in France and resisted the colonial powers openly. For example, in 1936 the party joined in the fifty-day strike against the government in Damascus, Aleppo, and Hums.[59] In the same year, however, the newly elected government in France banned the French Communist Party, thus exposing the Lebanese Communists to suppression and investigation.[60] In August 1940, the colonial authorities arrested thirty-four Lebanese Communists and put them on trial. It was only at the end of the pro-Nazi Vichy regime and after the Soviet Union joined the Allies against the Axis powers that Communist activities in Lebanon legally resumed.

The party enjoyed six years of open public activity (from 1942 to 1948) and seemingly basked in the international Communist and Soviet victories, which gave new rigor to its political and social programs. Four Communist candidates ran for Parliament in the Lebanese elections of 1943, but they received very few votes, possibly because they were unable to reach the Lebanese voters during the period when the party was banned.

The Communists devoted special attention to tobacco workers' strikes during the 1940s, lending guidance and advice to the Régie strikers (in particular men) to coordinate and unite their efforts.[61] The GCFUWE strove to maintain a unified vision among all parts and members of the Lebanese labor movement. It encouraged new unions to form and develop effective methods of coordination. As will become clear in the coming sections, the Régie workers sought GCFUWE support and started to link their demands to those of the larger labor movement. The Communist elements of the GCFUWE attempted to situate labor confrontations within a wider framework of class conflict.[62] It is difficult to ascertain the extent to which tobacco workers and other industrial workingwomen identified with these Communist unionists, but we know they came in contact with them during periods of labor agitation and strikes. Diffuse socialist views reached workingwomen through Communist unionists who came in close contact with them and their male colleagues during episodes of labor conflict, through popular venues such as the media, and very likely through male relatives and friends who were active in unions.[63]

Among the more militant Régie women, only two that I know of were active in the unions and were indirectly influenced by socialist views or methods of labor organization.[64] Many women expressed feelings of confusion and uncertainty about joining labor unions, stating that they were "uneducated" and "illiterate," and would not be able to "live up" to the unions' standards and goals. Most of them knew only indirectly—and usually through a male contact—about the GCFUWE and Communist Party's long-term objectives. Others seemed overburdened with domestic chores in addition to their Régie job, leaving them little time for other activities. A few also pointed to their fathers or husbands' aversion to women's involvement in any activity of a political nature that seemed "unladylike." On their part, unionists and Communists seemed uninterested in recruiting women into their ranks or making their meetings and circles more female-friendly and sensitive to women's domestic, family, and time constraints. Several Communist leaders found it divisive to address gender issues and rarely distinguished between male and female working-class cultures.[65] The Communist Party addressed its audience commonly in the plural masculine as "our male comrades" and "the workingmen of the countryside"; only rarely did it single out women as a group standing on its own. The party also discussed the growth of conscious social awareness in Lebanon at the hands of "male students and teachers, and the sons of the toiling industrial workingmen."[66] With the same male-centered language, party leaders urged their "countrymen" to bring a new "breed of men" to rule the country justly and democratically, noting that the "triumph of freedom in Lebanon rested in the hands of the sons of Lebanon."[67] The Lebanese Communist Party, which served as the "vanguard party," was expected to lead the workers' movements, although it had often suffered from a limited appeal to women. It is thus questionable whether the party played more than a marginal role in recruiting women workers and peasants into its ranks, and my findings cast serious doubt on the male intelligentsia's "missionary role" in propagating militancy among workingwomen.

It is safe to conclude that the particular work and societal arrangements experienced by the Régie workingwomen were more conducive to promoting their militancy and "consciousness" of their labor interests than were the union or the Communist Party. Moreover, the experience of anticolonial struggle and a wide-based national identity likewise contributed considerably to the development of rationalized methods of labor organization and protest.

The Final Stage of the 1946 Strike

The advanced level of organization and cohesion among the Régie workers in 1946 alarmed government officials, especially Interior Minister Sa'ib Salam, who decided to seize the company properties from workers' control because of what he expressed as his sympathy toward smokers' growing complaints for cigarettes. In reality a staunch opponent of the labor movement in general, Salam ordered the police to open the Régie depot by force.[68] Meanwhile, the Régie, in its continued efforts to isolate the Beiruti workers and to deny the legitimacy of their demands, tried to transfer cigarettes from its Damascus plant to market. Syrian workers there, however, blocked this move and declared solidarity with their Lebanese colleagues. The company then dispatched a truck to the Bikfaya branch to ship cigarettes to specified market locations.[69] Loaded with cigarettes and heading from Bikfaya to Beirut, the truck was intercepted by the Mar Mikhayil workers and prevented from being unloaded. These primarily female workers surrounded the truck and shouted their readiness to die rather than allow the truck to leave the depot. As a result, the truck retreated from Mar Mikhayil to another depot at Furun al-Shubbak, a neighborhood in East Beirut, where more than two hundred workers, again mostly women, slept on the ramp that connected the depot to the main street. A group of women workers obstructed the truck's path, their voices reverberating, "Let the truck pass over our bodies."[70]

The national police who escorted the truck tried to disperse the workers and clear the way. Numerous men and women rushed with their bare hands to prevent them from using their guns, only to find themselves being showered with bullets for no less than forty minutes. They could not hide or run away, and the place was soon filled with bleeding and dead bodies. Warda Butrus Ibrahim, one of the active women in the strike, was immediately killed, and her blood splashed on her fiancé, Sabi' Khunaysir, who stood next to her.[71] Lur Dib and Najim Hubayqa, a female worker and a male worker, were in a critical condition, and fifteen other workingwomen and twelve workingmen were wounded. The reports of the Hotel

9. Warda Butrus Ibrahim. On June 20, 1970, the URWE commemorated the martyrdom of Ibrahim, who was killed during the 1946 strike. *Source:* URWE records, Hadath, Lebanon. Reproduced by permission of the Union of the Régie Workers and Employees (Naqabat Muwazzafi wa 'Ummal Idarat Hasr al-Tabigh wa al-Tanbak).

Dieu hospital to which they were taken reveal that some of the injured suffered permanent damage and disabilities. Police bullets also hit several residents in the neighboring buildings. The police then arrested eight male workers and one woman worker.[72]

Scores of surviving workers attended to the wounded as they recovered and provided financial and social support for their families. The teams they organized visited the patients at Hotel Dieu hospital and raised funds to defray medical costs and the living expenses needed by the wives and children of the wounded.[73]

Popular Echoes and Social Recognition of the Strike

The strike was defeated, but not without significant cost to the company and important benefits to the workers. It set off a chain reaction across the country, and on June 28 the labor movement called upon Lebanese laborers everywhere to stop work for ten minutes as an expression of their solidarity with the tobacco workers and to condemn the actions of the Lebanese police.[74] Feelings of disbelief and horror at the government's heavy-handed treatment of the strikers swept over people in all walks of life. Representatives and members of political parties, social associations, workers' unions, and federations openly expressed their outrage at what they termed a "massacre." The high number of female victims particularly moved them. Hundreds of angry sympathizers congregated at Hotel Dieu hospital to denounce the Régie, France, and government officials, in particular Sa'ib Salam. The hospital hallway was filled with flowers and cards expressing sorrow and moral support.[75] Newspaper offices received hundreds of petitions, as did members of Parliament, who were urged to intervene in support of the workers.[76] For days, newspapers published pages of letters received from community and religious leaders, unions, and federations condemning the police action, in particular the armed attacks against women.

Salam found the national discourse an attractive medium for defending himself and discrediting the workers, and he accused them of disloyalty to the "nation" and of the fulfillment of "foreign" rather than local aspirations. He spoke of the disruption to the national economy that might have resulted from the continuation of the strike and invoked concerns for the collective welfare while glorifying the "national identity" of the Régie, which, he noted, contributed 95 percent of its profits to the public treasury.[77] But Salam was unable to show

how vital these alleged profits were to the development of the workers and the middle class, thereby demonstrating what Peter Gran argues is congruent with the premises holding up the tribal-ethnic state, "the [state] most resistant to the idea of allowing the formation of middle classes and the one most apprehensive about the idea of development."[78] More important for the Lebanese state specifically, it was not acceptable to allow women to cross any boundaries within the rigid, apartheid-like system of gender roles and "the sex-role stereotypy" because that would jeopardize the ethnic stratification that held the tribal-ethnic state together. Thus, the government seemed most vulnerable when it avoided discussing women's involvement in the strike, concomitantly revealing the potency of gender concerns in shaping the state's approach to the conflict.

The Lebanese government, embarrassed by the brutality of the police, was obliged to investigate the matter and minimize the widespread anger. George 'Aqil, the Mount Lebanon deputy, expressed concerns common among many parliamentarians when he sharply criticized Salam's policies and requested an immediate parliamentary session to question government officials.[79] Several deputies denounced the government's abuse of power and use of armed coercion to "quell a peaceful strike." Moreover, several deputies insisted that the Régie workers' demands were legal and that the government should accept them. As 'Aqil beseeched the deputies to pass a motion of no confidence in the government, it became evident that the strike and its repercussions were an early sign of the infant national state's fragility.[80] Historians have pointed to the 1956 "rose water" coup against the regime of Bishara al-Khuri and the 1958 confrontations with the Camille Chamoun government as the earliest indicators of the precarious foundation of the Lebanese state. However, in reality the 1946 strike was the earliest indicator that the Lebanese state and its defined national order were seriously challenged from "below" by protesting workers.[81]

The scope of support for the tobacco workers widened to include sympathizers from political parties that had once either opposed the workers or expressed only lukewarm support for their cause. This development gave the strike a decidedly nationalist image that set it apart from the state's brand of nationalism. Following the funeral service for Warda Butrus, mourners defiantly marched to Salam's residence, shouted Warda's name for hours, and denounced her killers. Warda was eighteen years old at the time of the strike. She had joined the Régie in 1944 at its Furn al-Shubbak branch and had become engaged to fellow worker Sabiʻ Khunaysir.[82] As striker Wasila Dubuq recounted in her description of the strike, the tobacco workers continued to organize demonstrations in front of Salam's residence, invoking the haunting memory of Warda throughout their painful one-month strike from June 11 to July 12, 1946.[83]

Rekindling the Flame: Not Without a Labor Law

The leading labor unions and federations' efforts to promote a new set of labor demands culminated in a meeting of the Labor Front (Jabhat al-ʻAmal), headed by Deputy Henri Pharoan and attended by the URWE and GCFUWE.[84] The Labor Front was founded during the early months of 1944 under the government's efforts to counterbalance the influence of communism in the labor unions. Two distinct but complementary demands surfaced: one exclusively relating to the tobacco workers and the other involving the Lebanese labor movement as a whole. With respect to the first, participants agreed to support fully the Régie workers' demands for a wage increase, financial compensation for the families of Warda Butrus Ibrahim and the wounded workers, wage payments for all the strike days, the return of all workers who were transferred outside Beirut during the strike, and, last, the release of all detained and imprisoned workers. Within the context of the labor movement as a whole, the participants and the delegates of various unions and federations agreed to intensify their campaign for the long-awaited labor laws, improve the methods for unifying and harmonizing workers' struggles, overcome political factionalism in the work environment, and, finally, propose direct discussion between the tobacco workers and the government.

On July 9, 1946, Saʼib Salam met with the delegation representing the tobacco workers.[85] Few tangible gains were evident after this meeting. Salam refused to pay the workers the earnings they lost during the strike because he feared it would encourage them and weaken their employers. He attempted to diffuse the issues by arguing that the workers' case fell under the jurisdiction of the Ministry of Finance, which refused any amelioration of the workers' status or their working conditions. The workers decided to carry through with their strike and to reinforce it with a general strike involving the entire public sector and national organizations throughout the country.[86] Several strikes had already erupted in various economic and commercial establishments, the most significant of which were those of the port, the railroad, the Central Bank (al-Bank al-Markazi), the breweries, and the workers of Beirut municipality.[87] Labor unrest was a real threat to Lebanese capitalists and put a great deal of strain on large sectors of society. As a consequence, the mounting pressure on the government, on top of images of its violent suppression of the strike, forced it to put in place formal mechanisms to settle labor disputes.

The government's readiness to reach a settlement was evident in the early days of July, when Salam met with the labor unions. The Régie and its workers soon reached an agreement, the terms of which included company grants to the workers equivalent to six weeks wages—although the Régie refused to pay the workers specifically for strike days. Needy workers would be given loans with low-interest rates to be paid back over a twelve-month period. Portions of the grant and loan were to be deducted automatically from their wages. The number of overtime hours also was increased to compensate for the interruption of work during the strike.[88] The Régie did not meet any other demands, including women's call for job permanency and equality with men in salary and benefits.

The violence inflicted on the workers and the death of Warda Butrus Ibrahim imposed new realities. In a society with deeply embedded tribal-social values wherein patriarchs saw themselves as providers and protectors of women and children, brutality toward women was considered cowardly and reprehensible—an offense to the honor system. Women were seen as "weaker" than men, who were "endowed" with the physical strength to engage and withstand armed attacks. Thus, Warda's murder not only brought shame to the government, but also left many observers with mixed feelings of admiration and surprise regarding the women's bravery. In the government's defense, spokesmen and some loyal journalists accused the male workers of intentionally placing women in the front line so that the men could hide behind them during clashes with the police. Yet even some newspapers that normally supported the state denounced its use of machine guns, invoked social norms of decency, and highlighted civil moral boundaries that state authorities should never violate.[89] On the one hand, it is possible that mass participation in the strike pointed to a widespread awareness of labor inequities and the exploitation of the working class at the hands of foreign and national capitalists. On the other hand, the government's decision to pass labor legislation may have been the culmination of diverse national concerns that simply converged in the form of support for the Régie workers.

Owing to the government's moral and political isolation at this time, the Parliament promulgated the long-awaited national labor law on September 23, 1946. The law provided workers for the first time with a number of rights, the most important ones limiting work to forty-eight hours weekly, allowing a fifteen-day yearly break, and offering paid sick leave. Women were to receive forty days of paid maternity leave.[90] The law also spelled out provisions relating to children, who were limited to working seven hours per day. Meanwhile, vague clauses watered down the legislation in regard to job promotion, wage increases, the right to strike, discharge from work, indemnities and family allowances, and, most important, the elimination of gender discrimination in pay, benefits, and treatment on the shop floor. Even though the government was forced to revise its policy on labor issues and come to the bargaining table, it appears to have used all its efforts to delay and subvert the process as well as to tailor many specifics within the labor legislation to its own interests and aspirations. The new legislation therefore largely nurtured the existing social configurations that perpetuated class and gender divisions and extended minimal benefits to the workers.

I believe, however, that the 1946 Régie strike strongly affected the Lebanese people's confidence in the government, which resigned at the end of the year. As for Salam, he was not appointed to any governmental position for five years after the strike.[91] Among wide sectors of Lebanese society, Salam's rule was seen as neocolonialist and autocratic. The British Foreign Ministry's assessment of him at the time reinforced these views and emphasized his unprincipled political tendencies: "Sa'ib Salam is himself regarded as a businessman and a fairly strong character . . . he is certainly not anti-British and in fact enjoys the reputation of being one of our men. . . . He can, however, be counted on to transfer allegiance, if there should be a conflict of interest, from us to the Americans."[92]

Workingwomen in Pursuit of Permanency

Women who had spoken out in the strikes were suddenly silenced in the legal negotiations and settlement process that witnessed the passage of the labor legislation.[93] Yet, owing to grave inequities and the arbitrary conditions under which women worked for the Régie, the women's demands were more urgent than the men's. Their primary goal was to be transferred from a temporary to a permanent status after completing the probationary period required by the Régie. But neither this period nor the duration of training was clearly stipulated by the new law, even though the Régie occasionally followed this probationary-to-permanency process for unskilled male workers. Compromised in the final legal settlements on July 15, 1946, around 350 temporary workers, mostly women, faced an uncertain future.[94]

The women tobacco workers' disappointment brings to mind the comparable disillusionment of women in other Arab societies when, after participating actively in labor and anticolonial struggles, they reaped few of the benefits accorded their male counterparts on the eve of dispute settlements or national independence.[95] Militant Algerian women known as the *mujahidat,* for instance, sacrificed a great deal during the war of independence against the French, but after independence they saw neither restructuring of the family nor an increase in women's authority relative to men.[96] In fact, many Algerian women were removed completely from many influential political positions after independence was gained in 1965 and thereafter had minimal presence in mass organizations and the Parliament. In the case of Palestinian women in Lebanon who joined the Palestine Liberation Organization (PLO), although their activism and at times militancy led to a decrease in family restrictions and patriarchal authority, particularly in the refugee camps, they nevertheless remained marginal to the PLO's executive posts and cadres, which had the potential to encourage women's economic independence and to prevent the male members from co-opting the women's goals, but did not fulfill that potential.[97]

The Régie's temporary women workers faced a novel situation wherein "nation," "citizenship," and the "law" were allied and interlinked in a complex and binding way that necessitated the use of new venues for expressing and achieving their goals. Women individually and collectively wrestled with the law, forcing the Régie to validate its policies. They did not partake in drafting the law, but they related their views and concerns on this issue to a male lawyer who negotiated on their behalf until the implementation of the law. By opting to throw themselves into the legal whirlwind to negotiate their labor conditions, these women apparently internalized some sense of "citizenship," although their view very likely deviated from the bourgeois version of "citizenship" and contested the state's control of the law.

Epilogue: Testing the Labor Law

With mixed feelings of excitement and frustration, several workingwomen took advantage of the labor law. They attempted to test the law's effectiveness in improving their working conditions and preventing employers from undercutting the few yet clear "inalienable rights" established by the law. As the following examples show, the implementation of the labor law was only a partial victory for the workers. Workingwomen and men sometimes achieved their goals, but for the most part the law fell short of providing just solutions and compensations for the workers.

Numerous women still faced great dilemmas in the Régie's leaf-sorting department and felt insecure about their financial prospects. The case of Wadad Brays is illustrative of these challenges. Brays joined the Régie on March 14, 1951. She sorted leaves for six months for a monthly salary of forty-four Lebanese pounds when the Régie, she claimed, abruptly discharged her without any reasonable justification or advance notice. Brays filed a lawsuit against the Régie, demanding sixty-six pounds in compensation, including, as the labor code stipulated, pay covering the one month she should have worked after learning of her impending dismissal and pay for qualified breaks, holidays, and her lawyers' fees. The Régie continued to argue that Brays was a seasonal worker and was not entitled to any compensation under Article 58 of the labor code. In addition, the Régie affirmed that when daily workers received their wages, they signed papers that clearly stated their status as daily or seasonal workers. Moreover, the middleman who hired these temporary workers informed them when hiring them that their tasks were transient and would end after the processing of the raw tobacco harvest.[98]

Temporary workingwomen such as Brays opted to use various legal channels to acquire the right to become permanent workers. The circumstances she lived through were vividly documented, first, in correspondence between the Ministry of Finance and the Ministry of Social Affairs and, second, in the surviving papers of a lawyer who handled the Régie's legal business. Meanwhile, in 1951 a group of temporary women workers, frustrated by the Régie's rejection of their demands for permanency and the URWE's indifference, turned to the GCFUWE and jointly filed a lawsuit against the Régie.[99]

The Régie's mandatory authority—the Ministry of Finance—argued that Article 58 denied workers any compensation if they were hired for a limited period of time. It stated that the Régie annually hired women for a few months to sort tobacco leaves; at the completion of this task, the Régie would discharge these seasonal hands and rehire them during the next tobacco harvest. The Ministry of Finance and the Régie refused to extend the contract to a full year, arguing that the raw tobacco harvest could not endure storage, especially during hot weather. Seasonal workers were not, in their view, eligible even for severance pay, a situation that deepened Brays' and other women's mistrust in the legal process and government protection.[100] Brays consequently lost the case and received no compensation.

Aside from seasonal workingwomen, other female and male workers also were deprived of permanent status. Unlike the seasonal workers, these workers were hired for more than six months. They, too, endeavored to interpret the labor codes to protect their interests during times when striking had not achieved the success they expected. The 1946 version of the Lebanese labor code stated that the period for training workers before they became permanent varied from a minimum of six months to a maximum of one year.[101] This specification was amended after several confrontations between labor and management. In most cases, the Régie violated the law and deprived the workers of benefits associated with permanency.[102] For years, hundreds of temporary workingwomen and men continued to petition the Lebanese authorities and the Régie to redress these injustices.

The case of Murra Sulayman al-Murr in the 1960s is one such example.[103] Al-Murr began working at Al-Qassuf tobacco factory on January 1, 1930, five years before the founding of the Régie. A December 1935 governmental decree (number 16/LR) gave the Régie the tobacco monopoly in Syria and Lebanon. The same decree enjoined the workers of factories now incorporated into the Régie to enter the Régie. Yet the decree was unclear regarding the starting date of permanency for those workers or whether the years of their service at their former tobacco factories should be taken into account.[104] At her retirement in December 31, 1962, al-Murr discovered that her end-of-work compensation did not include her years of work at Al-Qassuf tobacco factory. To gain her pension, al-Murr raised the issue with the Council of Labor Arbitration.

The Régie rejected al-Murr's request and maintained that she had quit work for a while before joining the Régie's workforce in April 17, 1935. But al-Murr proved that the short cessation of work occurred at the time of her transfer from the old tobacco factory of Al-Qassuf to the Régie. She provided the Council of Labor Arbitration with material evidence in support of the fact that the Régie had ordered her to cease work for a short period of time in 1935 until the process of folding the old tobacco factories into the Régie had been completed. The council ordered the Régie on June 13, 1963, to pay al-Murr the compensation owed to her, which it did.[105] This example is one of the few in which a workingwoman was able to win a legal challenge utilizing labor law.

Permanent women workers also strove to eliminate gender discrimination, monotony, and lack of promotion, and to achieve fundamental benefits. The Régie hired 'Alya Nasr al-Sayyah on September 2, 1947. She became a permanent worker several years later instead of six months later, as the administrative law of the Régie and the labor law stipulated. She did not receive the salary corresponding to her permanent post or the wage increases decreed in 1951 and 1953, the job promotions, and other fringe benefits such as transportation fees and the free boxes of cigarettes.[106] Moreover, al-Sayyah accused the Régie of nepotism because it gave a few of her coworkers, whose qualifications she matched, various benefits despite having started work long after she did. She also claimed that while working as a machine operator, she did not receive the wage increase or benefits associated with this rank; on the contrary, she continued to be paid the wage of a nonskilled worker. In sum, she demanded her rightful wage and retirement compensation and the concomitant fringe benefits.[107]

The issues raised in al-Sayyah's case were very common in other workers' claims; nonetheless, the standard company response, articulated through its lawyer, was one of total rejection. The lawyer pointed out that for legal claims to be addressed, the claim had to meet several criteria,[108] among them the necessity for a claim to be filed within a two-year period from the time an issue arises. In addition, the date of job permanency was a factor upon which most legal cases were built. Al-Sayyah insisted on her right to acquire job permanency, as stipulated by both the Lebanese labor law and the Régie's administrative law. The Régie, however, noted that both laws specified the training period as no less than six months rather than three, as al-Sayyah claimed. It also maintained that the labor law did not compel any employer to give a permanent job to a trainee at any time. Nonetheless, Article 74 of the labor law obliged the employer to offer severance pay for a trainee discharged after three months of starting work.[109] Despite that obligation, al-Sayyah lost her case.

10. Women operating machines at the Hadath factory, February 2, 1997. Photograph by the author.

As evident in these cases, Régie workingwomen were forceful in addressing their labor grievances during and after the 1946 strike. Despite supposedly gender-blind demands and male co-optation, women started to develop an awareness of their rights, which they again and again insisted must be spelled out in the body of the law.

Conclusion

On the eve of national independence in the early 1940s, labor unrest became entangled with the struggle for liberation from the French. At this time, workingwomen and men fought fervently on the side of the national elite, whose aspirations temporarily appeared to be comparable to their own. However, after independence, the national rationale for unity lost much of its impetus and a distinct challenge to the "nation" started to emerge from working-class groups.

At first, women opted to fight their grievances through legal institutions, mainly the courts. By taking advantage of this "rationalized" formal channel, women workers apparently internalized some of the main premises of national "citizenship" and sharpened their methods to improve their conditions.[110] But when legal means failed, they sought other routes to win their place in the commonly hostile world of male managers and statesmen. Their activism during the 1946 strike marked an early phase in their awareness of their interests as exploited workers and women. They emerged as pioneers in organizing strike committees, identifying their tasks, and boosting their fellow strikers' morale.

Women's militancy seemed to have been shaped by several distinct factors. The first was the workers' participation in anticolonial struggle and mass action against the French, which discouraged acquiescence and nurtured a collective national identity. The second was their internalization of the emerging ideas and experiences of "citizenship" and legal justice as a rubric for the relation between the Lebanese and their state. These two sources of militancy seemed to be common to both workingwomen and workingmen. Distinct labor and social conditions of various groups of women at the Régie apparently also encouraged female radicalism. On the one hand, temporary and seasonal workingwomen realized the centrality of the cheap, manual, nonskilled labor in tobacco manufacturing that devolved to them. It is reasonable to assume that because their work at the Régie lasted from three to nine months at the most, they must have also relied on familial and rural sources of livelihood. Deprived of stability, proper salaries, and benefits, they had the least to lose of all workers in instigating a strike. Permanent workingwomen, on the other hand, had a longer and more stable history at the Régie. They seemed agitated mostly by gender inequality in the bestowal of wages, rank, promotion, and benefits. These two groups' level of engagement in the strike and their leadership role attest to the emergence and rise of an empowering "tradition" of working-class womanhood. The gradual radicalization of tobacco workingwomen against the state did not seem to be determined by unionization, indoctrination, or affiliation with a political party. Tobacco workingwomen embraced the GCFUWE's general demands and were exposed to diffuse socialist ideas through its Communist leaders during episodes of intense labor conflict, but they looked with mixed humility and suspicion at labor unions and socialist parties because they believed one had to be educated and free and to have a particular political bent to attend union and party meetings and carry out their plans. The circles and organizations to which the unionists and Communists belonged concomitantly reinforced women's dependency and vulnerability, and undermined their confidence in themselves. The union and the party alike projected a sense of male hierarchy and sexual assertiveness, which made them less congenial to female membership.

The 1946 strike was pivotal in recasting the workers' political aspirations and deepening their belief that their sacrifices were making history. Yet afterward it left a less glittering impression among the women who were denied an equal status with men and could not overcome socioeconomic deprivation. Nonetheless, the strike became a vivid sign of women's public assertiveness and an open challenge to the state's authority in a place seen as created by men and for men. The workingwomen citizens' militancy against the state, in turn, became an occasion for contesting gendered perceptions and promoting an unconventional image of womanhood. Women were the first to revolt and therefore to advance a new and empowering image of the industrial workingwoman.

4

Rural Displacement and Migration among the Régie Workers, 1950–1980

MULTIPLE HISTORICAL FORCES shaped women and men's entry into the industrial sectors of Lebanese society following the demise of the French mandate and the consolidation of the first national state in 1946. Rural hardship and social dislocation exacerbated by governmental neglect defined the early national history of factory laborers, the shape of the industrial workplace, and its social and political character.

This chapter examines the historical circumstances and the ideological premises of the Lebanese system that molded the gender, sectarian, and regional composition of the workforce at the Hadath plant—the major and largest Régie branch—from the 1950s onward. Data on the Régie workforce, which are derived from company records and state censuses, unfortunately do not provide a consistent chronology, nor are they always broken down by gender. To bridge the chronological gaps, I relied on figures and tables provided by the United Nations and the Food and Agricultural Organization, informal estimates published in local newspapers, and statistical studies conducted by contemporary social scientists, in particular those affiliated with the American University of Beirut. On some occasions, I also drew upon oral histories that I collected during the 1990s.

Analysis of these data and a revisionist reading of the secondary literature on national Lebanese history and ideology allowed me to delineate the distinct social processes that shaped two interdependent facets of the Régie workforce. The first concerns the patterns of sectarian and regional representation at the Régie, and the second involves the propensity for workers at the Hadath branch in Beirut to organize labor and to sustain confrontations between the mid-1950s and 1970.

As we turn to the first of these two facets, it is important to recognize that from the mid-1950s to 1969, there was a distinct decline in agricultural revenues in the Lebanese countryside, few government-initiated agricultural reforms, land shortages, overpopulation, and dramatic urban prosperity that attracted rural-urban migrants from ʻAkkar in the North and the Biqaʻ Valley in the East and the South to Beirut. From 1969 onward, political instability and violence contributed to a new wave of migration from the South and the Biqaʻ to Beirut. The Lebanese state's development policies also proved to be a potent factor in transforming the Régie workers' regional and sectarian character. I examine governmental policies and economic planning in the light of the political ideologies that guided the state from the 1950s to 1964. These ideologies laid the groundwork for policies that accentuated rural displacement, which became the source of Beirut's industrial workforce. Two-thirds of the Régie's workers had moved either voluntarily or forcibly from Beirut's rural surroundings. All these factors set the stage for a social process that modified the sectarian and regional character of the people who worked at the Régie. The Shiʻi population, concentrated in the country's "peripheral" rural regions, bore the brunt of economic underdevelopment and government mismanagement, which eventually drove hundreds of thousands of them to the city. This may explain how the Shiʻis took over the Maronites' place as the largest sectarian group at the Régie during the 1960s.

The second facet is that workingwomen and men were engaged in frequent and intense labor confrontations between the mid-1950s and 1970, almost all of which emerged from the central branch of the Régie in Hadath. I believe this labor activism was closely related to the spatial dislocation and subsequent rural-urban migration experienced by much of the Régie workforce. These shared experiences appear to have encouraged a spirit of cohesion, social solidarity, and defiance among diverse religious groups of workingwomen and men. I also argue that the stability of the workforce and the interplay of strong familial and village ties among 40 percent of the workers enhanced their adaptability to the industrial setting and nurtured a propensity for collective action. Moreover, Beirut's urban landscape and its popular culture likely provided the means through which workers learned about the political system as well as how they discovered ways to express their grievances and attract the moral support of many sectors of Lebanese society. Migrant industrial workers of suburban Beirut also were often exposed to more politically radical musical and artistic performances than they had been in the countryside and were well placed to witness union demonstrations, student protests, labor agitations, and diverse opposition movements against the state. It is difficult to ascertain precisely the extent to which Beirut's popular spaces and activities influenced the workers' awareness and level of sustained protest against their employers, but I believe that the vast majority of Régie workingwomen and men expressed a vivid awareness of the audio-visual (television, radio, cassette players, and theater) performances, which openly attacked the capitalist system and railed against class exploitation and the state's detrimental social and labor policies. These forms of oppositional culture seldom appeared in the countryside.

From the French to the Lebanese Régie: Continuity and Change

The historical transition made by industrial workers from the French colonial period to the nationalist one recast the relationship between laborers and the state. The infant Lebanese polity was newly faced with legitimizing its control over capital and labor through legal means shaped both by the liberal economic neutrality that the polity formally advocated as well as by its system of sectarian and tribal stratification at both the civil and state level.

A "Lebanese republic" came into being in 1920 under the tutelage of the French. A constitution drafted in 1926 pronounced the "permanent" geographical boundaries of Lebanon and stated that the president of the Lebanese republic, elected by the French-formed Chamber of Deputies, had to swear loyalty to the "Lebanese nation."[1] The Constitution did not specify a ratio for proportional representation of the various Lebanese professions, nor did it identify particular governmental positions for each sect. Through the appointment of French-educated Christians to several official posts and the emphasis on Lebanese rather than Arab patriotism in the Constitution, the French obviously expected the pro-French Christian elite to play a foundational role in the postindependence state.[2] The mandate's sectarian preferences also were manifest in the encouragement of Maronite political leadership.

In the area of labor legislation, the French did not recognize any particular rights or needs for industrial workers and prohibited the establishment of unions. In the mid-1940s, during the post-French phase, labor unions, political parties, and civil organizations were permitted to form, mainly because they helped embellish the raison d'être of the modern Lebanese nation-state as a democratic republic supporting a liberal economy. Yet after 1946, despite the fact that the labor movement continued to work legally to achieve its goals, it was infiltrated by the government, which aimed to weaken the influence of the movement's leftists and Communists.[3] I explore this issue more fully in chapter 6 when I address the workers' strikes during the 1960s. Let it suffice herein to note that conflicts between the labor movement and the state appeared early on during the first national government of Bishara al-Khuri (1946–52). Al-Khuri felt that in order for Lebanon to succeed as an entrepreneurial, service-based, neutral entrepot in the region, the state must co-opt the labor movement and suppress workers' aspirations for a developed industrial sector with a system of social and health benefits, concerns representing the essentials of the tribal-ethnic hegemony.

With the emergence of the Lebanese National Pact (al-Mithaq al-Watani), which precipitated the demise of the French mandate in 1943, the nationalist elite, both Muslim and Christian, came to an agreement about the political status of Lebanon and its internal sectarian character. In short, Lebanon was to be a sovereign, neutral polity, with the Muslim and Christian elites expressing allegiance to its national foundations.[4] On the one hand, the Muslims were expected to resist any plans for fusing Lebanon with a larger Arab Islamic state. On the other hand, the Christians were expected to refrain from seeking the protection of Western powers, thus accepting Lebanon's Arab identity. The pact consolidated the practice of dividing government and parliamentary offices on a sectarian basis, with a Maronite designated president, a Sunnite prime minister, and a Shi'i Speaker of the House. It also maintained a Muslim-Christian ratio of five to six in the Chamber of Deputies.[5] From the very beginning, these agreements reflected the precarious nature of the new polity and its struggle to create a sense of cohesion and viable citizenship across religious communities and class lines.

With respect to the Régie, it is difficult to ascertain the distinct shifts experienced from the colonial phase to the national phase. Knowledge about the industrial workforce in Grand Liban, let alone the gender and sectarian composition of the Régie workforce, is seriously impeded by a lack of sources.[6] I can only confirm that a qualitative change occurred in 1959—a long while after independence—when the government took explicit steps to tighten its grip on the Régie by issuing a decree to revise and organize supervision over the Régie's administration and by appointing a permanent deputy to the executive board.[7]

The Régie's Gender and Sectarian Character

From 1958 to 1964, the Régie had seven branches: Hadath in Beirut; Bikfaya and Khinshara in Mount Lebanon; Tripoli and Batrun in the North; and Nabatiyya and Ghaziyya in the South. The two branches farthest from each other, Tripoli and Ghaziyya, were three hours apart by car. The central branch at Hadath was the largest, a maximum of two hours by car from all the remaining Régie branches. Among these seven branches, only the Hadath plant included all lines of tobacco production: sorting, preparing, manufacturing, packaging, and storing (table 6).

Two other branches—namely, Bikfaya and Tripoli—embraced light mechanization of manufacturing tobacco that required semiskilled labor in addition to sorting tobacco leaves, which was carried on largely by unskilled workers. The Tripoli branch produced mainly tombac (made for water pipes, *narjila*) for exportation, whereas the Bikfaya factory produced brands of cigarettes for the local market, mainly the Bafra brand.

Sufficient data on the religious identity and gender of the Régie workers at all branches, except the mixed and heterogeneous Hadath plant, have

TABLE 6. Production of tobacco across the branches of the Régie, 1958–1981

	Hadath	Bikfaya	Tripoli	Ghaziyya	Khinshara	Batrun	Nabatiyya
Sorting tobacco leaves	X	X	X	X			
Storing in warehouse	X		X	X		X	X
Preparing	X				X		
Manufacturing	X	X					
Packeting	X	X					
Tombac manufacturing			X				
Snuff manufacturing					X		

Source: Régie Personnel Department, "Listing du personnel par matricule, 1 octobre, 1981," Régie company records, Hadath.

proven useful in delineating a trend toward almost sectarian homogeneity. This delineation helps us understand why the major labor conflicts with the Régie emerged first in the sectarian heterogeneous Hadath branch, whereas the other sectarian homogeneous branches were either reluctant or slow to join in. For example, Bikfaya's workers were more than 90 percent Christian, but Tripoli's workers were mostly Muslim Sunni. It is noteworthy, however, that the two branches demonstrated comparable gender and occupational heterogeneity, being a mix of skilled and unskilled workers, and that women formed 54 percent of the workforce in Bikfaya and 50 percent in Tripoli. At the Ghaziyya plant in the South, where the majority of the workers were Shiʻi women, there were only two departments, sorting and storing, and no manufacturing was carried out. The storing of tobacco leaves was the single operation at the Batrun and Nabatiyya branches, and more than 95 percent of the workers were unskilled men. As for sectarian backgrounds, the workers at Batrun were predominantly Christians, and at Nabatiyya they were overwhelmingly Shiʻi Muslims. Finally, the production of tobacco at Khinshara in Mount Lebanon was semimechanized and specialized in chopping, grinding, and packaging tobacco for snuff. At Khinshara, 76 percent of the workers were unskilled women, and all of them were Christian.[8]

Between 1954 and 1987, more than 40 percent of the Régie workers were women (see table 4 in chapter 1). The employees who occupied the company's administrative posts were almost exclusively men drawn from wealthy and educated Lebanese families composed primarily of Sunni Muslims and Maronite Christians.[9] Thus, the highest-ranking positions at the Régie were dominated by men, and the lowest were held by women.

In terms of the Régie's sectarian makeup, Maronite women were a majority, making up 44 percent of the total female labor force in 1954 (table 7). Shiʻi women workers (21 percent) came next, then Greek Orthodox (13 percent), Armenian (11 percent), and finally Catholic (6 percent).[10] Sectarian minorities such as the Druze, the Syriac, and the Latin made up less than 2 percent. These figures show that although Christians formed the majority of the wealthiest class in Lebanon at the time, they also were present among the lower classes.[11] The Lebanese working class was not exclusively Muslim in composition. Indeed, a significant percentage of the Maronites went on to become "proletariat" and joined the ranks of industrial labor, as I show later in this chapter. Although there are no exact figures for the number of working-class Maronites nationally, I confidently consider their high number at a major industrial enterprise such as the Régie an indication of the existence of a significant lower-class component in the Maronite community.

During the 1960s, the Régie witnessed a remarkable increase in the number of Shi'i women workers. From 21 percent in 1954 to 42 percent in 1969, Shi'i women jumped to the first rank in the sectarian scale of the Régie female work-force. Maronite workingwomen ranked second (32 percent) in 1969, and Greek Orthodox women were third (10 percent). These patterns remained in force for the rest of the period (table 7), and I discuss the significance of this change later in this chapter.

TABLE 7. Sectarian background of Régie female workers, 1954–1987

	1954		1969		1981		1987	
	N	%	N	%	N	%	N	%
Christian Maronite	350	44	424	32	367	30	336	30
Muslim Sunni	18	2	79	6	102	8	95	9
Muslim Shi'i	168	21	554	42	532	43	481	44
Christian Catholic	50	6	64	5	77	6	73	7
Christian Orthodox	105	13	129	10	107	9	90	8
Muslim Druze	3	0	6	1	4	0	1	0
Armenian	86	11	53	4	27	2	18	2
Syriac	5	1	7	1	9	1	7	0
Christian Protestant	—	—	—	—	—	—	—	—
Latin	3	0	4	0	4	0	2	0
Chaldean	—	—	—	—	—	—	—	—
Muslim 'Alawite	—	—	1	0	1	0	1	0
Jewish	—	—	—	—	—	—	—	—
Total	788	100	1,321	100	1,230	100	1,104	100
Unaccounted for	153	16	105	7	—	—	5	1

Sources: List of union membership dues paid, 1954, URWE records, Hadath; Régie Personnel Department, "Liste nominative du personnel au 1-1-1969," "Listing du personnel par matricule, 1 octobre 1981," "Liste des rubriques de Paie, 13-12-1987," Régie company records, Hadath. Figures rounded to the nearest whole number.

Perpetual Struggle and Organized Confrontation at Hadath, 1954–1970

The highest frequency of attempted strikes and actual organized protests at the Régie took place between 1954 and 1965. Short-term strikes yielding little change in the work conditions occurred in 1954, 1955, 1958, 1959, and 1960.[12] More forceful strikes in terms of magnitude, scope, level of organization, and the nature of demands raised occurred in 1963 and 1965. All of these strikes started at the Hadath central plant and spread out to other branches. The men and women at Hadath proved to be the driving force for organized strikes and the masterminds behind plans to gather other branches into strike actions.

The immediate reasons for the frequency of labor agitations and militancy under leadership at the Hadath plant can be traced to two sets of factors, one pertaining to the structure, concentration, and composition of the workforce at the Régie, and the other to the workers' social origins and historical experiences. With respect to the first set of factors, Hadath hosted the largest segment of the Régie workforce and entertained the full scope of production instead of one or only a few industrial tasks. Moreover, by hosting the full and diverse range of ranks, the Hadath plant brought together the highest percentage of both low-ranking workers (and often temporary ones) and high-ranking administrative employees. This situation may have augmented and dramatized class conflict and more directly subjected Hadath workers than workers in other branches to the ramifications of such conflict. The Hadath plant's gender, sectarian, and regional heterogeneity also made it representative of all the branches from north to south. No other branch could claim such wide-ranging representation. It also is significant that there was an important measure of stability in the Régie labor force between 1954 and 1969, which may have permitted a constructive and sustained form of labor activism.

I believe that much of the Régie workforce's stability stemmed from patterns of age stratification among workingwomen and men between 1954 and 1969 (table 8). Women between the ages of twenty and thirty decreased almost by half over this period, whereas those between thirty-one and forty increased by 9 percent, and those between forty-one and fifty increased by 2 percent. Even more noteworthy was the 11 percent increase in the number of women between the ages of fifty-one and sixty. Overall, the change in age composition reflected a 20 percent decrease in workers thirty years old and younger. The remaining groups also attest to the aging nature of the workforce, especially those age sixty-one and older. This age group was absent in 1954, but by 1969 comprised almost 4 percent of the labor force.

The increase in the number of older women workers over the years and the concomitant decrease in the number of younger workers evidently contributed to the stability of the Régie's social character. Stability may have nurtured greater familiarity among workers, long-term awareness of institutional history, and increased knowledge of the professional, legal, and social world of fellow employees. Like kinship networks inculcated by emigrant workers following rural dislocation, stability may have minimized feelings of estrangement at the workplace and slowed the pace of cultural change for those new to the city, thus reinforcing conditions favorable to organized protest.

All these features of the Hadath plant do not, of course, in and of themselves endow it with a propensity for militancy or collective protest. To complete this picture, it is necessary to explore the impact of three central historical developments. The first development was formed around the shared experiences of rural poverty, displacement, and migration of Hadath workers. The second related to the familial and village bonds that prevailed among a considerable number of workers. The third was associated with the workers' adaptation to

TABLE 8. Age distribution among Régie female workers, 1954–1987

	1954		1969		1981		1987	
Age	N	%	N	%	N	%	N	%
15–19	35	7	—	—	1	0	—	—
20–30	218	44	297	24	150	12	58	5
31–40	113	23	394	32	286	23	168	15
41–50	126	26	340	28	394	32	381	34
51–60	2	0	145	12	331	27	342	31
61–	—	—	48	4	60	5	159	14
Total	494	100	1,224	100	1,222	100	1,108	100
Unaccounted for	449		202		8		1	

Sources: List of union membership dues paid, 1954, URWE records, Hadath; Régie Personnel Department, "Liste nominative du personnel au 1-1-1969," "Listing du personnel par matricule, 1 octobre 1981," "Liste des rubriques de Paie, 13-12-1987," Régie company records, Hadath. Figures rounded to the nearest whole number.

Beirut's urban political culture and with their exposure to the city's developing labor movement and the politicized environments of university campuses, unions, and factories.

Migration and the Proletarianization of Beirut's Suburbs, 1955–1980

From the mid-1950s to the early 1970s, the major rural regions of Lebanon—specifically the East (the Biqa'), the North (in particular 'Akkar), and the South—shared high rates of underdevelopment, population growth, unemployment, and illiteracy. These features were accompanied by a conscious governmental effort to marginalize the countryside and to strangle opportunities for social development and economic growth there, which in turn contributed to swelling numbers of depressed and unskilled rural residents. This situation subsequently prompted a major wave of migration to the urban centers, in particular Beirut, from the late 1940s onward, which further intensified beginning in 1975, when the Lebanese civil war erupted. At this time, the South, unlike other regions, became the stage for political instability and radicalization.[13]

Lebanon's countryside exhibited particular sectarian features, which were later reflected in people's rural-to-urban movements and were key in shaping both the nation's political culture and the extent to which people engaged in labor confrontations. The Biqa' had large Catholic and Orthodox Christian communities, but it also had an even larger Muslim community composed of Sunni and Shi'i. The South was predominantly Shi'i, but had a significant Sunni community and a smaller Christian one. The North had a mixed Muslim Sunni and Christian population of various denominations.

In the early 1950s, a large wave of migrants moved from these rural regions to the cities, especially Beirut, in reaction to the deteriorating conditions of peasant life caused by unchecked population growth, land shortages, and irresponsible government policies. In his study of industrial development in Lebanon during this time, Edmund Asfour, an economic analyst at the United Nations Relief and Work Agency, collected significant data about population growth and emigration that provide critical support for my observations about the expansion of the industrial workforce and the change in its sectarian and regional profile. Asfour found that Lebanon showed clear signs of increasing rural overpopulation, which subsequently pushed village residents to Beirut and other urban areas.[14] In addition, natural increases in the Muslim population outpaced increases in the Christian population.[15] It is possible that by the mid-1960s, Shiʻi Muslims already had become the largest sectarian group in Lebanon, with greater populations pressures developing among Muslims in the Shiʻi regions in the South and in the Biqaʻ than among their Christian counterparts.[16]

With respect to the material conditions of the countryside, the sharp difference in "the average income in the agriculture sector and the average for the whole population," according to Asfour, was not solely indicative of undeveloped cultivation methods, but was more importantly "an indication of excessive underemployment on the farm and disguised unemployment in rural villages."[17] In 1950, those engaged in agriculture—estimated at 40 to 50 percent of the population—earned no more than 19 percent of the total provisional national income, whereas the industrial population—estimated at 8 percent of the total population at the time—earned 13 percent of total income.[18] The possibility of improving the agricultural sector looked grim for Lebanon in comparison with neighboring Arab countries such as Syria and Iraq because of the decreasing returns on investments, a lack of supplies, and limited state support. For instance, the government took few measures to improve irrigation and increase the amount of land under cultivation as agricultural revenues from the Lebanese countryside continued to decline.[19] On the contrary, the urban service sector received much more state funding to encourage free exchange and trade policies.[20] As a consequence, internal migration and large-scale emigration became a manifestation of declining rural village populations and rapid urban population growth. Asfour notes that in 1951 approximately two to four thousand people emigrated by sea alone, most of whom "were from rural areas and were young people of between 15 and 45 years of age."[21]

The state neglected much needed agrarian reform and suppressed many socioeconomic problems faced by Lebanese civil society. Population growth led to land shortage in some areas of Lebanon. In the meantime, the expansion of domestic industry and development of urban centers offered new opportunities for marginalized peasants. In a study of the Biqaʻ Valley, a major rural region, during 1955–56, Charles Churchill noted that "of course underemployment was great. Except during planting and harvesting from April to November, men have no agricultural occupation. So for a full third of the year, at least, there is complete idleness for the great majority of the labor force." Moreover, around 2 percent of the agricultural workforce in Biqaʻ were small proprietors who hired laborers and rented small lots. Out of around 8,084 people surveyed by Churchill in the Biqa', 62 men and 7 women owned land. Tenancy and farm labor were the dominant patterns, whereas "the individual farmer" was "in the minority." There is clear evidence of the Biqa'is' involvement in nonagricultural occupations that Churchill categorized as "Other." At least 358 men and 87 women out of 8,084 were involved in such occupations. But it is important to note that Churchill's tables and observations seem incomplete because he did not define what these "Other" occupations were or explain the lack of data on the remaining 1,980 men and 1,366 women in the region.[22]

The erosion of the countryside's economy and the decreasing return on agricultural land persisted. In 1961, approximately 92 percent of peasants owned 5 or less hectares (12 acres), and less than half of one percent owned from 50 to 100 hectares (125 to 250 acres).[23] In less than a decade, capitalist development in the absence of rigorous plans for land reform led to a significant shift in the size and nature of ownership of agrarian land.[24] By 1973, the breakup of landownership because of inheritance and sale created many tiny lots that were insufficient for the subsistence of a rural household (a typical family of five). As a result, some peasants sold their land to work as agricultural laborers, and others moved to the city. This development affected the social composition of the peasantry owing to the shrinkage in the traditional stratum of small landowners and a significant increase in the fortunes and power of fewer landlords, with the holdings of an estimated 439 landowners exceeding those of 91,000 small peasants.[25] In the mid-1970s, the average monthly wage rates were 150 Lebanese pounds (U.S.$1.00 = 2.25 pounds) for female agricultural workers and 90 pounds for children, particularly in the Biqa' Valley and 'Akkar.[26] The agricultural male worker earned around 275 pounds per month. Industrial wages, by comparison, ranged from 500 to 3,000 pounds per month.[27] More important was the fact that 44 percent of the industrial workers in the Biqa', 35 percent in the South, and 24 percent in the North received less than the minimum wage (3,000 pounds per year).[28] By contrast, only 10 percent of the population of Beirut earned incomes that fell below the minimum wage.

It is important to note, however, that the Shi'i populations of the South and the Biqa', in particular, seemed to have carried the brunt of underdevelopment. This finding is clearly supported by a statistical survey in 1974 that showed that the Shi'is composed the highest percentage (32 percent) of all the Lebanese who received less than the minimum wage and had the highest rate of illiteracy in the country. The data further showed that the Biqaʿ and the South reflected the highest percentages of illiteracy, especially among women (37 percent and 26 percent, respectively), followed by the North (17 percent).[29]

Health and educational facilities in the rural districts, in particular the Biqaʿ, also were far from adequate. In 1970, only two public and one private hospital served Biqaʿ residents. There were severe limitations on the development of the infrastructure in the area as well. For example, in forty-five towns of the Biqaʿ, mules were the primary source of transportation, and only 5 percent of the inhabitants had running water.[30] The Biqaʿ also shared several features with the southern and northern parts of Lebanon, especially the ʿAkkar region, which had for decades formed a human "reservoir" for most industrial work, particularly at the Régie.

Under these challenging circumstances, rural women with large families found ample reason to seek waged work in the cities. The Lebanese case provides an interesting comparison with Arab women elsewhere, such as Algeria. Rural women in Algeria, unlike their middle- and upper-class counterparts in urban regions, had strong motives to avoid wage work. As Marnia Lazreg successfully shows, the small proportion of wage-earning rural women here (particularly in industry and services) stemmed from the fact that "despite its vagaries, Algerian socialism did result in providing health care to those who need it, medical drugs at low prices and free child immunization"—luxuries that proved hard to come by in most of rural Lebanon.[31]

The decreasing return on agricultural land in Lebanon was accompanied by significant development in the urban cities, in particular Beirut, which showed a rate of almost 5 percent of urban growth from 1965 to 1980. This rate of growth is relatively rapid when compared to urban growth rates in other Middle Eastern non-oil-exporting countries such as Egypt and Israel, which were almost 3 percent and 4 percent, respectively.[32] Between 1965 and 1980, rural-to-urban migration was decisive in driving Lebanese urbanization and played a greater part in accelerating the growth of cities there than in Turkey, Iran, Saudi Arabia, and Iraq.[33] Rural-to-urban migration in Lebanon accounted for 65 percent of urban growth, the second-highest proportion in the Middle East after that of the Yemen Arab Republic.

People moving out of Lebanon altogether also contributed to the deterioration of rural economies. From 1975 to 1977, the number of Lebanese immigrating to different parts of the world reached 745,760—almost half of whom (352,260) were permanently repatriated.[34] More important, the Lebanese Civil War also affected the industrial workforce in a profound manner. Around 60 to 70 percent of all Lebanese workers immigrated to various African, Asian, and American countries, but it is unclear what percentage returned.[35] By 1980, 88,050 migrant Lebanese workers were in Saudi Arabia and the Persian Gulf region.[36]

From 1969 onward, a Palestinian and Lebanese armed resistance to Israel emerged in the South. This region gradually became a stage for Israel's systematic military encroachments, attacks, and air raids. In addition to the rural poverty discussed previously, social dislocation owing to these conflicts became a primary catalyst in the disintegration of peasant life in the southern towns and triggered waves of migration to Beirut. The shifts in the sectarian identity of working-women and men at the industrial sites of Beirut during this time reflected this dislocation. Early on, the Shi'i youth in the South embraced the Palestinian cause. However, most Maronites in the area blamed the PLO and the leftist Lebanese National Movement for their political dislocation and accused both organizations of giving Israel a reason to transform the South into a war zone. Israeli reprisals in the South sought to insert a wedge between the Palestinians and the Lebanese, forcing the Lebanese government to take action against the PLO. The government's attempts to clamp down on Palestinian organizations, however, angered a large section of the working classes in rural Muslim regions.[37]

Israel's goals to destroy the PLO base and weaken the Lebanese Left proved extremely taxing to Lebanese workers. In 1976, Israel, taking advantage of the civil war, started large-scale military preparations and launched several attacks in the southern borderlands where Palestinian guerilla organizations and popular resistance had taken root. These attacks had a direct and long-term impact on workers, especially those employed in the tourist and hotel sectors. A number of firms and institutes started to lay off workers, three thousand at least, within a few days after the attacks, arguing that tourists would not be visiting Lebanon. This lay off in turn gave the owners of industrial firms engaged in carpentry, mechanics, printing presses, construction, and shoemaking a reason to control their profits by doing the same. These businesses asked the government's permission to dispense with half of their workforce or to decrease their workers' salaries by half.[38]

The change in the sectarian character of East and West Beirut illustrates the profound transformations caused by the processes of rural deterioration and forced migration to the city. In 1974, one year before the civil war began, the Shi'is composed only 16 percent of Beirut's total population and 33 percent of its suburban populace. Maronites formed 23 percent and 27 percent of these populations, respectively.[39] Yet within three years of the outbreak of the civil war, Shi'i immigrants to West Beirut and its suburbs reached 260,000 (76 percent) in a population of 304,000.[40] As explained earlier, rural-to-urban migration was evident during the 1950s and had drawn an increasing Muslim population from the "peripheral" areas, most notably Shi'is. This phase overlaps with the Camille Chamoun administration (1952–58) and reflects his government's economic policies and political outlook, as I discuss in a later section. In the early 1970s, however, political instability and the civil war, rather than government policies or deteriorating economic conditions, pushed young and old from the South to Beirut. Equally significant was the forced migration of Maronites (105,000 total) from 'Akkar, the Biqa', and the South to East Beirut following violent clashes among various factions and political parties. The Maronites formed 85 percent of East Beirut's overall population (125,000) between 1976 and 1978.

These trends in the sectarian restructuring of Beirut as a result of rural displacement and forced migration were also evident in the gradual shift in the regional origins of the Régie labor force from 1954 to 1969 (see table 9).

TABLE 9. Regional background of Régie workers, 1954–1969

| | 1954 | | | | 1969 | | | |
| | Female | | Male | | Female | | Male | |
Region	N	%	N	%	N	%	N	%
Beirut	131	15	170	16	91	7	156	9
Mount Lebanon	536	59	550	51	554	41	788	47
Northern Lebanon	30	3	75	7	89	7	213	12
Eastern Lebanon	76	8	75	7	255	19	194	11
Southern Lebanon	128	14	202	19	354	26	411	23
Non-Lebanese	1	0	4	0	3	0	6	0
Total	902	100	1,076	100	1,346	100	1,768	100
Unaccounted for	32	40	47	60	75	45	92	55

Sources: List of union membership dues paid, 1954, URWE records, Hadath; Régie Personnel Department, "Liste nominative du personnel au 1-1-1969," Régie company records, Hadath. Figures rounded to the nearest whole number.

Although female and male workers who came from Mount Lebanon remained the majority among Régie workers, it is clear that their proportion, along with those who originally came from Beirut, had significantly decreased by 1969. In contrast, the percentage of female and male workers coming from the "peripheral" South, North, and the East had increased. It is important to note that in 1954 the number of female workers from the East and Mount Lebanon slightly exceeded the number of male workers of the same regional background (table 9). Fifteen years later male workers from Mount Lebanon outnumbered female workers from that region, but the female workers from eastern and southern Lebanon became the majority in the Régie workforce.

Like the migrants from the "periphery," most Régie workers settled in the eastern and southern suburbs of Beirut, which formed the city's "belt of poverty" *(hizam al-bu's)*.[41] People from the Biqaʻ settled mostly in the eastern suburb known as al-Dahiya al-Sharqiyya, whereas those who came from the South settled in the southern suburb known as al-Dahiya al-Janubiyya. Nearly all were Muslims, both Shiʻi and Sunni. For safety reasons amid a deepening civil war, all Muslims of the eastern suburb of Beirut were displaced and consequently forced to take refuge in the southern suburb, where they eventually settled.[42]

Civil strife, death, and uprootedness made the *muhajjars'* (forced migrants) successful adaptation to urban life in Beirut rife with complications. Some migrants to Beirut's suburbs illegally built small rooms on public estates belonging to local municipalities or religious communities. Some also bought a few square meters and built their own lodgings or rented small apartments in buildings owned by wealthy Beiruti families. The average domestic situation consisted of seven family members living in a one-room shanty apartment (or, in a few cases, a two-room apartment), with a small kitchen and bathroom.[43]

Industrial firms, including the Régie, absorbed 75 percent of the laborers of these suburbs. The average monthly wage for a family of five in 1980 was 1,150 pounds (U.S.\$1.00 = 3.50 pounds). Deprived of a living wage and basic benefits to support self-sufficiency, the average household was unable to meet its basic needs. No less than 85 percent of dislocated families depended on the earnings of several members within these families, including husbands, wives, daughters, sisters, and children.[44]

All in all, the economic and political forces that enveloped rural workers between 1955 and 1980 interlocked in distinct ways that shaped workers' choices and outlook. These experiences cemented special ties among the Régie women and men, nurtured a spirit of collective confrontation and militancy, and, in combination, made the transition from rural to industrial labor for women less controversial and helped to justify the new order of things.

Government Policies and the Transformation of the Régie Workforce

It is difficult to understand the full ramifications of the decline in agricultural output and the growth of Beirut without taking into account state ideology and policy. Rural disintegration, displacement, and migration to the capital city in the 1950s were shaped largely by the policies of Presidents Bishara al-Khuri (1946–52) and Camille Chamoun (1952–58). This twelve-year period seemed to have laid the foundation for the socioeconomic changes experienced by the working classes in the North, the Biqaʻ, and the South, particularly for Shiʻi Muslims during the late 1950s and early 1960s. These presidents' economic plans had far-reaching effects on the social composition of the industrial workers of the major cities—including the workers at the Régie. For example, Muslim working-men and women, as a whole, reached their greatest numbers at the Régie between 1954 and 1969 (see table 7).

The Al-Khuri and Chamoun governments promoted Lebanon as a liberal, pro-Western, service-based polity in which the Maronite elite and a few of their Muslim allies enjoyed political and economic dominance. They focused their efforts on developing Beirut and Mount Lebanon, where Maronite Christians were concentrated. Little attention, if any, was devoted to the South, the Biqaʻ, or ʻAkkar because they seemed irrelevant to tourism, commercial planning, or banking and financial development. Only the industrial regions closest to the capital city received government investment and protection in the hope of strengthening transportation and banking facilities. Between 1950 and 1956, these policies did lead to a significant growth in some sectors: a 51 percent rise in the national income and a 34 percent increase in per capita income.[45]

Thanks to the Arab-Israeli conflict and the flight of capital and labor from the Arab nationalist countries, Lebanon also witnessed a marked expansion of its service sector and industrial output between 1955 and 1961. The number of waged workers in industry and agriculture together (43 percent) was indicative of the significance of capitalist relations in the economy at large (table 10). Yet owing to the emphasis placed on the service sector, industrial production and manufacturing did not compose a major part of the national economy.[46] Moreover, the government did not spend much effort in protecting or promoting the rights of Lebanese workers, 32 percent of whom remained seasonal and temporary waged workers, like many at the Régie.[47] Because of the general lack of comprehensive oversight and the government's resistance to progressive taxation, economic reforms, social welfare, and trade unionism, the Lebanese workers suffered through difficult periods of high inflation and poverty.[48]

In the 1960s, like Middle Eastern economic development researcher William Persen, political economist Charles Issawi was an unreserved admirer of "economic liberalism." As he attempted to praise the far-reaching achievements of the Chamoun era, he ironically exposed its problems. The Lebanese economy, Issawi noted, reflected the form of an "inverted pyramid." Most of the monetary output in the financial sector was reinvested in that sector or consumed.[49] The same historical forces that accounted for the enlargement of several economic sectors under "economic liberalism" caused sharper class divisions and inequalities and boosted urban centers at the expense of the rural regions.[50] This situation accounted for the expansion of the industrial workforce, including the Régie's.[51]

TABLE 10. Distribution of the Lebanese working population, ages 15 to 64, in various economic activities, 1959

	Independent and administrative staff		Workers	
	N	%	N	%
Agriculture	125,000	34	95,000	24
Industry, handicraft, & construction	12,000	3	75,000	19
Commerce, banking, & transportation	26,000	7	53,000	13
Various professions	20,000	5	28,000	7
Public administration	—	—	16,000	4
Seasonal & temporary workers	183,000	50	130,000	32
Total	366,000	100	397,000	100

Source: Joseph Lerbert, *Étude preliminaire sur les besions et les possibilities du développement du Liban*, cited in *Al-Qadiyya al-ZiraŞiyya fi Lubnan fi Dawş al-Mariksiyya* (The Agrarian Question in Lebanon from a Marxist Perspective)(Beirut: Manshurat al-Hizb al-ShuyuŞi al-Lubnani, ca. 1973–74), 382.

During the 1960s, the expansion of the Régie workforce and the shift in its sectarian character were further shaped by the economic policies of Fuad Shihab (1958–64), which remained in effect in the succeeding government of Charles Helou (1964–70), an ardent supporter of the Shihabist outlook and practices. Shihab believed that the development policies and governmental enterprises of his predecessor, Chamoun, benefited Beirut almost exclusively and encouraged the ascendancy of a Christian minority. Instead, Shihab planned to restore economic growth to the "peripheral" regions outside Beirut and to respond to the needs of their Muslim populations.[52] Shihabism failed, though, and the peripheral regions did not achieve the level of economic growth and expansion that would decrease rural-to-urban migration.[53] In the Régie's case, the Shihabist practices did not lead to the creation of rural branches comparable to the Hadath in terms of the scope of their industrial tasks and size. Moreover, none of the rural Régie branches specialized in manufacturing.

The Shihabist vision was mirrored in the composition of the semigovernmental Régie and was manifest in the company's plans to decentralize its production process by establishing branches in the "peripheral" districts of the South and the North, as well as in its attempt to preserve a Muslim-Christian balance in its workforce.[54] During Shihab's reign, the Régie planned to open new branches in the southern and northern districts. Between 1964 and 1969, when Helou was in power, several factories and warehouses emerged in Tripoli, Batrun, Bikfaya, Nabatiyya, and Ghaziyya. The South alone, where the Ghaziyya branch was located, was the source of 70 percent of the tobacco grown in the country.[55] As a result, the trend continued toward an increase in the number of Muslim workers at the Régie. More important, Shihabist practices signaled a shift from Chamoun's by attempting to instigate a new social balance based on an institutionalized sectarian formula (see table 16 in chapter 6). In truth, Shihabism was not a deflection of sectarianism, but rather a more pronounced implementation of it that accounted for and acknowledged the expanding Muslim population and the need to reconfigure its share in Lebanese government.

Ideology and National Narrative

Classical and liberal nationalist narratives about "Lebanon" shed light on the hegemonic system's local character. In their classical version, the narratives argue that Lebanon constitutes distinct religious groups that can be traced to disparate racial-cultural entities. Michel Chiha, a major proponent of this idea in the 1960s, stated that Lebanon's birth was a sublime attempt at coexistence among diverse religious traditions and races. Chiha surmised, "Lebanon is different from all Middle and Near Eastern, Mediterranean, and Western Asian countries. It survived, socially and politically, owing to a balance between religions and civilizations." Chiha proposed the establishment of a national assembly that would uphold the delicate balance among the various Muslim and Christian sects, and would offer each one "full representation" and political rights to prevent the domination of one over the others. He felt this step was necessary for the making of a nation *(umma)* whose economy was based on trade and business.[56]

There was no place in Chiha's theory, however, for a people *(sha'b)* united by other criteria of modern nationhood, such as a shared history or a common linguistic-cultural background that could appeal to all groups and classes.[57] Commerce and financial services were declared to be the principal functions of the Lebanese economy that linked it to the Arab world and Western countries. Chiha argued that such functions were compatible with the "natural" resources and the ideal geographical location of Lebanon on the Mediterranean. Throughout history, he noted, the people of Phoenicia, the cradle of modern Lebanon, had dominated international trade and mastered sea commerce. More important, Chiha theorized, the import-export trade led to cultural progress and ultimately to happiness.[58] He insisted that Lebanon did not possess the resources for industrial growth.

Chiha placed Lebanon's provinces hierarchically on the basis of their contribution to its formation and "civilizational" progress. He singled out Mount Lebanon as the national heartland. From a previously impoverished Mount Lebanon, Chiha reflected, "emerged a solid and powerful social and cultural structure that offered the Lebanese diasporas the most brilliant [figures] and best representation."[59] Beginning in the 1950s, liberal thinkers and artists understood episodic conflicts in Lebanon to be caused by external factors. It was therefore common to read and hear how the 1860 peasant upheavals in Mount Lebanon involving Druze-Maronite armed battles resulted from Ottoman or European intrigues or both.[60] The structural and therefore the internal contradictions that sustained the hegemony led to political outbursts. In 1958, thousands of Lebanese Muslims and Christians rose against the government of Camille

Chamoun demanding the severance of Lebanon's diplomatic ties with the Western superpowers, more political rights, and, most important, development of the impoverished rural Lebanese areas and the working classes.[61] Several Lebanese scholars and politicians blamed the crisis on Egyptian leader Jamal Abdel Nasser's (1952–70) pan-Arab policies and personal designs.[62] The 1975–90 Lebanese Civil War, too, appeared to others to have been triggered by one or a combination of the following factors: Palestinian military growth, Syrian subversive plans, and American intervention.[63]

The Rahbani brothers' popular plays during the 1950s and 1960s reflect the theme of foreign disruption of Lebanese harmony.[64] The Rahbanis' typical village, a model of peace and national solidarity, is undermined when a stranger (al-gharib) plants seeds of sedition and envy. Villagers turn against each other as families accuse rival families of instigating the conflict and sabotaging the village's stability and prosperity. Al-mukhtar, the village mayor, intervenes to reconcile the villagers' differences and harmonize their needs, blaming al-gharib, but not any member of the village, for the chaos. Although the reconciliation remains largely rhetorical, it keeps the social structure and the "balance" intact.[65] Solutions to problems come out of al-mukhtar's individual charisma and personal benevolence.

In the 1970s, this picture starts to change dramatically, particularly in the plays Ya'ish Ya'ish (Long Live, Long Live) and Al-Mahatta (The Train Station), which emphasize class tensions and gender disagreements at the expense of national unity. The Lebanese economy faced a crisis at the time (early 1970s) and seemed unable to reinvent itself. Idealist notions of Lebanon, in particular the Chihian discourse, were thus under scrutiny from liberal as well as radical thinkers.[66] A good example of this tendency appears in the work of the playwright and musician Ziad Rahbani. He exposed class rifts and mocked the value system of the bourgeoisie that aimed to legitimize the liberal economic system and, in connection with it, the tribal-ethnic hegemony. In his play Shi Fashil (What a Failure), Mr. Nur, a playwright, upholds the image of a united Lebanese nation divided by outsiders who range from Palestinians to Israelis, Americans, and Iraqis. Mr. Nur ironically fails to launch his play on stage because of the sectarian predicaments engulfing the actors. Abu al-Zuluf (a mythical figure in peasant songs) asks Mr. Nur: "What is the identity of the foreigner in your plays? You tell some people that the foreigners are the Palestinians, and you tell others that they are the Israelis."⁶⁷ Making the problem external to the Lebanese nation was meant to assert its viability and lack of contradictions. Yet contradictions abound in the way that distinct Lebanese groups constructed their identity and their relationship to the nation-state.

Different facets of the Chihian Lebanese cosmography and cultural mythology were also developed or reworked in art and music. A whole generation of lyricists sang the Lebanese "prodigy," a unique formation endowed with a republican morality and rural virtues. More important, there was a symbiosis between the implementation of Lebanon's socioeconomic arrangement and its artistic expression. In the late 1950s, the Rahbani brothers were moving firmly away from the long classical songs to shorter ones that lasted from three to five minutes. In Egypt, similar developments were under way, leading to the birth and popularization of the short rhythmic song.⁶⁸ The classical songs were characterized by a slower rhythm and fewer shifts in theme and tune, each song lasting from half an hour to more than an hour. The new Lebanese song had a faster rhythm and quicker beat aiming to achieve dramatic effects on listeners in almost a quarter of the time devoted to the classical ones. It seemed suitable for a society experiencing substantial shifts in its production and consumption patterns—and entering firmly into urbanity. At the same time, nostalgia toward the simplicity and purity of preindustrial life remained an important part of Lebanese songs and musicals.⁶⁹

Mawsim al-'Izz (Season of Glory), a Rahbani Brothers' musical first performed in 1960, centers on young men and women in a Lebanese village celebrating with optimism and conviviality the coming of the silk season. Shahin, a young village man, hopes to save enough money from his silk work to marry his beloved, Najla. One song in particular reflects the dominant social norms and moral values in 1960 Lebanon with regard to women's work and the expectations of patriarchy. Shahin sings,

We want to build a house
For the heart to rest in
And a young beautiful girl who would tie her belt [around her waist] to live in
She would weave and sit on the steps
I asked my heart: "What do you want?"
"I want," he said, "the beautiful girl whoever she is."
And we asked the beautiful girl: "What do you want?"
She said: "Build me an *'illiyi* [a high sitting room]."⁷⁰

Shahin wants stability, a house made for a couple, a house where the wife—who is a young inexperienced woman—"ties her belt" and reveals her feminine figure, tidiness, and modesty. She would spin her loom behind the very doorsteps of her house. Shahin, like other male peers, supports her work, but only if it is close to home. The young woman simply yearns for an 'illiyi that can be added onto the house, but at an elevation that will permit her to see more of the world while also signifying her higher social status. In this setting, both woman and man express an attachment to precapitalist value systems. Yet it is noteworthy that the woman expresses no direct romantic inclinations toward the man, even though by showing she will accept an 'illiyi rather than a house, which he wants to build, she is welcoming him into her life. She does not aspire to do factory work. This detail might reflect the ambivalence felt by many family heads of household, who continued to have doubts about women's work outside the home and its implications for gender relations and conjugal ties. As I read it, the song summarizes and idealizes the continuation of traditional labor patterns and gendered perceptions in Lebanon.

An excerpt of a few lines of prose from this same musical draws on a related theme, but this time the message has to do with the roles of women as mothers and lovers of the Lebanese nation. These lines address women silk workers:

In happiness embrace him [husband]
In sickness embrace him
And tell them [children]: Lebanon
All time: Lebanon
After God they should worship Lebanon.[71]

In other words, despite their new waged labor, workingwomen should not ignore their larger "family duties" as citizens and mothers of the nation. Such sentiments, again, functioned to reinforce traditional labor and gender roles.

Geographic Background, Family Clusters, and Village Ties at the Régie

To complete the historical picture I am presenting of Régie workers, it is important to assess how they compensated for rural displacement and the temporary loss of community as they embraced industrial work in Beirut. Kinship played a potent role in labor recruitment at the Régie and in the country at large, which in turn shaped workers' perceptions of their workplace, the relationships that grew within its confines, and the manner in which they addressed their needs and grievances. For almost three decades, from 1954 to 1981, immediate kinship and family ties bound no less than 40 percent of the Régie workers and employees. Among the remaining 60 percent of the workers, many were distant relatives on the maternal and paternal sides or nieces, nephews, and cousins of older workers (table 11).

The largest family clusters at the Régie were the Shi'i Zu'aytirs and Musawis as well as the Maronite Ja'ja's and Sab'alis. Except for the Sab'alis, these families migrated to Beirut's suburbs from the Biqa' region. These three family clusters also joined the Régie during its "old" days at the major Mar Mikhayil branch before it moved to Hadath in 1958. The Sab'alis came from Bikfaya in Mount Lebanon and worked at its branch. The concentration of a large number of workers belonging to one family, in some cases more than fifty, was noteworthy. In 1954, there were twenty-five Salibas (Greek Orthodox), twenty-two Sawayas (Catholic), and twenty and eighteen Khuris and Hilus (Maronite), respectively. The Burjawis (Sunni) and the Haydars (Shi'ite) formed the largest Muslim family clusters, totaling thirteen and twelve, respectively. The Maronite and Catholic families had a long-established tradition in tobacco planting and manufacture before the creation of the Régie. The Sawaya family, for example, had owned

TABLE 11. Clusters of families in the Régie, 1954–1981

No. family members at the Régie	1954		1969		1981	
	N	%	N	%	N	%
1	653	63	910	61	829	63
2–5	326	32	464	31	391	30
6–10	42	4	75	5	61	5
11 and more	12	2	26	2	33	2
Total	1,033	100	1,475	100	1,314	100
Unaccounted for	26	—	63	—	—	—

Sources: List of union membership dues paid, 1954, URWE records, Hadath; Régie Personnel Department, "Liste nominative du personnel, au 1-1-1969," "Listing du personnel par matricule, 1 october 1981," Régie company records, Hadath. Figures are rounded to the nearest whole number.

a number of small tobacco manufactures in Mount Lebanon and had bought shares in the Régie at the time of its inception.

Among the remaining 60 percent of the workers, more distant blood and village ties nevertheless still prevailed.[72] Some families also were initially part of larger family clusters and networks at the Régie. A recent ethnographic work on Lebanese families reveals that in 1954, twenty-eight Régie workers belonged to four different Maronite families—namely, the Daghirs (six) and their offshoot the Sasins (four), the Ghanims (seven), the Daws (two), and Matars (nine)—that were branches of one main family, the al-Ghassanis.[73] These families preserved vital social relations and exchanged benefits and services that were reinforced by marital alliances as well, despite the fact that the common line that netted their interests together was apparently more religious that familial or tribal.

By 1969, new Lebanese families, Christian and Muslim, had reshaped the social environment at the Régie. The Zu'aytirs, a Shi'i family, numbered nine workers in 1954, but claimed seventy-five in 1969, thus turning into the largest family cluster in the company.[74] The Zu'aytirs maintained a steady number at the Régie after the civil war, counting seventy-four workers in 1981. Another Maronite family, the Sab'alis, ranked second in size to the Zu'aytirs and claimed thirty-one Régie workers in 1981, followed by the Khuris, a Maronite family (twenty-nine). Next in size were the Sawayas (twenty-eight), and, finally, the Ja'ja's, whose number increased from two in 1954 to twenty-two in 1969. The Ja'ja's expanded still more, reaching fifty in 1981, thus outnumbering all the Maronite families at the Régie (table 11).

A number of early studies of tobacco manufacturing attributed a religious-parochial character to the workers' collective behavior.[75] These studies relied on French sources that focused almost exclusively on Mount Lebanon at the expense of other Lebanese regions and were thus misleading. Other studies interpreted the presence of large family clusters in industrial settings as an indication of the persistence of parochial ties that were antithetical to collective class action. Salim Nasr and Claude Dubar, for instance, asserted that despite the economic changes introduced by capitalism, "traditional" kinship ties, patron-client relations, and sectarian loyalties were still the dominant expressions of working-class identity in Lebanon.[76] Religious attachments and "other ties of birth," subalternists suggested in later studies, overcame class interests.[77] On the contrary, my research on tobacco workers affirms the interplay of kinship and sect in the workers' individual choices and collective actions, as was clearly demonstrated in the 1965 strike (see chapter 6). It is inadequate to consider these ties as inherent to each individual worker's social reality or even to view these realities as static. It is true that such ties exemplified the essence of the tribal-ethnic hegemony that prevailed in Lebanon, but in the case of tobacco workers there was a particular utility for familial and sectarian affiliations that changed over time with the rise of new social processes triggered by the dislocations described earlier in this chapter and by the new challenges of the work environment.[78]

In sum, the expansion of familial clusters, particularly among the Shi'is and Maronites, who shared a similar regional background and socioeconomic experiences, helped workers adapt to Beirut's urban setting and the industrial work culture, and carried political implications for their militancy.

Conclusion

The low mortality rate, dramatic population growth, and land shortage, combined with the absence of government development policies, caused a steady deterioration in the rural regions of Lebanon. Owing to combined global and local factors, the pace of urbanization pushed both men and women to seek work beyond the home and farm. I have examined these historical circumstances and social transformations from the 1950s to the 1970s through the experiences of the Régie's workingwomen and men.

The character of the Régie workforce was shaped by intertwined gender, regional, and sectarian heterogeneity. In terms of gender makeup, little change occurred from 1954 to 1981. The proportion of women to men remained relatively constant over thirty years. Female and male workers were drawn from the diverse Christian and Muslim communities of Mount Lebanon, 'Akkar in the North, the Biqa', and the South. Until the mid-1950s, Maronite Christians composed a major group at the Régie. This fact is particularly telling because it runs counter to the dominant popular and scholarly perception of the Maronites as a privileged "class" in the stratified Lebanese system. The Maronite elite had propagated an early image of its unique national mission in the Lebanese polity, had controlled the office of the presidency, and had shaped different government policies since independence. This fact also led many working-class Maronites to have a distorted self-image via close identification with the privileged members of their sect who had access to resources and social dominance. My research on the Régie shows, however, that the working class was as much a Maronite phenomenon as it was a Shi'i one. Maronite workers formed almost 44 percent of the Régie workforce up until the 1950s, but declined to 30 percent after 1969. The Maronites and the Shi'is were situated at the two polarized ends of the spectrum in terms of their political representation and access to state decision making, yet they cannot be seen as situated in mutually exclusive classes.

During the 1960s, the Régie experienced a major shift in the regional and sectarian composition of its working body. The Shi'is of the Biqa' and the South started to replace the Maronites as the largest religious group at the company. This regional-sectarian shift was caused by decisive historical developments in the areas dominated by Shi'is. The Shi'is, more so than the Maronites, carried a legacy of uprootedness and forced migration owing to the combined effects of rural poverty and demographic expansion amidst governmental neglect. From 1969 onward, the precursors to war and the civil war itself further accelerated forced migration and urban politicization.

I believe that the Hadath branch of the Régie became the cradle for the most collective protests because of its large size and full occupational scale, as well as its gender and sectarian heterogeneity, but even more so for the shared experiences of rural poverty and migration among its workers. In chapter 6, on the one hand I show that the sectarian, regional, and gender diversities did not hamper the workers' ability to organize successful protests, but on the other hand I highlight how Régie women and men's accounts and recollections reveal that Beirut's urban setting and some of the radical features of its popular culture might have encouraged workplace militancy.

5

Women Negotiate Family and Work

1950–1997

THE SOCIAL PROCESSES emerging from the intersection of powerful factors such as rural decline, overpopulation, urban growth, and failing development policies shaped the nature and social meaning of Lebanese women's waged labor between 1950 and 1970. Yet after 1970 new historical forces conditioned women's involvement in industrial labor and the tasks that devolved to them at factories. With the rise of neoliberalism during the early 1970s, rigorous modernization in several factories customarily associated with a female workforce had unexpected results for workingwomen. Meanwhile, the Lebanese Civil War (1975–90) caused the loss of income for thousands of industrial workingmen and the departure of a considerable number of them from Lebanon.

The first part of this chapter examines the level of women's participation in industrial labor nationwide between 1970 and 1985. I show that laws of the tribal-ethnic state, official decrees pertaining to workingwomen, and the hiring practices of industrialists and employers were shaped by concerns for moral propriety and social harmony as well as by a biased approbation of female aptitude and ability. The outbreak of the civil war in 1975 also had unexpected consequences for female waged work. Gender roles associated with patriarchal, patrimonial peasant ways of life came under new pressures as a consequence of economic and social crisis. The migration of thousands of families from war zones to Beirut, men's loss of income, and uprootedness loosened familial resistance to female paid work and led many women to seek employment.

Despite this change, the number of workingwomen in several industrial enterprises declined instead of rose. Much evidence shows that after the outbreak of the war, to compensate for significant shortages in the Lebanese male

116

workforce, major industries in Beirut turned to foreign male workers largely from India and Thailand instead of hiring more Lebanese women. In addition, the modernization of these industries during the early 1970s and the further mechanization of labor led to an abrupt modification in the gender composition of the workforce in favor of men. The discriminatory policies of hiring men had little practical basis because the majority of new male hires who replaced women came with no skills or previous experience. In the absence of governmental protection of Lebanese workers, in particular female ones, employers gave in to their deep-seated biases and misconceptions about women's suitability for mechanized labor.

The second part of this chapter focuses on women's adaptation to industrial labor between 1970 and 1990, and the strategies they devised to navigate the professional and personal pressures of home and the workplace. On the one hand, women utilized a wide range of kinship, village, and sectarian ties and sought the mediation of influential political leaders to strengthen their positions at the workplace and improve their rights and benefits. On the other hand, they gradually transformed and were transformed by their labor and the urban setting of Beirut, which entailed a restructuring of their social and personal worlds and brought them face to face with new hierarchies of gender. This new situation encouraged them to recast their relations to their husbands or other male relatives and to their male colleagues at the workplace. The Régie women's age patterns, marital status, and personal accounts illuminate the women's approach to patriarchal control and male authority and the extent to which they were shaped by industrial labor, residential mobility, partial separation from rural culture, and the pursuit of economic independence. Many women workers invested much effort in convincing their families to allow them to seek industrial labor in Beirut, whereas others defied their families outright to stay at the Régie. The city and factory emerged as alternative platforms on which some working-class women played out new identities and expanded their social networks.

Between Paternalism and Gendered Morality: State Laws for Workingwomen

Under the French mandate and the Lebanese state, legislation pertaining to women's waged work had a direct bearing on the nature and level of women's participation in industrial manufacturing, their work conditions, and their male employers' hiring policies.

Back in the early 1930s, the International Labor Organization recommended to the international community certain procedures to regulate women and children's employment.[1] The first legal document on labor relations that appeared in Lebanon on March 9, 1933, integrated few of these recommendations.[2] Under the French mandate in 1935, the colonial-system president promulgated a new law regulating women and children's employment in industrial plants. The law forbade children between the age of thirteen and sixteen from working in jobs classified as dangerous to their health. The provisions of this law also became the foundation of the 1946 labor code in independent Lebanon.[3] This code defined the legal principles for work relations, hiring practices pertaining to women and children, duration of work, vacations, salary, and dismissal from work.[4]

The nascent Lebanese tribal sectarian state interfered directly in the organization of women's work to safeguard the interests of the elite. The laws prohibited women's work in factories relating to manufacturing explosives, melting iron in chemical ovens, and dyeing. The Lebanese state also was quick to implement laws prohibiting women from driving "machines with big engines" and from engaging in alcohol production.[5] The 1946 law decreed that women receive a forty-day maternity leave with full pay and forbade employers from accepting their return to work before a minimum of thirty days. It also prohibited employers from discharging pregnant women. Although the maternity leave was modest, the state saw it as a first and necessary step in acknowledging the centrality of the mother-child relationship and its contribution to familial and social cohesion. In 1948, the state adopted further international agreements prohibiting work for women in the evening except in situations where the woman is working in a family business or dealing with products that can decay quickly.[6] This prohibition reflected the male society's social and moral considerations of the suitability of evening jobs for women, especially because husbands were usually at home in the evening and needed their attention and because of the association made between night work and illicit activities such as prostitution.[7] The laws also catered to employers by prohibiting lifetime contracts and vaguely requesting that "some compensation" be paid to the employee in cases of dismissal. In brief, the laws existing before 1950 left many labor conditions to the employers' discretion and imposed few restrictions on them.

In 1951, new state legislation was extended to workingwomen that aimed to define more clearly suitable workplace conditions. Employers were forced to provide separate restrooms for women and eating areas and facilities where women could take required breaks during each working day. Notwithstanding these legal changes in favor of women, the state continued its paternalistic approach to women workers and protected men's prerogatives in deciding the job opportunities for women. The law, for example, gave a woman the right to end her labor contract instantly upon marriage, but not in cases of illness or childbirth. Almost as if encouraging women to defer to their husband's will and domestic labor, the law demanded that a woman be compensated in full if she left upon marriage, on condition that she provide evidence of the marriage and notify the employer in a timely manner. This law applied to all women who had been working for more than a year.[8] In 1959, the government issued a legislative decree known as Nizam al-Muwazaffin (employees' law), stating that it promoted the principle of gender equality in rights and obligations, particularly in the public sectors. In practice, however, women received less recognition and fewer vacations and promotions in return for their work. They also became the primary victims of arbitrary dismissal and temporary employment.

An important development in the history of legal protection for workingwomen occurred in 1963 with the consolidation of the social security law, which required employers to provide health coverage and special benefits for expectant and new mothers. Nonetheless, many employers, particularly in the private sector, did not abide by this law and extended few benefits, with little interference from the government or rule-enforcement police.[9] Linda Lorfing and Julinda Abu al-Nasr found out that only two of the ten factories they surveyed in suburban Beirut in 1979 abided by the social security law, and the other eight forced their workers and employees to follow a special health plan devised to suit the employers' needs. Moreover, only six out of ten factories offered personal insurance or security against accidents at work.[10]

Even though legal regulations pertaining to workers emphasized gender equality and equal opportunity for all, they failed to detail what equality meant or to investigate whether factory owners and employers strove to achieve it. Despite clear discrimination against women in both the spirit and the application of the laws, male legislators and a few male and female legal experts, such as Ikram Haffar, praised the laws for reflecting "a concern for protecting society's interests or the desire to shield women physically and morally."[11] Haffar failed to realize how the law served the state's efforts to preserve a patriarchal moralism by narrowly defining the scope of women's labor and ensuring that men's superior position in conjugal and familial decision making was not jeopardized in the process.

The employees' law, improved in 1974 and consonant with the social security law, decreed that employers extend an undivided, fully paid, forty-day "maternity vacation" for women.[12] Employers were required to protect women from undertaking "dangerous, exhausting, or health-damaging" tasks. But this article was too vague and general to be effective in preventing the abuse of women's human rights. Hundreds of workingwomen mentioned physical stress and exhaustion among the primary and most common hardships in their industrial work.[13] Moreover, there is considerable evidence that employers still denied many workingwomen their maternity leave.[14]

In 1976, the Lebanese government signed the Arab Agreement concerning workingwomen, which supposedly obligated Arab states to adopt and implement advanced and improved labor laws. The agreement stated that every workingwoman was entitled to health insurance that must extend benefits to "her family."[15] Nevertheless, it was left for each Arab state to decide who comprised a woman's family members. The Arab Agreement also recommended better work conditions, an extended vacation, and rest for breast-feeding mothers, but the Lebanese government overlooked this feature and many others that could have improved women's work situation. Another area in the agreement that Lebanon neglected was the need to offer family grants to working mothers whose husbands were disabled. Few if any factories provided a day care center for the children of workers in Lebanon.[16] These issues surfaced in several of the Régie women workers' accounts. During the URWE's meeting on September 24, 1971, Wasila Dubuq, an executive member, pointed to the growing need for a day care center among married women workers and proposed the construction of one by the union. The latter accepted Dubuq's proposal and contacted Iqbal Dughan, a female lawyer working for the Régie, to study the proposal and report her findings to the URWE. In the following URWE meeting, however, there was no mention of the proposal or its fate. When I asked Dubuq about it, she blamed the civil war for preventing her and the unionists from pursuing this issue.[17]

In retrospect, most of the labor laws issued by the Lebanese government between 1951 and 1976 paid little attention to the conditions of female industrial labor and excluded many categories of female waged work. They also supplemented employers' power by leaving vague any statements about equality and compensation and by allowing each factory's management to decide the parameters of equity in salary, rank, promotion, and benefits. Yet the state was assertive in its paternalistic concern for the social order of Lebanese society, at the heart of which was the moral and physical suitability of certain forms of paid labor for women.

Lebanese Industrialists and the State: Marginalizing Women's Labor, 1970–1985

The limited and ambiguous areas in state legislation pertaining to female industrial labor, along with the legislation's paternalistic tendencies, were compounded by male industrialists' discriminatory hiring practices and flawed perception of women's abilities. In this section, I highlight how these practices and perceptions coincided with critical stages of industrial development and modernization in Lebanon and with a marked decline in the skilled and semiskilled male workforce caused by the devastating effects of the civil war and the loss of property and human life. These historical developments affected the level of women's participation in industrial labor in Lebanon and eventually obstructed an active and expansive role for them in industrial production. Despite the scarcity of quantitative data on women's performance in Lebanese industries, I utilize examples from the Régie, 1970s and 1980s surveys, and statistical studies conducted by, among others, Lorfing, Abu al-Nasr, Evelyn Richards, and Janet Hyde Clark. Clark and Lorfing's 1982 study is particularly noteworthy because it assessed women's work in fourteen factories in Beirut's suburbs between 1970 and 1982. Although largely descriptive in nature, it drew upon a number of national and international censuses and reports on Lebanese labor and laborers from 1965 to 1980 and offered new and valuable findings on the constituents of the female workforce as well as on women's status and potential role in the industrial sector.[18]

In the early 1970s, economically active women in Lebanon formed 18 percent of the national labor force. The largest clusters of workingwomen appeared in the areas of agriculture (23 percent); domestic service (23 percent); professional work, mostly teaching (21 percent) and industry (20 percent); and office work (10 percent).[19] In 1972, approximately 69 percent of all industrial workingwomen in Lebanon were concentrated in the textile industries, including garment production, tailoring, and rug making.[20]

In 1975, the outbreak of the civil war brought new realities to Lebanese industrialists and workers alike. The industrial sector suffered the loss of 20 percent of its fixed capital and the collapse of 250 factories with a capital base of one billion Lebanese pounds (U.S.$1.00 = 2.25 pounds).[21] The textile industry was hit particularly hard. Clark and Lorfing argued that the preponderance of women in textile jobs and other jobs dealing with food processing could be attributed to the jobs' connection with women's "traditional" or "natural" activities as nurturers, child raisers, cooks, weavers, and embroidery craftspersons.[22] Employers and state legislators defined "natural" manual dexterity, domestic-type tasks, and aptitude rather than achieved skills as the basis for the association between particular industrial tasks and women.[23] Yet these industries habitually associated with women witnessed an alarming decline in the number of women workers in this period, from fifty thousand before 1975 to roughly twelve thousand in 1981.[24] This decline is significant given the fact that Lebanon was at the same time witnessing a drain in its industrial workforce, which decreased from 130,000 to around 78,000 after the war.[25] During the same period, the percentage of the national Lebanese workforce laboring in the Persian Gulf, African, and Latin American countries increased from 7 percent to 25 percent and was mostly men. The uprooting of thousands of Lebanese from their homes following the sudden loss of income and growing inflation did not cause a decisive transformation in the gender composition of the Lebanese industry in favor of women. Although a devaluation of women's industrial capabilities existed before this period, the civil war factors pushed for a conscious and more systematic exclusion of women from numerous industrial tasks. The employers of fourteen factories in suburban Beirut went to great lengths to train male workers who displaced women. Between 1975 and 1982, according to Clark and Lorfing, there was an approximately "38 percent rise in the numbers of men employed and a fall of about 57 percent in the numbers of women."[26] Clark and Lorfing's data underscore management's willingness to invest in nonskilled or semiskilled men. Moreover, to compensate for the shortage of Lebanese male technicians, several food and thread factories turned to foreign workers instead of to women, and by 1982 nearly 64 percent of the male workforce was non-Lebanese. Lebanese employers hired Thais and Indians to run high-speed automatic spinning machines and food-packaging systems. In one thread factory, for instance, the entire male workforce was Indian. Another textile factory in a southern suburb of Beirut laid off 80 percent of its women in the early 1980s after transforming its production from discrete machine winding of cotton thread to automatic winding. A paint factory in the same location dispensed with most of its female workforce in 1983 after mechanization; women had composed 51 percent of the factory's total workforce before this point, but only six workingwomen remained there by 1982, and these women did not manufacture paints but simply assembled paint brushes by hand. Even food factories, which during the 1970s relied primarily on female output, started to curtail its hiring of women after the introduction of advanced machinery. In one dairy food factory, the percentage of workingwomen dropped from 98 percent to 15 percent between 1975 and 1982. The manager justified this decline by noting that "the job suited men only" because it involved operating controls for sterilizing milk and processing yogurt and cream cheese. Women's tasks on the production line were reduced to "putting lids on cartons." In comparison, clothing factories exhibiting a low level of mechanization in the 1980s continued to absorb inexpensive female labor and thus maintained a dominant female workforce.[27]

It is useful to compare the level of women's participation in Lebanese industry with the level in its counterparts in the Arab World. During the early 1980s, women supposedly composed only 9 percent of the overall Arab working population. This figure does not reflect the reality of female labor because so much of women's waged work goes unnoticed and is rarely included in statistical figures. Huda Zurayk also notes that the women's labor statistics produced by official Lebanese and Arab agencies are often erroneous because they are based almost exclusively on conventional market-based labor activities and fail to detect women's indirect contributions to the market economy.[28]

This problem is particularly evident regarding women's economic production in agricultural and familial settings. In this period, Arab women seemed most active in countries where the rural economy was central and agriculture labor was integral to the national income. In Iraq, for instance, women composed 66 percent of the agricultural workforce. In Yemen, they formed around 87 percent.[29] Even though Lebanese agriculture played a modest role in the national economy, approximately 25 percent of the Lebanese female population turned to waged labor in 1980. In Iraq, around 18 percent of the female population engaged in waged work, 15 percent in Jordan, and 8 percent in Libya. In comparison with nineteen Arab countries, Lebanon ranked third after Mauritania (28 percent) and the Sudan (21.7 percent) in the percentage of women in its national workforce.[30]

In addition to the particular modes of production, economic systems, and social structures of various Arab countries, government planning played a partial role in women's contribution to nondomestic labor. For example, the Iraqi government was committed to increasing women's input in various sectors of waged work and made this goal the basis for its official policies on workingwomen.[31] In Lebanon, the absence of such state planning and the gendered discrimination common on the shop floor impeded women's participation in industry.

It is clear that women's own motives and attitudes toward waged work did not in and of themselves determine the number of women in Lebanese industry. Several factories in Beirut, especially those providing relatively good working conditions, admitted that they received more job applications from women than they could accept and that they consciously solicited male workers instead.[32]

Women's Industrial Labor: Image and Social Reality

In 1988, Rose Ghurayyib attributed the hurdles in the way of women's employment to a "patriarchal capitalist" ideology and saw women's strife as part of a larger social malady generated by the control of national wealth by a handful of landlords, merchants, and government officials. For this reason, workers and low-income earners such as women were deprived of a fair share in education, employment, and social mobility. Men, according to Ghurayyib, controlled women's access to education and dominated all employment and job-training policies.[33] Despite the fact that more men than women demanded to be paid good salaries and to receive more fringe benefits, many employers embraced male workers as "more reliable" and noted that men did not tend to leave after marriage. Clark and Lorfing demonstrated that in every aspect of industrial work, the conditions experienced by men were generally superior to those experienced by women.[34]

It seems to me, however, that this situation created a vicious cycle wherein many women would end up in physically strenuous jobs with minimum pay and few benefits and thus have little incentive to hold on to their waged work, especially if someone, such as a potential husband, were to provide for them. I am not certain that the large number of workingwomen who preferred to leave their jobs after marriage reflected a gendered statement on industrial labor. On this basis, I disagree with Clark and Lorfing's conclusion that waged work hardly changed women's "traditional attitudes" toward their roles in society. First, I do not believe that the questions these researchers' raised and the data they collected measured this dimension adequately. For instance, Clark and Lorfing did not compare women's attitudes on job commitment and vocational training to the attitudes of men who occupied the same ranks as the women at the same factories. This comparison might have yielded a useful assessment about gender differences. I also found some of the women's personal views, as reported by the authors, indicative of a change in their aspirations toward economic and personal independence. For example, approximately one-quarter of the single women in the fourteen factories surveyed emphasized personal liberties as a central motive for work, expressed their love for their jobs, and insisted they would keep working after marriage. It would have been helpful to know what ranks these women occupied and what industrial tasks they carried out in comparison with the overwhelming majority of single women who preferred to quit their work after marriage. It is possible that working conditions played a larger role in this issue than the two scholars recognized. Moreover, almost all women interviewed stated that they "were eager for their teenage daughter to have some kind of vocational training." Clark and Lorfing, however, dismissed the latter statement, noting that "while this may represent a change in attitude, one suspects that it is less a relaxation of traditional bonds than an earnest desire on the women's part for their daughters to follow a respectable trade lest they find themselves in the same predicament as their mothers."[35]

The need for a "respectable trade" raises the possibility that women who quit their industrial work after marriage were motivated more by the discouraging nature of their work than by their deferment to their husbands or by their economic and social dependence. Clark and Lorfing did not address the role of the legal system generally or of state protection specifically, and they expressed a middle-class bias when they noted that "only the young and educated" were beginning to question the established value system relating to gender roles and women's status. Lorfing and Abu al-Nasr, in an earlier study done in 1979, found that half of the workingwomen they interviewed stated that they would stop work after marriage.[36] This means that the other half would continue to work after marriage, which is a noteworthy feature. In retrospect, therefore, other social processes, influences, and opportunities must be brought to bear in the analysis of the reality of women's industrial labor in Lebanon.

After the outbreak of the civil war, the state became marginalized, and the army was paralyzed by contentious factionalism. Even the state's role as legal arbitrator in labor grievances was suspended or minimized. In the absence of governmental intervention and weakened union resistance during the civil strife, the decision to dispense with female workers at little expense to the employers in the textile, garment, and food industries was triggered by rigorous mechanization and shrinking numbers of unskilled and manual laborers. The suppressed opportunities and discouraging ambience of work for women may have pushed women to seek other avenues of waged work, where they reckoned again with low salaries and strenuous working conditions to compete with their male counterparts.

In comparison with the textile, garment, and food factories in the Beiruti suburbs, the tobacco industry maintained a substantial female workforce. Permanent workingwomen at the Régie reached their largest numbers in 1980, when the management, thanks to the workers' struggles, granted permanency to 835 temporary workers, around 45 percent of whom were women.[37] Women formed around 43 percent of the total workforce in 1969, and 41 percent in 1981, a mere 2 percent decrease (see table 4 in chapter 1). These figures run counter to the dominant picture of industrial female labor in Lebanon during the 1980s. The difference in the Régie can be explained, first, by the centrality of manual, nonmechanized leaf sorting and packaging for tobacco manufacturing and by the fact that these jobs devolved to women; second, by employers' attempts to recognize women's ardently fought-for central demands; and third, by the improved labor conditions and circumstances in the Régie (relative to other factories) that encouraged a higher level of women's commitment to work and labor organizations.

Working at an industrial firm such as the Régie meant different things to different women. It shaped women's personal lives and altered their marital and communal experiences. For some, having a "stable" job preserved their marriages, but for others it deprived them of marital life, motherhood, and the self-esteem and social status associated with them.[38] However, for those who became exclusive industrial workers, it solidified their association with city life and a worker identity that may have been congenial to labor activism and provided the thrust to preserve their work and improve its conditions.

These situations shaped and were shaped by the cultural meaning that women gave to their domestic and paid labor. I do not propose that preindustrial values about women's factory work changed overnight or that all women found such work necessarily liberating, but that a tension had already been injected in the cultural image of women's domesticity. This tension opened a window to manipulation, selection, and differentiation in women's intentional choices. In the next section, I look closely at the ways in which the realities of industrial labor from the 1970s to the late 1980s influenced and were influenced by changes in women's attitudes and choices as reflected in features pertaining to their age and marital status while employed by the Régie.

Age and Marital Status: Social and Personal Meanings of Women's Industrial Labor

In 1970, a minority of workers (25 percent) in the Lebanese industrial sector fell between the ages of fifteen and twenty-four (see table 12). Second in rank came those fifteen years or younger, who composed 21 percent of the labor force. These statistics attest to the continued preponderance of youths employed as industrial workers. Several other sources reveal a concentration of children of both sexes in several industrial tasks that demanded minimal skill and training. Between 1972 and 1975, the majority of Lebanese workingwomen fell between the ages of twenty and twenty-five years old. Around 1974, nearly 30 percent of the workers in the plastics industry and 12.5 percent in al-Jabr cloth factory were children younger than fifteen. At a major shoe factory, Red Shoe, 50 percent of the workers were between the ages of fourteen and twenty.[39]

Up until 1979–80, more than 70 percent of the female industrial workforce in Beirut was twenty-four years old or younger.[40] Approximately 31 percent of the total female workforce in ten factories started industrial work at the age of fourteen, and 40 percent began between the ages fourteen and seventeen years. At least half of the married women, however, started work after age thirty.[41] Until at least the late 1970s and early 1980s, employers in several textile, garment, paint, and food factories expressed their preferences for young women younger than eighteen because the latter demanded fewer benefits and less compensation. Employers felt that young girls were easier to manipulate owing to their ignorance about their rights and their weaker abilities to confront management for better salaries and health coverage. Legislation dealing with social security and minimum wage, as Hyde and Lorfing noted, "only applies to those over 18 and is even then sometimes not respected." Meanwhile, the same employers preferred men to be older than eighteen because they would be more disciplined and avoid trouble on the shop floor.[42]

TABLE 12. Age distribution of Lebanese workers, 1970

	<15		15–24		25–34		35–64		65 and Older	
	N	%	N	%	N	%	N	%	N	%
Agriculture	4,665	26	17,385	15	14,370	11	53,940	22	11,250	48
Industry	3,645	21	30,330	25	24,240	18	35,355	15	1,860	8
Utilities	15	0	630	0	1,530	1	3,420	1	15	1
Construction	480	3	6,885	6	9,630	7	17,310	7	720	3
Commerce & hotels	1,470	8	17,805	15	21,600	16	45,645	19	5,025	21
Transport & communication	45	41	4,725	4	11,445	9	21,360	9	645	3
Finance & services	45	0	3,660	3	7,245	5	7,185	3	285	1
Other services	7,260	41	37,755	32	43,815	33	57,090	24	3,675	16
Indefinite professions	150	1	540	0	630	0	915	0	105	0
Total	17,775	4	119,715	23	134,505	25	2,220	45	23,580	100

Source: République Libanaise, Ministère du Plan, *L'enquête par sondage sur la population active au Liban*, vol. 2, *Tableaux de résultats, juillet 1970* (Beirut: Ministère du Plan, Direction Centrale de la Statistique, Nov. 1972), 156. Figures rounded to the nearest whole number.

At the Régie, child labor was suppressed possibly because the company's internal laws stipulated that prospective workers had to be eighteen years of age or older. This stipulation may have been made, in turn, because the nature of work at the Régie involved more skilled and highly mechanized tasks, particularly after the 1960s.[43] It seems to me that women literally stepped in and took the place of the now prohibited children, especially because women provided the Régie with satisfactory levels of labor at a pay level comparable to that of children—less than minimum wage. It is important to note, however, that workers younger than the stipulated age who were desperate for employment easily nullified the Régie's provision against child labor. Numerous women workers told me how they used their older sisters' photoless identification cards to gain employment at the company and continued to carry fraudulent identification papers until they became eighteen years old. These accounts reveal that between 1954 and 1987 the absence of child employees (younger than fifteen years old) from the Régie's statistical tables does not necessarily correspond completely to reality, at least for those between ages twelve and fifteen (see table 8).[44]

During the 1970s, industrial workingwomen tended to be single; in 1972, only 7 percent of all employed women in Lebanon were married.[45] In 1977, two years after the outbreak of the civil war, single women composed 80 percent of the female workforce at the Régie, but married women only 7 percent (see table 13).

Similar patterns were discerned elsewhere. In 1979, 83 percent of working-women in ten major factories in suburban Beirut were single.[46] Therefore, women who married and stayed at the factories during the 1970s and possibly early 1980s appear to be significantly fewer in number than those who married and left.

The National Committee for the Affairs of Lebanese Women (Al-Lajna al-Wataniyya li-Shu'un al-Mar'a al-Lubnaniyya) reported a significant increase in the number of single workingwomen during the late 1980s.[47] Evelyn Richards's statistical study corroborates this fact, showing that single workingwomen reached 82 percent of the overall Lebanese workforce during this period. Richards traces such an increase to a conscious planning on the part of capitalists and entrepreneurs to attract low-wage workers who tailored job descriptions and work requirements to single women.[48]

In the tobacco industry, however, this picture changed dramatically in the period between 1977 and 1986. The number of single women at the Régie dropped by 22 percent between 1977 and 1986, whereas that of married women increased by 15 percent (table 13). At the same time, the number of widowed women increased

TABLE 13. Régie female workers' marital status, 1977–1986

	1977		1986	
	N	%	N	%
Single	761	80	477	58
Married	66	7	182	22
Divorced	2	0	32	4
Widowed	121	13	126	15
Total	950	100	817	100
Unaccounted for	—	—	310	28

Sources: Al-Sanduk al-Watani lil-Daman al-IjtimaŞi (Bureau of Social Security), "Al-Riji: Al-MaŞlumat al-MutaŞalliqa bi al-Ujaraṣ wa al-Ashkhas al-KhadiŞin li Hadha al-Talab" (The Régie: Information Related to Workers and Persons Applying to Social Security), July 4, 1977, and Régie Personnel Department, "Liste des rubriques de paie, 1-12-1987," Régie company records, Hadath. Figures rounded to the nearest whole number.

by 2 percent. Although it was still difficult to achieve a stable and constant core of married workingwomen at the Régie, these figures reflect the older age of workingwomen and the high death toll among men because of the war.

It is possible that the increase in the number of married women among Régie workers was spurred by the loss of income resulting from their husbands' death or injury during the civil war. In addition, the company took special measures to accommodate workers from a wide array of sectarian groups, hoping to minimize the war's impact on productivity. For example, in 1986 the Régie implemented a special plan that decreed that, first, for safety reasons, Muslim workers did not need to work at the main branch in Hadath, a predominantly Christian area where their lives might be endangered by right-wing Christian militias. In the meantime, the Régie guaranteed the payment of their salaries in full. Second, Christian workers who could come safely to work in Hadath would be paid, in addition to their original wage, supplementary pay for overtime hours worked. Furthermore, the Régie hired additional young women and men to compensate for the absence of the Muslim workers. The new workers had no direct legal contact with the company because they were hired through a broker (the *iltizam* system) from the neighboring Christian areas of Hadath. The production of tobacco products skyrocketed, and sales reached their highest levels since the Régie's founding.[49] These measures protected the permanent workforce at the Régie but had a negative impact on the two hundred temporary workers, mostly women, hired by the company. The latter worked under life-threatening circumstances and were forced to sleep numerous times at the factory when the bombing of Beirut was heavy. In addition to the long hours of work and worsening conditions, these workers were deprived of the benefits extended by the company to permanent workers. They felt cut off from the rest of the workers and lacked legal and institutional protection. The only legal link they had to the company was through the broker who had hired them and who had no jurisdiction over their work conditions.

A third factor may be related to changes in women's attitudes in response to the civil war. During episodes of social unrest, war, inflation, and state absence, a job at the Régie was a stable source of income and, in some cases, a crucial supplementary source of money for working-class families. Many of the female workers' spouses were free laborers, farmers, or small-businessmen who, in most cases, received no health or educational benefits via their jobs (table 14).

TABLE 14. Occupations of female Régie workers' spouses, 1997

Occupation	N	%
Works in another institution	47	25
Is an employee (blue or white collar) in another institution	18	10
Skilled worker	57	31
Owner of small business	20	11
Farmer	12	6
Soldier	8	4
Free laborer	3	2
Worker at the Régie	17	9
Unemployed	4	2
Total	186	100

Source: Survey of 356 Régie workers (286 women and 69 men) conducted by the author in 1997. Figures are rounded to the nearest whole number.

Through the years, Régie workers made substantive gains in acquiring full medical coverage for a worker's family and financial aid for the education of their children.[50] These benefits, in my opinion, explained why significant numbers of women persisted in their work at the Régie after their marriage, particularly when their spouses were unemployed or were in jobs lacking health insurance coverage. In time, however, women began to reap important social and personal advantages from their labor that made them less inclined to give it up to conform to the demands of domestic labor, familial interests, or male authority. This development brings into question the notion that marriage and family, on the one hand, and waged work, on the other hand, were antithetical and irreconcilable among Middle Eastern women. I illustrate this point further in the cases of Muna Mawrid and Nayfa Farhan later in this chapter.

The older age at marriage for Régie women during the 1990s seems to reflect a social transformation and an increasing mistrust of marital demands and obligations among the urban working class amidst worsening economic conditions, inflation, and political disillusionment. In 1997, the largest group of workingwomen at the Régie, 28 percent, married between the ages of fifteen and twenty (table 15). The second-largest group (22 percent) was women who married between the ages twenty-six and thirty. But 26 percent of the Régie women were first married after they were thirty years old. It is noteworthy that by 1997

TABLE 15. Age of Régie female workers at first marriage, 1997

Years Old	N	%
1–14	10	5
15–20	53	28
21–25	35	19
26–30	41	22
31–35	27	15
36–40	14	8
41 and older	6	3
Total	186	100
Unaccounted for	2	

Source: Survey of 356 Régie workers (286 women and 69 men) conducted by the author in 1997. Figures are rounded to the nearest whole number.

the average age for marriage among men was only two years older than that for women, very likely because of the impact of the civil war.[51]

For many single women at the Régie, a job fulfilled basic economic needs until such time when they found a spouse who could relieve them of their financial burdens. But after these women started work, gained experience, and developed a complex set of social and personal relations with their coworkers, the work environment became more meaningful to them. Some women willingly decided to stay at work after marriage. A census conducted by Saʿid Hayik, a director in the Régie personnel department, revealed that unlike many of the earliest women recruits into the company who left their jobs after marriage, the next generation of women persisted in industrial labor during the 1980s and 1990s.[52]

Scholars have tried to discern whether social taboos or religious attitudes have been responsible for women's modest participation in industrial labor in the Arab world since the 1960s. Nadia Haggag Youssef argued in her 1974 study that factory work for women was considered taboo in Middle Eastern societies because of the kind of work women did and because their proximity to men was considered somewhat "promiscuous." Youssef noted that all industrial working-women were socially stigmatized, which explained why the majority of them remained unmarried.[53] Mona Hammam, Linda Layne, and Yusif Sayigh, among other researchers, similarly argued that this stigma encouraged single women to perceive their factory work as transitory until their marriage.[54]

In my opinion, however, the devaluation of industrial labor for women and the "honor" and family "integrity" associated with it for men did not remain unchanged in Lebanon. Women's participation in the industrial workforce was often impeded owing to the material and social conditions created by the civil war, the modernization of the industry, and government policy. Meanwhile, the worsening economy of the conjugal household—many of which survived uprootedness, migration, and inflation—paved the way for the development of new attitudes toward women's doing paid work. Moreover, historical analyses of various systems of production as well as the societal and state structures sustaining them show that patriarchal values and practices can be manipulated, violated, and changed. Deniz Kandiyoti emphasizes that the notion of a universal Muslim patriarchy is inadequate for explaining the social production of patriarchy or the complex and nuanced "reproduction" of women's subordination.[55] Some workers' families did impose certain restrictions on them. Yet the accounts by several Régie women indicate that some women started consciously and unconsciously to violate the social codes that once defined them within the rural unit.

To illustrate this complex and occasionally contradictory process, I present the cases of two Régie women, Nayfa F. and Muna M., who strove to overcome the mechanism of patriarchy and the gender structure nurtured by it. These cases underscore some of the strategies that women employed to surmount the control of their labor and sexuality by men.[56] They also show that women sometimes undertook serious negotiations with husbands and fathers because the women wanted to remain at the Régie. They equally reveal how tobacco labor enhanced some women's social position and mobility.

Women's Strategies: Between Home and the Workplace

> A woman can lose her marriage unjustly and helplessly, but she cannot lose her work.
> —Nayfa Farhan, Régie factory worker

Nayfa F., a Shi'i woman, was born in 1933 in Kafarila in southern Lebanon.[57] Like many of her female coworkers, she was illiterate because her parents, who owned some village land, had her work on their farm and found little use in sending her to school. When Nayfa turned twenty-one in 1954, she joined the

Régie, where she worked in the leaf department until retirement. It is possible that the physical abuse and exploitation experienced by Nayfa at the hands of her immediate family motivated her to seek industrial labor in Beirut. At first, her parents vehemently opposed her decision to join the Régie and beat her several times, insisting that she need not seek work outside the family's business. But they later succumbed to her resistance and reluctantly accepted her work at the Régie. After her father's death, she received her inheritance of land. Together with her salary at the Régie, this share allowed her to purchase jewelry (a common goal for people seeking to protect their money from devaluation over the years) and to buy an apartment in a suburban quarter in Beirut known as Burj al-Barajina.

After Nayfa was married in 1960, her husband, a government clerk, repeatedly demanded that she quit her job. Her refusal to do so became the source of struggles and resentment between the two. Meanwhile, they had five children together, and Nayfa's workload at home increased. She took her eldest daughter out of school and sought her assistance in the daily chores of cleaning and cooking. The conflict between Nayfa and her husband worsened, and the tensions mounted when her husband presented her with an ultimatum: remain married or carry on with her wage work. She planned to take a temporary unpaid leave from the Régie to see whether she could truly save her marriage and fundamentally alter her relationship with her husband. She concealed this decision from her husband, telling him instead that she had quit her job. She sold her jewelry and with the savings she received from her parents raised an amount of money equivalent to the Régie's compensation fees paid for those who quit. A year passed by, and Nayfa's relationship with her husband deteriorated even further, so she became strongly convinced that saving her marriage was a futile effort. Nayfa divorced in 1972 and returned to the Régie.

Nayfa's story shares many themes with other oral accounts from the Régie women. These women noted that their initial motive for taking wage work outside the confines of their homes was either to save some money for marriage or to help support their families during a crisis. Nonetheless, the women's subsequent experiences at work and the social and psychological benefits they reaped from it encouraged them to preserve their jobs for a longer period of time. Factory work and working-class identity, which many unskilled men associated with low social status, alternatively empowered several Régie women and compelled them to expand their roles beyond those of wife or daughter.

Independence and Social Conformity

My only condition for marriage was to keep my job.
—Muna M., Régie factory worker

Born in Beirut in 1946, Muna M. was a Sunni Muslim woman who worked at the Régie branch in Tripoli.[58] The untimely death of her father compelled her to leave elementary school in the fifth grade and look for a job to help her family. She took up several temporary, part-time jobs until she turned seventeen and found steady employment in the well-known Ghandour food-processing and chocolate factory in Beirut. After working for two years in Ghandour, she left there and joined the newly established Régie branch in Tripoli in 1965. Two years later she entered into a serious relationship with a man working at the same Régie branch, and he proposed marriage to her. He promised to buy her an apartment and provide fully for her if she were to quit her job and devote herself to her home. Muna refused his proposition, and for months he tried to persuade her to change her mind. Finally, her future husband abandoned his request, and Muna agreed to marry him under one condition: she would never quit her work at the Régie.

This is but one case among many in which female workers married after starting to work at the Régie, which meant that work had not obstructed their marriage opportunities. On the contrary, it gave married couples a sense of stability and to a large extent enhanced their economic status. Some women met their future husbands either at the Régie or in the city's wider social circles, which meant that women's factory work was also an occasion for meeting more men.

Many Régie women spoke to me of their families' initial opposition to their adoption of industrial labor. Some fathers, brothers, and husbands of Régie women saw factory work as too "public" for women and disruptive to the gender balance, religious piety, and social harmony. Others, however, were persuaded by male family or village members who worked at the Régie to send their daughters and sisters there. They were reassured by these Régie men and some Régie women that the girls and women would be working well within ethical boundaries. Other families gave in to their daughters' wishes on condition that they be accompanied by women acquaintances to and from the Régie. The first women from a particular family or town to begin work at the Régie often faced more parental prohibitions, which normally faded during periods of dire poverty and sheer necessity.

Underlying the men's opposition, however, were subtle fears of replacing male with female labor and undercutting skilled men's positions. The gender war coincided with the Régie's praise of women's commitment to work, "compliance" with rules, and "reasonable expectations" with respect to salary.[59] This fear of female labor was vividly manifest in 1954, when a large group of Régie men protested vehemently to the Ministries of Labor and Finance that men were being substituted with women at the Régie.[60] This social process, in turn, was given new cultural meaning by the threatened yet stronger male population. The domesticity argument said that a woman's place was in her home next to family men and not commingling—with no clear physical or sexual boundaries—with strange and thus "menacing" men.

Uses of Kinship: Industrial Adaptation and Social Control

As explained in the previous chapter, familial and village ties were an integral part of the social world of Régie workers. In this section, I show how working-women manipulated kinship, sectarian, and village ties in their gradual adaptation to urban life and in strengthening their position within the Régie.

Women figured prominently among the company's major family clusters—mainly the Zu'aytirs, the Ja'ja's, the Musawis, the Sab'alis, and so on—who belonged to the last category in table 11 (eleven and more family members at the Régie). The leaf department of the Hadath plant employed forty-two Zu'aytir workingwomen out of a total of seventy-four Zu'aytir family members at the plant in 1981. The remaining thirty-two Zu'aytirs were a mix of skilled and unskilled women and men distributed over several departments, except for administration.[61] In comparison, there were only three women among the fifty Ja'ja's employed at the Régie, two of whom worked in the leaf department.[62] The remaining Ja'ja's were workingmen who were barely skilled and a few others who, unlike the Zu'aytirs, held administrative positions.

Women composed almost half the total number of Musawis working at the Régie—namely, nine out of twenty. These women were concentrated in the leaf and factory departments. Only two of the Musawi men held administrative positions in the technical and tobacco expertise sections. Finally, among the Sab'alis, twenty-four workingwomen and seven workingmen were located in the leaf and factory departments of the one-building branch in Bikfaya, their hometown.[63]

Overall, the women formed a significant core of at least three of the four family clusters and almost half of all the family clusters added together.

These features of the Régie workforce and the oral accounts by several Régie workingwomen reveal the multifaceted and complex use of kinship and religious networks, first, to attain employment; second, to control workplace conditions and the value of labor; and third, to demand respectability. In the 1960s and later, a major trend in the scholarship on Lebanese labor presented the cultivation of kinship relations by workers as a sign of "retardation" in their national, civic, and class consciousness that thwarted any attempts to "modernize" the Lebanese people along professional rather than sectarian lines. Sociologist Samir Khalaf advocated this view. He viewed Lebanese nationalism as a superior and ideal form of consciousness that was diametrically opposed to kinship or sectarian identity, which he relegated to an inferior rank. In 1968, he wrote that "as an extension of kinship attachments and a communal life marked by close and intimate association and factionalism, social interaction at all levels of the society is characterized by a high degree of personal jealousies and kinship feuds. Lebanese legend and history is [sic] replete with accounts revealing the vindictive and vulnerable nature of interpersonal relations." He concluded that these "personal allegiances and loyalties" were invariably given priority at the expense of social interests and individual needs.[64] Guilain Denoeux, like Khalaf, presented the provincial leader, the za'im, and his hybrid, the ra'is (informal leader), as the prototypes for a political leadership in the Middle East that generated a consenting and largely passive clientele.[65]

In opposition to these assumptions, I found that kinship and familial ties were not antithetical to class behavior or action and that the workers used them effectively at times to achieve their goals. Workingwomen cultivated vital connections with local and national za'ims to solicit support in problems relating to their professions, work conditions, and personal lives. Suad Joseph found in the early 1980s that the women and men in Camp Trad, a working-class neighborhood in Beirut, "participated in a common political culture, the central feature of which was the manipulation of personal networks across all other boundaries to achieve basic life needs."[66] Thus, workingwomen were active participants in informal networks—kinship and friendship, for example—which they utilized for their own good. The type of social associations they established among themselves and with men were purposeful and multifunctional. If men seemed helpless actors in this patron-client paradigm, as Khalaf depicted them, working-class women, as Joseph saw them, were enmeshed in a social nexus with each other to "create solidarity with other women for economic purposes; exchange information, goods and support with other women to preserve and reproduce their class position; offset the divisiveness of their menfolk to reinforce the status quo; control other women; and construct hierarchical relations."[67]

With the decision to move from village to suburb came women's utilization of kinship connections to settle and find a job in their new world. The nature of the economic infrastructure and poor governmental planning meant a failure to absorb the overwhelming number of young and displaced migrants to the city. Not everyone was able to immigrate to Latin America, Africa, and Western industrial countries, and many were left to struggle in a Lebanese job market with few openings. Even with the aggressive policies of capitalist expansion in the 1950s, one had to utilize whatever resources were at one's disposal. Workers turned to provincial and sectarian loyalties neither because "nepotism," as Thomas Stauffer noted in 1955, was the only method of job recruitment in Beirut nor because industrial life had not matured among Middle Eastern workers.[68] Lebanese workingwomen and men found a supportive base in kinship and neighborhood ties during their adaptations to industrial life, job recruitment and training, and the social challenges of the novel urban environment.

Mediating Kin: The Case of Najla J.

Najla J., a Maronite woman, was born in 1931 in a village called Dayr al-Ahmar in eastern Lebanon. Her father worked in several public vocations until he finally settled in a job as a school principal. Unlike many of his fellow townsmen, he believed in the value of education and sent all his children to school. Najla, however, was ill disposed to school education and did not continue beyond her second elementary class.[69]

When Najla turned eighteen, she contemplated a change in her life at Dayr al-Ahmar. She learned about a job opening at the Régie through one of her women relatives. At first, she was hesitant, but the father of that relative, himself a skilled worker at the Régie, continued to encourage her until she was finally convinced to join. Najla's parents were initially strongly opposed to her decision, but she kept reminding them of all the able and morally "well-protected" young women who joined the Régie. They agreed to allow her to try this work for only a certain time, during which she would find out for herself that it was unsuitable. They were concerned mostly about Najla's decision to move to Beirut, close to the Régie, living on her own and away from them. To accomplish her goal without agitating her parents, Najla decided to take two of her siblings to live with her in Beirut. Najla's sister worked at the Régie for four years and left when she got married, and her brother took up work at Beirut's airport.

At the Régie, Najla joined the leaf-sorting department as a temporary or seasonal worker. Several months later the company transferred her to the manufacturing department. In the meantime, her parents kept asking her to quit, but she held firmly to her job. Her memories of the earliest months at the Régie and the influence that industrial work had on her outlook and self-esteem were noteworthy. She recalled that although she was illiterate and unskilled, she was neither intimidated nor overwhelmed by the nature of her work in the manufacturing department. She described her work as "easy," and she felt happy and important by the warm attention she received from the Régie managers, who belonged to the Sawaya family. Like Najla, the Sawayas were Maronites and shared indirect marital ties with her family.

The good treatment she received initially from the Sawayas began to change. She understood that sectarian and marital ties ran thin when it came to the Sawayas' class interests and capitalist gains. Friction with the foreman occurred frequently and intensified with the introduction of new machines in the manufacturing department in 1958. Mechanization caused a significant increase in the pace of production, which led to a restructuring of industrial tasks. When the foreman decided to substitute another woman for Najla to operate a new machine, Najla's frustrations turned into open conflict with management. She resorted to legal channels to maintain her job as an operative, but she realized that because she was a temporary worker with no permanent status, the law did not protect her or entitle her to remain an operative.

This reality alerted Najla to her insecure position at the Régie and the importance of achieving permanency. Along with six other temporary workingwomen, she formed a delegation to present their grievances. Their delegation sought the assistance of a literate workingman, who wrote four petitions on their behalf to the prime minister, Sami al-Sulh, and other government officials asking them to take immediate action against the Régie. Al-Sulh asked another government official, to handle their case and deal directly with the Régie administration. As the women's delegation was preparing to meet with that official, Najla realized that the latter was married to a distant cousin of hers. Conscious of the importance of kinship ties, Najla eagerly explained to him her blood ties with his wife to ensure his commitment to her and her women colleagues. The official promised to support their collective demand for permanency.

The news of the women's meetings with the official and then with the prime minister reached the ears of the Régie administration. The latter openly accused Najla and her colleagues of plotting against the company and agitating the workers. The women were not moved by the management's intensified investigations and its constant talk about their "disloyalty" and "unruly" behavior. Along with the pressures exerted by the government official, the women's organized opposition started to bear fruit, and the Régie was eventually forced to grant them job permanency.

Najla and her colleagues emerged from this process with more than job permanency. Their collective efforts, planning skills, and the achievement of their goal honed their characters and instilled in them a sense of daring, strength, and independence. Najla earned the reputation of being a "daredevil," a headstrong and trusted activist. She became a source of inspiration for her fellow Régie women, including those in her family and religious sect.

Several Régie women identified a relative as their first source of knowledge about the Régie and as an assistant in their job recruitment. Georgette A. joined the Régie in 1942 through the mediation of a young man from her village, Zihilti, in Jizzin. Georgette N. joined the Régie in 1959 through the mediation of a French woman friend who convinced her employers to hire Georgette in her place because she was quitting. Samiah 'A. was encouraged by her sisters-in law to apply when the Régie started to hire new workers. Theresa A. joined the Régie through the mediation of the Régie's director in the 1970s, who was a friend of her father. Wahiba W. was hired by the Régie through her mother-in law, and Haniya A. through her paternal uncle, who was the head of a department at the Régie in 1980. Huriya 'I. was encouraged by women from her own village and family to join the Régie. Louisa G. joined the Régie through an acquaintance of her neighbors, Tawfiq M.[70] Other Régie men and women sought the mediation of local and national political leaders not merely to find a job at the Régie, but to resolve problems with the management. Their stories also reveal the intersection of powerful political figures in the Régie's business affairs.

Untied and Without a "Back": The Case of In'am A.

In'am A., a Shi'i woman, was born in Ba'labak in 1944 to a family of twelve.[71] The whole family worked at farming the land until 1955, when In'am's brother eloped with a woman from a large rival family. To avoid rekindling the feuds between them and their in-laws, the family migrated to al-Zalqa, a suburb in eastern Beirut. The mayor of al-Zalqa, who was an old friend of the family, helped them rent a small apartment, and the men and women worked at his small factory for four years. After the mayor died and the business dwindled, the family was forced to seek another source of income. Along with her mother and sisters, In'am founded a bakery, where they sold bread and pastries and gave all their profits to In'am's father. In 1958, In'am's brother, through the patronage of an influential local leader, solicited the support of President Chamoun to get him a job at the Régie. Through yet another form of patronage or familial connection, In'am's brother forged identification cards for In'am and her sisters that increased their ages by at least four years so that they could be employed by the Régie.

In'am's very young sisters could not be counted on for protection inside the Régie and had not cultivated the kind of connections in Beirut for times of need. In'am's early experiences at the Régie evoked feelings of frustration and alienation when she faced other women workers' aggressive competition and harassment, particularly from those who had many immediate relatives at the workplace. In telling her story, she strongly emphasized that she was not "tied" to any family cluster and had no "back"—that is, the protection of relatives to whom one could turn to at the workplace. On one occasion, a Christian woman operative whom In'am was assigned to assist hit her with a machine drawer, and In'am was seriously injured and hospitalized. Feeling helpless and unwelcome by her women colleagues, she decided to conceal the facts from the management and reported that she was responsible for the accident because she slipped on the floor. She thought that because "she was going to spend her entire life at the Régie," she did not want to make enemies.

In the meantime, she demanded to be transferred to another department, claiming to be disabled and unfit to work as an operative even though she had trained for several years and had passed the qualifying exams. After referring her to a doctor, who found her perfectly fit for the work, management refused her request to be transferred from the factory to the leaf department. One hot summer day, In'am deliberately rubbed her body with Abu al-Shanab, a potent cream medication known to cause severe skin inflammation during heat. She was hospitalized and allowed to rest for twenty-four days, after which the Régie transferred her to the leaf department. There she faced yet another problem when the male foreman sexually harassed her on the first day of work. She realized that she could not keep hoping or dreaming of having strong relatives at the Régie to defend her and decided to take matters into her own hands. The following day she brought a knife with her and threatened to kill the foreman if he ever harassed her again. Like most women who were concerned about their social reputation and wanted to safeguard their "moral" image, In'am did not discuss the incident of sexual harassment with her employers or with other workers. From that day on, however, she hid a knife in her sleeve when she passed through the Régie factory's security check.

In'am's case clearly indicates that abuse, physical attack, and sexual harassment experienced by individual workingwomen on the shop floor could be prevented by familial backing or connection to influential managerial or political figures. The fact that In'am did not have an older and more established group of relatives at the Régie made her more susceptible to verbal and physical harm. Her inability to stand her ground against other workingwomen's harassment of her may have impeded her upward occupational mobility, which would have been translated into a higher rank and a better salary.

Conclusion

The wide range of domestic and agricultural activities in which women participated, including waged labor, attest to women's significant contribution to the Lebanese rural economy. These activities also show that social rejection of paid labor is associated with the middle and upper classes rather than with the working class, where female labor was commonly indispensable to the survival of the rural family.

Nonetheless, full-time factory work that demanded a spatial separation of women from the patrimonial-patriarchal household was not achieved without confrontations and negotiations. As women workers moved from village to city, they devised new strategies to adapt to the new work culture and social setting.

Women's low level of participation in industrial labor in comparison to that of men, as I have tried to show, was not independently determined by social taboo or female subordination to patriarchal control. Rather, it was shaped largely by paternalism, the devaluation of women's acquired skills, and the new hierarchies of gender produced in state legislation and Lebanese industrialists' hiring policies. The dramatic shortage in the number of skilled and semiskilled men in Lebanon's workforce owing to the civil war did not encourage employers to recruit Lebanese women, but rather to call upon foreign male workers. A large number of women applied to these factories, but only a fraction of them attained the jobs they sought. Under these circumstances, the vast majority of industrial workingwomen ended up in the lowest-ranking, manual, physically challenging jobs, which promised modest or little benefits and unfavorable work environments. I conclude that such circumstances and not women's "traditional" deferment to male protection and dependence may have discouraged them from remaining in their jobs after marriage. I also demonstrate, based on the personal statements of industrial workingwomen in the tobacco, textile, and food-producing factories, that industrial labor transformed women's self-image and social roles. Many seemed to become more assertive in challenging male authority and in fighting abusive spousal and parental control. Many of the women who entered the tobacco factories were motivated primarily by stark necessity, but some also were driven at least in part by hopes of personal autonomy and adventure.

Kinship, village ties, and influential political leaders' mediation played no small role in women's adaptation to the industrial environment and manipulation of familial control. Provincial ties were not necessarily antithetical to the development of rationalized identities based on class, profession, or gender. Instead, they served workers' interests and helped them cope with transitional social phases. All in all, women's labor history entertains a range of contradictory choices regarding reselection, renewal, or abandonment of preindustrial values.

6

"Qati' al-Arzaq min Qati' al-A'naq"

Gendered Boundaries and Class,
Tobacco Women's Struggle, 1960–1965

DURING THE TWO DECADES following their first major strike in 1946, tobacco women became more sophisticated in their labor activism and more savvy in the formulation of their short- and long-term objectives, all of which led to their militant clashes with the Régie and the tribal ethnic state in 1963 and 1965. This chapter delineates the historical developments unfolding during this phase of women's militancy, the nature of their labor demands, the approach they took to achieve them, and the social and political implications of their radicalization.

For the first time in their history, tobacco women staged strikes that spread into the various departments and branches of the Régie. The women confronted their employers' suppression of their human and labor rights, reshaped their own leadership, spearheaded labor conflicts, and sometimes took control of the organization of the strike. This state of affairs was a far cry from the experiences of the earlier generation of Régie workingwomen, whose demands during the 1946 strike were undermined and later diffused in 1950 through futile lawsuits and negotiations. Unlike previous instances of protest, the women of the 1960s resisted manipulation or sabotage by the Régie's upper male stratum and high-ranking skilled employees, and succeeded in making women's needs central to the strike's agenda.[1] This development was an important instance of gender taking priority over class, or, more specifically, of women working against a male-led class action. As I show, although more workingwomen became unionized and drawn to socialist ideals, the majority expressed growing doubts regarding the URWE's reliability and its commitment to their goals. They also questioned the position of skilled workingmen and employees in the Régie's higher administrative ranks, who supported URWE decisions.[2] By 1963, Régie women openly rejected the URWE's leadership and began forging an alliance with the underprivileged strata of the male workforce, the blue-collar workers. The call for job permanency and equality advanced by both temporary workingwomen and permanent male workers became the pole around which the entire militant experience revolved.

Between 1960 and 1970, industrial workingwomen also faced a changing sociopolitical and economic climate. These conditions were characterized by substantial economic growth, internal struggles among various elements of the tribal-ethnic hegemony over their envisioned modes of governmental reform, and the oppositional politics of secular and leftist political parties. As I discuss more fully later in the chapter, these developments brought to the fore a complex set of social experiences on the shop floor—and in family life—that shaped and were shaped by women workers' work culture, experiences, and outlook.

In this chapter, I raise questions pertaining to the scholarship on working-class identity in general and on class-based activity in an Arab–Middle Eastern society in particular. One prevalent trend in this scholarship is the cultural approach, in particular the subaltern variation that lays major emphasis on cultural and perceptual forces in shaping workers' identity.[3] Dipesh Chakrabarty is a major proponent of this approach and argues that the "subaltern classes [carry] in their own heads" religious affiliations and familialism that invariably work against the development of rationalized national and class identities.[4] Yet I have learned through a close examination of the 1963 and 1965 Lebanese strikes that there is ample evidence to counter not only Chakrabarty's ahistorical position, but also his problematical notions attributing key causal connections between the particular content of workers' minds and their identity-making activities as well as his stereotypical analyses of workers' supposedly naive appreciation of their relationships to religious and other groups. Instead, the strikes showcase workers' ongoing adaptation to industrial work culture and urbanity, and bring into relief the complex, wide-ranging identities among the players involved in these class-based actions. I present several case studies of Régie women and men to illustrate their creative and intentional use of sect, informal social networks, and kinship to counteract state repression and strengthen their own and their peers' labor commitments.

Another prevalent trend in the scholarship can be seen in Marxist Lebanese writings, which entertain two divergent approaches to the development of class consciousness among Arab workers. The first approach is based on a universal, unilinear evolutionary model of societal development that moves from traditional phases to modern ones. The coexistence of both traditional and modern elements within one society is seen as merely temporary, giving way to the final triumph of modernism and, in Marxist terms, to advanced levels of workers' class consciousness.[5] The second approach views the labor protests that broke out during and after French colonial rule as the beginning of an evolutionary transformation from the simple and spontaneous to the most complex, mature stage of class action. The proponents of this view, however, argue that modern or rational types of labor organization attracted workers in "traditional" societies because of their similarity to communal, religious, and charitable associations and because workers perceived union leaders to be like their former religious or informal provincial leaders.[6] Again, however, a closer examination of the 1963 and 1965 strikes shows that these rigid models of Lebanese workers' awareness fail to capture the complexities of the workers' experiences in general and the nature of workingwomen's labor activism in particular.

Gender Discrimination on the Shop Floor: The Strikes of 1963

To clarify the realities surrounding the 1963 and 1965 strikes, it is vital to understand the history of Régie labor conflicts between 1946 and 1963. Workingwomen and men struck on many occasions, most notably in 1947, 1954, 1955, 1958, 1960, and 1961. In general, the strikers' goals in these strikes varied from an increase in salaries and compensation, family allowances, loans, medical benefits, and sick leave to more fundamental demands such as job permanency.[7] Almost all of these strikes were organized by the URWE, were economic in type, and ended without violence or police intervention. The duration of the strikes ranged from one to thirty-three days.[8] Workers won many of these concessions, except for job permanency, which remained a long-denied demand of the mostly female temporary workers. In the URWE's negotiations with management, this particular demand was constantly compromised in favor of others pertaining to the permanent workers.

By 1963, five hundred Régie women had achieved permanent status, but the remaining one thousand were still temporary.[9] Temporary workingmen formed a small section of the blue-collar workers. Like their female counterparts, these men were denied basic benefits and privileges, such as participation in the paid annual break, a health plan, the thirteenth-month bonus or production bonus, and paid weekend breaks. Moreover, temporary and permanent women workers encountered similar discrimination because unlike the Régie (white-collar) administrative staff, they were not allowed to receive paid weekend breaks and holidays before completing five years of work.[10] Indeed, permanent women workers faced additional hardships and lagged behind their male counterparts in benefits, receiving lower wages and fewer rewards even when performing the same or additional tasks.

Despite commonalities in the conditions and overall grievances among workers, the agenda for the strike planned in June 1963 reflected diverse objectives. According to the biographical account of an anonymous tobacco workingman, self-described as "'Amil Tabigh" (Tobacco Worker), the permanent and temporary Régie women aspired to achieve "equal pay for equal work" and the job permanency that they had called for incessantly since the 1940s.[11] They consciously attempted to reverse their position of marginality and inferiority not merely in relationship to their employers, but also within the labor force itself. Women's assertion of their particular rights did not undermine class cohesion, but introduced instead unconventional forms of class-based action and leadership.

The men joined the workingwomen in requesting protection against arbitrary discharge and recurring abuse by their employers, which the law only vaguely addressed. Indeed, these and other requests for a social security system and housing, the improvement of labor laws, and free education for workers' children were tied to the call for unity among all workers nationwide, reflecting an awareness of the link between the Régie workers and the Lebanese labor movement at large.[12] Instead of focusing narrowly on their specific grievances against the Régie, 'Amil Tabigh and his coworkers called for the preservation of allowances and the right to unionize. Régie workers had attained both demands already, but the demands' recurrence on their agenda was a sign of the their solidarity with workingwomen and men nationwide. The labor demands specific to tobacco workers included free medical, health, and dental treatment, an increase in the coverage of transportation expenses, and the "fourteenth-month" production bonus.[13]

In early June 1963, the Régie's management decided to transfer forty newly admitted women from various departments and branches to the Hadath factory plant. Such transfers were customarily made to bestow permanency on workers. The remaining temporary workingwomen who were thus arbitrarily excluded from permanency denounced the Régie's inconsistent and irrational practices and accused it of nepotism and sectarian favoritism. Hundreds of outraged women and men who had been working for more than ten years at the Régie and had waited desperately to become permanent now initiated a wildcat strike, causing a work stoppage in all departments of the company, which originated in the Hadath plant and later spread to all branches nationwide.[14] The women who spearheaded the strike faced a much different workplace and political environment from the one their earlier counterparts had encountered. Union and Communist activism were making inroads among Lebanese workers in the 1960s. To be sure, Communist ideas were not dispersed merely through formal party organs, but on a popular level through a generation of Communist musicians, radio broadcasters, newspaper reporters, and artists, and this political ambiance discouraged women's acquiescence.

Government supporters' attitudes toward women's radicalism were ambivalent and complex. On the one hand, they presented the Régie workingwomen as uncontrollable strikers whose unharnessed behavior threatened to disrupt state order and interests at the Régie. The official press noted their determined behavior in "invading" the Hadath administrative building as well as in annoying and "expelling" the high-ranking administrative employees from their offices.[15] On the other hand, this same press persistently downplayed women's leadership role in the strike, either by lumping them with the workingmen under the Arabic term 'ummal or by noting that male agitators "took refuge behind workingwomen" and used them to force "their colleagues to stop work."[16] A more complex version of this dual and ambivalent approach to women's radicalism was the claim that Communist workingmen placed women "at the forefront of the strike lines" and "exploited them," insinuating that women were passive and easily manipulated by men.[17] These depictions and others carried significant undertones, revealing the state's vulnerability, the Régie's political impotence, and, in turn, gendered weakness as these portrayals struggled to restore among these workingwomen the dominant gender structure.[18]

As I discussed in chapter 3, Régie women developed an exemplary form of leadership vested in informal women's groups nurtured in part by kinship and village ties, friendship, bonds of sociability, and a common labor history. More

11. The administration building of the Hadath factory, February 2, 1997. Photograph by the author.

than half of the Régie workforce had direct and indirect familial and kinship ties. Women constituted a significant section of at least three of the four major family clusters at the Régie and almost half of all the family clusters added together (see chapter 5).[19] Among the women's groups were the periodic delegations sent to the Régie's management to protest mistreatment and harmful conditions at the workplace, the non-URWE committees composed of women workers and aimed at assisting fellow female colleagues who were laid off or who faced medical or social emergencies, and the strike committees organized and led exclusively by women.[20] Women's social groups, which departed from the formal male-based trade unions and the Communist Party, have unfortunately not been studied or discussed to date in the literature.

Many common facets of their lives fostered the shared sense of mission and cohesion among these Régie women. Most of the women were concentrated in the leaf-sorting and assembling departments, and rural poverty and the deterioration of peasant life in the East (Biqa'), the North ('Akkar region), and the South were important experiences they shared at this time. Unlike the earliest women recruits into the company, many women working between 1954 and 1969 were more commonly linked by age and marital status, whether they were married when they entered the Régie or remained there after marriage (see table 15 in chapter 5).[21] At this time, women began to reap important social and personal advantages from their labor, which made them less inclined to give it up to conform to the demands of domestic labor, familial interests, or male authority.

The Régie's workforce had reached its largest size in the 1960s, and this era was the "golden" one for the Régie, both in terms of production and profit. From 1955 to 1965, the annual sale of tobacco increased almost twofold.[22] Yet resentment among workers at this time ran rampant because their wages and benefits did not witness a similar increase. The women also seemed disappointed with the URWE's earlier record of caving in to the management and trying to appease government officials. For instance, despite numerous workers' insistence that they continue with their strike during July 1963, the URWE tried to diffuse it and belittled its effect.[23] The URWE declared publicly that it was surprised by the strike of 150 workers in early August, which it branded as "illegal."[24] The URWE noted that it could not adopt such an unauthorized strike even if the strikers' motive was just. A short editorial in the daily newspaper Al-Nahar expressed an unusual sympathy toward the Régie workers by condemning both the Ministry of Labor and the union for failing to resolve the workers' grievances or even to give them satisfactory answers to their questions.[25] In the meantime, a marked breakdown in the relations between workers and employers at numerous industrial sites made 1963 "the year for the flourishing of strikes," as declared by Al-Nahar.[26]

The 1963 crisis at the Régie, caused by the arbitrary decision to offer permanency to just forty out of one thousand temporary workers, had important ideological and practical ramifications for the state. Within the state bureaucracy and the Parliament, government officials continued to observe sect-based political balances despite the state's broader emphasis on merit and qualifications, which were the principal precepts of the "reform" policy of President Fuad Shihab (1958–64).[27] By applying its Shihabist merit-sect formula in hiring and promotion practices, the Régie's attempt to offer permanency to these forty women violated the government's reformist standards (table 16).[28]

In addition, although this merit-sect formula did not specify ratios of female to male workers, it indirectly favored men. In spite of the government's broader ideological agenda, and in defense of sectarian balance and employers'

TABLE 16. Sectarian ratios recommended by the Lebanese government for employment at the Régie, 1958–1964

Religious sect	%
Maronite	27
Armenian Catholic	1
Chaldean	0
Syrian Catholic	0
Syrian Orthodox	0
Protestant	1
Latin	0
Armenian Orthodox	4
Greek Catholic	6
Greek Orthodox	10
Sunni	23
Shi'i	20
Druze	7
Total	100

Source: "Pourcentage des confessions au Liban" (Percentage of the Lebanese Confessions), private collection of Jacques Dagher, Beirut. Figures are rounded to the nearest whole number.

discrimination against women, the president and prime minister considered the workingwomen's demands for equal pay and job permanency as a threat to and a violation of state policy.[29]

When the news of the wildcat strike reached the URWE, it quickly informed the Régie management and the Ministry of Finance that the permanency accorded to only forty workers was irrational. The strikers hoped to bring about a fair and impartial consideration of the status of all part-time women workers and make seniority and merit, rather than sectarian affiliation, the basis for assigning permanency. The brief negotiations that ensued between management and the URWE culminated in a common pledge made by the government and the Régie to amend the provisions concerning permanency and base them on seniority. As a gesture of good will and with the URWE's encouragement, the workers ended the strike.[30] All permanent women and men workers had lent their full support to the strike even though temporary workers were never considered part of the URWE because they had to be permanent to become unionized.[31] These developments raise critical questions regarding nonunionized workers' role in and contribution to the labor movement in the 1960s. Workers across gender and rank, whether unionized or not, contested the arbitrary nature of the hiring scale and the policy of job upgrading at the Régie in their pursuit of an objective and standardized system of permanency and promotion.

The 'Amil Tabigh memoirs offer rare insight into the views of the male workers who supported the women's strike.[32] He saw the need to preserve the quality, "respect, and pride" in the tobacco profession as the overwhelming motive behind the men's support of the strike. Other statements in the memoirs, however, suggest that the men hoped that by improving and stabilizing the women workers' status, they could prevent the Régie from hiring unskilled and low-wage women laborers, who the men felt had in the past caused the discharge of qualified and skilled men—a perspective shared by many of the Régie workingmen whom I interviewed.[33] In short, many striking skilled male workers appropriated women's demands to enhance their own working conditions and to safeguard their future interests.

During the initial settlement reached between the URWE and the Régie, the government pledged to change the provisions of permanency, but it did not act on its pledge, so 3,600 workers struck again on June 17, 1963.[34] Yet the workers soon learned that the URWE preferred to suspend the strike in order to give ample time for negotiations with the Ministry of Finance, whose director had just arrived from a trip to the United States. URWE head Jean Tuwayni's language and tone of voice were conciliatory. Meanwhile, the Régie, in an attempt to diffuse the mounting opposition, expressed its inclination to extend job permanency to some 165 workers and examine the demands of some other women who were eligible to become permanent.[35] The URWE was not willing to adopt the strike, and, moreover, Jean Tuwayni showed his readiness to call off the strike to give management more time to assess its strategy.[36] As time passed with little progress being made, the blue-collar workers again insisted on striking. On July 6, they marched out of their work sites to denounce the indifference the Régie had expressed toward their insecure job posts and its selective criteria for determining seniority.[37]

The workers called for the Régie's fulfillment of ten central conditions:

1. Canceling the transfer of the forty workers to the Hadath plant and establishing an objective scale for promotion based on qualifications and seniority;

2. Paying transportation expenses for all permanent workers;

3. Using seniority as the key criteria to transform the status of the greatest possible number of women from seasonal or part-time to permanent workers;

4. Offering women workers twenty-one days of annual paid break similar to that of their male coworkers;

5. Increasing the apportioned monthly amount of cigarette packets given to female workers from twenty to forty-five, the amount male workers normally received;

6. Promoting permanent female workers according to their seniority;

7. Extending paid Sunday and holiday breaks to workers and employees on an equal basis;

8. Implementing a free health plan, including dental care;

9. Curbing the abusive powers of the directors of various departments and sections; and

10. Paying for strike days and eliminating any punitive measures.[38]

In response, the Régie accused the workers of instigating riots and threatened to discharge any "unruly" women and their male colleagues who dared to disrupt production or challenge management's authority. Unwilling to compromise, but aiming to fend off the workers' mounting pressure against the company, the management decided to close the Hadath factory indefinitely.[39]

Camaraderie

The closing of the Hadath plant threatened to paralyze the strike and prepared the way for a confrontation with the Lebanese police. The workers realized that to achieve any success, their strike must be launched on the company's premises, but the plant's main gate was locked with a metal chain and blocked by Régie's security guards and the police. In telling me of these events, a number of women recalled vividly the incidents that unfolded on July 6, 1963, noting that the workers openly asserted their right to work and tried first to gain the sympathy of the police and persuade them to open the gates—but to no avail.[40] Aloud and in one voice the workers repeated the proverb "Qati' al-arzaq min qati' al-a'naq": to cut off one's livelihood is to cut off one's head. One group sought to lift morale by singing about their unity and pride in their resistance to their employers. The songs and slogans, exhorting the police to disregard their orders and sympathize

12. The main entrance to the Hadath factory, February 2, 1997. Photograph by the author.

with the workers, who were poor like them, encouraged the increasingly agitated crowd of workers. A group of them, mostly women, then moved forward in the direction of the main gate. Several voices were heard calling for 'Alya F., a thirty-year-old woman worker known for her extraordinary physical strength. 'Alya came forward quickly and started pressing her left shoulder on the gate. She was soon supported by other men and women in a pushing contest with the police force on the opposite side of the gate. Outnumbering the security guards and police, and excited by 'Alya's courage and the chanting of slogans, the protesters broke open the gate. Numerous workers rushed to occupy various production sites, and a few, including a thirty-nine-year-old woman named Masihiyya N., engaged in fistfights with the police. Masihiyya successfully disarmed a police-man and ran away with his gun.[41]

Inside the factory, workingwomen and men formed a delegation to advance and negotiate for their demands with Albert Janis, a Frenchman acting as the company's director-general. Janis promised to examine the strikers' demands and withhold punitive measures; he even guaranteed payment for the strike days. Aware of past disappointments and broken promises, the workers' delega-tion requested a formal statement from Janis that the company was committed

13. The factory building, Hadath, February 2, 1997. Photograph by the author.

to a fair settlement. In the meantime, the workers held a series of meetings that concluded with the decision to end the strike and resume work at the Régie until the company reviewed their requests.[42]

After waiting for three months, the workers started to doubt the Régie and Finance Ministry's sincerity. They recognized a disturbing familiarity in the Régie's reaction and remembered that when they had threatened to strike in October 1961, the Régie had also at that time quickly met with the URWE and expressed its willingness to consider workers' demands seriously. A week after the three months' wait in 1963, however, the Ministry of Finance sent the workers an official confirmation that their central demands would be met.[43] It granted a minority of permanent and skilled women workers some benefits, such as the extensions of weekly and yearly paid breaks, and established production bonuses for machine operators equivalent to the cash value of one month's salary. In addition, permanent workingwomen and men expected to achieve improved conditions for job promotions, health benefits, and wage increase.[44]

Yet neither of the two fundamental demands pertaining to the women— namely, job permanency for temporary workers and equal pay for the permanent ones—was included among the agreed-to demands in 1963. Both questions had apparently been discarded in the early stages of negotiation between the URWE and the Régie. The agreement also neglected the most vital demand for promotion among senior workers, in particular those who had been working at the Régie for more than twenty years.[45] As 'Amil Tabigh maintained in his memoirs, the strikers made the issue of seniority central to their agenda and strove to establish it as the sole criterion for job promotion.[46] The women's attempt to stage a wildcat strike in October 1963 showed their lack of faith in the URWE, whose leadership they viewed with suspicion, if not contempt. This distrust resulted from the URWE's failure to treat their demands seriously, much less to acknowledge them, and from the growing alienation that most women workers felt because of their almost total lack of representation on the URWE's executive council. Indeed, the agreement reached by the URWE and the Régie continued to sustain the formula of sectarian "balance" in the hiring and promotion policies, which catered to the interests of a few skilled workers but antagonized hundreds of others, most of whom were women.

Unfortunately, neither the daily newspapers nor the URWE reports provide the full text of the 1963 agreement or its details. The URWE male leadership evidently did not seriously address the transient workingwomen's call for permanency. The union did integrate this call into its list of demands, but only as a tactic to mobilize as many women workers as possible to help buttress its bargaining power in general vis-à-vis the Régie.

Company and Union Between the Shihab and Helou Regimes

The 1965 strike coincided with a turbulent episode in Lebanon's history, characterized by growing sociopolitical opposition to Fuad Shihab's governmental reforms and the 1964 rise to power of President Charles Helou (1964–70). The competition between different wings of the sectarian and tribal ruling class had direct implications for the Régie's labor policies and the union's actions. Throughout the Shihabi and Helou administrations, women workers in two production sections—the sorting and stemming departments and the main factory—continued to protest against the discrimination and inequalities they suffered in comparison to their male coworkers with regard to salaries, rights, and benefits.

As the company union, the URWE offered membership to permanent Régie workers exclusively and aimed to organize labor for the benefit of capital and

14. *Al-farz* building from outside, Hadath factory, February 2, 1997. Photograph by the author.

the male working elite. Its executive council consisted of two divisions, the consultative and the executive. The former included six posts occupied by workers' representatives, whose role was confined to deliberation. The executive division comprised six posts assigned to Régie administrative staff. Control over URWE policies and resolutions evidently remained in the hands of the active members, who also could cast their vote on whether and when to strike.[47] It is worth noting that ever since the URWE's inception, its leadership had been drawn from the Régie's high-ranking male directors and supervisors.[48] In contrast, only one seat on the executive council was reserved for a female representative of the women workers, even though they made up more than 40 percent of the company's labor force.[49] In line with the discrimination experienced by women laborers on the factory floor, this female representative's responsibility was merely to communicate the union's decisions and instructions to female Régie workers.[50]

The Régie soon reneged on some of its earliest guarantees to the workers, most notably its pledge not to punish any of the ringleaders of the 1963 strike. Instead, it transferred to remote branches several workers who had spearheaded the strike and expressed their intention to run for the union's executive council in the next election.[51] In addition to the workers' eroding confidence in their union, after 1963 the influence of leftist ideologies, in particular Communist ones, found its way into their circles. The growing numbers of subscriptions taken out to the Communist daily newspaper *Al-Nida'* by women and men workers highlight the peak of Communist influence in 1965.[52] During March and April 1965, police reports and official declarations published in the daily newspapers *Al-Hayat* and *Al-Nahar* repeatedly emphasized the Communist influence among Régie workers.[53] The Lebanese police claimed to have "confiscated Communist flyers and documents" from Régie workers such as 'Ali Subayti, Ilyas al-Dibs, 'Ali 'Awadah, Nimr Saliba, and Musa Husayn.[54] These men apparently worked closely with As'ad 'Aql, head of a leftist trade union known as the Liberation Labor Front (Jabhat al-Taharrur al-'Ummali), which in turn was affiliated with the Progressive Socialist Party, led in Lebanon by Kamal Junblat. It turns out that the Régie's transfer of the activist workers seems to have been orchestrated with the union's help as a preemptive move to curb the growing influence of communism at the Régie.[55]

During the 1960s, many Régie workers also became affiliated with the Christian-based, right-wing Phalange Party (known as "al-Kata'ib"), founded in 1936 by Pierre Gemayyel, who was inspired by Francisco Franco, the Spanish Fascist.[56] Most of the Phalange members were Maronites concentrated in Mount Lebanon and Beirut.[57] Even though the party insisted that it had few if any upper-class affiliates, many of its members were affluent businessmen, middle-class merchants, and professionals. Despite its opposition to all forms of socialism, the Phalange Party declared its commitment to a "fair" system of social security.[58] The dramatic rise in labor radicalism and socialist influence during the 1960s may have pushed Phalange leaders to modify their slogans and actions to hold onto their lower-class members. John Entelis also argues that the party's 1960 electoral victory might have shaped its political orientation: "Having tasted power, first in the streets during the 1958 disturbances then in government . . . and, finally within parliament from 1960 on, the LKP [Lebanese Kata'ib Party] began to moderate some of its ideological rigidity in favor of compromise and cooperation with its political opponents. By so doing the party became more effective as an institution of popular and now greater legitimate appeal."[59]

Pierre Gemayyel, during his service as a cabinet member from 1960 to 1964, introduced the social security bill and advocated a partial welfare system. The

Phalange Party also maintained that "labor unions are a basic factor in securing justice and consolidating national unity."[60] Gemayyel devoted special attention to the Régie crisis and expressed open support for the workers demands, in particular those that pertained to the Christian workers or that meshed with socioreligious beliefs.[61]

The mounting tensions between labor and management and the gradual radicalization of Régie workers mirrored to a great extent the social and economic changes unfolding outside the company's gates. The 1964 campaign to reelect Fuad Shihab for a second presidential term ended in defeat, but the political controversy surrounding his project to modernize the Lebanese state did not. The election of Charles Helou to the presidency in August 1964 ushered in a new political era during which focused efforts were made first to undermine Shihabism and then to thwart any improvements in the circumstances of the workers and other underprivileged social groups.[62] The labor movement did not remain impartial to the rift between the old and the new ruling elite. It became polarized between those who fiercely defended the gains, however modest, attained by the labor movement under Shihab, on the one side, and those who embraced anti-Shihabism, on the other.[63] The Régie workers' labor agitations and protests during the mid-1960s served the proponents of Shihabism, who insisted that reforming the state would reverse the destructive effects of the ongoing use of subjective, nonrationalized criteria as the basis for distributing raises and promotions in industries, including the Régie.

The 1960s were a tumultuous time for Lebanon's economy, marked by major commercial and monetary setbacks and advances. One sign of the times was the 1966 bankruptcy of Entra Bank, a major edifice of the Lebanese financial world. In addition, political schisms unfolding at the state level were worsened by increasing social inequalities: 4 percent of the Lebanese population lived lavishly; 30 percent lived below the poverty level; and the remaining 66 percent were either well-to-do (middle class) or lived with financial uncertainties.[64] At the popular level, the political polarity between Shihabism and its opponents was compounded by inflation, which reached unprecedented levels during early 1965. The price of meat and vegetables multiplied five to six times in a relatively short period, and the price of clothes soared on the eve of the Easter holiday.[65] Meanwhile, economic expansion, particularly in industry, was driven in part by more investments of national and foreign capital, higher levels of mechanization, better legal sanctions, and state support. New income tax laws exempted for six years all industries founded in the major cities between 1964 and 1970.[66] Industries founded in rural areas were tax exempt for ten years. The government also promised older industries similar exemptions if they revamped themselves and produced new commodities.

During the mid-1960s, labor agitation and strikes spread through various public sectors, including the Transportation Department, the Central Bank, and, most important, the state-run elementary and secondary schools. Like tobacco workers, teachers called for wage increases to balance inflation, the right to unionize, and permanency for part-time, transient, and seasonal workers.[67] Yet none of these strikes received attention from the government and the business elite or threatened the gendered and class structures the way the 1965 Régie strike did.

The Lenten Fasting: The Straw That Broke the Camel's Back

Critical labor demands were not the only types of concerns that brought workers together against the Régie management. Sacred holidays and religious ritual seemed important rallying points around which two thousand workers harmonized their demands and goals.[68] In March 1965, with the advent of the Lenten fasting that normally precedes the Easter holiday, the Régie's Christian workers sought to leave work an hour earlier than the formal clock-out time of 2:30 in the afternoon. Several years earlier, the Muslim workers had been extended a similar privilege during Ramadan, the holy month of fasting, when they could leave at 1:00 in the afternoon. On Fridays, the Muslim workers were also allowed to leave work at 11:00 in the morning to perform congregational prayer. The Muslim workers openly supported their Christian colleagues and argued that the fulfillment of the latter's request would instill a sense of sectarian equality at the Régie.[69]

On March 6, 1965, a small delegation of Christian workers led by Sabi' Khunaysir, the late Warda Butrus Ibrahim's fiancé, approached factory director Raymond Zalzal with their request. But Zalzal insulted and humiliated the group, prompting a fistfight with Khunaysir.[70] The administration then had Khunaysir arrested, accusing him of disparaging behavior, agitating against management, and violating the company's law and order.[71]

The news of the confrontation with Zalzal and the subsequent arrest of Khunaysir outraged the workers, and they hurriedly declared a strike. Muslims at the

Régie proclaimed their full support for their Christian colleagues and described the incident as "demeaning to the company's working family." The Christian workers insisted on the right to leave work at 1:00 P.M. during the Lent fasting, Zalzal's transfer to another branch, Khunaysir's release, the reinstatement of workers transferred to other branches after the 1963 strike, and the implementation of the government-approved wage increases.[72]

The Régie denied that Khunaysir had been detained and expressed its inclination to discuss the workers' requests after they resumed work. When Khunaysir was freed, however, the workers gathered around him in the Hadath plant's courtyard, cheering jubilantly and pledging to carry on with the strike.[73]

One may argue that in this situation, labor demands alone did not unify the Muslim and Christian protesters. Neither the administration's manipulations of "religion" nor an outside force dictated such a move. But it is misleading to assume that a pure concern for religious piety and the observance of the fast was behind the workers' protests. When I discussed this question with numerous workers, it became clear that the overwhelming majority of them consciously realized the potency of religious arguments. They felt that when culturally "packaged," their demand for a few free hours during Ramadan and Lent were difficult for the Régie's management to refuse.

The URWE was perplexed and appeared helpless during the workers' independent initiatives to continue the strike. The pamphlets the URWE issued at the time revealed its surprise at the announcement of the 1965 strike—as it had been by the 1963 strike.[74] The URWE publicly declared that it would not support the workers' cause as long as the strike went on. From the first day of the strike, the URWE urged the strikers to return to their posts and embrace "legal" channels— that is, the union—to solve their disputes with the management.[75]

The Women Take Command:
"In March, Take Your Cows out to the Fields"

By calling on its members to end the strike, the URWE tested the limits of its authority over both workers and administrative staff. Yet to the URWE leader's chagrin, all the productive sectors across rank and gender were swiftly mobilized for action.[76] Already manifest were signs of broad union affiliation and improved plans for collective actions in pursuit of the workers' goals. Women workers, in particular, were eager to take up the cause and build on their past experiences. Back in 1946, Asma Malkun had headed a strike committee and was critical in coordinating the striking women and men workers' tasks. With her male coworkers, she had struggled to obtain a license for the union in 1947 and thereafter represented women workers in the URWE executive council until 1965. Sa'da Nasif and Josephine Shidyaq were the first women unionists not only at the Régie, but in any Lebanese industrial plant. To gain a sense of how far women's protest style had come by 1965, it is useful to relate the 1965 strike as seen through Nuhad Z.'s eyes.[77]

Nuhad Z. had joined the Régie in 1956 at the age of fourteen and rebelled openly against the Régie in both 1963 and 1965. She recalled how she and her fellow women strove to preserve the potency of the 1965 strike and to maintain a unified front against management. Women such as 'Alya F., Samira J., Fatima N., Josephine D., and Masihiyya N. dispatched delegates to the offices of the administrative staff asking them to leave their offices and join the strikers at the courtyard. Nuhad recounted that the women marched with their sticks, knocking on each office door and summoning them by a famous peasant saying, "Bi adhar nazzil baqaratak 'ad-dar": "In March, take your cows out to the fields."[78] This saying historically referred to the practice of taking one's cows out to pasture in the spring after housing them in stables all winter. In the current context, the women used it to emphasize the workers' responsibilities toward the strikers. The white-collar employees showed only lukewarm support for the women protesters, but being aware of the strikers' anger and frustrations, they avoided confronting them and left the company building with the hope that security forces would soon put an end to the protest.[79] While the workers were gathered in the courtyard, their sense of authority gained momentum as letters of support from various departments of the plant started to pour in. The government continued to downplay women's role in the strike by accusing "disruptive male elements" of pushing women to invade the administrative building at Hadath.[80] The Régie, for its part, held several meetings with the workers' delegates in which the company insisted on an end to the strike as a prerequisite for further discussion.[81]

The tobacco workers then decided to meet directly with the minister of finance, and as they marched en masse in the direction of the ministry, people on the streets started to take an interest and inquire about their cause. The workers' march soon became a spontaneous occasion for people from all walks of life to express their resentment against the government's failings, and non-Régie workers soon came to march alongside the Régie workers, chanting their slogans and carrying their banners. The event turned into a huge demonstration. The workers' delegation met with Andre Tuwayni, the general director of the Ministry of Finance, who seemed impressed by the popular support the workers had garnered. Tuwayni recommended that the workers cooperate with the URWE to secure tangible results and persuaded them to organize another meeting among the workers, the URWE, and the Ministry of Finance.[82]

Despite the workers' open challenge to its authority, the URWE welcomed Tuwayni's initiative, and a meeting was held among the three groups, which yielded a number of gains for the workers.[83] The URWE seemed on friendly terms with Andre Tuwayni, with whom it had exchanged favors in the past, and it also was in awe of his links to the authorities and wanted to resolve the problem on amicable terms. Although some of the workers' gains were not expected to take effect until the workers ended the strike, management was inclined to fulfill one set of demands immediately, which included permitting Christian workers to leave work at 1:00 P.M. during the Lenten fast, extending to female workers the same holidays and breaks accorded to the men, allocating to women the same number of cigarettes provided to men, creating a cafeteria for workers at the plant, canceling any punitive measures against the strikers, and paying wages for the strike days.[84]

Yet the URWE failed to secure permanency for women and equal pay for equal work. These critical goals were left for future discussion between the workers and the administration. The URWE warned the workers that if they did not accept the settlement, it would absolve itself of any commitment to promote its implementation.[85] At this juncture, the strike took on a new character, marked by a forceful commitment to the standardization of holidays and breaks across gender, religion, and occupation. In a remarkable move, the Christian workers decided to drop their Lenten fasting demand and instead to embrace the goals of the whole Régie family of workers. New requests had now risen to the top of the strikers' agenda.

The tobacco workers took a few days to study the URWE's proposed settlement, one that soon revealed an explicit marginalization of women's objectives, in particular the request for equal minimum wages for women and men. The women immediately formed their own delegation to meet with the URWE at the last stage of the Régie-worker deliberations.[86] To the URWE and their male colleagues, the women emphasized the urgency and primacy of their requests, refusing to accept the salary, benefit, and promotion preferences given to men at the Régie. The women spurned any compromise and insisted on written evidence of the URWE's commitment to their cause. They wanted all permanent women workers to receive the minimum wage and asked for a systematic policy on wage increases; payment of the fifteenth-month bonus; an allowance to cover transportation expenses of seasonal and part-time workers; the extension of the same holidays to all workers; the right to depart from work at 1:00 P.M. during the Christian Lenten fast and at 11:00 A.M. on Fridays; the reinstatement of all transferred workers to their previous positions at the Hadath plant; and, finally, the cancellation of all punitive measures against the workers.[87]

The women evidently neither abandoned the men's requests nor separated them from their own core demands. Like the men, they embraced the request to transcend parochial and gender divisions and preferential treatment by calling for the standardization of breaks and holidays for all workers. Their gendered rebelliousness was not merely a departure from a male-dominant class, but a redefinition of class itself. It emphasized that men and women's class awareness and militancy stemmed from a variety of similar and dissimilar grounds, that workingwomen were just as capable of engaging in labor radicalism as men, and that in spite of the absence of a tradition of party affiliation among women they were just as proficient in rigorous and articulated labor action.

The women's organized efforts and uncompromising stance had multifaceted implications. First, they marked women's unprecedented active involvement not merely at the beginning of the strike, but also during the negotiation and settlement phase. Second, they took the initiative away from the URWE and put it in the hands of the women themselves. Third, they proved women's ability to advance radical labor demands that emphasized particular gender-based issues, but in the interest of a gender-balanced notion of class. Their insistence on an equal minimum wage in the end posed a serious threat to the Régie's time-honored policy of manipulating gender differences among workers. The women's stance ultimately reinvigorated the strike and boosted the Lebanese labor movement as a whole.

During the 1960s, the greater Lebanese political arena—marked by social conflicts, ineffective governmental policies, and an expanding urban working class frustrated by ongoing uncertainty—exerted both subtle and direct influence on women's radicalism. This period specifically brought an upsurge in the appeal of secular Arab nationalist parties (Nasserite, Ba'thist, Progressive Socialist Party, Communist) propagating leftist demands for social justice and the elimination of class exploitation. Several cabinet members' affiliation with these leftist organizations provided a basis of support for Communists' open activism. At this time, the Lebanese Communist Party strove to protect and support the industrial working classes. Party leaders insisted on the fulfillment of all the strikers' demands and tried to prevent conservative elements in the URWE from forcing workers to reckon with less than their rightful share.[88] Sources allied with the administrative staff claimed that the Communists were responsible for the strikers' insistence on a 15 percent increase in their salaries instead of the 8 percent allotted by the government.[89] The Ministry of Information and top-ranking state officials declared that the Communists among the workers were posing a "threat to their colleagues" and pressuring the workers to continue their strike. "Leftist extremists," they noted, were also behind the women's invasion of the administrative building of the Hadath plant.[90] Right-wing opposition to the strike ran editorials with headlines such as "Workingmen and Women Are Sacrificed for Leftist Extremists," "The Communists Exploit the Strike of the Régie Workingmen and Women," and "Women at the Forefront of the [Strike] Lines."[91] A comparison of articles about the strike and announcements by both the strikers and the government clearly shows that the Lebanese Communist Party was directly involved in the 1965 strike at the Régie. Nonetheless, Communist influence must not be exaggerated in the workingwomen's case because none of the women was a party affiliate. As I mentioned earlier, although women's militancy received clear support from the Communists and may have been fused with popularized socialist ideals, such militancy was shaped outside the party's formal channels in the day-to-day development of the strike and through interaction with male Communist colleagues.

It is significant, though, that the workers expressed a greater commitment to the Communists than to the URWE. Leftist activities among the Régie workers, one newspaper wrote, jeopardized the "union's self-control" and as such allowed for the expansion of the strike against the URWE's will.[92] Government officials noted that the workers' attempt to declare a strike twice during the first week of March despite the union's disapproval attested to the increase in leftist activities among workers.[93] This was not a recent development, for two years earlier the Régie had transferred five of the workers from Hadath to peripheral branches owing to their marked leftist activism. Moreover, the Lebanese police accused approximately twenty workers arrested by the end of the 1965 strike of being Communist agitators.[94]

At the same time, the Phalange also was gaining ground at the Régie owing to its support of the Christian workers' demands. When the Régie strike emerged in March 1965, Pierre Gemayyel submitted a memorandum to the prime minister in support of extending a break for the Christian workers during Lent. It was clear both to him and to the government that such a request served merely as a prelude to a more extensive and fundamental list of labor demands, the most important of which was permanency for "workingwomen and men."[95] Gemayyel therefore seemed prepared to support the strike, despite the party's conservative politics, lest he alienate hundreds of his Christian followers and their families, who stood united with their Muslim counterparts on the strike's goals. Several workingwomen noted that it was common for Phalange members at the Régie to express a strong commitment to the labor movement and to fight in unison with all their coworkers irrespective of their political affiliations.

On the Shop Floor and in the State Bureau:
Gendered Bargaining and Social Taboo

For the first time in the history of the workers' struggle against management, the call for an equal minimum wage for women workers became the central objective of a Régie strike. As the workingwomen at the Régie sharpened their protest methods and bargaining efforts, they gave greater emphasis to their position as women, diverting from their earlier practices of emphasizing a male-based class solidarity, as they did during the strike of 1963. It soon became clear that the Régie's intransigence on the issue of equal pay for equal work bespoke a more fundamental gender bias at the state level. By denying women the right to receive the same pay for doing the same tasks as men, the state was objecting to any alteration of the society's gender structure and any challenge to the basic ideological premises of the tribal-sectarian hegemony. Indeed, gender inequalities varied in form and intensity throughout Lebanese society, but through the state's legal agency they often became a tangible political reality. In general, not all cultural constructs receive the same level of support from the state. Some are put to more use than others, a fact that some subalternists largely overlook as they ironically give the state an all-encompassing place in their analytical frameworks.[96]

In 1965, the beginning daily wage for a workingwoman at the Régie was 2.85 Lebanese pounds (a little more than one U.S. dollar), and her work month comprised twenty-five days. Even after she became permanent, her salary did not exceed 100 pounds per month, compared to the country's legal minimum monthly wage of 145 pounds per month. She was also deprived of the paid weekly breaks and holidays enjoyed by her male counterparts. These blatant inequities played a key role in radicalizing women in their effort to settle disagreements with the management and the government.[97]

The available sources on the 1965 strike make evident that the 350 workers accused of kindling the strike and radicalizing the whole workforce worked exclusively in the Régie's factory section.[98] Almost all those who were detained by the police came from this section. Workers came from various Muslim and Christian sects, and women were clearly the preponderant sex among the strikers.[99]

The debates over gender equality and the violent termination of the strike (which I describe later) revealed the state's fear of tampering with gender roles. It is noteworthy that the state's rejection of equal pay for equal work was unchallenged by large sectors of society, even upper-class feminists. Responses ranged from lukewarm encouragement to outright rejection of what most men perceived as a reconfiguration of gender roles not only at the workplace, but in the home as well. The outcry from various echelons of Lebanese society against the 1946 shootings of "harmless" women by armed policemen was nowhere repeated in 1965 during the Régie women's fearless and well-organized struggle. Yet most of the Régie's workingmen, in particular those affiliated with leftist parties, continued to lend the women unwavering support. The leadership of the 1965 strike, too, continued to command solidarity with the women, which meant that men and women's demands were seen as inseparable.[100] To the press, the Régie administration voiced its willingness to discuss these grievances through the union's legal channels, but only after the workers ended the strike. The Régie dismissed the payment of the minimum wage to workingwomen as "unreasonable and impossible."[101] In a later press communiqué, the government also described the women's demands as "dangerous" and rejected them because they "transcended the authority of the URWE and the Ministry of Finance." The government further argued that it would not resolve the tobacco workers' needs through the narrow prism of the Régie, but rather through the wide angle of the "well-being of the entire Lebanese economy."[102] Purportedly to safeguard the country's prosperity and prevent an economic "disaster," the government also opposed work leave during the Lenten fast, which it anticipated would cost the Régie and the public treasury no less than two hundred hours of work each year.[103] This figure was greatly exaggerated, and the loss actually equaled less than one hundred hours each year. The dramatization of the damage to the national economy reflected the government's real fears of giving in to the women's demand.

This issue of women's minimum wage became the center of a heated debate over women's rights and social positions not merely in industrial or agricultural labor, but in all economic sectors. Numerous political leaders and religious dignitaries pressed upon the Régie their objection to any changes in the working conditions at the company and particularly to any attempts to correct the wage disparities between women and men. They vehemently opposed offering to women workers salaries comparable to those of men and asserted that such an action would cause social "upheaval."[104] These conservative voices argued that paying women and men equal wages would lead to equality in other domains, thus jeopardizing male superiority and privileges that contributed to their communities' stability. They warned, "Don't create for us a revolution regarding the question of equal wages for women workers."[105] The government declared, "One glance at the strikers' demands is sufficient to prove how dangerous they are!"[106]

Faced with deep-rooted social and economic discrimination, the women realized that paid labor was merely a step on the long and arduous path to social justice and genuine liberation. In 1946, the tobacco women had capitalized on the massive social support they gained after Warda Butrus Ibrahim's death. In stark contrast, in 1965 the Régie administration may have benefited from conservatives' gender bias in suppressing the demand for wage equality. The Régie and the government, in their shared fear of equivalent challenges from underprivileged groups and impoverished sectors, hurried to quell the strike and contain its repercussions.

As the ultimate authority over the Régie, the Lebanese government orchestrated a multifaceted campaign against the strike that involved the French directors, the URWE, parliamentary leaders, the press, the police, and even the Lebanese army. On March 16, 1965, President Charles Helou convened a meeting of top government officials to discuss the strike.[107] For the same purpose, he met with two French Régie officials, Paul Duphenieux, the president of the board of directors, and Albert Janis, the general director.[108] The meetings revolved around the work leave request for religious holidays, but made no mention of women's demand for equal pay. The government entertained two options: allow all workers, Muslims and Christians, to quit work at 11:00 A.M. on Fridays, when Muslim workers go for prayer, or eliminate this privilege for Muslim workers and allow them instead to leave on Fridays to pray with the understanding that they would return to work immediately afterward.[109] The government decided to implement the second option.

A week after these meetings, the URWE delivered a leaflet stating that the government would consider it a violation of the labor law to quit work before the end of the official work day at 2:30 P.M.[110] The outraged workers declared the strike again. The government responded by closing down all of the Régie plants and deploying the army to the company's central offices to protect it from the "vandalizing acts" by "subversive" and "leftist elements."[111]

The size of the army force deployed at the Hadath plant and along the roads leading to it indicated how seriously the government was taking this labor revolt. Army tanks were stationed at the factory's main gate, and a few battalions of artillery were set up around the adjacent hills.[112] Approximately 150 workers arrived at the Hadath plant from the Régie offices in Burj Hammud Beirut to reinforce the strike, but the police prevented them from entering.[113] Orders were given to the military to arrest any employee or worker who called for a strike or demonstration.[114] Lebanese labor law had decreed that striking was workers' "sacred right," but only after attempts to use legal and peaceful means were exhausted and with the union's approval. The place seemed like a battlefield as the whole neighborhood of the Hadath plant was put under martial law.

Workers were surprised by the tight security and the military measures taken against them around and inside the company. Scores of women nonetheless gathered with their male colleagues at the courtyard of the Mar Mikhayil warehouse and attempted to defy police orders, but when they tried to cross over the roadblocks to enter the warehouse by force, the policemen directed water hoses at them.[115]

Meanwhile, the workers of the Hadath plant also were prevented from crossing security barriers. They decided on another method that involved marching on foot toward the presidential palace at Sin al-Fil, thirty minutes away from Hadath, where they sought to present their case to the president.[116] The police, however, relentlessly chased them through the quarters and streets leading to Sin al-Fil. Many women and men were brutally beaten and seriously injured, and in one case police aggression led to a woman worker's miscarriage and permanent physical damage to another. The secret police terrorized the community of Hadath as it searched its houses for hidden workers, dragging out and arresting twenty men and women.[117]

Popular Echoes of the Strike

The tobacco workers' clashes with the government became a national event that pushed to the forefront the tensions of labor, nation, and gender. The lives of a significant number of Lebanese people were closely tied to working conditions at the Régie. Government figures show that up until 1963, more than three hundred thousand people were involved in tobacco production, and around three thousand were directly employed by the Régie.[118] Régie workers and their families, like those in other industrial firms, experienced a dramatic deterioration in the quality of their lives during the 1960s. Many of them gradually developed a deepseated animosity toward the affluent few "at the top" and the "government of the millionaires." Their demands echoed the distress of thousands of others outside the Régie, who felt spontaneously drawn to the 1965 strike.

Hundreds of people from all walks of life, including ministers and deputies, expressed their support for the strikers through letters and petitions to leading newspapers. Several national women delegations visited the URWE center to express solidarity with the Régie workers. Local associations and national professional organizations visited the offices of the major newspapers, denouncing the government's brutality and intransigence. Petitions and delegations from various districts and major towns poured into the regional city halls urging provincial leaders and deputies to intervene on behalf of the Régie workers.[119] Various demonstrations erupted, the most significant of which brought together the workers' families and friends to denounce openly the government's cruel suppression of the demands being made.[120]

The major labor syndicates, however, were divided on the strike. The renewal of the strike and the government's reaction revealed profound differences between the two central poles of the labor movement, the leftist faction led by the Liberation Labor Front and its liberal rival the Labor Union (Al-Itihad al-'Ummali). The former fiercely attacked the government and its actions, but the latter mobilized more than sixty-six labor unions and syndicates to support the government, denounce the strike, and call for the dissolution of the Liberation Labor Front, which it held responsible for encouraging the protest and disturbing the nation's economic stability. Taking a compromise position, the URWE criticized the government's actions, but also faulted the workers for their imprudent strike.[121]

The government mobilized various media tools for the confrontation with the workers and orchestrated a press campaign to justify its suppression of the strike. Its propaganda depicted the strike as a leftist, foreign conspiracy against the "national integrity and stability of the country" and only mildly criticized the Shihab administration for introducing some "destructive" and "disruptive" labor and social reforms. The military repression was described as necessary against the "mutiny" at the Régie and the authority of the state.[122] Prime Minister Haj Husayn al-'Uwayni attempted to undermine the strikers' struggle by accusing them of harboring "subversive elements" who did not relate to any labor cause. He threatened that the Régie would remain closed until all leftist workers who had instigated the strike were arrested.[123] 'Abdul 'Aziz Harfush, a Communist and a leading activist in the strike, refuted these accusations, stating that his fellow workers had spontaneously renewed the strike after the government reneged on its promises.[124]

The major newspapers were divided in their attitudes toward the strike and the government. Some editorials absolved the government of any responsibility and blamed the unrealistic plans of former President Fuad Shihab.[125] Kamil Muroeh, the head of the daily newspaper *Al-Hayat,* praised the social and political regulations of the Lebanese system of government, commenting that its benefits exceeded by far those in its Arab counterparts. Alluding to the Communists, Muroeh claimed that the confrontations between the workers and their employer were the results of schemes plotted outside Lebanon to undermine Lebanese democracy, obstruct the free-market capitalist system, and instigate a class struggle.[126] It soon became evident that the strike was another platform for the political struggle between the Shihabist national elite and its successor, which was using the Shihabist period and its shortcomings as a way to diffuse its own problems. Indeed, the daily newspaper *Al-Nahar* expressed government sentiments as it blamed the Shihabist presidency for failing to redistribute wealth or deliver justice to the workers.[127]

Furthermore, the reports' focus on leftists in general and on Communists in particular underscored a considerable increase in workers' Communist Party affiliations since the 1940s. Among party members were Hasan Hamid, 'Ali Subayti, Ahmad 'Abdallah, and 'Abdul 'Aziz Harfush, who played a major role in organizing the 1963 and 1965 strikes. The Communist Party mobilized its rank and file to support the strike and rallied a large number of political and social leaders to help halt the repressive campaign against the tobacco workers. Three of the party's leaders, George Hawi, George Batal, and Khalil al-Dibs, together with two Communist Régie workers, Hasan Hamid and 'Ali Subayti, were intercepted at a police roadblock in 'Ayn al-Rimmani, a Beiruti suburb, when returning from a meeting with Kamal Junblat, the head of the Progressive Socialist Party, to solicit a wider popular support for the strike.[128] Subayti and the Communist leaders were arrested, but Hamid managed to escape.

The newspaper *Al-Anwar* attacked the government for its violent actions and for the false allegations against "dangerous leftists" made by several politicians as a pretext for crushing the strike. The root of the social problem, the newspaper noted, was not the alleged struggle between the Left and the Right, but rather the struggle between the overwhelming majority of the people seeking basic social benefits and a "greedy, obstinate capitalist minority attempting to eat up everything."[129] *Al-Jarida* similarly denounced the baseless claims that the government made to justify its suppression of the Régie workers, who did not pose a threat to either foreign investors or the Lebanese economy, even though the workers were supported by leftist and radical parties.[130] Finally, Junblat provided his unconditional support to the Régie workers by stating that their needs amounted to no more than a small fraction of the illicit money that "the rich and the covetous elite had accumulated."[131] *Al-Anba'*, the Progressive Party's newspaper, presented the Régie crisis as a symptom of the fundamental struggle between the Right and the Left in Lebanese society.[132] Junblat and a few leftist government deputies publicly declared that their relations with the government would depend to a large extent on its approach toward the Régie workers. More significant, these deputies clearly pointed to workingwomen as the central protagonists in this strike and acknowledged the legitimacy of their struggles, questioning "the government's use of armed force against a workingwoman who had asked the state to apply a law that the parliament had passed less than two months ago specifying that the minimum monthly wage was 145 pounds. A workingwoman cannot accept a monthly salary that does not exceed 100 pounds."[133]

The strike was on the agenda of a series of parliamentary meetings that convened in May 1965. Heated arguments ensued among deputies over the strike's identity, political character, and implications. The debates dragged on for another month, when prominent deputies denounced Minister of Labor Edward Hunayn for his failure to provide a satisfactory and dignified solution to the workers' problems.[134] A number of right-wing and conservative deputies continued to cast the strike as a "foreign plot" that threatened to crack the foundations of the social order.[135] What had started out as a simple request for an additional five or six free hours per week during the month of Lent had turned into not only a vehicle for major labor protest, but also a battleground for vying factions in the Parliament and government. The countercampaign launched from within the government helped boost the image of the strikers, who were delighted to see the tale of "leftist conspiracies" dissolve with the assertion of their human and labor rights.

Kinship, Sect, and Social Networks

Actual and fictive kinship ties and sectarian links provided vital sources of support and protection for the strikers during the police clampdown. Despite government propaganda to subvert the strike, the public embraced its cause and supported the numerous workers who fled the Lebanese secret police. Family members, distant relatives, friends, and acquaintances were ready to offer their protection and risk their safety to take in the fugitives and offer financial and psychological comfort for the families left behind. Civil disobedience to state authority and silent resistance to coercion became manifest in the cohesive circles of family and sect and in the webs of kinship and informal social networks.

Take, for example, the Zu'aytir clan, the largest family cluster at the Régie, with around two hundred of its members, women and men, permanent and temporary, working there in 1965. The Zu'aytir Shi'ite clan, which resided in Fanar, a working-class neighborhood in Beirut, was known for its members' loyalty to each other and to friends and work associates. The government tried not to intimidate Zu'aytir clan members directly, but sought instead to confront their allies. Fanar gradually came to be seen as a formidable *qal'a* (fortress) safe from police chases or interrogation.[136] For security reasons and to share the economic burdens, Zu'aytir households took turns hosting fugitive strike leaders. A Zu'aytir member was expected to resist any cooperation with the police and to deny any knowledge about the hiding workers.[137]

'Abdul 'Aziz Harfush, a Shi'ite and one of the strike leaders wanted by the police, took refuge with the Zu'aytirs for more than a week. The men and women of Fanar offered him their hospitality, and Régie workingwomen kept him abreast of all the developments at the Régie and his family up to date on his safety. Meanwhile, a renowned figure and deputy, Da'as Zu'aytir, who belonged to the family who sheltered Harfush, openly attacked the government and helped provide some solutions to the Régie workers' grievances.[138]

The experiences of Ilyas Lattuf, a Maronite Christian Régie worker and ringleader, further illustrates the function of sect, informal social networks, and kinship in counteracting state repression and strengthening workers' solidarity and labor commitments. In the absence of his extended family in Beirut, Lattuf sought refuge with the influential Ja'ja's, who lived in the town of Kafarshima, adjacent to the Hadath Régie plant. The Ja'ja' Maronite family had more than one hundred permanent and temporary workers at the Régie, the second-largest family cluster. Like the Zu'aytirs, the Ja'ja's were active during and after the strike, using whatever political means and lobbying tactics at their disposal to enhance the cause of the strike. Their strong family loyalty was believed to have had a major impact on the decision of the district attorney, who belonged to the Ja'ja' family, to declare Lattuf innocent of all government indictments, which hung over his head while he remained in hiding.[139]

Imprisoned Régie workers, too, exhibited high morale and optimism regarding the strike's effectiveness, mostly because they felt assured by their families, friends, and colleagues' assistance. Fatima N., a skilled woman worker and leader, was arrested while distributing leaflets during the strike. While in prison, she felt that most inmates treated her with great affection and deference, the treatment earned by a heroine. Even the male guards, she noted, avoided directing insults and slanders at her, which they normally and systematically did with other inmates. She was strongly encouraged by her parents' support and their efforts to contact political and religious leaders to release her and her comrades from prison.[140]

Ending the Strike

The government's decision to shut down all the branches of the Régie was part of an organized plan in cooperation with the company's directors and some international experts to deny the strikers any of their requests.[141] It sought to punish the "unruly tobacco workers" and consequently to thwart any future insurrection on the Régie's shop floor as well as at any other factories. To implement the plan, the Régie called upon the workers at the Tripoli, Khinshara, and Bikfaya branches to resume work as usual on March 30, 1965. Anyone who did not comply was to be discharged from work, as stipulated by the Régie's labor and administrative regulations.[142] The following day the government ordered the opening of the Hadath plant, except for the factory area that had been the central stage of the strike, and simultaneously advertised for new workers, or scabs, to compensate for the shortage of laborers. The Régie was ready to dismiss any insubordinate laborer.[143]

As workers reached the company's entrance on their way to work, the police treated most of them harshly and interrogated them. The police also arrested a score of other workers who were accused of agitating against the management and circulating Communist leaflets.[144] The security forces also demanded answers to questions that dealt with their future actions, such as "How would you act in the occurrence of a strike?"[145] By intimidation, threats, and interrogation, the government and the Régie spread an atmosphere of fear aimed at breaking down the workers' defiance. In the meantime, as the list of detained Communists grew, the official government press lamented the loss of governmental profits, estimated at four million Lebanese pounds daily.[146] This official press tried hard to blur the reality about the Régie's profits that the unofficial press had publicized since 1963—namely, that around twenty thousand toiling families were living on thirty-eight pounds per month (between fifteen and seventeen U.S. dollars) so that the government could have a "legitimate source of profit equaling twenty million pounds per year" and "a handful of stockholders [could have] two and a half million pounds, and five merchants another one million pounds."[147]

The Régie, backed by the government, attempted to use more humiliating measures to subdue women workers, not merely by threatening to discharge them from work, but by prohibiting them from resuming work on the same day as their male coworkers.[148] Given the women's leading role during the strike and their demand for equal pay, the government apparently anticipated the recurrence of disturbances at the company. The majority of workers expressed their opposition to the discrimination against the women and forced the Régie to allow them all— men and women—to resume work together.[149]

A month later the government and the Régie dismissed 290 temporary women workers who had participated in the strike.[150] The issue of the minimum wage for female workers lingered for two more years. In December 1967, a strike broke out, and the Régie was compelled to give permanent women workers the minimum wage and additional benefits. Nonetheless, the situation of the dismissed 290 temporary women workers was not discussed.[151]

In brief, the 1963 and 1965 strikes heralded a new journey for tobacco women from legal claims to militancy against unjust working conditions inflicted upon them by the company and sanctioned by the state. In spite of these developments, the popularity of the Shihabist reforms and their emphasis on sectarian balance, accompanied by relative economic gains for the bourgeoisie, affected the outcome of the 1963 walkout. The latter turned into an occasion for reconciliation between the high-ranking male laborers and management at the women's expense. In 1964, the Helou regime brought to power a new configuration of the tribal-sectarian ruling elite that was staunchly protective of capitalism and unwilling to pursue even the partial and mild reforms of the Shihabist era. Despite the regime's sharpened weapons for coercion and suppression, however, Régie women workers demonstrated an unprecedented level of organizational and collective discipline that promoted their cause and eventually brought their demand for equal minimum wage to fruition.

Conclusion

It took more than twenty years for tobacco women workers to receive the minimum wage specified by the labor law of 1946. As I have shown, this process was shaped by new political conditions and social developments in the lives of industrial workingwomen. The 1940s labor conflicts unfolded in a country that was slowly evolving from its colonial past and lacked the freedom to develop advanced forms of labor organization. However, the strikes of the 1960s highlighted workingwomen's improved collective action and sustained militancy, and underscored a significant level of unionization and party membership among workingmen.

A complex phase in the relationship between the workingwomen and the company union, the URWE, unfolded during the 1960s. These women expressed their mistrust of the URWE (with its conciliatory approach toward management), acted independently of it, and resisted its numerous requests to end their strikes. Furthermore, workingwomen at the Régie rejected attempts to manipulate their input in the strikes and their radicalism just to strengthen the position of skilled, high-ranking workingmen. Their awareness of their distinct needs as women and not merely as workers marked their conscious dismissal of the URWE's decisions and their collective steps to take control of the settlement process with the Régie.

Unlike the URWE, the Communist Party was influential among the Régie workers and was directly involved in the 1965 strike. I have shown that the striking women trusted and welcomed the input of their Communist colleagues and upheld a number of labor demands advanced by the Communist Party, in particular the call for a 15 percent increase in their salary. It is also possible that the Régie workingwomen were influenced initially by diffuse socialist ideas and demands for improving working-class standards of living—alongside agitations against the state present in the popular culture of the 1960s—and later by the actions of Communist workingmen at the Régie. Among the general public and in the language of a number of leftist politicians, the 1965 strike was an ideological struggle between the Right and the Left. The fact that a right-wing party such as the Phalange would endorse the Régie workers' demands, expressed in Christian sectarian terms, attests to the ability of this party's working-class members to stand in solidarity with their Muslim counterparts and influence the position of their own leaders in their favor.

A close look at women workers' labor practices during this phase proves the invalidity of the cultural approach, in particular the subaltern variation that lays major emphasis on "cultural and perceptual variables," especially religion.[152] Even though, as Chakrabarty correctly asserts, gender coexists with nation and class, he treats all three as reified entities that are almost intrinsically biological, carried "by the subaltern classes in their own heads."[153] I argue that, instead of this static biologism, familial bonds and religious ties were undergoing change and that their affects on women's choices and behavior varied on the basis of class, locale, and political history. Moreover, workers lived multiple experiences of class, sect, and gender that were not always mutually exclusive.[154] The Régie workingwomen as such did not have a uniform or fixed experience of "culture." Rather, they shaped and were shaped by particular arrangements of "culture" based on their social position as women and workers, their regional background, and their individual histories. We need to focus on these arrangements that were refracted onto the shop floor where tobacco women fought their daily battles. This multifaceted, ever-changing, intention-driven, and processual view of culture—as opposed to a unilineal, stage-driven view of culture as the organizing machine of history—helps us to understand the context in which women at times utterly rejected male paternalism, but at other times manipulated it to achieve their goals.

Sectarian and occupational divisions did not deter Lebanese working-women from fighting for sexual equality in salary, promotion, and benefits. Gendered consciousness neither substituted for nor sabotaged class awareness. Rather, it was enriched and cast in unconventional forms by the hands of women whose commitment to their own needs as well as to those of their leftist male colleagues and of the labor movement at large grew out of their historical circumstances shaped by their temporary work status, marital status, migrant backgrounds, experiences with the decline in the value and status of rural labor, their relative dependence on industrial labor, and their embrace of urban life. As images of workingwomen ranged from being "invaders" of public property and "gadflies" to "victims" of male Communist activism, the strikers and society at large took notice of the potency of a gendered awareness of working-class grievances and women's attempts to reverse these grievances. The campaigns marked by the tobacco women's struggles had implications far beyond the factory doors, reaching to diverse groups in Lebanese society, who contributed additional energy and revitalization through their own opposition to the state. These supporters realized the broad implications of the Régie women's militancy, the significance of their thrust to push the limits of gender boundaries, and the positive advances likely to result from their attempts to redefine women's roles both publicly and politically.

Conclusion

THE INDUSTRIAL TRANSFORMATION of Mount Lebanon during the nineteenth century caused modest developments in women's work culture, experiences, and the gendered division of labor. Unlike the case in other parts of the Ottoman Empire, the rise of the silk *karkhana*s in Mount Lebanon did not of itself lead to a profound rearrangement of work patterns or gender relations. Even though rural women in general engaged in paid labor and performed mixed farm and domestic work, they remained part of extended family networks and enmeshed in a social world structured largely by patriarchal values. When they became full-time silk workers, the women of Mount Lebanon were neither spatially separated from their families nor conceptually distanced from the regional, preindustrial perceptions of the sexual division of labor. The gender hierarchy on the shop floor was never completely divorced from its counterpart in the village setting, where male relatives' authority persisted. From the time women entered the silk factory to the time they returned home, they were subject to religious and parental supervision of their labor and personal lives. Male employers who depended greatly on female labor tried to accommodate religious authorities by imposing *moral* codes of conduct and *ethical* standards through strict on-the-job sexual segregation. The most that women achieved in altering their gender roles during this phase was an early adaptability to industrial modes of production and work patterns.

The rise of tobacco manufacturing and the decline of the silk industry in the late nineteenth century gave rise to new work patterns and social experiences. Workingwomen reacted to the new changes by a conscious and vocal resistance to mechanization. Government inspectors, trade unionists, and socialists alike marginalized and largely ignored the gendered meaning of this resistance. The women, though, gradually developed skills in collective social organization that

179

were pertinent to their waged workplaces. They confronted threats of unemployment, for instance, by uniting their efforts and working closely with the labor unions and their male leaders. They moved away from demonizing machinery to demanding essential economic compensation, benefits, and security.

Syrian and Lebanese elite women resisted the creation of the French tobacco monopoly, the Régie, albeit from a distinct class and ideological position. Within the feminist framework of their resistance, the question of gender was yoked to a discourse on anticolonialism and national progress. The elite women denigrated paid labor and gave voice to male fears that industrial workingwomen were undercutting men's opportunities in the job market. They hoped to instill among the men of their class modern views of women's centrality in the family structure and sexual equality within the domestic domain, aiming all the while for *respectability* and the valorization of women's domestic labor. Much of their efforts were devoted to philanthropy, welfare, and charity work.

Factory women took quite a different position. These women renegotiated their gender roles within the workplace and household, and started to derive their identity from industrial labor processes and working-class experiences. Feminist writers' publications that called for a more active role for women in public and national affairs did not, however, impact the world of the overwhelmingly illiterate workingwomen. Instead, episodes of nationalist uprisings and open anticolonial resistance during the early twentieth century helped bring factory women in touch with the feminists' public declarations, which instilled a short-lived sense of sisterhood and solidarity among most women.

On the eve of national independence in 1943, labor unrest became entangled with the liberation struggle against the French, which led to the consolidation of the Lebanese state. Workingwomen and men fought on the side of the national elite, whose aspirations they believed were congenial to their own. Following independence, however, the rationale for national unity and harmony lost much of its fervor. A distinct challenge to the idea of a Lebanese *nation* came from identities rooted in *class* and spread among workers in major industrial undertakings. Workingwomen citizens' militant protests against the state, in turn, became an occasion for contesting sexual inequality and preindustrial perceptions of women and their economic roles. The Régie workingwomen developed a rationalized approach to their grievances against management and manipulated legal channels to reach their aims. Against the preponderant view that the state dominates all aspects of the legal discourse, I have shown that other social strata engaged in and shaped this discourse. Law making was a mutual process defined by relations of opposition to the state as well as by participation in processes of *citizenship* that united workingwomen and men.

Women's radicalism during the 1946 strike was decisive in forcing the Lebanese government to pass new labor laws. Their militancy appears to have shaped and been shaped by their participation in ongoing anticolonial struggles and their social and working experiences as temporary and permanent Régie workingwomen. Like their male counterparts, workingwomen participated in the struggle against French colonialism, which enhanced the development of their wide-based collective identity. In addition, as workingwomen adopted broad citizen-based identities and began using the legal language of citizenship, so grew their understanding of ways to organize their labor meaningfully and powerfully.

The instability in which many of these women lived and worked likely contributed to the ways in which their radicalism developed. For example, many temporary workingwomen were very likely forced to rely on family support, farmwork, or other source of paid labor to supplement their modest income from the Régie. Temporary workingwomen, on the one hand, without economic

15. Ready to leave work at the Hadath factory, February 2, 1997. Photograph by the author.

stability, equitable salaries, or benefits, had the least to lose in confrontations with management. Permanent workingwomen, on the other hand, had more to lose in their labor protests but demonstrated their commitment to overcoming gender discrimination and exploitation in salary, rank, and benefits. These factors in combination discouraged women's acquiescence and nurtured an emboldening sense of community among them.

At the same time, neither formal unionization nor membership in leftist parties had a direct impact on women's radicalism during the 1940s. In some ways, many women seemed both confused and intimidated by labor unions and socialist parties, believing that one had to be educated, politically bent, and truly autonomous to join them. In other ways, the union and the parties reinforced many women's sense of dependency and vulnerability because they rarely considered female membership, let alone leadership, vital to their long-term goals. Moreover, the dominant male hierarchy, worldview, and sexual assertiveness projected by the membership of both types of organizations made the organizations less congenial to female membership. For instance, several Communist ideologues found it contradictory and divisive to address gender issues, let alone to distinguish between male and female working-class cultures. In retrospect, neither the male intelligentsia's *missionary role* nor political indoctrination radicalized Lebanese industrial workingwomen. Instead, these workingwomen intentionally created their own distinct forms of activism and *unruliness,* and struck out on their own terms to alter gender imbalances at the Régie.

Up until the 1950s, farm and factory were interlinked in particular labor processes that made it difficult to assess gender relations within either sphere exclusively. For many, family production and agricultural work functioned as a safety valve against the fluctuations of the market economy. Single peasant women and mothers alike started to experience intensification in their work and a decline in their status as women's social standing became more commonly tied to their earning power in the market economy. In the midst of increases in urban growth, industrialization, overpopulation, and political instability, socioeconomic power gradually shifted from the countryside to the city, fostered by the government's failed agricultural policies and general neglect of the periphery. Rural-to-urban moves undertaken by many Lebanese between the mid-1950s and 1970 explain the preponderance of rural roots among the Régie workingwomen and men. Migrants originating primarily from impoverished peasant areas in

'Akkar, the Biqa', and the South set up housekeeping in and around Beirut. The Shi'i population of the South, in particular, suffered from government neglect and persistent Israeli raids and incursions into their villages, where a strong Palestinian-Lebanese resistance movement against Israel resided. During this period, the Shi'ites started to replace the Maronites as the largest religious group at the Régie because of this situation.

Powerful historical circumstances cemented the ties among the Régie workers, particularly between the largest two sectarian clusters, the Shi'ites and the Maronites, drawn from the Biqa', 'Akkar, and the South. The two shared a legacy of rural displacement owing to economic deterioration and political dislocation caused by armed confrontations between the Israeli army and the Lebanese-Palestinian resistance and then, beginning in 1975, by the Lebanese Civil War. I believe that these common experiences and memories among the largest and most representative segment of the workforce explain to a large extent the propensity for radicalism at the Hadath branch between the mid-1950s and the 1970s. The sectarian, regional, and gender diversities evident at the Hadath factory did not prevent its workforce from acting cohesively and effectively in pursuit of its class interests. The Hadath branch also exhibited large family clusters and village ties that apparently enhanced the solidarity among workers during strikes and labor conflicts. It also is possible that Beirut's popular culture at the time, within whose rubric Hadath workingmen and women lived, encouraged open resistance and protest against social and economic injustice. The artistic and musical life of Beirut in particular carried strong messages against the state's economic policies, class differences, and capitalist greed. Plays and broadcasted radio programs by leftist artists were immediately accessible to workers and seemed to have been an integral part of their social education.

Rural women who traveled to Beirut in pursuit of industrial work may have faced less resistance from their families than did middle- and upper-class women because their financial need was greater and they had a much longer tradition of paid labor. Thus, the emphasis on Islamic conservatism and patriarchal authority as the sole determinants of Arab women's low level of participation in paid labor proves inadequate. A close look at the statistical figures for several factories in Beirut between 1970 and 1977 clearly shows that a very high percentage of lower-class women sought paid work particularly after the outbreak of the civil war and the departure of hundreds of skilled male workers to Arab and other countries.

However, many women were turned down by Lebanese employers in factories traditionally known to rely on a female workforce. The employers expressed a clear preference for hiring foreign male workers. Some of the workers were skilled, but many had to undergo special training to operate the machines and carry out certain tasks. Moreover, mechanization led to the displacement of unskilled women workers in favor of men as a result of consistent gender discrimination and a devaluation of women's abilities. Male employers blocked women's opportunity to train for new tasks the way men did. The paternalistic spirit inherent in state laws reinforced the employers' biases against women and gave them much liberty in tailoring job hiring, contracts, and procedures to their own needs. At the Régie, women received benefits and wages that fell far below those of their male counterparts. They lived through worse and more complex forms of capitalist exploitation than did their male colleagues. A subtle gender war had ensued with the introduction of inexpensive female labor, which undermined the skilled male workers' position and stability. Meanwhile, the Régie's management tried to exploit young and inexperienced workingwomen by singing the virtues of *modest expectations* and *complacency* for women.

It took more than twenty years for tobacco women workers to receive the minimum wage specified by the labor law of 1946. The 1940s labor unrest unfolded in a country that was slowly evolving from its colonial past and facing serious economic and political problems. In contrast, unionization and politicization of many industrial workingmen who were affiliated with various liberal, nationalist, and leftist parties accompanied the strikes in the 1960s. The right-wing nationalist Phalange Party and the Communist Party were among those with the largest following at the Régie. Parties with less-significant representation at the Régie were the Syrian Nationalist Party, the Free Nationalists Party, and the Progressive Socialist Party. During the 1965 strike, many workingwomen already were members in the company union, the URWE, but none was affiliated with leftist organizations. They realized, however, the significant role that the Communist Party played in supporting the strike. During the daily struggles to achieve their goals and organize their efforts in 1965, they were in direct contact with their Communist colleagues and seemed to have been influenced by the popular articulation of socialist ideas in the media. It is important to note that in several Lebanese towns, the Communist Party received more of a general following and sympathy than actual paid memberships during the mid-1960s.

Furthermore, the local political cultures of the South and Beirut were receptive to proletarian ideals of resistance and opposition to the state.

Outside the gates of the Régie, the 1965 strike received national attention when leading politicians perceived it as a struggle between right and left that would ultimately determine relations with the working class, disgruntled political groups, and even the state's leftist deputies. The official media launched a secondary war against Communists and the workingwomen who led the 1965 strike, presenting them as undisciplined and unpatriotic accomplices and a threat to national welfare. State representatives and the Régie management were mostly alarmed by the workingwomen's relentless confrontational actions even after the end of the strike. They tried hard to marginalize these actions, claiming that the women's Communist male colleagues had deliberately placed them at the front lines of the strike. In other instances, the official press denounced women's leadership roles during the strike as irrational and reckless aggression. Yet, in fact, women became hardened by the exploitative policies of their employers on the shop floor and by the state's consistent violation of their rights. They became aware of the attempts by the upper stratum of their male coworkers to marginalize the women's interests and to appropriate their radicalism to strengthen the men's own positions. The women's awareness of their distinct needs as women and not merely as workers was evident in their open dismissal of the URWE's advice and their decision to take immediate control of the settlement process with the Régie.

The multiple experiences of religion, class, and gender did not always contradict each other on the shop floor. The manipulation of actual and fictive kinship ties or religious and regional bonds helped workers adapt better to industrial life, stand strong against state coercion, and negotiate some of their class interests. Without sabotaging their exclusive interests, the women transcended sectarian and occupational divisions in pursuit of sexual equality in wages, promotion, and benefits. Gendered consciousness did not substitute for class awareness, but rather enriched it and recast it in new terms. This relationship was illustrated in the women's combined commitment to fulfill the demands pertaining both to them and to the leftist male strikers. At no time did they express their suspicion of the Communists at the Régie or their indifference to the long-term goals of the labor movement, despite the fact that most of them avoided formal membership in leftist organizations. In essence, an understanding of class formation remains incomplete without a serious qualitative statement about gender. By looking at work-based conflicts through the lens of gender, one also learns how gender acted as a source both of unity and of division in labor movements. Whereas the tobacco workingwomen deferred at times to male labor unionists in resolving their conflicts with management, they did not find it unusual to strike for demands not shared by their male colleagues.

The Régie workingwomen utilized kinship networks, religious affiliation, and village ties to meet new social challenges on the shop floor and in their urban homes. Preindustrial values continued to influence the women's world, taking on new dimensions in the industrial setting of Beirut. Even though the peasant women who poured into the tobacco factories were motivated primarily by stark necessity, they in the process came to enjoy personal autonomy and a sense of adventure. They began to postpone marriage as a result of the transformation of their social world and the widening of their personal horizons. It is true that many if not most were able neither to overcome completely their socioeconomic deprivation nor to achieve fully their personal or social liberation. Nonetheless, during their efforts to eliminate their marginal position, industrial workingwomen added new chapters to women's history in the Middle East. Their militancy gave the labor movement and the postcolonial history of Lebanon new meanings by highlighting both the empowerment of women and working-class actions as vital and interdependent elements of social change and by reversing the image of women as *silent*. Striking was pivotal in recasting women's gender identity and political aspirations as well as in deepening their belief that their sacrifices made history. Women's strikes became vivid signs of their public assertiveness, strength, and ability to take over highly controlled, masculinized political spaces—even if only briefly. The women were clearly the first to revolt, and, recognizing this fact, we can more clearly and realistically see and understand the powerful images and empowered actions of these key historical industrial workers.

Notes | Selected Bibliography | Index

Notes

Introduction

1. Peter Gran, *Beyond Eurocentrism: A New View of Modern World History* (Syracuse, N.Y.: Syracuse Univ. Press, 1996), and Peter Gran, "Organization of Culture and the Construction of the Family in the Modern Middle East," in *Women, the Family, and Divorce Laws in Islamic History*, edited by Amira El Azhary Sonbol, 64–80 (Syracuse, N.Y.: Syracuse Univ. Press, 1996).

2. Much of the Lebanese scholarship on the formation of the Lebanese nation-state presents contradictory and often divisive narratives. Scholars such as Mas'ud Dahir, Ghassan Salami, Wajih Kawtharani, and Kamal Salibi disagree on whether Lebanon was a historically justified national entity, who benefited from its creation, and when and how a Lebanese people with a viable national identity evolved. See Mas'ud Dahir, *Tarikh Lubnan al-Ijtima'i: 1914–1926* (The Social History of Lebanon: 1914–1926) (Beirut: Dar al-Matbu'at al-Sharqiyya, 1984), 20, 37–38; Ghassan Salami, *Al-Mujtama' wa al-Dawla fil-Mashriq al-'Arabi* (Society and State in the Arab East) (Beirut: Markaz Dirasat al-Wihda al-'Arabiyya, 1987), 14; Kamal Salibi, *A House of Many Mansions: The History of Lebanon Reconsidered* (Berkeley and Los Angeles: Univ. of California Press, 1988), 201–4. Writing in the 1940s, literary Muslim figures such as Omar Farroukh and Zaki Naqqash claimed that the concept of historical Lebanon was a false fabrication; contemporary right-wing Christian ideologues believed Lebanon to have been "eternal and everlasting"; and Christian ideologues of the Syrian Nationalist Party denounced Lebanonism, in favor of a Syrian national identity, as merely mythical and purely "imagined." See Nicola Ziadeh, "The Lebanese Elections, 1960," *Middle East Journal* 24 (1960): 367–81. Based on this scholarship that is representative of the main ideological trends in Lebanon, it is difficult to endorse all aspects of Engin Deniz Akarli's thesis in *The Long Peace* that an embryonic "nation-state" had formed in Mount Lebanon by 1920. He feels that the fact that Ottoman Mount Lebanon, the historical and geographical heartland of modern-day Lebanon, enjoyed a semi-independent political regime between 1861 and 1920 that promoted social integration and a common political culture and that paved the way for a Lebanese nation after French rule. Akarli is correct in discerning a strong "Lebanonist" regionalism among the Maronite aristocracy of Mount Lebanon during the late nineteenth century. See Engin Deniz Akarli, *The Long Peace: Ottoman Lebanon, 1861–1920* (Berkeley and Los Angeles: Univ. of California Press, 1993), 1–2, 82–84, and 100–101. Many members of the Maronite elite played a leading role in the political

history of Mount Lebanon and Grand Liban, embellishing the image of Maronite liberty and self-hood, which they claimed was denied under past Muslim rules. The Maronite literati's scholarly production on provincial nationalism, much like its counterparts in other Arab regions after the division of the Ottoman Empire among European powers, furnished an "ideological justification" for the territorial divisions implemented by the colonial powers and for "forging a new identity for the local elites." See Rifa'at Abou-El-Haj, "The Social Uses of the Past: Recent Arab Historiography of Ottoman Rule," *International Journal of Middle East Studies* 14 (1982), 185–87, 188, 192. Abou-El-Haj asserts that national imaginations are a function of internal social formations in Arab society rather than being the ultimate reason for the creation and durability of the provincial national state. In chapters 1 and 2 of my study, I highlight the form in which this process unfolded in Ottoman Mount Lebanon and Grand Liban.

3. "Ya Alf Sawm wa Sala 'Ala al-Riji" (We Offer a Thousand Prayers and Fasting to Return to the Days of the Régie), *Lisan al-Haal*, May 23, 1930, 1.

4. Ministère des Affaires Étrangeres (MAE), Paris, Syrie-Liban, 1930–40, Situation au Liban, vol. 550, Apr. 9, 1935. Under the banderole system, tobacco products, which did not carry official stamps purchased from the Ministry of Finance, were not admitted into the market. In the old Ottoman Régie, where the banderole system was in effect, owners of tobacco workshops bought the stamps from government offices and affixed them to the packets of tobacco. See Donald Quataert, *Social Disintegration and Popular Resistance in the Ottoman Empire, 1881–1908: Reaction to European Economic Penetration* (New York: New York Univ. Press, 1983), 14.

5. See Ippei Yamazawa, "Raw-Silk Exports and Japanese Economic Development," in *The Textile Industry and the Rise of the Japanese Economy,* edited by Michael Smitka (New York: Garland, 1998), 302–6. Yamazawa points to the effects of the silkworm disease epidemic in Europe on Japanese and Chinese silk production from the 1850s to the early nineteenth century. See also Isma'il Haqqi Bey, ed., *Lubnan: Mabahith 'Ilmiyya wa Ijtima'iyya* (Lebanon: Social and Scientific Studies) (Beirut: Majmu'ah mina al-Udaba', 1918), 401, and Donald Quataert, *Ottoman Manufacturing in the Age of the Industrial Revolution* (Cambridge, U.K.: Cambridge Univ. Press, 1993), 17–18, 125.

6. Paul Saba, "The Creation of the Lebanese Economy—Economic Growth in the Nineteenth and Twentieth Centuries," in *Essays on the Crisis in Lebanon,* edited by Roger Owen (London: Ithaca Press, 1976), 18.

7. Ibid., 18, 21–22.

8. Carolyn Gates, *The Historical Role of Political Economy in the Development of Modern Lebanon* (Oxford, U.K.: Centre for Lebanese Studies, 1989), 8. In chapter 1, I discuss the economic transformation that took place in Lebanon during the late nineteenth century that led to the destruction of the local silk industry and the repercussions of that loss on Lebanese society at large.

9. Régie Personnel Department, "The Development of the Size of the Régie Working Force, 1959–1972," Régie Co-Intéressee Libanaise des Tabacs et Tombacs, company records (hereafter "Régie company records"), Hadath and Beirut, n.d.

10. Stephen Hemsley Longrigg, *Syria and Lebanon under French Mandate* (London: Oxford Univ. Press, 1958), 340.

11. "RÉGIE CO-INTÉRESSÉE LIBANISE DES TĀBĀC ET TOMBĀCS. ASSEMBLÉE GÉNÉRALE ORDINAIRE DES ACTIONNAIRES DU 26 Juin 1953. RAPPORTS présentés par le Conseil d'Administration et par les Commissaires de Surveillance, Exercice 1953)" (annual report of the Régie Board of Directors and Budget Commission presented to the General Assembly on June 26, 1953), private collection of Jacque Dagher, former Régie administrative officer, Beirut.

12. Emile Dirani, "Taqrir ila Wizarat al-Maliyya Hawl Awdaaʻ al-Riji" (A Report to the Ministry of Finance on the Situation of the Régie), typed manuscript, Nov. 17, 1971, 50, Régie company records, Beirut.

13. The 1935 concessionary law did not provide any right for the renewal of the concession. Ibid., 59.

14. Ibid.

15. "RÉGIE CO-INTÉRESSÉE LIBANISE DES TĀBĀC ET TOMBĀCS. ASSEMBLÉE GÉNÉRALE ORDINAIRE DES ACTIONNAIRES DU 30 Mai 1968. RAPPORTS présentés par le Conseil d'Administration et par les Commissaires de Surveillance, Exercice 1968" (annual report of the Régie Board of Directors and Budget Commission, presented to the General Assembly on May 30, 1968), private collection of Jacques Dagher, Beirut.

16. The amount of the American tobacco in these two brands was 80 percent. Ibid.

17. Saʻid Hani, *Al-Diyar,* June 3, 1993, 7. This trend was intermittently interrupted from 1985 to 1991, when the tobacco factory at Hadath worked under extraordinary conditions, produced the national brands of cigarettes, and surprisingly managed to procure profits for the company. See George Hubayqa, "Nataʼij ʻAmal Idarat Hasr al-Tabigh Khilal Fatrat al-Ahdath" (The Outcome of the Operations of the Régie during the War), typed manuscript, Hadath plant, 1994, 5, Régie company records, Hadath.

18. For a detailed account of the relationship among the Lebanese tobacco farmers, the Régie, and the Lebanese government, see Hassan Fakhr, "Fadaʼih al-Riji" (The Scandals of the Régie), *Al-Hurriyya,* no. 560 (May 4, 1971): 9, and Saʻid Ghabris, "Al-Tabigh wa Rihlat al-Qahr mina al-Harir ila al-Riji" (The Tobacco and the Journey of Misery from Silk to the Régie), *Al-Safir,* Dec., 12, 1977, 6.

19. Ramkrishna Mukherjee, *Society, Culture, Development* (New Delhi: Sage, 1991), 47–52.

20. The analytical framework I developed in this area owes much to the insights and intellectual challenges provided by Rifaʻat Abou-El-Haj in his seminar on comparative formation of modern nation-states in 1995–96.

21. A good example of this scholarship is reflected in the following sources: Ruth F. Woodsmall, *Study of the Role of Women: Their Activities and Organizations in Lebanon, Egypt, Iraq, Jordan, and Syria* (New York: International Federation of Business and Professional Women, 1956), 5; Yusif A. Sayigh, "Management-Labour Relations in Selected Arab Countries: Major Aspects and Determinants," *International Labour Review* 77 (Jan.–June 1958), 523, 534; Nadia Haggag Youssef, *Women and Work in Developing Societies* (Berkeley, Calif.: Institute of International Studies, 1974), 30, 38, 82, 86. Youssef argues that "the nature of Islam as a religious system" was responsible for maintaining the primacy of kinship control, which explains in turn the low participation of women in paid labor. See also Mona Hammam, "Women and Industrial Work in Egypt: The Chubra el-Kheima

Case," *Arab Studies Quarterly* 2, no. 1 (winter 1980), 51, 62; Nadia Hijab, *Womanpower: The Arab Debate on Women at Work* (New York: Cambridge Univ. Press, 1988), 87–88.

22. Peter Gran, "The Failure of Social Theory to Keep Up with Our Times: The Study of Women and Structural Adjustment Programs in the Middle East as an Example," paper presented at the Thirty-fourth Annual Meeting of the Association of Muslim Social Scientists, Sept. 30, 2005, Temple Univ., 3. Thanks to Professor Gran for allowing me to quote from this valuable paper, which he gave to me at the meeting.

23. Valentine Moghadam, *Modernizing Women: Gender and Social Change in the Middle East* (Boulder, Colo.: Lynne Rienner, 1993), 5, 14. See also Maryam Poya, *Women, Work, and Islamism: Ideology and Resistance in Iran* (London: Zed Books, 1999), 1–2, 17. Poya's work on Iranian women shows that the state's position on women's employment and gendered division, which underwent significant change, was not determined by religion. Ivy Papps contributes to this undertaking by highlighting comparable and similar patterns in women's employment in Middle Eastern and Western countries. Thus, he explains that male employers in four Middle Eastern countries discriminated consciously and unconsciously against women on the basis of pregnancy, much like the case in other developing countries. Ivy Papps, "Attitudes to Female Employment in Four Middle Eastern Countries," in *Women in the Middle East: Perceptions, Realities, and Struggles for Liberation*, edited by Haleh Afshar (New York: St. Martin's Press, 1993), 97.

24. My findings in this area concur with Vinay Bahl's in *The Making of the Indian Working Class: The Case of the Tata Iron and Steel Co., 1880–1946* (New Delhi: Sage, 1995).

25. Erik Jan Zurcher, "Preface," in *Workers and the Working Class in the Ottoman Empire and the Turkish Republic, 1839–1950*, edited by Donald Quataert and Erik Jan Zurcher (New York: Tauris Academic Studies, 1995), 9.

26. See Dipesh Chakrabarty, "Labor History and the Politics of Theory: An Indian Angle on the Middle East," in *Workers and Working Classes in the Middle East: Struggle, Histories, Historiographies*, edited by Zachary Lockman (Albany: State Univ. of New York Press, 1994), 332.

27. Suad Joseph, "The Politicization of Religious Sects in Borj Hammoud, Lebanon," Ph.D. diss., Univ. of Michigan, Ann Arbor, 1975. Joseph correctly questions Fuad Khuri's assumption that Lebanese society lacks class conflict, which Khuri strictly confines to organized conscious and collective activity against the dominant classes. See also Mahdi 'Amil, *Madkhal ila Naqd al-Fikr al-Ta'ifi: Al-Qadiyya al-Filastiniyya fi Idyulujiyat al-Burjuwaziyya al-Lubnaniyya* (Introduction to the Refutation of Sectarian Thought: The Palestinian Cause in the Ideology of the Lebanese Bourgeoisie) (Beirut: Dar al-Farabi, 1985), and Fuad Khuri, "Sectarian Loyalty among Rural Migrants in Two Lebanese Suburbs: A Stage Between Family and National Allegiance," in *Rural Politics and Social Change in the Middle East*, edited by Richard Antoun and Iliya Harik, 198–213 (Bloomington: Indiana Univ. Press, 1972). Ussama Makdisi argues in his recent study that sectarianism was a manifestation of the modernization process that unfolded in Ottoman Mount Lebanon after the 1860 "intercommunal" violence. See Ussama Makdisi, "After 1860: Debating Religion, Reform, and Nationalism in the Ottoman Empire," *International Journal of Middle East Studies* 34, no. 3 (2002), 604.

28. Joan W. Scott, "On Language, Gender, and Working-Class History," *International Labor and Working-Class History* 31 (spring 1987): 1–13. Scott argues that gender analysis was an "alternative" and not merely an "augmentation" of class analysis.

29. See Steve Smith, "Class and Gender: Women's Strikes in St. Petersburg, 1895–1917, and in Shanghai, 1895–1927," *Social History* 19, no. 2 (May 1994), 141–42.

30. Gran, "The Failure of Social Theory," 5, 7–8.

31. Ibid.

32. USAID was formed to obstruct the Soviet Union's aims and the nationalist liberation movements in the "Third World." It was associated with the Marshall Plan reconstruction of Europe after World War II and the Truman administration's Point Four Program. In 1961, President John F. Kennedy signed the Foreign Assistance Act into law and created USAID by Executive Order. Since that time, USAID has been the principal U.S. agency to extend assistance to countries recovering from disaster, trying to escape poverty, and engaging in democratic reforms. See http://www.usaid .gov/about_usaid/.

33. Nagat M. El-Sanabary, introduction to *Women and Work in the Third World: The Impact of Industrialization and Global Economic Interdependence,* edited by Nagat M. El-Sanabary (Berkeley: Center for the Study, Education, and Advancement of Women, Univ. of California, 1983), vii.

34. I explain this issue in chapter 1.

35. Chandra Mohanty, *Feminism Without Borders: Decolonization Theory, Practicing Solidarity* (Durham, N.C.: Duke Univ. Press, 2003), 17, 20.

36. See Deniz Kandiyoti, "Islam and Patriarchy: A Comparative Perspective," in *Women in Middle Eastern History: Shifting Boundaries in Sex and Gender,* edited by Nikki R. Keddie and Beth Baron (New Haven, Conn.: Yale Univ. Press, 1991), 23–42.

37. See Elizabeth Thompson, *Colonial Citizens: Republican Rights, Paternal Privilege, and Gender in French Syria and Lebanon* (New York: Columbia Univ. Press, 2000), 19, 25. Thompson convincingly shows that patriarchy underwent a serious crisis during World War I because of male conscription in the Ottoman army and famine. When men were away, women managed the family economy single-handedly, only to be faced by large waves of locusts that "stripped the [fields] of everything green."

38. Kandiyoti, "Islam and Patriarchy," 27–28. See also Deniz Kandiyoti, "Contemporary Feminist Scholarship and Middle Eastern Studies," in *Gendering the Middle East: Emerging Perspectives,* edited by Deniz Kandiyoti, 1–27 (Syracuse, N.Y.: Syracuse Univ. Press, 1996).

39. The following are general studies dealing with labor movements and unionized workingmen and indirectly touching on workingwomen's activism: Jacques Couland, *Al-Haraka al-Naqabiyya fi Lubnon: 1919–1946* (The Syndicate Movement in Lebanon: 1919–1946) (Beirut: Dar al-Farabi, 1974), in French, *Le mouvement syndical au Liban, 1919–1946* (Paris: Éditions Socials, 1970); Ilyas al-Buwari, *Tarikh al-Haraka al-'Ummaliyya wa al-Naqabiyya fi Lubnan: 1908–1946* (The History of the Labor and Unionist Movement in Lebanon: 1908–1946), 3 vols. (Beirut: Dar al-Farabi, 1908–80); 'Ali al-Shami, *Tatawwur al-Tabaqa al-'Amila fi al-Ra'ismaliyya al-Lubnaniyya al-Mu'asira* (The Development of the Working Class within Modern Lebanese Capitalism) (Beirut: Dar al-Farabi, 1981); Mustafa al-'Aris, *Mustafa al-'Aris Yatadhakkar* (Mustafa al-'Aris Remembers) (Beirut: Dar

al-Farabi, 1982); Claude Dubar and Salim Nasr, *Al-Tabaqat al-Ijtima'iyya fi Lubnan: Muqaraba Susyulujiyya Tatbiqiyya* (The Social Classes in Lebanon: An Applied Sociological Approach) (Beirut: Mu'asasat al-Abhath al-'Arabiyya, 1982).

40. Among studies that devote special attention to workingwomen, Donald Quataert's work sheds light on the labor activities and social protest of women who worked as loom operators in rug production in western Anatolia. See his article "Machine Breaking and the Changing Carpet Industry of Western Anatolia, 1860–1908," *Journal of Social History* 16 (spring 1986): 473–89. Quataert also addresses the gendered division of labor and the transformation of silk weaving in Anatolia during the age of the Industrial Revolution. He notes, for instance, that women seemed to be for the most part subsistence workers, whereas men worked as commercial weavers of cotton, wool, and other textiles. Quataert, *Ottoman Manufacturing*, especially the introduction and the conclusion. See also Gunseli Berik, *Women Carpet Weavers in Rural Turkey: Patterns of Employment, Earnings, and Status* (Geneva: International Labour Office, 1987). Sherry Vatter highlights a women's cottage industry in Damascus during the nineteenth century that involved craftwork in European-style cotton hosiery, knitted stockings, and embroidery. The fact that women did not participate in collective work-based organizations, she notes, "undermined their ability to protest at low wages and poor working conditions." Despite the advantages that the hiring of women brought to the merchants, displaced workingmen's resistance may have prevented the textile sector from becoming feminized in its entirety. Sherry Vatter, "Militant Textile Weavers in Damascus: Waged Artisans and the Ottoman Labor Movement, 1850–1914," in Quataert and Zurcher, 50–53.

41. See Assef Bayat, "Historiography, Class, and Iranian Workers," in Lockman, ed., *Workers and Working Classes in the Middle East*, 178; Yavuz Selim Karakişla, "The Emergence of the Ottoman Industrial Working Class, 1836–1823," in Quataert and Zurcher, 16–17. Assef Bayat made important statements in this regard, and back in 1995 Donald Quataert set this vision as an agenda for future labor historians, stressing the need to assess the transformations in the forms and significance of unorganized labor and "labor movements that did/do not espouse left-wing ideologies." Donald Quataert, "Introduction," in Quataert and Zurcher, 17.

42. Joel Beinin and Zackary Lockman, *Workers on the Nile: Nationalism, Communism, Islam, and the Egyptian Working Class, 1882–1954* (Princeton, N.J.: Princeton Univ. Press, 1987), 5, 21. Beinin and Lockman studied Egyptian textile and transport workers (tramways and railways) who played a leading role in the labor movement, and they make valid observations about "the best-organized" men. Like Jacques Couland and Ilyas al-Buwari, however, they overlook a substantive section of the working class and, more important, end up generalizing almost exclusively about workingmen. They examine the shop floor, the union, and the political party as central vehicles for the development of workers' class "consciousness."

43. Irene Lorfing and Julinda Abu al-Nasr, *Dirasa Istitla'iyya Hawla al-'Amilat fi al-Masani' fi Dawahi Bayrut, 1979* (A Survey of Workingwomen in the Factories of Beirut's Suburbs, 1979) (Beirut: Institute of Women's Studies in the Arab World, Beirut Univ. College, 1979).

44. Janet Hyde Clark and Irene Lorfing, *Tasks of Women in Industry* (Beirut: Institute of Women's Studies in the Arab World, Beirut Univ. College, 1987).

45. See Quataert, "Machine Breaking and the Changing Carpet Industry," 481–83. Quataert throws light on the riots led by Greek and Armenian women in Usak and neighboring villages in western Anatolia in 1908. When the spinning factories eliminated these women's livelihood, the women rose up against government authority, carrying off the wool and wrecking the engines of the Anatolian carpet industry.

46. See Eric Hobsbawm, *Nations and Nationalism since 1780: Programme, Myth, Reality* (Cambridge, U.K.: Cambridge Univ. Press, 1990), 145, 148. Hobsbawm states that it is "likely that the radicalization of the working classes in the first post-war Europe may have reinforced their potential national consciousness." A slightly modified version of this process can be discerned in Lebanon, whose people also struggled against colonization. See also Beinin and Lockman, 17. The latter confirm that some Egyptian trade unions even insisted that workers should play a decisive role in the national movement.

47. Hobsbawm, *Nations and Nationalism,* 88.

1. From Loom to Puff: Women and Waged Labor in Colonial Lebanon

1. Modern-day Lebanon is made up of Beirut, Mount Lebanon, the North, the South, and the Biqa' region in the East. The secondary scholarship had until recently marginalized the place of the last three in the formation of modern Lebanon and its history. See Haqqi Bey; Sa'id Himadeh, ed., *Economic Organization of Syria* (Beirut: American Univ. of Beirut, 1973); Couland, *Al-Haraka al-Naqabiyya;* Dubar and Nasr; Iliya Harik, "Nushu' Nizam al-Dawla fi al-Watan al-'Arabi" (The Formation of the State System in the Arab World), *Al-Mustaqbal al-'Arabi* 99 (1987): 77–93; Dahir, *Tarikh Lubnan al-Ijtima'i;* Kamal Salibi, *The Modern History of Lebanon* (New York: Praeger, 1965); Leila Tarazi Fawaz, *An Occasion for War: Civil Conflict in Lebanon and Damascus in 1860* (London: Center for Lebanese Studies, 1994); Charles Issawi, *The Middle East Economy: Decline and Recovery* (Princeton, N.J.: Markus Wiener, 1995).

2. Akarli, 1–2, 78–81. Akarli argues that the implementation of the Mutasarrifiyya, a relatively autonomous political regime in Ottoman Mount Lebanon between 1861 and 1920, led to several sociopolitical changes that laid the ground for the formation of an embryonic "nation-state" in that region in 1920.

3. In the nineteenth-century agrarian Lebanon, the senior man had the ultimate authority over all members of his patrilineal-patrilocal extended family. His authority was consolidated by an ownership system that included land, house, animals, and the tools for farming. The role of the family's female members was confined mainly to the household, where they contributed to the family's subsistence and were considered symbols of its honor and prestige. A Middle Eastern woman had the right to inherit and own property. However, the extent to which she could transfer her productive property when she married into another family depended on the economic integrity of her patrilineal family. See Kandiyoti, "Islam and Patriarchy," 31, 32.

4. The desperate need for cash pressured peasant families to violate the social taboo imposed on factory work for women. Despite the tedious work in the silk *karkhana,* long hours, noisy machines,

bad ventilation, and tight discipline, silk work provided women with wages that increased their buying power and relatively improved their bargaining position within their families. Akram Khater, "'House' to 'Goddess of the House': Gender, Class, and Silk in the 19th-Century Mount Lebanon," *International Journal of Middle East Studies* 28 (Aug. 1996), 331, 332, 334.

5. Later in this chapter I explain how peasant families engaged in *al-muni* (food preservation) throughout the year for food consumption during winter. As for the religious rituals that helped women workers learn organizational skills, I refer to the role of Muslim Shi'ite women in 'Ashura' commemorating Imam Husayn, who was killed in 680 Karbala' at the hand of the Umayyad ruler Yazid. For an excellent study of 'Ashura', see Augustus Richard Norton, *Hezbollah* (Princeton, N.J.: Princeton Univ. Press, 2007), 50–59. As I show in chapter 3, women workers resorted to the hall of a nearby church to organize themselves and coordinate their actions during the 1946 strike. I refer to religion or to the church not as an institution or as a set of beliefs, but simply as a source for inspiration and as a value system that emphasizes sacrifice. Hannih Dib, a leading female tobacco worker, strongly believes that Jesus Christ was the first socialist in the world. Hannih Dib, interview, Mar. 6, 1997, Ghaziyya, Lebanon. It can also be argued that Christian workers' familiarity with the church, the Sunday Mass, or other religious rituals such as Easter celebrations acquainted them with mobilizational skills and methods needed to organize the strike.

6. The British and French imperial powers forced the Ottomans in 1881 to make several concessions in connection to the payment of the empire's debts after the implementation of the Ottoman Public Debt Administration.

7. For an elaborate study of that period, see Ussama Makdisi, *The Culture of Sectarianism: Community, History, and Violence in Nineteenth-Century Ottoman Lebanon* (Berkeley and Los Angeles: Univ. of California Press, 2000).

8. The British on their part supported the Druze Muslims, although indirectly, for the British role in Mount Lebanon was minor to that of the French. See Makdisi, *The Culture of Sectarianism*, 61, 71.

9. Akarli, 51–52.

10. Owing to the regulations imposed by the European powers on the Ottoman Empire in the 1860s, Mount Lebanon enjoyed a semiautonomous status, which prevented any central government from regulating the cultivation and manufacturing of tobacco. Yahe Karyergatian, "Monopoly in the Lebanese Tobacco Industry," master's thesis, American Univ. of Beirut, 1965, 19–23.

11. Khater, "'House' to 'Goddess of the House,'" 329.

12. See "Tableau de l'industrie des habitats de Beyrouth et des principaux Bourgs qui en dependent," in Charles Issawi, *The Fertile Crescent, 1800–1914: A Documentary Economic History* (New York: Oxford Univ. Press, 1988), 382.

13. Fawwaz Taraboulsi, *In Kan Baddak Ti'shaq: Kitabat fi al-Thaqafa al-Sha'biyya* (If You Wanted to Love: Writings in Popular Culture) (Beirut: Dar al-Kunuz, 2005), 22–23.

14. Gran, "The Failure of Social Theory," 3.

15. See Quataert, *Ottoman Manufacturing*, 107–33. Quataert's discussion of raw-silk production and silk cloth in the Ottoman Empire offers much evidence in support of women's waged labor

during the age of the Industrial Revolution. See also Suraiya Faroqhi, "Labor Recruitment and Control in the Ottoman Empire (Sixteenth and Seventeenth Centuries)," in *Manufacturing in the Ottoman Empire and Turkey, 1500–1950*, edited by Donald Quataert (Albany: State Univ. of New York Press, 1994), 38–39. See also Haqqi Bey; Afif I. Tannous, "Social Change in an Arab Village," *American Sociological Review* 6 (1941): 650–62; Maurice Chehab, *Dawr Lubnan fi Tarikh al-Harir* (Lebanon's Role in the History of Silk) (Beirut: Manshurat al-Jami'a al-Lubnaniyya, 1968); Couland, *Al-Haraka al-Naqabiyya;* al-Shami; Dubar and Nasr; al-Buwari, vol. 1; Dominique Chevallier, *La société de Mont Liban a l'époque de la Révolution Industrielle en Europe* (Paris: Libraire Orientale P. Geuthner, 1982), translated into Arabic as *Mujtama' Jabal Lubnan fi 'Asr al-Thawra al-Sina'yya fi Urubba* by Muna Abdullah 'Aquir (Beirut: Dar al-Nahar, 1995); Khater, "'House' to 'Goddess of the House.'"

16. Donald Quataert, "Introduction," in Quataert, ed., *Manufacturing in the Ottoman Empire,* 2. As Quataert notes, many scholars recognize manufacturing "only when it [is] urban-based and either guild-organized or located in a factory setting."

17. Al-Buwari, 1:47–48.

18. Ibid., 1:45.

19. Hani Fahs, "Mu'jam al-Qarya al-Saghir" (Shorter Dictionary on the Village), *Al-Safir,* Dec. 29, 2000, 1. Translations of non-English-language material are mine unless otherwise noted.

20. Ibid.

21. Ibid., 2.

22. Issawi, *The Fertile Crescent,* 382.

23. For a survey of the silk manufacturers in nineteenth-century Mount Lebanon, see Ibrahim Bey al-Aswad, *Dalil Lubnan* (The Guide to Lebanon) (Ba'abda, Lebanon: Al-Matba'a al-'Uthmaniyya, 1906). Maurice Chehab estimated the number of workers in the traditional and modern silk manufactures as being between 12,000 and 14,000. See Chehab, 50.

24. Khater, "'House' to 'Goddess of the House,'" 327.

25. Ibid., 329. See also Quataert, *Ottoman Manufacturing,* 109–11. As Quataert explains, workers in different parts of the Ottoman Empire suffered from European economic competition. Nonetheless, certain Ottoman industries rose even as others fell.

26. Saba, 3.

27. Chevallier, *Mujtama' Jabal Lubnan,* 396. Chevallier describes Lebanon's early-modern economy as primitive and agrarian but makes no assessment of the modes and means of production to support his view.

28. Irina Smilianskaia found that Mount Lebanon specialized in sericulture, Latakia in the cultivation of tobacco, the Biqa' Valley and Hawran in wheat, and Sayda and the adjacent areas in cotton. See Irina M. Smilianskaia, "From Subsistence to Market Economy, 1850s: Razlozhenie feodalnikh otnoshenii v Sirii I Livane v seredine XIX v" (The Disintegration of Feudal Relations in Syria and Lebanon in the Middle of the Nineteenth Century), in *The Economic History of the Middle East, 1800–1914: A Book of Readings,* edited by Charles Issawi (Chicago: Univ. of Chicago Press, 1966), 228. On the beginning of capitalism in eighteenth-century Mount Lebanon, see Richard

van Leeuwen, *Notables and Clergy in Mount Lebanon: The Khazin Sheiks and the Maronite Church* (Leiden: E. J. Brill, 1994).

29. Saba, 2. In comparison with Chevallier and Issawi, Saba advances a clearer and more detailed picture of economic development in Lebanon.

30. Ibid., 3.

31. Ibid., 4.

32. Taraboulsi, *In Kan Baddak Ti'shaq*, 30.

33. Ibid.

34. Ibid., 17.

35. Chevallier, *Mujtama' Jabal Lubnan*, 380, 396.

36. 'Amil, *Madkhal Ila Naqd al-Fikr al-Ta'ifi*, 12.

37. Chevallier, *Mujtama' Jabal Lubnan*, 393.

38. The first steam machines in silk production were introduced in al-Qurayya manufacture, *karkhana*, in 1862. See Chehab, 49.

39. Haqqi Bey, 517–18. Chevallier notes that in 1851 the wages of male workers varied between four to five piasters, whereas those of female workers did not exceed one piaster. See Chevallier, *Mujtama' Jabal Lubnan*, 392.

40. Chehab, 50.

41. Haqqi Bey, 517–18.

42. Chehab states that yearly consumption of wood for some silk manufactures was enormous, reaching around 150,000 kilograms. See Chehab, 50.

43. Khater, "'House' to 'Goddess of the House,'" 340.

44. Ibid.

45. Ahmad Khalifa, *Status of Women in Relation to Fertility and Family Planning in Egypt* (Cairo: National Center for Social and Criminological Research, 1973), 133–34.

46. Chehab, 50–51.

47. See Akarli, 27–30.

48. Ibid., 30–33.

49. See Chevallier, *Mujtama' Jabal Lubnan*, 395; Khater, "'House' to 'Goddess of the House,'" 327. Ibrahim al-Aswad points to Druze Muslim owners of silk factories around 1906. See al-Aswad, *Dalil Lubnan*, 543, 553, 560, 561, 563, and 572.

50. Saba, 18.

51. See Ippei Yamazawa, "Raw-Silk Exports and Japanese Economic Development," in *The Textile Industry and the Rise of the Japanese Economy*, edited by Michael Smitka (New York: Garland, 1998), 302–6; Haqqi Bey, 401; and Quataert, *Ottoman Manufacturing*, 17–18, 125. Japanese raw-silk exports thrived owing to their low price and the rapid technological developments in Japan's sericulture and silk-reeling industries during the late nineteenth century.

52. MAE, Nantes, Syrie-Liban, 1918–40, "A SON EXCELLENCE Monsieur le Haut Commissaire de la Republique Franaise en Syrie et au Liban," Nov. 29, 1933, carton 719.

53. George Hakim, "Industry," in Himadeh, ed., *Economic Organization of Syria*, 137; Haqqi Bey, 365.

54. Couland, *Al-Haraka al-Naqabiyya*, 147.

55. See Mustafa Bazzi, "Tatwwur al-Hiraf wa al-Sinaʿat al-Shaʿbiyya fi Jabal ʿAmil" (The Development of Handicrafts in Jabal ʿAmil), in *Al-Muʾtamar al-Awwal lil-Thaqafa al-Shaʾbiyya fi Lubnan* (The First Convention of Popular Culture in Lebanon) (Beirut: Ministry of Culture, 1993), 402–6.

56. Ibid, 344–45.

57. Dahir, *Tarikh Lubnan*, 41; Haqqi Bey, 365; Couland, *Al-Haraka al-Naqabiyya*, 45. From the late nineteenth century onward, the exportation of raw tobacco to Egypt grew dramatically. It ranged from 1.2 to 1.5 million kilograms between 1878 and 1883. Taxes on tobacco sales generated around 7.5 million French francs per year for the treasury of Mount Lebanon, and silk generated 12 million francs. See Joseph Antoine Labaki, *Mutasarrifiyyat Jabal Lubnan: Masaʾil wa Qadaya, 1861–1915* (Self-Rule of Mount Lebanon: Issues and Matters, 1861–1915) (Beirut: Dar al-Karma, 1995), 253.

58. Haqqi Bey, 403.

59. MAE, Nantes, Syrie-Liban, Apr. 20, 1935, carton 719.

60. A conversation between Monsignor Elias Richa, a Maronite bishop, and an anonymous tobacco manufacturer. MAE, Nantes, Syrie-Liban, Mar. 19, 1935, carton 718.

61. MAE, Nantes, Syrie-Liban, "A son Excellence Monsieur le Haut Commissaire de la République Francaise en Syrie et au Liban, Beyrouth," Nov. 29, 1933, carton 719.

62. This information is based on the 1937 report "Rapport à la société des nations sur la situation de la Syrie et du Liban" (Conditions of Work in Syria and the Lebanon under French Mandate), *International Labour Review* 34 (Apr. 1939): 513–17.

63. Chevallier, *Mujtamaʿ Jabal Lubnan*, 393; al-Buwari, 1:80.

64. Mikhael Afandi Melhem, "Ziraʿat al-Tabigh," *Al-Muqtataf* 6 (June 1881), 31.

65. The French authorities submitted a yearly report to the League of Nations on the economic, social, and political conditions of their colonies. See Couland, *Al-Haraka al-Naqabiyya*, 147, and *Sawt al-ʿUmmal*, 1 (Mar. 7, 1930): 1, and 1 (Apr. 17, 1930): 6.

66. MAE, Nantes, Syrie-Liban, 1918–40, "Chkrallah Abdallah: Fabricant de Tabacs-Chiah (Liban)," Beirut, Nov. 29, 1933, carton 719.

67. "Al-Tabigh," *Al-Jaysh* (Jan. 1985): 31.

68. Muhammad Said al-Qasimi, *Qamus al-Sinaʿat al-Dimashqiyya* (Dictionary of Damascene Industries) (Paris: Mouton, 1960), 337.

69. Chehab, 68.

70. Barbara Nemer, "An Industrial Solution for Bekaa's Burley Tobacco," master's thesis, Holy Spirit Univ.–Kaslik, Beirut, 1997, 13.

71. Ibid.

72. For these demonstrations, see *Sawt al-ʿUmmal* 1 (Mar. 17, 1930): 1.

73. Jacqueline des Villettes, *La vie des femmes dans un village Maronite libanais ain el Kharoube* (Tunis: Imprimerie N. Bascone et S. Muscat, 1964), 105.

74. Ibid.

75. G. Hakim, "Industry," 171–72.

76. Ibid.

77. Fuad al-Shimali, "Qadiyyat 'Ummal al-Dukhkhan: Muzaharat al-'Amilat fi'l-Saray" (The Question of Tobacco Workers), Al-'Ummal 7 (Nov. 26, 1930): 6.

78. Mitri Qindlaft, "Al-Mar'a wa al-Ma'mal" (Women and the Factory), Al-Muqtataf (Dec. 1913): 537.

79. Sawt al-'Ummal 1 (Mar. 17, 1930): 1.

80. Ibid. The GTUTW urged the Lebanese workers to unite and enroll in the trade unions and Arab workers elsewhere to form representative committees to combat unemployment.

81. The modern history of Syria and Lebanon is rich with socioeconomic and national revolts that presented a serious threat to the local and regional authorities of the time. The most significant revolts were the 1840 and 1860 Christian peasant revolts, the 1920 and 1936 Shi'ite peasant uprisings against the French, and the 1925 Syrian revolt against the French. For a significant study on the first, see Yusif Ibrahim Yazbek, Al-Judhur al-Tarikhiyya lil-Harb al-Lubnaniyya (The Historical Roots of the Lebanese Civil War) (Beirut: Dar Nawfal, 1993). On the 1925 Syrian Arab revolt, see Michael Provence, The Great Syrian Revolt and the Rise of Arab Nationalism (Austin: Univ. of Texas Press, 2005).

82. For a detailed discussion of the famine and its impact on Lebanese women, see Elizabeth Thompson, 19–39.

83. Al-Shimali, 6.

84. MAE, Nantes, Syrie-Liban, 1918–40, "Li Ma'ali Sahib al-Fakhama al-'Amid al-Sami Lil-Jumhuriyya al-Ifransiyya fi Suriyya wa Lubnan" (To Majesty High Commissioner of the French Republic in Syria and Lebanon), Feb. 5, 1935, carton 718.

85. Ibid.

86. MAE, Nantes, Mandat, Syrie-Liban, 1918–40, "Pour le Haut Commissaire sur la Compaanie LIBANO-SYRIENNE," Mar. 14, 1934, carton 866.

87. Hakim, "Industry," 126.

88. Ibid., 134.

89. Al-Buwari, 1:145. For more on the banderole tobacco system, see Quataert, Social Disintegration, 13–18.

90. "Min Akhbar al-Saraya," Lisan al-Haal, Jan. 1, 1930, 3.

91. "'Ummal al-Tabigh wa Rahmat al-Hukuma,'" Lisan al-Haal, June 17, 1930, 3.

92. Al-Shimali, 6.

93. Ibid., 1.

94. "Ya Alf Sawm wa Sala 'ala al-Riji."

95. Ibid.

96. MAE, Paris, Syrie-Liban, 1918–40, "Le rétablissement du Monopole des Tabacs dans les États du Levant sous Mandat français," Jan. 24, 1935, vol. 550.

97. The French formed an official commission to supervise and control their colonies' fiscal policies, the Compte de Gestion des Services d'Interet Communs. See George Hakim, "The Fiscal

System," in Himadeh, ed., *Economic Organization of Syria*, 335; MAE, Nantes, Syrie-Liban, 1918–40, "CONFERENCE DES INTERETS COMMUNS, SÉANCE," Feb. 1935, carton 696.

98. MAE, Paris, Syrie-Liban, 1918–40, "Le rétablissement du Monopole des Tabacs dans les États du Levant sous Mandat français," Jan. 24, 1935, vol. 550.

99. In 1928, these principal manufactures were (location names, given after the manufactures' names, are as spelled in the document cited): Abboud Melhem, Jounieh; Abou Ghanem Elie, Furn-el-Chebak; Abou Hayla, Bekfaya; Abou Zeid, Jounieh; Abou Rahal Freres, Bekfaya; Andraos, Bekfaya; Awad Joseph, Furn-el-Chebak; Bacha Saadallah, Chuah; Bellama Freres, Bekfaya; Bellane Sleiman, Jounieh; Chammoun Mansour, Jounieh; Daher Abdallah & Cie, Chouair et Zahle; Freyha Freres, Fleuve de Beyrouth; Gemayel et Abouzakheme, Bekfaya; Haidar Ibrahim Aziz, Hadet; Hakim Naoum, Jounieh; Kassouf Jean et Freres, Khonchara et Zahle; Kamle Said, Tayoune; Khouri Fouad et Philippe, Jounieh; Lattouf Amine, Wadi Chahrour; Nakib O., Chiyah; Noun et Kamel Noun, Furn-el-Chebak; Saba Freres, Anfa; Saleh Nehme, Chiyah; Sawaya Semean et Fils, Chouair et Zahle; Semaan, Bekfaya; and Ziade Assad, Damour. See MAE, Nantes, *L'indicateur: Libano-Syrien*, 1928–29, Per 356, 15–16.

100. MAE, Paris, Syrie-Liban, 1918–40, "NOTE SUR LA SITUATION DE LA FABRIQUE DES TABACS & CIGARETTES NAKAD, TRABOULSI & C A BEYROUTH," n.d., vol. 550. The Andraous and Traboulsi factories together contributed 276,000 out of 1,700,000 kilograms of Syria and Lebanon's annual tobacco production.

101. A number of carton box and cardboard factories emerged to complement the making of cigarettes. French archival sources refer to two such factories, the Chikhani and the Zaccour. MAE, Nantes, Syrie-Liban, 1918–40, "Requete de W. Michel Zaccour," June 24, 1935, carton 719. The Zaccour factory employed 130 to 150 workers.

102. Ibid. The Andraous factory had 200 workers, and the Traboulsi employed 140.

103. See also Karyergatian, 26.

104. The company in question consisted of the Libano-Syrian Tobacco Company, a Syrian entrepreneur named Osman Charbati, and a number of Lebanese entrepreneurs such as Hanna Qasouf and Brothers, Sema'an Sawaya and Sons, and Munib Sukkari. See *Al-Iqtisadi* (May 1977), 12.

105. MAE, Nantes, Syrie-Liban, 1918–40, "CONFERENCE DES INTERETS COMMUNS, Reunion," Jan. 29, 1935, carton 696.

106. The four groups that constituted the Libano-Syrian Tobacco Company were: (1) the French group, which included Le Credit Foncier d'Algerie et de Tunisie, La Compagnie General des Colonies, La Régie Co-Intéressee des Tabacs du Maroc, La Banque de L'Union Parisienne, and La Banque Française de Syrie; (2) the Franco-Suisse group, which was composed of La Compagnie Generale Financiere des Tabacs dans Laquelle la Société Generale; (3) the Libano-Syrian group, created from various visible Lebanese and Syrian people; and (4) the Anglo-American Egyptian group, consisting of La Société Anonyme des Tabacs et Cigarettes de Syrie et du Liban, La British American Tobacco, and the Maison Matossian. MAE, Nantes, Syrie-Liban, 1918–40, "Pour le Haut Commssaire le COMPAGNIE LIBANO-SYRIENNE DES TABACS," Mar. 14, 1934, carton 866.

107. In 1951, decision-making and executive power was transferred from the French high commissioner to the Ministry of Finance in Lebanon and Syria. However, the post of general director

202 | Notes to Pages 23–25

remained in French hands until 1970. Tensions between the Régie and the Ministry of Finance persisted until 1991, when the Lebanese government took over the Régie. Meanwhile, the Régie was expected to remit annually a minimum of 22 million French francs to these states, equivalent to what they received under the banderole system.

108. MAE, Paris, Syrie-liban, 1918–40, "A Son Excellence Monsieur de Laboulaye, Ambassadeur de France a Washington, D.C. (Etat-Unis)," Apr. 21, 1935, vol. 551.

109. Ibid.

110. MAE, Paris, Syrie-Liban, 1918–40, "On Excellence MONSIEUR LE MINISTRE DES AFFAIRES ENTRANGERES (Levant)," Feb. 1, 1935, carton 718.

111. Ibid.

112. Antoine 'Arida, *Lubnan wa Faransa: Watha'iq Tarikhiyya Asasiyya Tabruz Dawr Bikriki fi Muwajahat al-Intidab al-Faransi wa al-Ihtikarat al-Faransiyya* (Lebanon and France: Important Historical Documents Underscoring the Role of Bikirki in Confronting the French Mandate and French Monopolies), translated by Faris Ghassub (Beirut: Dar al-Farabi, 1987), 63. Prior to 'Arida's ascendancy to the patriarchal seat, 'Arida and a French investor obtained from the French a license to start a major cement company, which employed hundreds of workers and was producing 180 tons of cement in 1930. See *Al-Manara* 6, no. 1 (Jan. 1930), 69; *Al-Massara* 15, no. 4 (Apr. 1929), 268. In 1931, when 'Arida became the Maronite patriarch of Lebanon and the Levant, he sold his share to a Jewish investor. See MAE, Nantes, Syrie-Liban, 1918–40, no title, Mar. 19, 1935, carton 718.

113. 'Arida, 61.

114. MAE, Paris, Syrie-Liban, 1918–40, "EXPOSE DES MOTIFS DU PROJET D'ARRETE INSTITUNT UN MONOPOLE FISCCAL DES TABACS," Apr. 13, 1929, vol. 320.

115. MAE, Nantes, Syrie-Liban, 1918–40, "INFORMATION NO. 46/SS," Sept. 12, 1934, carton 718, and MAE, Paris, Syrie-Liban, 1918–40, "Monopole des tabacs," Jan. 28, 1935, vol. 550. Among these owners were Osman Charabati, Ruchdi Souccari, and George Sahnaoui in Syria, as well as Dimitri Saba, S. Sawaya Fils, Joseph and Habib Abihaila, and Semaan Freres in Lebanon.

116. This description is based on a documented meeting between an anonymous Lebanese tobacco manufacturer and 'Arida. MAE, Nantes, Syrie-Liban, 1918–40, no title, Mar. 11, 1935, carton 718.

117. MAE, Paris, Syrie-Liban, 1918–40, "Monopole des tabacs," Jan. 27, 1935, vol. 550.

118. MAE, Paris, Syrie-Liban, 1918–40, "SALLOUM FRERES (ALEP, SYRIE)," Mar. 21, 1935, vol. 550.

119. MAE, Paris, Syrie-Liban, 1918–40, "Monopole des tabacs, Beyrouth," Jan. 26, 1935, vol. 550.

120. At the Interet Communs meeting held on January 25, 1935, Lebanon was represented by two French officials, M. Lafond and M. Tallec (financial counselor); the Lebanese secretary of state, Abdallah Beyhum; and the director of finance, Amir Chehab. The French delegates, M. Lavastre, M. Roux, and M. Joubert (financial counselor), and the minister of finance, M. Hindie, represented the state of Syria. Two French officials, Governor M. Schoeffler and M. Banoist (financial counselor), also represented the state of Lattakia, and two French officials, M. Durieux and M. Cabars (director

of financial services in the Sandjak of Alexandretta), represented the state of Alexandretta. Finally, the French colonel Devic and the governor represented the state of Jabal al-Duruz. MAE, Nantes, Syrie-Liban, 1918–40, "CONFERENCE DES INTERET COMMUNS, Reunion," Jan. 29, 1935, carton 696.

121. For the petition of the tobacco farmers of Tyre, Bint Jubayl, and Halta-Batrun, see MAE, Nantes, Syrie-Liban, 1918–40, "TELEGRAMME, Bent Jebeil," Jan. 10 and Jan. 20, 1935, carton 1066.

122. Ibid.

123. See the study of Gabriel Manassa presented to the deputy of the French high commissioner on February 15, 1935. MAE, Nantes, Syrie-Liban, 1918–40, "A Monsieur LAFOND, Délègue du Haut-commissaire, aupres du Gouvernement libanais," Feb. 15, 1935, carton 718. French colonial policy in Syria aimed to appease the 'Alawites by offering them positions in the army and government. See Hanna Batatu, *Syria's Peasantry, the Descendants of Its Lesser Rural Notables, and Their Politics* (Princeton, N.J.: Princeton Univ. Press, 1999).

124. MAE, Nantes, Syrie-Liban, 1930–45, "INFORMATION No. 4029, SURETE GENERALE," Dec. 3, 1934, carton 718.

125. MAE, Nantes, Syrie-Liban, 1930–45, "Li-Ma'ali Sahib al-Fakhama," Feb. 5, 1935, carton 718.

126. French High Commissioner, *Cahier de Charges du Monopole des Tabacs et Tombacs*, 16/LR (Beirut, 1935), in Arabic: *Daftar Shurut Ihtikar al-Tabigh wa al-Tanbak*, 16/LR, Nov. 1935 (Beirut: 'Azar Press, 1944), 21, Union of the Régie Workers and Employees (URWE) records, Hadath and Beirut.

127. It is hard to believe that these figures include the seasonal and agricultural tobacco workers.

128. MAE, Paris, Syrie-Liban, 1918–40, "TELEGRAMME NO. 366, Beyrouth," June 27, 1935, vol. 551. It is not clear from the French sources whether the workers at the Hanna Chikhani and Michel Zaccour factories for cigarette wraps and carton boxes were among the 200 workers expected to become unemployed.

129. *Le Jour*, June 4, 1935, 1.

130. Michel Zaccour was a member of the Lebanese Parliament. MAE, Nantes, Syrie-Liban, 1918–40, "NOTE: pour monsieur le conseiller aux affaires financières, Beyrouth," June 24, 1935, carton 719.

131. République Libanais, Ministère du Plan, *L'enquête par sondage sur la population active au Liban*, vol. 2, *Tableaux de Résults, juillet 1970* (Beirut: Ministére du Plan, Direction Centrale de la Statistique, 1972).

132. See *Al-Thaqafa al-Wataniyya*, Sept. 25, 1970, 20.

133. Jacque Dagher, interview, Jan. 1, 1997, Ba'abda, Lebanon.

134. *Al-Hurriyya*, Sept. 7, 1970, 9.

135. *Al-Hayat*, Nov. 21, 1970, 5.

136. *Al-Hurriyya*, Sept. 7, 1970, 9.

137. Along with resignation, death also explains the figures related to the quitting of jobs at the Régie. The 1995 census shows that 341 workers (17 percent) died. The average age at death was fifty-six for 243 male workers and fifty-four for 98 female workers. Data about the age of the remaining 33

workers were missing. Five percent were dismissed, 53 percent retired, 9 percent resigned, 2 percent married, 12 percent left for unclear reasons, and 1 percent for health problems. See the 1995 census, Régie personnel department, May 26, 1995, Régie company records, Hadath and Beirut.

138. Several Régie male workers related such views about women to me during my fieldwork in Beirut in 1997. Their comments refer to their perceptions of their female colleagues in general and were not related to any particular events or to labor protests through which the Régie workers lived.

2. Domesticity and Waged Labor: Gendered and Class Polemics in Colonial and Postcolonial Times

1. This conclusion is in consonance with the thesis of Joan W. Scott and Louise Tilly's essay "Women's Work and the Family in Nineteenth-Century Europe," *Comparative Studies in Society and History* 17, no. 1 (Jan. 1975): 36–64.

2. Mukherjee, *Society, Culture, Development*, 52; see also Marnia Lazreg, *The Eloquence of Silence: Algerian Women in Question* (New York: Routledge, 1994), 11–16.

3. Lazreg, *The Eloquence of Silence*, 13–15.

4. Isma'il Ibrahim, *Al-Sahafa al-Nisa'iyya fi al-Watan al-'Arabi* (Women's Journalism in the Arab World) (Cairo: Al-Dar al-Dawliyya lil-Nashr wal-Tawzi', 1996), 51–53; Nahawand al-Qadiri, "Nash'at al-Sahafa al-Nisa'iyya al-Lubnaniyya, 1892–1920" (The Rise of Lebanese Women's Journalism), *Al-Fikr al-'Arabi* 10, no. 58 (1989), 150–52, 163. Around eleven magazines for women were founded primarily by women between 1892 and 1925. With few exceptions, these women referred to themselves as "Lebanese" and distinguished between a "Lebanese" and a "Syrian" audience even in the case of those whose magazines were issued in Beirut before the foundation of Grand Liban in 1920. These eleven magazines and their founders were: *Al-A'mal al-Yadawiyya* (Handicrafts) by Fasila; *Al-Hasna'* (The Beauty) by Jurji Baz; *Al-A'mal al-Jadida* (The New Actions) by Angelina Abu Shaqra from 'Amshit in Mount Lebanon; *Al-Mar'a al-Suriyya* (The Syrian Woman) by 'Afifah Karam; *Fatat Lubnan* (The Young Woman of Lebanon) by Salma Abi Rashid, a Lebanese from Wadi Shahrur; *Minerva* by Marie Yani; *Al-Fatat* (The Young Woman) by Muhammad al-Baqir; *Al-Fajir* (Sunrise) by Najla' Abi al-Lam'; *Al-Hayat al-Jadida* (The New Life) by Habbuba Haddad; and *Al-Mar'a al-Jadida* (The New Woman) by Julia Demeshkie. Of these nine magazines, only two were founded by men (Jurji Baz and Muhammad al-Baqir). Two additional women's magazines emerged between 1892 and 1925: *Fatat al-Watan* (The Country's Woman) by Maryam al-Zammar from Zahle and *Al-Khidr* (A Woman's Chamber) by 'Afifa Saab from Choeifat. One magazine, *Al-'Arus* (The Bride), was issued in Damascus at the time by Marie 'Ajami.

5. Al-Qadiri, 155–57.

6. See "Al-Mar'a wa al-Shaja'a" (Women and Courage), *Al-Hasna'* 3, no. 3 (Dec. 1911): 124–27. The author of this article signs herself as "a Lebanese" and writes from the town of Bishmizzin in northern Lebanon. See also al-'Amiriyya, "Al-Mar'a wa al-Siyasa" (Women and Politics), *Al-Mar'a al-Jadida* 7, no. 2 (Feb. 1925): 52–53; S. M., "Ila al-Sayyida al-'Amiriyya" (To the 'Amiriyya Lady), *Al-Mar'a al-Jadida* 7, no. 4 (Apr. 1925): 141–42.

7. See Beth Baron, *The Women's Awakening in Egypt: Culture, Society, and the Press* (New Haven, Conn.: Yale Univ. Press, 1994), chap. 5.

8. Gran, "The Failure of Social Theory," 7–8.

9. Leila Ahmed, *Women and Gender in Islam* (New Haven, Conn.: Yale Univ. Press, 1992), chaps. 3 and 4.

10. Muhammad Jamil Bayhum, "Al-Mar'a wa al-Sana'i'," (Women and Trades), *Al-Hilal* (July 1894), 923, 926. Bayhum came from a Sunni Muslim background.

11. Mitri Qindlaft, "Al-Mar'a wa al-Ma'mal" (Women and the Factory), *Al-Muqtataf* 43 (Dec. 1913), 537, 540–41. Qindlaft came from a Christian background.

12. Amira Zayn al-Din, "Nazra 'Umumiyya" (A General Glance), *Al-Hasna'* 2, no. 2 (Aug. 1910), 65–67; "Nazra fi al-Mar'a wa Ta'thir al-'Adat" (A Glance at Women and the Influence of Customs), *Al-Hasna'* 7, no. 3 (Jan. 1911), 270.

13. Jamila Bitar, "Al-Mar'a wa ma Yumkin an Ta'maluhu" (Women and What They Can Achieve), *Al-Hasna'* 3, no. 7 (Jan. 1911): 268–69. This essay was based on a speech marking Saint Catherine's day that Bitar delivered at a well-known women's school, Zahrat al-Ihsan, in Beirut.

14. "Ila Hakim Biladi wa Ibn Biladi" (To the Governor of My Country and My Countryman), *Al-Mar'a al-Jadida* 7, no. 9 (Sept. 1925), 352.

15. "Ila Ibnat Biladi: La Huquq Jadida Natlubuha" (To the Daughter of My Country), *Al-Mar'a al-Jadida* 4, no. 6 (June 1924), 231.

16. In 1925, the total population of Lebanon was 700,000, of which 64 percent were women. See "Ila Hakim Biladi," 352.

17. *Al-Mar'a al-Jadida* was the first women's magazine to come out in French Lebanon. It was first issued in 1921 by Julia Tu'ma with the assistance of her husband, Badr Dimashqiyya, who signed as "Demeshkie." Tu'ma was born in 1882 in the town of al-Mukhtara in Mount Lebanon to a Christian family and received her education at the American School in Sidon and later at a school in Choeifat in Mount Lebanon. She worked as a teacher in Lebanon and Palestine and became the chief administrator of Al-Maqasid Islamic School in Beirut. Tu'ma was known for her strong personality and stood up to the male members of her family, who opposed women's work outside the household. Dimashqiyya came from a Muslim background, but little is known about his educational and social background. They were married in 1913, and in 1917 Tu'ma founded an organization for women in cross-sectarian marriages. Later on, she founded a literary salon in Beirut that organized various intellectual and artistic activities until 1920. With Evlyn Tuwayni, Tu'ma established in the early 1920s the Women's Union (al-Itihad al-Nisa'i), which played a significant role in the political campaign for the independence of Lebanon in 1943. Tu'ma and Dimashqiyya personally funded *Al-Mar'a al-Jadida* and organized and published it in their house garden. The magazine issues stopped in 1928 when Tu'ma became ill. She passed away in 1954. See Ghassan Tuwayni, "Zawaj Julia Tu'ma Dimashqiyya wa Majallatuha Namuzajan" (The Marriage of Julia Tu'ma Dimashqiyya and Her Magazine Are a Good Example), *Al-Nahar* (Feb. 5, 2001): 5; Emily Faris Ibrahim, *Adibat Lubnaniyyat* (Lebanese Women Writers) (Beirut: Dar al-Rihani, 1964), 81–84; Nadia al-Jurdi Nuwayhid, *Nisa' min Biladi* (Women from My Homeland) (Beirut: Al-Mu'assasa al-'Arabiyya lil-Dirasat wa al-Nashr,

1987), 110–12. Nuwayhid's work is simply a compilation of biographical sketches of famous Syrian and Lebanese women from the late nineteenth century to the the mid-1980s. She collected these sketches from Arabic newspapers and magazines and made no additions or few changes. Nuwayhid's work thus almost seems to be a primary source. Emily Ibrahim, however, was a Lebanese literary figure and scholar who in the 1960s highlighted the careers and lives of leading Lebanese women novelists and journalists to establish for herself and educated women like her a sense of historical continuity in women's achievements and a feminist pride in a "Lebanese" heritage of female creativity and power. Ibrahim's work thus attempted to give women writers of the early twentieth century a wider scope of influence and importance. I have tried to present, however, a different reading of upper-class women's journalism and its overarching themes and debates. I argue that these themes and debates were of use to these women's own class and expressed specific gender configurations of relevance to the Syrian and, later, Lebanese national elite.

18. *Al-Mar'a al-Jadida* 4, no. 6 (June 1924), 231.

19. Ibid., 233.

20. Fatat al-Furat, "Kalima Naziha" (An Honest Word), *Al-'Irfan* 19 (Mar. 1930), 326.

21. *Al-Mar'a al-Jadida* 4 (n.d.), 230.

22. MAE, Nantes, Syrie-Liban, 1918–40, "FERMETURE DES SOUKS, INFORMATION NO. 540," Feb. 16, 1935, carton 1066.

23. MAE, Nantes, Syrie-Liban, 1918–40, "RENSEIGNMENTS," Feb. 28, 1935, carton 1066.

24. MAE, Nantes, Syrie-Liban, 1918–40, "INFORMATION NO. 1624," May 22, 1935, carton 1066.

25. This information was based on the union's letter to the French high commissioner, Comte De Martel, on Dec. 15, 1935. See MAE, Nantes, Syrie-Liban, 1918–40, "INFORMATION NO. 1292," Apr. 19, 1935, carton 718.

26. Nuwayhid; E. F. Ibrahim.

27. Baron, *The Women's Awakening in Egypt,* 189.

28. Ibid.

29. MAE, Nantes, Syrie-Liban, 1918–40, "INFORMATION NO. 1292," Apr. 19, 1935, carton 718. The leaflet text was preserved in French in these archives.

30. Ibid.

31. Nikki R. Keddie, "Introduction," in *Religion and Politics in Iran: Shi'ism from Quietism to Revolution,* edited by Nikki R. Keddie (New Haven, Conn.: Yale Univ. Press, 1983), 9.

32. MAE, Nantes, Mandat, Syrie-Liban, 1918–40, "Li-Ma'ali Sahib Fakhamat al-'Amid al-Sami" (To Mr. High Commissioner), Feb. 5, 1935, carton 718.

33. Mervat Hatem, "Class and Patriarchy as Competing Paradigms for the Study of Middle Eastern Women," *Comparative Study of Society and History* (1987), 812.

34. I elaborate on this point in my discussion of the 1946 strike, which I study in the next chapter.

35. Gran, "The Failure of Social Theory," 3.

36. See Couland, *Al-Haraka al-Naqabiyya;* al-Shami; and al-Buwari.

37. See "Working Conditions in Handicrafts and Modern Industry in Syria," *International Labour Review* 29, no. 3 (Mar. 1934), 408. Although this report's findings are approximate, they are reliable and useful if one takes into account that the number might have included not only women who worked in manufacturing, but also women who worked in the agricultural sector of tobacco as well. Even if randomly produced, this figure of 10,000 confirms that women's involvement in the tobacco industry was significant given that the total number of industrial workers was 200,000.

38. "Conditions of Work in Syria and the Lebanon under French Mandate," *International Labour Review* 39, no. 4 (Apr. 1939), 514.

39. Ibid., 514–15.

40. "Women's Work in the Lebanon," *International Labour Review* 58, no. 3 (Sept. 1948), 395.

41. In a mission headed by Father Joseph Lebert, IRFED issued a work of seven volumes entitled *Étude preliminaire sur les besoins et les possibilités du développement du Liban*. See Wade R. Goria, *Sovereignty and Leadership in Lebanon, 1943–1976* (London: Ithaca Press, 1985), 59–63.

42. The table refers to "various activities," which normally includes collective family work.

43. "Free profession" is a category that means independent work such as family or private business, peddling, and a number of skilled jobs such as dressmaking, hairdressing, tutoring, and so on.

44. Charles Churchill, "Village Life of the Central Beqa' Valley of Lebanon," *Middle East Economic Papers* (1968), 46–47, table 10, "Occupation of Household Members in Thirteen Villages in the Biqa' by Sex in 1955–56."

45. For an elaborate study on the informal work done by women, see Elizabeth Fernea and Richard Lobban, *Middle Eastern Women and the Invisible Economy* (Gainesville: Univ. of Florida Press, 1998).

46. 'Adnan Salameh interview, Aug. 24, 1996, Dearborn, Michigan. The Salameh family was active in tobacco planting.

47. République Libanais, *L'enquête par sondage*. I examined this census in its French and Arabic versions. As in the case of most censuses, the two versions were issued around the same time. Most labor studies in Lebanon after 1972 have utilized *L'enquête*'s tables and statistics. Al-Shami's *Tatawwur al-Tabaqa al-'Amila* and Dubar and Nasr's *Al-Tabaqat al-Ijtima'iyya* are only a couple of examples. The shortcomings of the census in table 3.3, however, lie in its limited time scope (1970) and the absence of any data on religion in a country characterized by a multisectarian social composition and resided over by a tribal-ethnic state.

48. République Libanaise, *L'enquête par sondage*, 157, table 14.10, "The Distribution of Working People According to Occupation, Age, and Gender."

49. Ibid., table 6.1, "The Distribution of Female Laborers According to Occupation," 1970.

50. Faroqhi, "Labor Recruitment," 38, and Donald Quataert, "Ottoman Manufacturing in the Nineteenth Century," in Quataert, *Manufacturing in the Ottoman Empire*.

51. Quataert, "Ottoman Manufacturing," 95.

52. Waddah Sharara, *Dawlat Hizbullah: Lubnan Mujtama'an Islamiyyan* (The State of Hizbullah: Lebanon Made into an Islamic Society) (Beirut: Dar al-Nahar, 1996); Zaynab Z., interview, Feb. 13, 1997, Hadath.

53. In'am A. interview, Feb. 20, 1997, Hadath.

54. Latifa H. interview, Feb. 25, 1997, Ghaziyya, Lebanon.

55. Munira S. interview, Feb. 10, 1997, Hadath; Dibi K. interview, Feb. 19, 1997, Hadath; Fatima Z. interview, Mar. 1, 1997, Hadath.

56. Scott and Tilly, 43–44, 45–46.

57. Nuha M. interview, Dec. 29, 1997, Hadath; Tamam H. interview, Dec. 28, 1997, Hadath; Safiya Z. interview, Mar. 2, 1997, Hadath; Nelly J. interview, Mar. 2, 1997, Hadath; and Fatima S. interview, Mar. 4, 1997, Hadath.

58. Scott and Tilly, "Women's Work and the Family," 48–50.

59. Sharara, *Dawlat Hizbullah,* 77–78.

60. Rose Ghurayyib, "Al-Mar's wa al'Amal: Mushkilat wa Ma'uqat" (Woman and Work: Problems and Obstacles), in *Adwa' 'ala al-Haraka al-Nisa'iyya* (Highlighting the Modern Women's Movement: Studies and Essays), edited by Rose Ghurayyib (Beirut: Institute of Women's Studies in the Arab World, 1988), 328–32.

61. 'Adnan Muroeh, "Tanzim al-Usra wa al-Mar'a al-'Amila fi Lubnan" (Family Planning and the Workingwoman in Lebanon), in *Al-Mar'a wa al-'Amal fi Lubnan* (Women and Labor in Lebanon) (Beirut: Institute of Women's Studies in the Arab World, Beirut Univ. College, 1980), 50.

62. Lorfing and Abu al-Nasr, 66. The ten factories surveyed had 470 women and 483 men. A sample of 205 women became the basis for this study and its generalizations. In this sample, around 171 women were single, 19 were married, and 15 were widowed and divorced. See page 54 of Lorfing and Abu al-Nasr's study.

63. Scott and Tilly, 42–43.

64. Even during the nineteenth century, Turkish, Greek, and Arab women in the Ottoman Empire confronted familial and social resistance to their involvement in industrial work. Donald Quataert shows that nineteenth-century Armenian and Turkish women joined the mills at Bursa after particular "negotiations" and the issuance of "morality decrees" by local religious leaders. Full-time industrial labor, which separated the women from the household, thus did not seem to be a simple continuation of earlier mixed-labor tasks. Rather, it created a significant social break with the rural setting. In the 1860s, women who left home resided in special dormitories to work at spinning mills. The effect on their lifestyle and pattern of spending was revealing, for they were accused, as Quataert explains, of laying out "too much of their earning in dress," even though they received only one-half of the regular spinners' wages in the silk factory. See Quataert, "Ottoman Manufacturing," 127.

65. Henry 'Azzam, "Al-Mar'a al-'Arabiyya wa al-'Amal: Musharakat al-Mar'a al-'Arabiyya fi al-Qiwa al-'Amila wa Dawruha fi 'Amaliyat al-Tanmiyya" (Arab Women and Work: The Participation of Arab Women in the Workforce and Their Role in the Process of Development), *Al-Mustaqbal al-'Arabi,* no. 34 (Dec. 1981), 77. 'Azzam was the regional consultant of the International Labour Organization and its branch in the Middle East.

66. Ibid., 77–78, 78–84.

67. Al-Shami, 151.

68. Most of the anthropological and sociological studies providing data on women's lives in Lebanon go back to the 1960s. During the civil war period (1975–90), few such studies were made, which explains the dates of the following works. These studies place much emphasis on cultural determinants. Woodsmall, who associated the social and economic restrictions on Arab women with Islam, noted that the mild patterns of sex segregation in Beirut and the rarity of the veil could be explained by the presence of a large Christian population in Lebanon (Woodsmall, 5, from 1956). See also Y. Sayigh, "Management-Labour Relations in Selected Arab Countries," 523, 534 (from 1958); Lee L. Bean, "Utilisation of Human Resources: The Case of Women in Pakistan," *International Labour Review* 97, no. 4 (Apr. 1968), 397; C. Rossillion, "Cultural Pluralism, Equality of Treatment, and Equality of Opportunity in the Lebanon," *International Labour Review* 98, no. 3 (Sept. 1968), 228; and Youssef, 30, 38, 82, 86 (from 1974). For comparative studies on women and labor in other Arab countries, see Hammam, "Women and Industrial Work in Egypt," 62, and Linda Layne, "Women in Jordan's Workforce," *MERIP Reports* 9 (Mar.–Apr. 1981), 22.

69. Layne, 22.

3. At the Legal Frontiers: "Unruly" Workingwomen Between Colonial Authority and the National State, 1940–1946

1. Indeed, tobacco production carried the interests of a significant segment of Lebanese society, estimated in 1963 to be 300,000 persons, or 12 percent of the total population. These numbers were reported in the official census conducted by the government and revealed by Al-Wakala al-Wataniyya lil-Anba' (National News Agency), and they were quoted in the daily newspaper *Al-Nahar,* June 30, 1963, 6.

2. The labor law was the paramount demand raised by the GTUTW in its concluding statement at its general conference of November 1930. The full statement was published in *Al-'Ummal* 7, no. 2 (Dec. 1, 1930),7.

3. Al-Buwari, 1:230.

4. Philip S. Khoury, *Syria and the French Mandate: The Politics of Arab Nationalism, 1920–1945* (Princeton, N.J.: Princeton Univ. Press, 1987), 584–92.

5. This notion is prevalent in the standard history textbooks of the Lebanese public schools.

6. For an illuminating study of the Arab scholarship on the modern nation-state and its social foundations, see Abou-El-Haj, "The Social Uses of the Past."

7. P. Khoury, 592.

8. Couland, *Al-Haraka al-Naqabiyya,* 337–38.

9. MAE, Nantes, Syrie-Liban, 1930–40, "INFORMATION NO. 4029," Jan. 3, 1934, carton 718.

10. Ibid.

11. Jacques Dagher interview, Jan. 28, 1997, Ba'abda, Lebanon.

12. *Chartouni vs. the Régie,* C/I.P.C. (Beirut, 1941); a copy of this case was found in the MAE, Nantes, Syrie-Liban, 1930–45, Sept. 28, 1943, carton 1107.

13. The report "'Ummal Sharikat al-Riji" was part of a series published on February 1, 1938, in a local newspaper and republished in al-'Aris, 422–23.

14. See Couland, *Al-Haraka al-Naqabiyya*, 303–4. As for the strike of the Régie workers on December 29, 1943, see MAE, Nantes, Syrie-Liban, 1930–45, "INFORMATION," Dec. 18, 1943, and "INFORMATION," Dec. 29, 1943, carton 1107.

15. The question of the amelioration of work conditions and the founding of a labor law came to occupy a central position on the agenda of the attempted and carried-out strikes from 1943 to 1946. For an overview of the strikes that occurred during this period, see al-Buwari, 1:261–88, and Couland, *Al-Haraka al-Naqabiyya*, 338–75.

16. MAE, Nantes, Syrie-Liban, 1930–45, "INFORMATION," Oct. 5, 1943, carton 1107.

17. MAE, Nantes, Syrie-Liban, 1930–45, "INFORMATION," Sept. 28, 1943, carton 1107.

18. See Couland, *Al-Haraka al-Naqabiyya*, 308–9.

19. Ibid.

20. Several European investors, mostly French, were granted economic concessions in the Levant during the French colonial period, 1918–46. These concessions targeted the most lucrative economic segments of the countries in question. The companies included, to name only a few, the Société des Tramways et d'Electricite, the Régie Co-Intéressee Libano-Syrienne des Tabacs et Tombacs, the Régie Générale des Chemins, and the Banque de Syrie au Liban. See P. Khoury, 486, and Couland, *Al-Haraka al-Naqabiyya*, 337–38.

21. Couland, *Al-Haraka al-Naqabiyya*, 313–15.

22. A number of demands were common to all of these strikes. The regulations regarding work hours and their decrease to eight per day was a chief demand, in addition to gaining the right of unionization, finding a labor court, stopping illegal and arbitrary discharge from work, gaining family allowances, and setting a scale for wage increase. In general, all of these demands attested to the workers' growing awareness of a labor code. For an overview of these demands and the strike that occurred from mid-1943 to mid-1945, see Couland, *Al-Haraka al-Naqabiyya*, 357–87, and al-Buwari, 1:213–34.

23. Couland, *Al-Haraka al-Naqabiyya*, 358.

24. Al-Buwari, 1:217.

25. Ibid., 1:238.

26. Ibid., 1:219.

27. Ibid., 1:223, 225.

28. Ibid., 1:227–28.

29. Ibid., 1:223–25.

30. P. Khoury, 613–17, and William L. Cleveland, *A History of the Modern Middle East* (Boulder, Colo.: Westview Press, 2000), 214.

31. Couland, *Al-Haraka al-Naqabiyya*, 384, and al-Buwari, 1:263.

32. The persistent autonomy and influence that the foreign or concessionary companies exerted in the process of founding a labor law is exemplified even in the structure of the Ministry of Social Affairs, formed on June 1, 1951, which later became the Ministry of Labor. The former was divided

into four departments: Labor Department, Trade Unions Department, Concessionary Companies Control Department, and, finally, Department of Social Affairs. Joseph Donato, "Lebanon and Its Labour Legislation," *International Labour Review* 65, no. 1 (Jan. 1952), 73. The concessionary companies maintained their independence in applying their own provisions despite the founding of the national labor law.

33. Al-Buwari, 1:273.

34. Couland, *Al-Haraka al-Naqabiyya*, 317–18; al-Buwari, 1:256; al-'Aris, 179.

35. Al-Buwari, 1:256.

36. Ibid., 1:275.

37. Quoted in Al-'Aris, 179–80.

38. In the 1940s, Albert H. Hourani believed that all social reforms that had taken place in Lebanon and Syria since the turn of the twentieth century were attributable to the state's initiative rather than to the people's. See Albert H. Hourani, *Syria and Lebanon: A Political Essay* (London: Lebanon Bookshop, 1946), 82. See also Donato, 73–92; Robert J. Lampman, "The Lebanese Labor Code of 1946," *Labor Law Journal* (July 1954), 497; and Benjamin T. Hourani, "Unionism in the Lebanese Labor Code of 1946," master's thesis, American Univ. of Beirut, 1959, 27. For a leftist perspective, see Couland, *Al-Haraka al-Naqabiyya*, 414–21, and al-Buwari, 1:264–74.

39. See the writings of Communist ideologues and activists such as Ibrahim Mustafa, "Tatawwurat Bunyawiyya Hamma" (Important Structural Developments), *Al-Tariq* 40, no. 1 (Feb. 1981): 95–106; al-Buwari; Yusuf Khattar al-Hilu, *Awraq min Tarikhuna* (Pages from Our History) (Beirut: Dar al-Farabi, 1988); and Artin Madoyan, *Hyati 'ala al-Mitras* (Life at the Barricade) (Beirut: Dar al-Farabi, 1986).

40. A number of Régie workingmen I interviewed preferred to remain anonymous. Interviews by the author, Beirut, Mar. and Apr. 1997.

41. See note 39 of this chapter.

42. Even though the official date for Lebanese independence from the French was 1943 following the United Nations declaration of Lebanese independence, the complete evacuation of all French administrative and military personnel did not occur until 1946.

43. The demands included promulgating a labor law, protecting workers from the punitive measures taken by their employers, granting a wage increase and job permanency one year at the most after the employee starts work, establishing a fixed procedure for wage increase and promotion, paying workers' wages on a monthly instead of a daily or weekly basis after four years of service, and, finally, granting the workers paid sick days and weekly and yearly breaks. See al-Buwari, 1:268–69.

44. Ibid., 1:270.

45. *Al-Nahar*, June 4, 1946, 4.

46. *Al-Nahar*, June 15–16, 1946, 2. In the early 1950s, Edward W. Samuell Jr. reported that in 1947 the Régie workforce was made up of 1,500 permanent and 350 temporary workers, but he did not provide any information on the percentage of workingwomen. See Edward W. Samuell Jr., "A Contribution to the Study of Lebanese Labor Syndicates," Ph.D. diss., American Univ. of Beirut,

1952, 96. Newspaper reports that covered the 1946 strike indiscriminately referred to the workers in the masculine plural as *'ummal.*

47. Al-Buwari, 1:278, 321.

48. The electricity workers, whose number did not exceed 1,000 in 1947, gained the right to form their syndicate only a month before the Régie workers did on July 10, 1947. The URWE founding members were Elias Sawaya, Sharif Shikhani, Jean Tuwayni, Farid Sharbil, Anis Iskandar Abdullah, Asma Malkun, and Husayn Ali Qasim. At the time of its formation, the union comprised 1,850 female and male members. In 1947, the union's executive board included the following members: president, Jean Tuwayni; vice president, Mahmud Subuh; secretary, Hafiz al-Munzir; treasurer, Munir 'Alam al-Din; accountant, Fayiz Sallum; and advisors, Halim Ruhanna, Adib Sawaya, Joseph 'Ajil, Asma Malkun, Ahmad Diyab, Yusuf al-Qasuf, and Nasib Nasr. See Samuell, 85, 96. On another note, the scholarship on labor in Lebanon and the Middle East refers to workers as "blue-collar laborers" and to employees as "white-collar laborers" or "staff."

49. *Al-Nahar,* June 27, 1946, 2.

50. Ibid.

51. Michael al-'Azar, a typographical worker, witnessed and recorded the organizational procedures and the day-to-day development of the 1946 tobacco workers' strike. Al-'Azar gave his notes to Ilyas al-Buwari, who included them in his book *Tarikh al-Haraka,* together with newspapers reports covering the strike. See al-Buwari, 1:321–34; see also Couland, *Al-Haraka al-Naqabiyya,* 399.

52. Al-Buwari, 1:323–24.

53. My interviews with numerous Régie men and women were replete with such depictions, expressed in colloquial Lebanese, carrying multiple political and sexual connotations.

54. Alexander Flores, "The Early History of Lebanese Communism Reconsidered," *Khamsin* 7 (1980), 12; Karim Muroeh, *Al-Muqawama* (The Resistance) (Beirut: Dar al-Farabi, 1985), 20.

55. Al-Buwari, 1:115, and Muhammad Dakrub, *Judhur al-Sindiyana al-Hamra'* (The Roots of the Red Oak Tree) (Beirut: Dar al-Farabi, 1985), 77.

56. Madoyan, 51–55. Al-Shimali devoted significant efforts in forming and developing strong labor unions in Lebanon and was at times criticized by the Communist Party as being more of a unionist than a socialist ideologue.

57. Al-Buwari, 1:137; Dakrub, 92.

58. K. Muroeh, 29–30.

59. Madoyan, 70–71.

60. Michael Suleiman, "The Lebanese Communist Party," *Middle Eastern Studies* 3 (Jan. 1967), 138–39; Madoyan, 188–89.

61. K. Muroeh, 38; al-'Aris, 177–82.

62. Al-'Aris, 111.

63. Nuqula al-Shawi, *Kitabat wa Dirasat* (Studies and Writings) (Beirut: Dar al-Farabi, n.d.), 172–74.

64. Mainly Wasila Dubuq (interviewed Jan. 27, 1997, Beirut) and Hannih Dib (interviewed Mar. 6, 1997, Ghaziyya, Lebanon).

65. Few leftist scholars who wrote historical evaluations of different phases of Communist activism in Lebanon made mention of women's issues and gendered dimensions of class. See, for example, Jacques Couland, "Nahwa Tarikh 'Ilmi lil-Haraka al-'Ummaliyya fi al-'Alam al-'Arabi" (Toward a Scientific History of the Labor Movement in the Arab World), *Al-Tariq* 38, no. 1 (Feb. 1979): 127–52; and I. Mustafa.

66. *Al-Shuyu'iyyun al-Lubnaniyyun wa Muhimmat al-Marhala al-Muqbila* (The Lebanese Communists and the Missions of the Coming Period) (Beirut: Manshurat al-Hizb al-Shuyu'i al-Lubnani, ca. 1969), 72–73.

67. Al-Hilu, 141, 150.

68. Ibid., 278. Salam was also known for his slogan "Siyasat al-hazim wa al-'azim" (The policy of firmness and determination), which summarized the Interior Ministry's outlook during his years of service.

69. Although the Bikfaya plant was a major branch of the Régie, the strike committee did not control it.

70. Quoted in *Al-Nahar,* June 30, 1946, 2.

71. Sabi' Khunaysir's traumatic experiences at the death of Warda, his fiancé, impacted his overall relationship with the management and augmented his rebelliousness. Wasila Dubuq interview, Jan. 27, 1997, Beirut. Dubuq was Warda's colleague and one of the leading women activists who clashed with the police during the 1946 strike.

72. *Al-Nahar,* June 30, 1946, 1.

73. Al-Buwari, 1:330.

74. Ibid., 1:324.

75. *Al-Bayraq,* June 29, 1946, 1.

76. Ibid., 2.

77. *Al-Nahar,* June 28, 1946, 1.

78. Gran, "The Failure of Social Theory," 8.

79. *Al-Bayraq,* June 30, 1946, 2.

80. Ibid., 1–2.

81. Fahim Qubain, *Crisis in Lebanon* (Washington, D.C.: Middle East Institute, 1961); Salibi, *The Modern History of Lebanon*; Michael Hudson, *The Precarious Republic: Political Modernization in Lebanon* (Boulder, Colo.: Westview Press, 1985); Malcolm Kerr, "Lebanese Views on the 1958 Crisis," *Middle East Journal* 15, no. 2 (spring 1969): 211–17; Jonathan Randal, *The Tragedy of Lebanon: Christian Warlords, Israeli Adventurers, and American Bunglers* (London: Hogarth Press, 1983); Helena Cobban, *The Making of Modern Lebanon* (London: Hutchinson, 1985).

82. Wasila Dubuq interview, Jan. 27, 1997, Beirut. Dubuq gave me a brief biography of Warda Butrus.

83. Ibid.

84. The Labor Front encompassed the unions of the commerce workers, bank employees, port employees, taxi drivers, and the railroad workers. Al-Buwari mentions that the URWE did not join the Labor Front or the GCFUWE. See al-Buwari, 1:218.

85. *Al-Nahar,* July 2, 1946, 2.

86. *Al-Nahar,* July 10, 1946, 2. For the intention to call for a general strike, see *Al-Bayraq,* July 8–9, 1946, 2. *Al-Bayraq* denounced the pretext Salam used to avoid payment for the strike days and pointed to the huge amount of revenues that poured into the treasury from the Régie's business, estimated yearly at 20 million Lebanese pounds. *Al-Bayraq* showed that the amount of revenues that could be lost by the government during strike was much larger than the amount of money the workers had asked for in compensation for the strike days. It concluded that it was not worthwhile for the government to continue in its intransigent position. Salam's position, however, emanated from the state's efforts to discipline and control labor struggles, a position that was not simply derived from their miscalculation of costs and revenues. See *Al-Bayraq,* July 10, 1946, 1.

87. Al-Buwari, 1:281.

88. *Al-Nahar,* July 2, 1946, 4. *Al-Bayraq* claimed that the government agreed to give compensation to Warda Butrus Ibrahim's family, not to take any punitive measures against the strikers, and to reinstate all the fired workers in their jobs. See *Al-Bayraq,* July 14, 1946, 2.

89. See the essay by Gebran Tueni, the chief editor of the newspaper *Al-Nahar,* in the June 29, 1946, issue, page 1.

90. Couland, *Al-Haraka al-Naqabiyya,* 416.

91. Goria, 64.

92. Quoted in ibid., 82 n. 31. The quotation is from a letter from Chapman Andrews, the British ambassador in Beirut, to Anthony Eden, the British secretary of state, on December 28, 1951.

93. The delegation of Régie workers that met with Sa'ib Salam consisted of four workingmen: Jean Tuwayni, Bahjat Nasif, 'Ali Nasir al-Husayni, and Edmund Faris. *Al-Nahar,* July 5, 1946, 2.

94. The number of temporary workers in 1947 was 350. See Samuell, 96.

95. See Julie M. Peteet, *Gender in Crisis: Women and the Palestinian Resistance Movement* (New York: Columbia Univ. Press, 1992); Lazreg, *The Eloquence of Silence;* and Valentine M. Moghadam, ed., *Gender and National Identity: Women and Politics in Muslim Societies* (London: Oxford Univ. Press and Zed Books, 1994).

96. Cherifa Bouatta, "Feminine Militancy: *Moudjahidates* during and after the Algerian War," in Moghadam, ed., *Gender and National Identity,* 23.

97. See Peteet, 147, 160–64.

98. *Wadad Brays vs. the Régie,* URWE case no. 827, Beirut, 1954, RégieURWE records, Hadath.

99. Andre Tuwayni, Ministry of Finance to the Ministry of Social Affairs, Feb. 1, 1952, URWE records, Hadath.

100. Ibid.

101. "The Administrative Law and Regulations of the Régie: 1979," n.d. (ca. 1979), 1, URWE records, Beirut. It was not until 1979 that a three months' period was stipulated in the labor law, after which an employer had either to keep the trainee permanently or to discharge her or him from work.

102. These associated benefits ranged from paid sick leave to weekly and yearly breaks, health benefits, transportation fees, a production bonus, a family allowance, wage increases, retirement plans, and other related issues.

103. The seventy cases I studied were classified into four basic categories: job permanency, retirement compensation and other allowances, promotion rights, and the correction of the birth date.

104. French High Commissioner, *Cahier de Charges du Monopole des Tabacs et Tombacs*, 1935, URWE records, Hadath.

105. *Council of Labor Arbitration v. the Régie*, the case of Murra Sulayman al-Murr, no case number, URWE records, Hadath, 1965.

106. Workers who did not smoke were entitled to receive the equivalent cash value of these cigarettes. This amount was added to their basic salary, thanks to the URWE's endeavors.

107. *'Alya Nasr al-Sayyah v. the Régie*, no case number, al-Khoury legal case records, Beirut, 1991.

108. *The Régie v. 'Alya Nasr al-Sayyah*, no case number, al-Khoury legal case records, Beirut, n.d. Al-Khoury, the Régie attorney, listed in his reply to al-Sayyah a number of factors that would normally substantiate a legal case. He stated that filing a claim in a timely manner and providing physical evidence in the form of official documents were essential in establishing a legal claim against the Régie. Numerous Régie workers lost their claims simply because they could not get their primary documents, which they had left behind in changing residence during the civil war. Abdul 'Aziz Harfush interview, July 4, 1995, Burj al-Barajina, Lebanon.

109. *The Régie v. 'Alya Nasr al-Sayyah*.

110. Couland, *Al-Haraka al-Naqabiyya*, 435.

4. Rural Displacement and Migration among the Régie Workers, 1950—1980

1. Salibi, *The Modern History of Lebanon*, 166–67; Longrigg, 178–79.

2. Salibi, *The Modern History of Lebanon*, 167.

3. Al-Buwari, 1:276–77, 2:107–8.

4. See Salibi, *The Modern History of Lebanon*, 187–88.

5. Hudson, 44–46.

6. There is a brief reference in *Hayat al-'Ummal* to the Régie's gender composition in the 1930s, denoting that "most" of the workforce was made up of women. No exact numbers were given or any further elaboration.

7. Dirani, Régietyped manuscript, Nov. 17, 1971, 50, Régie company records, Hadath. Dirani was a financial investigator commissioned by the Ministry of Finance to investigate the financial, commercial, and administrative conditions at the Régie, to suggest alternative plans to modernize the factories and marketing procedures, and to increase profits.

8. Husayn Subayti, the director of the industrial department at the Régie, described to me the configuration of the tobacco production process among the various Régie branches. Husayn Subayti interview, Mar. 11, 1997, Beirut. The workers' sectarian and gender distributions at these branches were deduced from Régie Personnel Department, "Listing du personnel par marticule, 1 octobre, 1981," Régie company records, Hadath.

9. By "workers," I mean the blue-collar laborers, and by "employees," I mean the white-collar staff.

10. I rounded up the figures to near one-tenth.

11. See Charles Issawi, "Economic Development and Liberalism in Lebanon," *Middle East Journal* 18, no. 3 (summer 1964), 288–89.

12. I briefly discuss the causes and outcomes of these strikes in chapter 6.

13. Suad Nur-al-Din asserts that the migration from South Lebanon to Beirut started out before Lebanon's independence in 1943 and intensified after the 1948 war between Arab countries and Israel. The impact of the 1948 war on the southerners was significant because many of them lost their jobs in Palestine or their lands on the Al-Hula Plain and, most important, because the shipping business shifted from the Haifa seaport to Beirut. See Suad Nur-al-Din, "Al-Nuzuh al-Sukkani mina al-Janub: Nazif Mustammir Munzu ma Qabla al-Istiqlal" (The Displacement of the Population from the South: A Movement That Started before Independence), *Al-Safir*, May 12, 2008, 8.

14. Edmund Asfour, "Industrial Development in Lebanon," *Middle East Economic Papers* (1955), 1. By 1960, the infant mortality rate in Lebanon was 7 percent (70 per 1,000 live births) in comparison to 13 percent (130 per 1,000) in Syria. Thus, despite the poor health conditions in rural Lebanon, the national health standards were steadily improving, which in turn signaled a greater population growth. See Alan Richards and John Waterbury, *A Political Economy of the Middle East: State, Class, and Economic Development* (Boulder, Colo.: Westview Press, 1990), 106. With respect to this work, I have utilized mostly its statistical tables, which the authors reproduced or put together on the basis of a large number of statistical reports provided by the World Bank, the Food and Agriculture Organization, and the United Nation Children's Fund on the Middle East, among others.

15. Richards and Waterbury, 106.

16. Although there were no official censuses for the Lebanese population from 1932 until 1970, a few scholars have attempted to come up with approximate estimates of the size of sectarian groups. See Hudson; Richards and Waterbury, 97. In 1974, Imam Musa al-Sadr provided the following census data: Shi'ite, 970,000; Sunni, 690,000; Maronite, 496,000; Druze, 342,000; Greek Orthodox, 230,000; and Catholic, 213,000. Cited in Shafiq al-Rayyis, *Al-Tahaddi al-Kabir: 1975–1976* (The Big Challenge) (Beirut: Dar al-Masira, 1978), 184.

17. Asfour, 2.

18. Ibid. Asfour relies on monographs on the national income of Lebanon provided by Albert Y. Badre and the staff of the Economic Research Institute of the American University of Beirut.

19. 'Adnan Fahs, *Al-Zuruf al-Iqtisadiyya lil-Harb al-Ta'ifiyya al-Lubnaniyya* (The Economic Circumstances of the Lebanese War) (Beirut: Dar al-Nahar, 1979), 35–41. Fahs emphasizes the government's failure to implement agricultural plans, such as the Litani Plan to improve agricultural output in Lebanon and prevent large-scale emigration in the 1950s.

20. Asfour, 3. See also Fahs, 44–46.

21. Asfour, 1; Fahs, 47.

22. Churchill, "Village Life of the Central Beqa' Valley of Lebanon," 8. Charles Churchill was an associate professor of public health and statistics at the American University of Beirut during the 1950s. In 1955, the School of Public Health at the university started a field-training program for public-health students in the Biqa' Valley. The program directors realized that in order for the

students to gain experience in the region's health problems, elementary data about its people must be acquired. Thus, Churchill started a census based on a sample of thirteen villages, eight of which were surveyed in 1955 and five in 1956.

23. Richards and Waterbury, 150, table 6.4.

24. *Al-Qadiyya al-Zira'iyya fi Lubnan fi Daw' al-Mariksiyya* (The Agrarian Question in Lebanon from a Marxist Perspective) (Beirut: Manshurat al-Hizb al-Shuyu'i al-Lubnani, ca. 1973–74).

25. Ibid., 21.; Fahs, 33.

26. Fahs, 33. Communist Party records give lower daily wage rates for men and women in the early 1970s. They show that men's average daily wages were seven Lebanese pounds, the women's three to four pounds, and the children's one and a half. See *Al-Qadiyya al-Zira'iyya*, 104.

27. Fahs, 69, 93.

28. See Nabil Khalifa, *Al-Shi'a fi Lubnan: Thawrat al-Dimughrafiyya wa al-Hirman* (The Shi'ites in Lebanon: The Revolution of Demography and Deprivation) (Beirut: Markaz Byblus lil-Dirasat wal-Abhath, 1984), 47.

29. Ibid., 48–50; *Al-Qadiyya al-Zira'iyya* (the 1974 survey), 214–21.

30. *Al-Qadiyya al-Zira'iyya* (the 1974 survey), 214–21. The Biqa' region was more than 41 percent of the total size of Lebanon. The Biqa' Plain alone was 170,000 hectares (420 million acres), or approximately 52 percent of the total agricultural area in Lebanon. Most of the fertile lands were owned by a handful of families such as the Rizks, Bustruses, Eddis, and Skafs. The agricultural products of the Biqa' composed 30 percent of the total agricultural production in Lebanon. In the 1960s, the total Biqa' population was 368,000; of this total, 65 percent lived in villages and therefore relied completely on agriculture, and the rest lived in towns. *Al-Qadiyya al-Zira'iyya*, 104–5, 166–67, 223.

31. Lazreg, *The Eloquence of Silence*, 162.

32. Richards and Waterbury, 264, table 10.1.

33. Ibid., 265.

34. Fahs, 29.

35. Ibid.

36. See Roger Owen, *Migrant Workers in the Gulf* (London: Minority Rights Group, 1992), cited in Richards and Waterbury, 382.

37. Samih Farsoun, "Student Protests and the Coming Crisis in Lebanon," *MERIP Reports* 19 (1973), 11–12. Many workers had appropriated the goals of the Palestinian resistance movement to push for social and economic reforms in Lebanon. They relied on the Palestinian presence to launch an effective opposition against the government.

38. Al-Buwari, 2:297–98.

39. N. Khalifa, 69–71.

40. Ibid.

41. Community studies were almost absent from the works of the social scientists who studied Lebanon. For this part of my study, I relied on what the daily newspapers, especially *Al-Safir*, reported on concerning the social circumstances and hardships of the immigrants in the Beiruti suburbs.

42. The population of the southern suburb, an area that did not exceed twenty-five square kilometers, had multiplied 166 times in forty-seven years (from 1928 to 1975). See Ilyas 'Abbud, "Dahiyat al-Muhhajjarin" (The Suburb of the Forced Migrants), *Al-Safir* (Aug. 4 and 5, 1980), 7. 'Abbud's study unfortunately does not provide specific figures of population increases between 1965 and 1975, which might help us locate the particular factors leading to this increase during each decade or so.

43. Ibid.

44. Ibid.

45. William Persen, "Lebanese Economic Development since 1950," *Middle East Journal* 12 (1958), 277–78. Persen studied in Beirut and worked for financial institutions there from 1953 to 1957. He integrated a great deal of statistical data on Lebanese economic development between 1950 and 1956 based on the Lebanese government's *Bulletin Statistique Timestriel* and the U.S. Department of Commerce's *The World Trade Information Service*. No further information is provided about these sources. Persen utilized the figures and tables in these sources to propagate the view that Lebanon's economic prosperity stemmed from its geographical and cultural advantages. These advantages were defined by the country's "Christian outlook," which meant "that it was less tied to the cultural deadweight of hundreds of years of lack of change." Persen was clearly driven by the need to extol the virtues of the Lebanese state and its biases, thus overlooking the serious political and economic setbacks it witnessed as a result of policies impelled by such an outlook.

46. See also Richards and Waterbury, 74. Table 3.11 assesses sectoral distribution of the labor force in the Middle East (in percentages) from 1950 to 1980. In 1960, the highest percentage of workers could be found in the service sector (39 percent). Agricultural and industrial workers formed 38 and 23 percent of the total workforce, respectively. The table shows a 17 percent decline in the agricultural workforce between 1950 and 1960, and a 3 percent increase in the industrial workforce, in contrast to a 14 percent increase in the number of those working in the service sector.

47. There is also a lack of statistics on illegal workers, especially Palestinian refugees who in certain industrial settings made up the majority of the labor force.

48. During the first three months of 1960 alone, about twenty labor strikes erupted in Lebanon. See Issawi, "Economic Development," 285.

49. Ibid.

50. Most of the money generated from the financial sector was reinvested in it. Moreover, only a small amount of the gross national product was generated from industry and agriculture.

51. Unfortunately, we do not have a geographic breakdown of Régie employment before 1968 to assess the extent to which these shifts in geographic-sectarian variables are reflected in the Régie workforce.

52. Basim al-Jisr, *Fouad Chihab: Dhalika al-Majhul* (Fouad Chihab: The Unknown) (Beirut: Sharikat al-Matbu'at lil-Tawzi' wa al-Nashr, 1988), 84–85.

53. For a recent critique of Shihabism and Chihism, see Albert Daghir, "Dawr al-Dawla al-Tanmawi: Mata Tajawuz al-Chihiyya" (The Developmental Role of the State: Beyond Chihism), "Qadaya" section, *Al-Nahar* (June 12, 2008): 3.

54. The Shihabist government recommended a formula for a fair representation of the Lebanese sects in the Régie's employment policy; see table 16 in chapter 6.

55. "RÉGIE CO-INTÉRESSÉE LIBANISE DES TÂBÂC ET TOMBÂCS. ASSEMBLÉE GÉNÉRALE ORDINAIRE DES ACTIONAIRES du 15 Juin 1966. Rapports présentés par le Conseil d'Administration et les Commissaires de Surveillance. Exercise 1965," 5; "ASSEMBLÉE GÉNÉRALE ORDINAIRE DES ACTIONAIRES du 8 Juin 1967. Rapports présentés par le Conseil d'Administration et les Commissaires de Surveillance. Exercise 1966," 5; "ASSEMBLÉE GÉNÉRALE ORDINAIRE DES ACTIONAIRES du 30 Mai 1968. Rapports présentés par le Conseil d'Administration et les Commissaires de Surveillance. Exercise 1967," 5; "ASSEMBLÉE GÉNÉRALE ORDINAIRE DES ACTIONAIRES du 26 Mai 1969. Rapports présentés par le Conseil d'Administration et les Commissaires de Surveillance. Exercise 1968," 5; and "ASSEMBLÉE GÉNÉRALE ORDINAIRE DES ACTIONAIRES du 26 Mai 1970. Rapports présentés par le Conseil d'Administration et les Commissaires de Surveillance. Exercise 1969" (annual reports of the Régie Board of Directors and Budget Commission presented to the General Assembly on June 15, 1966; June 8, 1967; May 30, 1968; May 26, 1969 and May 26, 1970), Jacques Dagher's private collection, Beirut.

56. Michel Chiha, *Politique intérieure* (Beirut: Éditions du Trident, 1964), 261–63, 242, 90, 257–58. For a critical study of Chiha's history and ideas, see Michelle Hartman and Alessandro Olsaretti, "The First Boat and the First Oar: Inventions of Lebanon in the Writings of Michel Chiha," *Radical History Review* 86, no. 1 (2003): 37–65. And for a thorough and critical study of Chiha's thoughts, see 'Amil, *Madkhal ila Nadq,* 141. 'Amil rightly criticizes Chiha's notion of "sectarian balance" by highlighting the fact that Chiha designed the legislative authority as the place to achieve the sectarian balance. Moreover, 'Amil points out that the sectarian balance formula did not also apply to the state's executive power, which remained a monopoly for the Maronite bourgeoisie. He concludes that maintaining a sectarian balance in the legislative authorities does not mean an "equal management of the state," but rather a form of hegemony that the Maronite bourgeoisie enjoyed beginning with the creation of Lebanon in 1946. The executive power, according to 'Amil, dominated the legislative power because the Constitution gave more privileges to the Christian president of the republic than to other branches of state powers. This hegemonic reality remained intact until 1989, when the Ta'if Agreement mildly modified this distribution of powers at the expense of the Maronite president of the republic.

57. In the 1970s and 1980s, a host of Lebanese thinkers and scholars, among them Elie Salem and Samir Khalaf, articulated a more complex version of the Chihian notion of the primacy of racial-ethnic reality in Lebanon. Salem, who served as the minister of foreign and expatriate affairs from 1982 to 1988, and Khalaf, a Lebanese sociologist, attributed the persistence of sectarian and family affiliations to the fact that Lebanon in principle consisted of disparate communities with diverse traditions. See Elie Salem, *Modernization Without a Revolution: Lebanon's Experience* (Bloomington: Indiana Univ. Press, 1973), 5, 6, and Samir Khalaf, *Lebanon's Predicament* (New York: Columbia Univ. Press, 1987), 115.

58. Michel Chiha, *Propos d'économie libanaise* (Beirut: Éditions du Trident, 1965), 335, 39, 281.

59. Ibid., 324.

60. Yusuf al-Sawda, *Fi Sabil Lubnan* (For the Sake of Lebanon) (Beirut: Manshurat Lahd Khatir, 1988), 223–28; Hikmat Albert Haddad, *Lubnan al-Kabir* (Greater Lebanon) (Beirut: Dar Nazir Abdu, 1996), 12, 47.

61. *Al-Hizb al-Taqadumi al-Ishtiraki: Rubu' Qarin mina al-Nidal* (The Progressive Socialist Party: A Quarter Century of Struggle) (Beirut: Dar al-Bayan, 1974), 135–52.

62. Kamal Salibi, *Crossroads to Civil War: Lebanon 1958–1976* (New York: Caravan Books, 1976), 2; Fahim Qubain, *Crisis in Lebanon* (Washington, D.C.: Middle East Institute, 1961), 35–37, 45.

63. Qubain, 53. See also Farid El Khazen, *The Breakdown of the State in Lebanon, 1967–1976* (Cambridge, Mass.: Harvard Univ. Press, 2000), 6; Samir Khalaf, *Civil and Uncivil Violence in Lebanon: A History of Internationalization of Communal Conflict* (New York: Columbia Univ. Press, 2002), 204–31; and Ghassan Tueni, *Une guerre pour les autres* (Paris: J. C. Lattes, 1985).

64. The Rahbani brothers, 'Asi and Mansur, were mainstream playwright-musicians who composed more than twenty musicals beginning in the late 1950s. The Rahbanis' songs and musicals captured the Lebanese people's imagination and memories and became cultural classics. Most of these musicals were performed in Ba'labak and Beirut and were broadcast by Lebanese public radio and television stations. Their overarching theme was that if the people learned wisdom, they could make Lebanon stronger and immune from outside challenges. Fairuz (Suad Haddad), "Lebanon's ambassador to the stars," was the major singer and actress in these musicals, whom the Lebanese consider a "desexed goddess, an undeniably virtuous prophet." See Elise Salem, "Imagining Lebanon Through Rahbani Musicals," *Al-Jadid* 5, no. 29 (fall 1999): 4–6.

65. Reconciliation was the concluding theme of the Rahbani Brothers' musicals, especially *Jisr al-Qamar* (1962), *Al-Layl wa al-Qindil* (1963), *Baya' al-Khawatim* (1964), *Jibal al-Suwwan* (1969), *Ya'ish Ya'ish* (1970), and *al-Mahatta* (1973). See Nabil Abu Murad, *Al-Akhawan Rahbani: Hayat wa Masrah, Khasa'is al-Kitaba al-Dramiyya* (The Rahbani Brothers, Life and Theater: The Characteristics of Playwriting) (Beirut: Dar Amjad lil-Nashr wa al-Tawzi', 1990), 234, 238.

66. Umar al-Zi'inni (1895–1961) stands out as the pioneer of the sarcastic songs that targeted the government, supported the poor, and called for unity against tyranny. His impact on numerous popular singers, playwrights, composers of musicals, and talk show hosts was obvious. For a study of al-Zi'nni, see Al-Zi'inni al-Saghir, *Umar al-Zi'inni Moliere al-Sharq* (Umar al-Zi'inni, the Moliere of the Orient) (Beirut: Mu'asasat Jawad lil-Tiba'a wa al-Taswir, 1980). Shushu (Hassan 'ala' al-Din) (1939–75), "the sarcastic philosopher," continued in al-Zi'inni's footsteps. However, in the early 1970s, Shushu created what came to be known as Masrah al-Sha'ib (the People's Theater). His plays did not spare any Lebanese government or political leader, focused on corruption and nepotism, and constantly exposed the government's class-based socioeconomic policies. For a study on Shushu and his plays, see Faruq al-Jammal, *Shushu: "Akh Ya Baladna"* (Shushu: "Alas, Our Country") (Beirut: Dar al-Afaq al-Jadida, 1981). The golden era of this genre was the 1970s, when Lebanon witnessed the rise of revolutionary singers such as Marcel Khalifah, Khalid Habir, Ahmad Qa'bur, and Butrus Ruhana, as well as playwrights and actors such as Roger 'Assaf, Masrah

al-Hakawati, Rafiq 'Ali Ahmad, Ya'qub Shidrawi, and Ziad Rahbani (the son of 'Asi Rahbani and Fairuz)—to name but a few. Poets were no less important, including 'Abbas Baydun, Khalil Hawi (d. 1982), Shawqi Bzay', Muhammad Abdallah, Mahmud Darwish (Palestinian), Samih al-Qasim (Palestinian), Tawfiq Zayyad (Palestinian), Nizar Qabbani (Syrian, d. 1998), and Muzzafar al-Nuwwab (Iraqi). For a study on the cultural life of Beirut in this period, see Abidu Basha, *Bayt al-Nar: Al-Zaman al-Di'i' fi al-Masrah al-Lubnani* (The Fire House: The Missing Period in the Lebanese Theater) (Beirut: Riyad el-Rayess, 1995), and Samir Kasir, *Histoire de Beyrouth* (Paris: Fayard, 2003).

67. Ziad Rahbani, *Nazil al-Surur; Bil'nisbi la Bukra Shu? Filim Amiriki Tawil; and Shi Fashil* (Inn of Happiness; So, What about Tomorrow? Long American Film; and What a Failure (Beirut: Mukhtarat, 1994), 200–203.

68. Arab composers' initial task was to separate the Arab music from the Ottoman and European influence, a task championed first by Sayid Darwish and later by Muhammad Abdul Wahhab, Muhammad al-Qasabji, Zakariyya Ahmad, and others. Then in 1932 an international conference was held in Cairo to discuss Arab music, during which the conferees agreed to prohibit the use of any European musical instrument in Arabic music. In the 1940s, with the independence of the Levantine states, it became inappropriate for the music of these states, especially Lebanon and Syria, to remain an echo of Egyptian music. In this historical context, we can then locate the beginning of the Rahbani school of music and its contribution to the country's national identity. This beginning also was supported by the public radio station, which started a policy of "lebanonizing" the wording of songs by changing it from the Egyptian dialect. For more discussion on this topic, see Ilyas Sahhab, "'Asi al-Rahbani: Al-Khalfiyya al-Tarikhiyya wa al-Mukawwinat al-Shakhsiyya wa al-Bidayat" ('Asi al-Rahbani: The Historical and Personal Background and the Beginnings), *Al-Tariq* 45, no. 6 (Dec. 1986), 216–17.

69. Abu Murad, 78.

70. Rahbani Brothers, *Mawsim al-'Izz* (Beirut, 1960).

71. Ibid.

72. Numerous interviews I conducted with workingwomen and men at the Régie in 1997 confirmed this information.

73. Ahmad Abu Sa'd, *Mu'jam Asma' al-Usar wa al-Ashkhas wa Lamahat min Tarikh al-'A'ilat* (The Dictionary of Names of Families and Persons and Glimpses from the Histories of the Families) (Beirut: Dar al-'Ilim lil-Malayin, 1997), 312.

74. These figures were deduced from the 1954 and 1969 censuses, Régie company records, Hadath.

75. Couland, *Al-Haraka al-Naqabiyya*, 111–14, 150; Labaki; and Hakim, "Industry," which treats the history of Mount Lebanon during the last decades of the Ottoman Empire as the history of modern Lebanon without a serious study of the history of the provinces that were annexed to Lebanon in 1920, a point I discuss in chapter 2.

76. Dubar and Nasr, 7.

77. Dipesh Chakrabarty, "Class Consciousness and the Indian Working Class: Dilemmas of Marxist Historiography," *Journal of Asian and African studies* 23, nos. 1–2 (1988), 28. Subalternists of the this period argued that the policy for the recruitment of industrial workers in India was based on ethnic considerations, caste relations, and village ties. They claimed that working groups, distinguished by religion and language, engaged in several communal riots. These assertions suggest that "Third World" workers' aspirations rarely served their immediate class interests.

78. Rifa'at Abou-El-Haj brought to my attention the process of "social utility" and its dynamic manifestation within a particular historical context. See Abou-El-Haj, "The Social Uses of the Past," 185–201.

5. Women Negotiate Family and Work: 1950–1997

1. See Donato, 75.

2. 'Abd al-Salam Shu'ayb, "Al-Mar'a al-'Amila fil-Qanun al-Lubnani" (The Workingwoman in Lebanese Law), in *Al-Mar'a wa al-'Amal fi Lubnan*, 15–18. The first legal document focused on agricultural workers and housemaids but devoted no special articles to women.

3. MAE, Paris, Syrie-Liban, 1930–40, "Qanun Yakhtas bi Istikhdam al-Awlad wa al-Nisa' fi al-A'mal al-Sina'iyya" (A Law Pertains to the Employment of Children and Women in Industrial Labor), Apr. 17, 1935, vol. 2921, 1–8.

4. 'Abd al-Salam Shu'ayb, 18–19. Even though the code offered some protection for employees and workers against arbitrary dismissal, it excluded (Article 7) agricultural workers and domestic workers working in houses and state offices, the overwhelming majority of whom were women.

5. Ibid., 21–22. Even though the state signed several international and intra-Arab agreements to protect workers rights and promote women's well-being at the workplace, few articles in such agreements were integrated into the national body of labor law.

6. Ibid. In the absence of data, it is difficult to delineate how workingwomen reacted to this class bias and the paternalism inherent in these laws or whether they were aware of the existence of these characteristics and their ramifications.

7. Ibid. Women drawn mostly from the middle and upper classes who ended up working in administrative positions, art, music, and theater were exempt from these laws.

8. Ibid., 23–24. See also Ghurayyib, "Al-Mar'a wa al'Amal," 330.

9. 'Abd al-Salam Shu'ayb, 19.

10. Lorfing and Abu al-Nasr, 59.

11. Quoted in 'Abd al-Salam Shu'ayb, 26.

12. Ibid., 27.

13. Several women tobacco workers whom I interviewed mentioned how ill they became as a result of their work at the Régie; see also Lorfing and Abu al-Nasr, 62. Although the latter source provides evidence for the late 1970s, it is nonetheless indicative of how little labor law has developed in the direction of implementing just work conditions for women.

14. Ibid., 60–61. Even in the late 1970s, many employers neglected state laws and continued to overlook women's maternity leave.

15. 'Abd al-Salam Shu'ayb, 35–36.

16. Of the ten factories Lorfing and Abu al-Nasr surveyed in suburban Beirut, only one provided a day care center, and that was because 90 percent of its workers were women. See Lorfing and Abu al-Nasr, 59.

17. Minutes of the URWE meetings, Sept. 24, 1971, 190, URWE records, Hadath, and Wasila Dubuq interview, Jan. 1, 1997, Beirut.

18. Clark and Lorfing, 1–2.

19. République Libanaise, Ministère du Plan, 163, table 14.12, "The Distribution of Female Workers According to Occupation."

20. Irene Lorfing, "Women Workers in Lebanese Industry," in El-Sanabary, ed., 183.

21. Marwan Iskandar and Elias Baroudi, "Industry," in *The Lebanese Economy in 1981–82*, edited by Marwan Iskandar and Elias Baroudi (Beirut: Middle East Economic Consultants, 1982), 12–16.

22. Clark and Lorfing, 10, 12–13.

23. Ibid., 10–11.

24. Ibid.; see also République Libanaise, Ministère du Plan.

25. Henry 'Azzam and Diana Shaib, *The Women Left Behind: A Study of the Wives of Lebanese Migrant Workers in the Oil Rich Countries of the Region* (Beirut: Work Employment Program Research, International Labor Organization, 1980), 1–3.

26. Clark and Lorfing, 38.

27. All of these examples come from ibid., 25–37.

28. Huda Zurayk, "Dawr al-Mar'a fi al-Tanmiyya al-Ijtima'iyya al-Iqtisadiyya fi al-Buldan al-'Arabiyya" (Women's Role in Social-Economic Growth in Arab Countries), in *Al-Mar'a al-'Arabiyya: Bayn Thuqul al-Waqi' wa Tatallu'at al-Taharrur* (Arab Women: Between Reality and Emancipation) (Beirut: Markaz Dirasat al-Wihda al-'Arabiyya, 1999), 98–99.

29. 'Azzam, "Al-Mar'a al-'Arabiyya," 57–58.

30. Zurayk, "Dawr al-Mar'a fi al-Tanmiyya al-Ijtima'iyya," 91–92, 101. See also Huda Zurayk and Haroutune K. Armenian, eds., *Beirut 1984: A Population and Health Profile* (Beirut: American Univ. of Beirut, 1985).

31. Henry 'Azzam related these figures on the basis of documented data produced at a United Nations international conference convened in Copenhagen, July 14–30, 1980. See 'Azzam, "Al-Mar'a al-'Arabiyya," 57.

32. Ibid., 40, 45–46.

33. Ghurayyib, "Al-Mar's wa al'Amal," 328–32.

34. Clark and Lorfing, 46.

35. Ibid.

36. Lorfing and Abu al-Nasr, 65.

37. Régie Personnel Department, "Listing du Personnel par Matricule," Oct. 1, 1981, Régie company records, Hadath.

38. Several Régie women workers whom I interviewed expressed these concerns.

39. *Al-Thaqafa al-Wataniyya,* no. 17 (Sept. 15, 1974), cited in al-Shami, 227 n. 74.

40. Lorfing, 185.

41. Lorfing and Abu al-Nasr, 55.

42. Clark and Lorfing, 40.

43. The only extant copy of these laws is that of 1979. The Régie's employment policy, however, was issued long before 1979. The first official French law for the Régie did not include any specification for employment except for one provision stating that 98 percent of the workforce was to be recruited from the local population. See "The Administrative Law and Regulations of the Régie: 1979," 2, URWE records, Hadath.

44. It would have been useful to compare the age configuration of the Régie workingwomen in 1969 (see table 8 in chapter 4) to that of their counterparts in all the Lebanese industrial sectors during 1970, but there was a discrepancy in the time period.

45. Lorfing, 183–84.

46. Lorfing and Abu al-Nasr, 54.

47. Al-Lajna al-Wataniyya li-Shu'un al-Mar'a al-Lubnaniyya, *Waqi' al-Mar'a al-Lubnaniyya, 1970–1995, Arqam wa Ma'ani* (The Lebanese Women, 1970–1995: Figures and Significance), vol. 1 (Beirut: Al-Lajna al-Wataniyya li-Shu'un al-Mar'a al-Lubnaniyya, 1997), 33. This source does not provide a statistical table.

48. Evelyn Richards, "Al-Mar'a wa al-'Amal fi Lubnan" (Women and Work in Lebanon), in Ghurayyib, *Adwa' 'ala al-Haraka,* 335.

49. George Hubayqa interview, Mar. 3, 1997, Hadath, Lebanon. Hubayqa presumably masterminded this plan and prepared the report on the development of the national tobacco production during the war years, 1975 to 1991.

50. Wasila Dubuq interview, Jan. 1, 1997, Beirut. See also Gabi Tabrani, "Al-Naqabat Lam Ta'ud Lil-Rijal: Al-Mar'a Aydan Asbahat Naqabiyya" (Trade Unions Are No Longer for Men: Women Also Became Unionists), *Al-Hawadith,* no. 933 (Sept. 1974): 73–74.

51. From the results of a questionnaire I gave to 356 Régie workers in 1997: 286 female and 69 male.

52. Sa'id Hayik, Régie Personnel Department, "The Retirement and Work Leave Census, 1935–1995," Hadath factory, 1995, Régie company records, Hadath.

53. Youssef, 30, 38.

54. See Hammam, "Women and Industrial Work in Egypt," 62; Layne, 22; and Y. Sayigh, "Management-Labour Relations," 523, 534. Sayigh's work is too theoretical to yield useful findings, and he used Western criteria as the ideal standards.

55. Kandiyoti, "Islam and Patriarchy," 23–24.

56. Ibid., 27–28. I tried here to focus on "women's strategies" as an active and historically developing entity that Deniz Kandiyoti proposed for an adequate analysis of male exploitation and material dominance of women's labor.

57. Nayfa F. interview, Mar. 9, 1997, Hadath. All details about Farhan come from this interview.

58. Muna M. interview, Mar. 27, 1997, Hadath. All details about Mawrid come from this interview.

59. Some of the administrators at the Régie and many workingmen I interviewed, in particular those who protested the replacement of male labor by female labor in 1954, related these observations to me.

60. From an interview with a leading male Régie worker who participated in this protest and preferred to keep his identity anonymous, January 1997, Hadath.

61. Régie Personnel Department, "Listing du personnel par matricule," 1981, Régie company records, Hadath.

62. Régie personnel department's "Listing du personnel par patricule" of 1981 (Régie company records) did not provide the corresponding Régie department for more than half of the workers belonging to the Ja'ja' family.

63. Ibid.

64. Samir Khalaf, "Lebanese Labor Unions: Some Comparative Structural Features," *Middle East Economic Papers* (1968), 132.

65. Guilain Denoeux, *Urban Unrest in the Middle East: A Comparative Study of Informal Networks in Egypt, Iran, and Lebanon* (Albany: State Univ. of New York Press, 1993), 3. Denoeux examines the growing notion among scholars of Third World urbanization that rapid urbanization of Middle Eastern cities intensified the effectiveness of informal networks, which were responsible for aborting any sociopolitical upheaval. Denoeux adopts a theoretical framework similar to Samir Khalaf's.

66. Suad Joseph, "Working-Class Women's Networks in a Sectarian State: A Political Paradox," *American Ethnologist* 10 (Feb. 1983), 16.

67. Ibid., 4.

68. Thomas B. Stauffer, "The Industrial Worker," in *Social Forces in the Middle East,* edited by Sydney Nettleton Fisher (New York: Cornell Univ. Press, 1955), 88–89. Although this article is old, it is among the few available representative sources of the general approach that social scientists of the time took toward the interplay of familial and sectarian loyalties at the industrial workplace. Stauffer denied the possibility of the slightest comparison between Western and Eastern labor categories. He believed that the "motives and satisfactions of workers in two societies may be only very vaguely comparable, and any attempt to reduce the data of the two systems to comparable tables may cast more shadow than light, introducing obscurities of method into our understanding, when there are none in our subject" (84). My own findings and conclusions refute such claims.

69. Najla J. interview, Feb. 6, 1997, Ashrafiyya, Lebanon. All details about Najla Ja'ja' come from this interview.

70. Georgette H., interview, Mar. 21, 1997, Hadath; Georgette N., interview, Mar. 23, 1997, Hadath; Samia 'A., interview, Mar. 5, 1997, Hadath; Theresa R., interview, Mar. 4, 1997, Bikfaya,

Lebanon; Wahiba W., interview, Mar. 17, 1997, Hadath; Haniya A., interview, Mar. 11, 1997, Hadath; Huriya ʻI., interview, Jan. 30, 1997, Hadath; Louisa G. interview, Feb. 6, 1997, Hadath.

71. Inʻam A. interview, Feb. 20, 1997, Hadath. All details about Inʻam A. come from this interview.

6. "Qatiʻ al-Arzaq min Qatiʻ al-Aʻnaq": Gendered Boundaries and Class, Tobacco Women's Struggle, 1960–1965

1. A number of newspapers related that workingwomen "invaded the administrative building in Hadath," expelling the high-ranking administrative employees from their offices and locking them out of the company's main gates. See *Al-Hayat,* Mar. 30, 1965, 7. These administrative employees evidently favored compliance with the URWE's decision to end the strike and expressed only marginal support for the women's demands. In reaction, the latter forced them to leave their offices and express solidarity with the strike. See also *Al-Nahar,* Mar. 6, 7, and 19, 1965, all p. 6; *Al-Hayat,* Mar. 16 and 30, 1965, both p. 7. "Upper stratum" refers to the male white-collar employees who staffed the Régie's administration and received the highest salaries in the company. Except for Iqbal Dughan, who was the first woman to occupy an administrative post in 1967, all supervisory offices in several production departments and factories were given to men. During confrontations between workers and the Régie, these employees almost always sided with the management. In my opinion, this upper stratum conformed to what is known as a "labor aristocracy," as described by Eric Hobsbawm in *Labouring Men: Studies in the History of Labour* (New York: Weidenfeld and Nicolson, 1964), 272–316. See also Iqbal Dughan inteview, Jan. 28, 1997, Hadath, Lebanon.

2. I explained in a previous chapter that I use the term *employees* to refer to the Régie administrative staff—in other words, the white-collar workers in the high administrative ranks. I distinguish this group from the blue-collar workers.

3. See Ramkrishna Mukherjee, "Illusion and Reality: A Review of Ranjit Guha," *Sociological Bulletin* 37, nos. 1–2 (Mar.–Sept. 1988), 129.

4. See Chakrabarty, "Labor History and the Politics of Theory," 332.

5. Al-Buwari, 2:183. Al-Buwari saw the labor protests of the 1960s as a laborers' renaissance and noted that the workers had formed a full-fledged class.

6. Couland, *Al-Haraka al-Naqabiyya,* 445–48.

7. Al-Buwari, 2:26, 120, 141, 175–76.

8. Ibid.; *Al-Thaqafa al-Wataniyya,* May 12, 1960, 6, and June 8, 1961, 9.

9. The Régie workforce in 1963 totaled 3,281. Régie Personnel Department, "Size and Salaries of the Régie Working Force, 1959–1972," n.d., Régie company records, Hadath.

10. *Al-Thaqafa al-Wataniyya,* May 17, 1963, 1. This weekly labor periodical depicted the working conditions and the gender composition of the Régie workforce in 1963 and covered news about the Lebanese labor movement. It was the major organ of several labor unions, syndicates, and federations, especially the leftist National Confederation of Labor Unions (Al-Ittihad al-Watani

lil-Naqabat). The periodical's reports unfortunately lacked elaborate or quantitative data on the percentage of employees and laborers or differences in salaries among various categories of workers. The "thirteenth-month bonus" refers to when in 1962 the Régie granted its permanent labor force a production reward equivalent to one month's salary. The company considered this reward separate from the base salary.

11. Ibid., 1–3. In 1963, *Al-Thaqafa al-Wataniyya* published a biographical account written during the same year by an anonymous author who referred to himself as "'Amil Tabigh." This account allows us to view the 1963 strikers closely.

12. Ibid., 3.

13. In 1963, the workers demanded another production bonus, a "fourteenth-month bonus," owing to a marked increase in their production and the company's profits.

14. *Al-Thaqafa al-Wataniyya*, June 13, 1963, 1.

15. *Al-Hayat*, Mar. 27, 1965, 7.

16. *Al-Hayat*, Mar. 30, 1965, 7.

17. Ibid.

18. *Al-Nahar*, Mar. 7, 1965, 6, and Mar. 26, 1965, 6.

19. There were nine Zu'aytirs, a Shi'i family, working at the Régie in 1954, a number that grew to seventy-five in 1969, thus turning into the largest family cluster. A similar increase was evident among the Maronite Sab'ali, Khuri, Sawaya, and Ja'ja' families. See chapter 4.

20. Najla J. interview, Feb. 6, 1997, Ashrafiyya, Lebanon; Wasila Dubuq interview, Jan. 27, 1997, Beirut; and Fatima N. interview, Feb. 6, 1997, Shiyyah, Lebanon.

21. Sa'id Hayik, Régie Personnel Department, "Retirement and Work Leave Census, 1935–1995," 1995, Régie company records, Hadath.

22. "Vente annuelle de produits manufactures," Record Group 2, Jacques Dagher's private collection, Beirut.

23. *Al-Nahar*, July 11, 1963, 6.

24. *Al-Nahar*, Aug. 10, 1963, 6.

25. *Al-Nahar*, Aug. 17, 1963, 6.

26. In a report evaluating the year's labor agitations and conflicts, *Al-Nahar* discussed the development of the labor crisis at the Régie from June until October 1963. See *Al-Nahar*, Oct. 31, 1963, 5–6.

27. Shihab had risen to power following the 1958 revolt against Chamoun's government, which he accused of forming a corrupt oligarchy that exploited the public sectors of the economy and that nurtured the interests of a bourgeois coterie of businessmen, bankers, and entrepreneurs. Shihab attempted to curb nepotism and corruption and to implement rationalized administrative practices by staffing the state bureaucracy with qualified and educated employees. The Shihabist reforms, however, had marginal effects and failed to overcome sectarianism and tribalism, which designated a specific number of posts for each religious community in each particular profession. In other words, the share of each sectarian group—Maronite, Shi'ite, Sunnite—in the political and public administration did not change. Instead, the qualifications of the candidates eligible for occupying

these posts were amended. See Waddah Sharara, *Al-Silm al-Ahli al-Barid: Lubnan, al-Mujtama' wa al-Dawla, 1964–1967* (The Cold Civil War: Lebanese Society and State), 2 vols. (Beirut: Ma'had al-Inma' al-'Arabi, 1980).

28. Jacques Dagher interview, Jan. 28, 1997, Ba'abda, Lebanon. Dagher claimed that it was easier to find and hire Maronite and Shi'ite workers than Druze or Protestants, so the Régie had to wait months and sometimes years before employing or promoting workers from one sect, however qualified, until an equivalent number of workers from another sect was secured. The merit-sect formula also prevented workers from obtaining employment at the Régie or from being promoted if they belonged to a religious sect whose numbers were in excess of the allocated percentage.

29. *Beirut Daily Star,* Mar. 30, 1965, 1; *Al-Nahar,* Apr. 6, 1965, 5.

30. In addition, the pledge stated that the promotion for the forty workers would be postponed until such time when the whole issue of permanency could be examined. *Al-Thaqafa al-Wataniyya,* June 13, 1963, 1.

31. Therese H. interview, Mar. 18, 1997, Hadath.

32. *Al-Thaqafa al-Wataniyya,* July 11, 1963, 5.

33. Ibid.

34. Régie management refused to promote the workers and threatened to close the factories to penalize them for their rebelliousness. Thus, it can be argued that the Régie aborted the government's pledge to the URWE. Ibid., 1; *Al-Nahar,* July 16, 1963, 6.

35. *Al-Nahar,* Oct. 31, 1963, 5.

36. *Al-Thaqafa al-Wataniyya,* July 11, 1963, 5; *Al-Nahar,* June 30, 1963, 6.

37. *Al-Thaqafa al-Wataniyya,* July 11, 1963, 5.

38. Ibid.

39. Ibid., *Al-Nahar,* Oct. 31, 1963, 5.

40. Wasila Dubuq, Najla J., Fatima N., Nuhad Z., and several other women related this encounter to me.

41. Both women workers, Naddaf (b. 1924) and al-Fann (b. 1933), were alive at the time of my research in Beirut but were unable to elaborate on this incident for reasons of health and old age. Younger men and women workers who participated in the strike described the incident in detail. See also *Al-Nahar,* July 11, 1963, 6.

42. The news reports stated that the general director composed a *bayan* (statement) in which he included his pledge to support the demands, not to persecute any worker because of his or her role in the strike, and to pay them for the days of the strike. See *Al-Nahar,* July 16, 1963, 6; *Al-Thaqafa al-Wataniyya,* July 18, 1963, 3; *Al-Nahar,* Aug. 17, 1963, 6.

43. *Al-Thaqafa al-Wataniyya,* Oct. 17, 1963, 1; *Al-Nahar,* Oct. 31, 1963, 6.

44. *Al-Thaqafa al-Wataniyya,* Nov. 7, 1963, 3.

45. *Al-Thaqafa al-Wataniyya,* Dec., 19, 1963, 1, 5.

46. Ibid.

47. These proportions have never reflected the real configuration of the Régie workforce. The blue-collar workers always made up no less than two-thirds of that workforce. Magda Rizkallah-Boulad, "La Régie des Tabacs et son syndicat," *Travaux et Jours* 44 (July–Sept. 1972), 55.

48. Ibid., 56.

49. Wasila Dubuq interview, Jan. 27, 1997, Beirut, Lebanon; see also Gabi Tabrani, "Al-Naqabat Lam Ta'ud Lil-Rijal . . . Al-Mar'a Aydan Asbahat Naqabiyya," *Al-Hawadith* (Sept. 27, 1974): 73–74.

50. Iqbal Dughan interview, Jan. 28, 1997, Hadath.

51. 'Abdul 'Aziz Harfush interview, July 4, 1995, Burj al-Barajina, Lebanon; *Al-Thaqafa al-Wataniyya*, Mar. 19, 1964, 1.

52. Several newspapers noted that industrial workers, without prior notification or the company union's approval, started the numerous strikes that erupted in Lebanon during the 1960s. Such action was a vivid sign of the workers' doubts about and frustrations with the union. See *Al-Nahar*, July 16, 1963, 6, Aug. 10, 1963, 6, and Oct. 31, 1963, 5–6; *Al-Hayat*, Mar. 7, 1965, 7. Ahmad 'Abdallah interview, Jan. 29, 1997, Wadi al-Zini, Lebanon. 'Abdallah, a principal Communist Régie worker, confirmed that seventy-five tobacco workers (a little more than 2 percent of the total labor force) subscribed to *Al-Nida'* during that year. Magda Rizkallah-Boulad also asserted the substantial growth in the number of Communist and Phalangist affiliates at the Régie. See Rizkallah-Boulad, 61.

53. *Al-Hayat*, Mar. 9, 1965, 5, and Mar. 14, 1965, 3.

54. *Al-Hayat*, Mar. 30, 1965, 7.

55. 'Abdul 'Aziz Harfush interview, July 4, 1995, Burj al-Barajina, Lebanon.

56. Rizkallah-Boulad, 61.

57. Michael Suleiman, *Political Parties in Lebanon* (Ithaca, N.Y.: Cornell Univ. Press, 1967), 240–41. See also John P. Entelis, *Pluralism and Party Transformation in Lebanon, Al-Kata'ib, 1936–1970* (Leiden: E. J. Brill, 1974), 49–51.

58. Suleiman, *Political Parties in Lebanon*, 243–44.

59. Entelis, 141–42.

60. Suleiman, *Political Parties in Lebanon*, 244.

61. *Al-Hayat*, Mar. 16, 1965, 7.

62. Before becoming president, Fuad Shihab (1958–64) was the Lebanese army's commander in chief. In the political factionalism and schisms of the 1958 crisis, Shihab was praised for preserving the army's neutrality and impartiality, which won him the confidence of all social groups. His ascendancy to the presidency was also influenced by the agreement between the U.S. administration and the Egyptian leader Jamal Abdul Nasir to prevent a civil war in Lebanon. For an assessment of the Shihabist epoch, see Sharara, *Al-Silm al-Ahli*.

63. Ibid., 591.

64. From an article by Basim al-Jisr in *Al-Jarida*, Mar. 26, 1965, 7. Al-Jisr based his figures on IRFED findings for 1965.

65. *Al-Thaqafa al-Wataniyya*, Apr. 15, 1965, 1.

66. Salim Zabbal, "Lubnan fi Maydan al-Sina'a" (Lebanon in the Field of Industry), *Al-'Arabi* 131 (Oct. 1969), 74–75.

67. Sharara, *Al-Silm al-Ahli*, 618–20.

68. *Al-Nahar*, Mar. 6, 1965, 6.

69. *Al-Hayat*, Mar. 7, 1965, 7. Sa'id Hayik interview, Mar. 1, 1997, Hadath. Hayik was among the few Christian workers who formulated this demand.

70. Jacques Dagher interview, Feb. 3, 1997, Ba'abda, Lebanon. Dagher was an administrative officer at the company in 1965. He reported that Raymond Zalzal was known for his ill temper and rough character and that the Lebanese army, to which Zalzal had belonged before joining the Régie, had not tolerated his personality and had discharged him from service.

71. *Al-Hayat*, Mar. 7, 1965, 7; *Al-Thaqafa al-Wataniyya*, Mar. 11, 1965, 1, 6.

72. *Al-Nahar*, Mar. 6, 1965, 6. This newspaper listed gender equality in wage and rank at the top of the workers demands. See also *Beirut Daily Star*, Mar. 7 and 8, 1965, 1; *Al-Thaqafa al-Wataniyya*, Mar. 11, 1965, 6; *Al-Hayat*, Mar. 7, 1965, 7. The Régie's deliberate attempts to issue falsified reports about the nature and outcome of Khunaysir's encounter with Zalzal augmented the crisis. *Al-Hayat*, a daily Lebanese newspaper, dismissed the account of Khunaysir's arrest as mere "rumors" and complied with the Régie's official story that Khunaysir had been resting at his house following the medical advice of the Régie's doctor. *Al-Thaqafa al-Wataniyya*, however, related a more accurate account, stating that the Régie security guards arrested Khunaysir following a confrontation he had with Zalzal. To prevent insurrection among the workers, Jean Tuwayni, the head of the URWE, and Khunaysir visited the factory and attempted to diffuse the workers' suspicions regarding the latter's arrest.

73. *Al-Thaqafa al-Wataniyya*, Mar. 11, 1965, 6.

74. URWE, "Bayan ila al-Mudribin" (A Statement to the Strikers), Mar. 9, 1965, URWE records, Hadath; *Al-Hayat*, Mar. 7, 1965, 7.

75. URWE, "Bayan ila al-Mudribin."

76. In 1965, the total number of the Régie workforce was 3,562, out of which 733 were administrative staff, or white-collar employees, and 2,703 were blue-collar workers. See "The Development of Size and Salaries of the Régie Working Force, 1959–1972," n.d., Régie company records, Hadath.

77. It was impossible to obtain a clear and definite date when Sa'da Nasif and Josephine Shidyaq became URWE members.

78. Nuhad Z. interview, Mar. 5, 1997, Hadath.

79. Jacques Dagher interview, Feb. 3, 1997, Ba'abda, Lebanon.

80. *Al-Hayat*, Mar. 30, 1965, 7.

81. *Al-Thaqafa al-Wataniyya*, Mar. 11, 1965, 1, 6; *Al-Hayat*, Mar. 11, 1965, 5.

82. *Al-Thaqafa al-Wataniyya*, Mar. 18, 1965, 4.

83. Andre Tuwayni was the cousin of URWE leader Jean Tuwayni. To some extent, this relationship facilitated the contacts between the URWE and the Ministry of Finance, the mandatory authority over the Régie, and was at times beneficial to the male workers, who most often compromised their female colleagues' interests.

84. *Al-Thaqafa al-Wataniyya*, Mar. 18, 1965, 4; *Al-Hayat*, Mar. 16, 1965, 7.

85. URWE, "Bayan ila al-Mudribin," Mar. 13, 1965, URWE records, Hadath; *Al-Nahar*, Mar. 12, 1965, 6.

86. *Al-Thaqafa al-Wataniyya*, Mar. 18, 1965, 1, 5.

87. *Al-Nahar*, Mar. 19, 1965, 6. Other requests were included in this statement, such as the implementation of a health plan and the rewarding of equal grants to all workers and employees. The latter request was the center of disputes between blue-collar workers and white-collar employees because the latter were constantly given the largest share of grants and rewards.

88. *Al-Nahar*, Mar. 13, 1965, 3.

89. *Al-Nahar*, Mar. 7, 1965, 6.

90. Ibid., and *Al-Nahar*, Mar. 26, 1965, 6.

91. *Al-Nahar*, Mar. 7, 1965, 6; Mar. 13, 1965, 3; and Mar. 26, 1965, 6.

92. *Al-Hayat*, Mar. 9, 1965, 5.

93. Ibid.

94. *Al-Hayat*, Mar. 30, 1965, 7, and Mar. 31, 1965, 5.

95. *Al-Hayat*, Mar. 16, 1965, 7.

96. See Chakrabarty's discussion of the history of "citizenship," which, in his opinion, underwrites and circumscribes working-class histories. Chakrabarty, "Labor History and the Politics of Theory," 326–37.

97. Fadl al-Haj, "Dawafi' Idrab 'Ummal al-Riji" (The Motivations of the Régie Workers' Strike), *Al-Thaqafa al-Wataniyya*, Mar. 18, 1965, 1, 5.

98. *Al-Nahar*, Apr. 1, 1965, 6. When the strike ended, the Régie decided initially to allow all workers to return to their jobs, "except those who worked in the factory," both temporary and permanent, because it accused them of starting the strike. Three days later, however, and owing to pressure from the rest of the workforce, the Régie allowed them to resume work.

99. *Al-Hayat*, Mar. 7, 1965, 7; Mar. 16, 1965, 7; and Mar. 30, 1965, 7.

100. Several female and male workers—in particular Ilyas Lattuf, a Phalangist worker, who assumed a leading role in the 1965 strike—confirmed this fact. Ilyas Lattuf interview, Jan. 31, 1997, Hadath.

101. *Beirut Daily Star*, Mar. 10, 1965, 3.

102. *Beirut Daily Star*, Mar. 30, 1965, 1. The first quote was included in the Labor Liberation Front statement published in *Al-Thaqafa al-Wataniyya*, Apr. 15, 1965, 8. See also *Al-Hayat*, Mar. 30, 1965, 7.

103. *Al-Nahar*, Mar. 30, 1965, 9.

104. See *Al-Hayat*, Mar. 30, 1965, 7.

105. Jacques Dagher interview, Jan. 28, 1997, Ba'abda, Lebanon.

106. *Al-Hayat*, Mar. 30, 1965, 7. See also *Al-Nahar*, Apr. 6, 1965, 6.

107. *Beirut Daily Star*, Mar. 16, 1965, 3.

108. *Al-Nahar*, Mar. 17, 1965, 6.

109. *Al-Hayat*, Mar. 16, 1965, 7.

110. URWE, "Bayan ila al-Mudribin," Mar. 25, 1965, URWE records, Hadath.

111. *Al-Nahar,* Mar. 26, 1965, 1; *Beirut Daily Star,* Mar. 26, 1965, 3.

112. 'Abdul 'Aziz Harfush interview, July 4, 1995, Burg al-Barajina, Lebanon.

113. *Al-Hayat,* Mar. 30, 1965, 7.

114. *Beirut Daily Star,* Mar. 27, 1965, 2.

115. *Al-Nahar,* Mar. 26, 1965, 6, and Mar. 27, 1965, 6.

116. *Al-Nahar,* Mar. 27, 1965, 6.

117. *Al-Thaqafa al-Wataniyya,* Apr. 1, 1965, 6. The description of these incidents was included in a letter sent by a group of Régie workers to several newspapers, political and community leaders, and some Parliament members.

118. By "tobacco production," I mean farming, trading, and manufacturing. Moreover, the 300,000 represented more than 12 percent of the total Lebanese population, which counted around 2.5 million in 1963. See *Al-Nahar,* June 30, 1963, 6.

119. Ibid.

120. *Al-Thaqafa al-Wataniyya,* Apr. 1, 1965, 6.

121. *Al-Nahar,* Mar. 30, 1965, 6, 9. The same newspaper reported that As'ad 'Aqil, the leader of the Liberation Front, was arrested and charged with insulting the government.

122. *Beirut Daily Star,* Mar. 27, 1965, 1; *Al-Nahar,* Mar. 28, 1965, 1.

123. *Beirut Daily Star,* Mar. 28–29, 1965, 1.

124. 'Abdul 'Aziz Harfush interview, July 4, 1995, Burj al-Barajina, Lebanon. Unfortunately, we have no contemporary police records or union reports documenting these incidents.

125. Ghassan Tuwayni, "Hiwar ma' al-Dawla" (A Dialogue with the Government), *Al-Nahar,* Mar. 28, 1965, 1.

126. "Fatih Ma'amil al-Riji fi al-Manatiq" (The Opening of the Provincial Branches of the Régie), *Al-Hayat,* Mar. 30, 1965, 7.

127. *Al-Nahar,* Mar. 28, 1965, 1.

128. Ibid; *Al-Nahar,* Mar. 28, 1965, 6; *Al-Hayat,* Mar. 30, 1965, 7.

129. *Al-Anwar,* Mar. 30, 1965, 1.

130. *Al-Jarida,* Mar. 30, 1965, 1.

131. *Al-Thaqafa al-Wataniyya,* Apr. 1, 1965, 8; George Batal interview, Feb. 5, 1997, Beirut; 'Ali Subayti interview, Jan. 29, 1997, Kafarsir, Lebanon.

132. *Al-Nahar,* Mar. 28, 1965, 6, and *Al-Anba',* Mar. 26, 1965, 2.

133. *Al-Hayat,* Apr. 4, 1965, 5.

134. During this session, Kamal Junblat asked Deputy Edward Hunayn, the minister of labor, if he could live on the forty- to sixty-pound monthly salary that temporary tobacco workers were paid. See *Al-Thaqafa al-Wataniyya,* May 20, 1965, 1.

135. *Beirut Daily Star,* Apr. 2, 1965, 1.

136. This information is based primarily on the account provided by Nuhad Z., a woman worker who joined the Régie in 1956 at the age of fourteen and exhibited open rebellion to the Régie

and the government during the 1963 and 1965 strikes. Unfortunately, we do not have police records to verify or compare these accounts. Nuhad Z. interview, Mar. 5, 1997, Hadath.

137. Ibid.

138. 'Abdul 'Aziz Harfush interview, July 4, 1995, Burj al-Barajina, Lebanon.

139. Ilyas Lattuf interview, Jan. 31, 1997, Hadath.

140. Fatima N. interview, Feb. 6, 1997, Shiyyah, Lebanon.

141. *Al-Thaqafa al-Wataniyya,* Apr. 1, 1965, 7. See also Ilyas Lattuf interview, Jan. 31, 1997, Hadath.

142. *Al-Nahar,* Mar. 30, 1965, 6.

143. *Al-Nahar,* Apr. 1, 1965, 6; *Al-Hayat,* Apr. 1 and 2, 1965, 4; *Beirut Daily Star,* Mar. 30, 1965, 1, 2.

144. *Al-Hayat,* Mar. 30, 1965, 1.

145. 'Ali Subayti interview, Jan. 29, 1997, Kafarsir, Lebanon.

146. *Al-Hayat,* Mar. 30, 1965, 1.

147. *Al-Nahar,* June 30, 1963, 6. This article was one of the few independent editorials by Antun al-Gharib that ran in the *Al-Nahar,* which was for the most part sympathetic to the government's position.

148. *Al-Thaqafa al-Wataniyya,* Apr. 1, 1965, 7.

149. *Al-Nahar,* Apr. 4, 1965, 6.

150. *Al-Thaqafa al-Wataniyya,* May 20, 1965, 1, 7.

151. *Al-Thaqafa al-Wataniyya,* Dec. 7, 1967, 1, 7.

152. Mukherjee, "Illusion and Reality," 129.

153. Chakrabarty, "Labor History and the Politics of Theory," 332.

154. Ibid.

Selected Bibliography

Archival Sources

Dagher, Jacques (former Régie administrative officer). Private collection, Beirut.

Al-Khoury, Joe 'Issa (attorney). Legal cases in Lebanon, documentation, 1974–92, Beirut.

Ministère des Affaires Étrangeres, Nantes. *L'indicateur: Libano-Syrien,* 1928–29, Per 356.

Mandat, Syrie-Liban, 1930–45, cartons 696, 718, 719, 866, 1066, 1107.

Ministère des Affaires Étrangeres, Paris. Levant, Syrie-Liban 1918–40, vols. 320, 550, 551, 696, 718, 1066, 2921.

Régie Co-Intéressee Libanaise des Tabacs et Tombacs. Company records, 1959–97, Hadath and Beirut.

Union of the Régie Workers and Employees (URWE). Records, 1954–92, Hadath and Beirut.

Interviews

Abdallah, Ahmad. Interview, Jan. 29, 1997, Wadi al-Zini, Lebanon.

A., Haniya. Interview, Mar. 11, 1997, Hadath, Lebanon.

A., In'am. Interview, Feb. 20, 1997, Hadath, Lebanon.

A., Samia. Interview, Mar. 5, 1997, Hadath, Lebanon.

'Aqil, Badi'. Interview, Jan. 23, 1997, Hadath, Lebanon.

Atrisi, Kamal. Interview, Mar. 1, 1997, Hadath, Lebanon.

Batal, George. Interview, Feb. 5, 1997, Beirut, Lebanon.

D., Hannih. Interview, Mar. 6, 1997, Ghaziyya, Lebanon.

Dagher, Jacques. Interviews, Jan. 28, 30, 1997, and Feb. 3, 21, 1997, Ba'abda, Lebanon.

Dubuq, Wasila. Interview, Jan. 27, 1997, Beirut, Lebanon.

Dughan, Iqbal. Interview, Jan. 28, 1997, Hadath, Lebanon.

F., Nayfa. Interview, Mar. 9, 1997, Hadath, Lebanon.

G., Louisa. Interview, Feb. 6, 1997, Hadath, Lebanon.

H., Georgette. Interview, Mar. 21, 1997, Hadath, Lebanon.

Harfush, 'Abdul 'Aziz. Interview, June 20, 1995, and July 4, 1995, Burj al-Barajina, Lebanon.

H., Latifa. Interview, Feb. 25, 1997, Ghaziyya, Lebanon.

H., Tamam. Interview, Dec. 28, 1997, Hadath, Lebanon.

H., Therese. Interview, Mar. 18, 1997, Hadath, Lebanon.

Hayik, Saʻid. Interview, Mar. 1, 1997, Hadath, Lebanon.

Hubayqa, George. Interview, Mar. 3, 1997, Hadath, Lebanon.

I., Huriya. Interview, Jan. 30, 1997, Hadath, Lebanon.

I., Kamila. Interview, Feb. 8, 1997, Hadath, Lebanon.

J., Najla. Interview, Feb. 6, 1997, Ashrafiyya, Lebanon.

J., Nelly. Interview, Mar. 2, 1997, Hadath, Lebanon.

K., Dibi. Interview, Feb. 19, 1997, Hadath, Lebanon.

K., Thurayya. Interview, Feb. 22, 1997, Hadath, Lebanon.

Lattuf, Ilyas. Interview, Jan. 31, 1997, Hadath, Lebanon.

M., Muna. Interview, Mar. 27, 1997, Tripoli, Lebanon.

M., Nuha. Interview, Dec. 29, 1997, Hadath, Lebanon.

N., Fatima. Interview, Feb. 6, 1997, Shiyyah, Lebanon.

N., Georgette. Interview, Mar. 23, 1997, Hadath, Lebanon.

R., Theresa. Interview, Mar. 4, 1997, Bikfaya, Lebanon.

Salameh, ʻAdnan. Interview, Aug. 24, 1996, Dearborn, Michigan.

S., Fatima. Interview, Mar. 4, 1997, Hadath, Lebanon.

S., Munira. Interview, Feb. 10, 1997, Hadath, Lebanon.

Subayti, ʻAli. Interview, Jan. 29, 1997, Kafarsir, Lebanon.

Subayti, Husayn. Interview, Mar. 11, 1997, Hadath, Lebanon.

T., ʻItaf. Interview, Feb. 15, 1997, Ghaziyya, Lebanon.

W., Wahiba. Interview, Mar. 17, 1997, Hadath, Lebanon.

Z., Fatima. Interview, Mar. 1, 1997, Hadath, Lebanon.

Z., Mashhadiyya. Interview, Mar. 10, 1997, Hadath, Lebanon.

Z., Nuhad. Interview, Mar. 5, 1997, Hadath, Lebanon.

Z., Safia. Interview, Mar. 2, 1997, Hadath, Lebanon.

Z., Zaynab. Interview, Feb. 13, 1997, Hadath, Lebanon.

Government Documents

Institut International de Recherches et de Formation en Vue de Développement (IRFED). *Besoins et possibilités de développement du Liban* (The Requirements and Possibilities of Development in Lebanon). Beirut: Ministère du Plan, 1960.

Lebanese Republic (Ministry of Social Affairs) and the United Nations. *Al-Jadawil al-Ihsa'iyya li-Masih al-Muʻtayat al-Ihsa'iyya lil-Sukkan wa al-Masakin: 1994–1996*

(The Statistical Lists of the Survey of the Variables for Residences and Residents, 1994–1996). 2 vols. Beirut: Lebanese Ministry of Social Affairs, Oct. 1996.

République Française. Ministère des Affaires Étrangeres. "Rapport à la Société des Nations sur la situation de la Syrie et du Liban" (Conditions of Work in Syria and the Lebanon under French Mandate). *International Labour Review* 34 (Apr. 1939): 513–17.

République Libanaise. Ministère du Plan. *L'enquête par sondage sur la population active au Liban.* Vol. 2, *Tableaux de résults, juillet 1970.* Beirut: Ministère du Plan, Direction Centrale de la Statistique, Nov. 1972.

Memoirs and Writings of Labor Activists

Al-'Aris, Mustafa. *Mustafa al-'Aris Yatadhakkar* (Mustafa al-'Aris Remembers). Beirut: Dar al-Farabi, 1982.

Al-Buwari, Ilyas. *Tarikh al-Haraka al-'Ummaliyya wa al-Naqabiyya fi Lubanan: 1908–1946* (The History of the Labor and Unionist Movement in Lebanon). 3 vols. Beirut: Dar al-Farabi, 1908–80.

Dakrub, Muhammad. *Judhur al-Sindiyana al-Hamra'* (The Roots of the Red Oak Tree). Beirut: Dar al-Farabi, 1985.

Hamdan, Kamal. "'Amal al-Mar'a fi Lubnan wa Masahat al-Tamyiz Baynaha wa Bayna al-Rajul" (Women's Work in Lebanon and the Extent of Discrimination). Unpublished manuscript, Beirut, 1997.

Al-Hilu, Yusuf Khattar. *Awraq min Tarikhuna* (Pages from Our History). Beirut: Dar al-Farabi, 1988.

Al-Hizb al-Taqadumi al-Ishtiraki: Rubu' Qarin mina al-Nidal (The Progressive Socialist Party: A Quarter Century of Struggle). Beirut: Dar al-Bayan, 1974.

Madoyan, Artin. *Hayat 'ala al-Mitras* (Life at the Barricade). Beirut: Dar al-Farabi, 1986.

Al-Mu'tamar al-Naqabi al-'Am al-Khamis (The Fifth Trade Union Conference). Publication of the General Labor Syndicate. Beirut: Manshurat al-Itihad al-'Ummali al-'am, 1992.

Slaybi, Ghassan. "Fi Zuruf Tabalwur al-Dawr al-Naqabi al-Watani: Al-Ittihad al-'Ummali al-'Am wa al-Harb" (The Conditions for the Crystalization of the Role of National Unionism: The General Syndicate of Lebanese Workers and the War). Unpublished manuscript, Beirut, 1992.

Newspapers and Periodicals

Al-Ahrar al-Musawwarra (Beirut, 1926–30)
Al-Anba' (Beirut, 1965)

Al-Anwar (Beirut, 1962–80)

Al-'Asifa (Beirut, 1933)

Al-Bayraq (Beirut, 1928–46)

Beirut Daily Star (1965)

Dirasat 'Arabiyya (Beirut, 1965–74)

Al-Diyar (Beirut, 1993)

Al-Haris (Beirut, 1930)

Al-Hasna' (Beirut, 1910–11)

Al-Hawadith (Beirut, 1974)

Al-Hayat (Beirut, 1946–80)

Hayat al-'Ummal (Beirut, 1978, 1980–1981, 1989)

Al-Hilal (Cairo, 1894–1900)

Al-Hurriyya (Beirut, 1971)

Al-Iqtisadi (Beirut, 1977)

Al-'Irfan (Beirut, 1930–57)

Al-Jarida (Beirut, 1965)

Al-Jaysh (Beirut, 1985)

Le Jour (Beirut, 1935)

Lisan al-Haal (Beirut, 1930)

Al-Liwa' (Beirut, 1978)

Al-Majalla al-Ijtima'iyya (Cairo, 1977)

Al-Majalla al-Qada'iyya (Beirut, 1987)

Majallat al-'Amal al-Dawliyya (Beirut, 1973–74)

Al-Manar (Cairo, 1988)

Al-Manara (Beirut, 1930)

Al-Mar'a al-Jadida (Beirut, 1925)

Al-Massara (Beirut, 1929–33)

Al-Muqtataf (Cairo, 1881–1913)

Al-Mustaqbal al-'Arabi (Beirut, 1970–89)

Al-Nahar (Beirut, 1943–2008)

Al-Nida' (Beirut, 1930–80)

Al-Safir (Beirut, 1974–2008)

Sawt al-'Ummal (Beirut, 1930)

Al-Tariq (Beirut, 1980–81)

Al-Thaqafa al-Wataniyya (Beirut, 1967–74)

Al-'Ummal (Beirut, 1930)

U.S. News & World Report (1958)

Arabic Secondary Sources

'Abbud, Ilyas. "Dahiyat al-Muhhajjarin" (The Suburb of the Forced Migrants). *Al-Safir,* Aug. 4–5, 1980, 7–9.

'Abd Al-Baqi, Huda. *Mu'anat al-Mar'a wa al-Awlad: Dirasa Hawla Ba'd al-Qawanin wa al-Zawahir al-Ijtima'iyya fi al-Mujtama' al-Lubnani* (The Suffering of Women and Children: A Study of Some of the Laws and Social Phenomena Prevalent in Lebanese Society). Beirut: Dar al-Muruj, 1989.

'Abd Al-Fadil, Mahmud. *Al-Tashkilat Al-Ijtima'iyya wa al-Takwinat al-Tabaqiyya fi al-Watan al-'Arabi* (The Social Structures and the Class Formations in the Arab World). Beirut: Markaz Dirasat al-Wahda al-'Arabiyya, 1988.

Abul-Rus, Iliya. "Waqi' Al-Haraka Al-Naqabiyya fi Lubnan" (The Reality of the Trade Union Movement in Lebanon). *Dirasat 'Arabiyya* 11, no. 1 (Oct. 1965): 98–114.

Abu Murad, Nabil. *Al-Akhawan Rahbani: Hayat wa Masrah, Khasa'is al-Kitaba al-Dramiyya* (The Rahbani Brothers, Life and Theater: The Characteristics of the Playwriting). Beirut: Dar Amjad lil-Nashr wa al-Tawzi', 1990.

Abu Sa'd, Ahmad. *Mu'jam Asma' al-Usar wa al-Ashkhas wa Lamahat min Tarikh al-'A'ilat* (The Dictionary of Names of Families and Persons and Glimpses from the Histories of the Families). Beirut: Dar al-'ilim lil-Malayin, 1997.

Abu Shaqra, Na'il. *Al-Tahuwwulat al-Iqtisadiyya wa al-Ijtima'iyya fi Mujtama' Jabal Lubnan, 1550–1900: Namudhaj 'Ammatur-Jizzin, Dirasa Muwwathaqqa* (The Socioeconomic Transformation in Mount Lebanon Society, 1550–1900: The Case of 'Ammatur-Jizzin, a Documented Research). Beirut: Dar Isharat lil-Tiba'a wal-Tawzi', 1999.

Ajami, Marie. *Dawhat al-Dhikra: Majmu'a Mukhtara* (Genealogy of Memory: A Selected Set). Damascus: Wizarat al-Thaqafa wa al-Siyaha wa al-Irshad al-Qawmi, 1969.

'Amil, Mahdi. *Fi al-Dawla al-Ta'ifiyya* (The Sectarian State). Beirut: Dar al-Farabi, 1986.

———. *Madkhal ila Naqd al-Fikr al-Ta'ifi: Al-Qadiyya al-Filastiniyya fi Idyulujiyat al-Burjuwaziyya al-Lubnaniyya* (Introduction to the Refutation of Sectarian Thought: The Palestinian Cause in the Ideology of the Lebanese Bourgeoisie). Beirut: Dar al-Farabi, 1985.

Al-'Amiriyya. "Al-Mar'a wa al-Siyasa" (Women and Politics). *Al-Mar'a al-Jadida* 7 (Feb. 1925): 52–53.

'Arida, Antoine (Patriarch). *Lubnan wa Faransa: Watha'iq Tarikhiyya Asasiyya Tabruz Dawr Bikriki fi Muwajahat al-Intidab al-Faransi wa al-Ihtikarat al-Faransiyya* (Lebanon and France: Important Historical Documents Underscoring the Role of Bikirki in Confronting the French Mandate and French Monopolies). Translated by Faris Ghassub. Beirut: Dar al-Farabi, 1987.

Al-Arqash, 'Abdul Hamid. *Al-Haraka al-'Ummaliyya al-Tunisiyya, 1920–1957.* Damascus, Syria: Markaz al-Abhath wal-Dirasat al-Ishtirakiyya fil-'Alam al-'Arabi, 1988.

Al-Aswad, Ibrahim Bey. *Dalil Lubnan* (The Guide to Lebanon). Ba'abda, Lebanon: Al-Matba'a al-'Uthmaniyya, 1906.

———. *Tanwir al-Adhhan fi Tarikh Lubnan.* Beirut: Dar Lahd Khatir, 1930.

'Aziz, al-Sayid Jasim. "Hawla Dawr al-Tabaqa al-'Amila: Maqulat Tarikhiyya . . . wa Mu'dilat" (On the Role of the Working Class: Historical Problems and Issues). *Dirasat 'Arabiyya* 8 (Aug. 1972): 72–84.

'Azzam, Henri. *Al-Mar'a al-'Arabiyya wa al-'Amal* (The Arab Woman and Work). Beirut: Markaz Dirasat al-Wahda al-'Arabiyya, 1982.

———. "Al-Mar'a al-'Arabiyya wa al-'Amal: Musharakat al-Mar'a al-'Arabiyya fi al-Qiwa al-'Amila wa Dawruha fi 'Amaliyat al-Tanmiyya" (Arab Women and Work: The Participation of Arab Women in the Workforce and Their Role in the Process of Development). *Al-Mustaqbal al-'Arabi,* no. 34 (Dec. 1981): 76–89.

Al-Baqari, Mahir. *Al-'Amal fi al-Islam* (Work in Islam). Alexandria, Egypt: Matba'at Dar Nashr al-Thaqafa, 1970.

———. *Al-'Amal wa al-Qiyam al-Khuluqiyya fi al-Islam* (Work and Moral Values in Islam). Alexandria, Egypt: Matba'at Dar Nashr al-Thaqafa, 1988.

Baqraduni, Karim. *La'nat Watan: Min Harb Lubnan ila Harb al-Khalij* (A Nation's Curse: From the Lebanese War to the Gulf War). Beirut: 'Abr al-Sharq lil-Manshurat, 1991.

Al-Bar, Muhammad 'Ali. *'Amal al-Mar'a fil-Mizan* (Assessing Women's Work). Riyadh, Saudi Arabia: Maktabat al-Riyadh, 1994.

Barakat, Halim. *Al-Mujtama' al-'Arabi al-Mu'asir* (The Modern Arab Society). Beirut: Markaz Dirasat al-Wahda al-'Arabiyya, 1984.

———. "Al-Nizam al-Ijtima'i wa 'Alaqatuhu Bimushkilat al-Mar'a al-'Arabiyya" (The Social System and Its Relationship to the Problems of Arab Women). *Al-Mustaqbal al-'Arabi* 4 (1981): 51–63.

Basha, Abidu. *Bayt al-Nar: Al-Zaman al-Di'i' fi al-Masrah al-Lubnani* (The Fire House: The Missing Period in the Lebanese Theater). Beirut: Riyad el-Rayess, 1995.

Bashshur, Najla' Nasir. *Al-Mar'a al-Lubnaniyya: Waqi'aha wa Qadayaha* (The Lebanese Woman: Reality and Questions). Beirut: Dar al-Tali'a lil-Tiba'a wa al-Nashir, 1975.

Bayhum, Muhammad Jamil. "Al-Mar'a wa al-Sana'i'" (Women and Trades). *Al-Hilal* (July 1894): 923–26.

Bayruti, Lucien. *Dirasa li-Awda' al-'Amil al-Sina'i fi Lubnan* (A Study of the Conditions of the Industrial Worker in Lebanon). Beirut: Lebanese Univ., 1969.

Al-Baz, Shahida. "'Amal al-Mar'a: Adat Taharuriha wa Taharur al-Mujtama'" (Women's Work: The Tool for Their Liberation and That of Society). *Al-Manar* 48 (Dec. 1988): 80–91.

Bazzi, 'Abbas. "Bint-Jubayl 1936: Al-Intifada wa al-Iqta'" (Bint-Jubayl 1936: The Uprising and Feudalism) *Dirasat 'Arabiyya* 5 (Sept. 1969): 72–88.

Bazzi, Mustafa. "Intifadat Bint-Jubayl wa Jabal 'Amil fi al-'Awwal min Nisan 1936" (The Bint-Jubayl and Jabal 'Amil Uprising: April 1, 1936). *Dirasat 'Arabiyya* 28 (Sept.–Oct. 1992): 65–92, and 29 (Nov.–Dec. 1992): 61–82.

———. "Tatawwur al-Hiraf wa al-Sina'at al-Sha'biyya fi Jabal 'Amil" (The Development of Handicrafts in Jabal 'Amil). In *Al-Mu'tamar al-Awwal lil-Thaqafa al-Sha'biyya fi Lubnan* (The First Convention of Popular Culture in Lebanon), 401–22. Beirut: Ministry of Culture, 1993.

Bitar, Jamila. "Al-Mar'a wa ma Yumkin an Ta'maluhu" (Women and What They Can Achieve). *Al-Hasna'* 3, no. 7 (Jan. 1911): 268–69.

Chehab, Maurice. *Dawr Lubnan fi Tarikh al-Harir* (Lebanon's Role in the History of Silk). Beirut: Manshurat al-Jami'a al-Lubnaniyya, 1968.

Chevallier, Dominique. *Mujtama' Jabal Lubnan fi 'Asr al-Thawra al-Sina'yya fi Urubba* (The Society of Mount Lebanon in the Age of the Industrial Revolution in Europe). Translated by Muna Abdullah 'Aquir. Beirut: Dar al-Nahar, 1995. A translation of *La société du Mont Liban à l'époque de la Révolution Industrielle en Europe.* Paris: Libraire Orientale P. Geuthner, 1982.

Chiha, Michel. *Lubnan al-Yawm* (Lebanon Today). Translated by Ahmad Beydoun. Beirut: Dar al-Nahar, 1994.

Couland, Jacques. *Al-Haraka al-Naqabiyya fi Lubnan: 1919–1946* (The Syndicate Movement in Lebanon). Beirut: Dar al-Farabi, 1974.

———. "Nahwa Tarikh 'Ilmi lil-Haraka al-'Ummaliyya fi al-'Alam al-'Arabi" (Toward a Scientific History of the Labor Movement in the Arab World). *Al-Tariq* 38, no. 1 (Feb. 1979): 127–52.

Daghir, Albert. "Dawr al-Dawla al-Tanmawi: Mata Tajawuz al-Chihiyya" (The Developmental Role of the State: Beyond Chihism) *Al-Nahar: Qadaya*, June 12, 2008, 3

Dahir, Mas'ud. *Al-Judhur al-Tarikhiyya lil-Mas'ala al-Ta'ifiyya al-Lubnaniyya* (The Historical Roots of the Sectarian Question in Lebanon). Beirut: Ma'had al-Inma' al-'Arabi, 1981.

———. *Tarikh Lubnan al-Ijtima'i: 1914–1926* (The Social History of Lebanon: 1914–1926). Beirut: Dar al-Matbu'at al-Sharqiyya, 1984.

Dubar, Claude, and Salim Nasr. *Al-Tabaqat al-Ijtima'iyya fi Lubnan: Muqaraba Susyulujiyya Tatbiqiyya* (The Social Classes in Lebanon: An Applied Sociological Approach). Beirut: Mu'asasat al-Abhath al-'Arabiyya, 1982.

Fahs, 'Adnan. *Al-Zuruf al-Iqtisadiyya lil-Harb al-Ta'ifiya al-Lubnaniyya* (The Economic Circumstances of the Lebanese War). Beirut: Dar al-Nahar, 1979.

Fahs, Hani. "Mu'jam al-Qarya al-Saghir" (Shorter Dictionary on the Village). *Al-Safir,* Dec. 29, 2000, 1.

"Fatih Ma'amil al-Riji fi al-Manatiq" (The Opening of the Provincial Branches of the Régie). *Al-Hayat,* Mar. 30, 1965, 7.

Fa'ur, 'Ali. *Al-Mar'a al-Lubnaniyya fi Muwajahat al-Harb wa al-'Unf wa al-Tahadiyat al-Ijtima'yya wa al-Iqtisadiyya* (The Lebanese Woman Confronts War, Violence, and the Social and Economic Challenges). Beirut: Jam'iyat Tanzim al-Usra fi Lubnan, 1995.

Al-Furat, Fatat. "Kalima Naziha" (An Honest Word). *Al-'Irfan* 19 (Mar. 1930): 320–26.

Ghalib, Edward. *Zira'at al-Tabigh wa Intajuhu* (The Planting and Production of Tobacco). Beirut: Dar al-Mashriq, 1965.

Ghurayyib, Rose. "Al-Mar's wa al'Amal: Muskilat wa Ma'uqat" (Woman and Work: Problems and Obstacles). In *Adwa' 'ala al-Haraka al-Nisa'iyya* (Highlighting the Modern Women's Movement: Studies and Essays), edited by Rose Ghurayyib, 328–33. Beirut: Institute of Women's Studies in the Arab World, 1988.

————, ed. *Adwa' 'ala al-Haraka al-Nisa'iyya: Maqalat wa Dirasat* (Highlighting the Modern Women's Movement: Studies and Essays). Beirut: Institute of Women's Studies in the Arab World, Beirut Univ. College, 1988.

Haddad, Georgette. "Nahwa Dirasa Susyulujiyya Liharaka Ijtima'iyya Fallahiyya: Namudhaj Harkat Muzari'i al-Tabigh fi Janub Lubnan, 1973" (Toward a Sociological Study of a Peasant Social Movement: The Case of the Movement of the Tobacco Farmers of South Lebanon, 1973). *Dirasat 'Arabiyya* 18 (May 1982): 126–29.

Haddad, Hikmat Albert. *Lubnan al-Kabir* (Greater Lebanon). Beirut: Dar Nazir Abdu, 1996.

Al-Haj, Fadul. "Dawafi' Idrab 'Ummal al-Riji" (The Motivations of the Régie Workers' Strike). *Al-Thaqafa al-Wataniyya,* Mar. 18, 1965, 1, 5.

Hakim, Yusuf. *Bayrut wa Lubnan fi 'Ahd Aal Uthman* (Beirut and Lebanon during the Ottoman Rule). Beirut: Al-Matba'a al-Kathulikiya, 1926.

Haqqi Bey, Isma'il, ed. *Lubnan: Mabahith 'Ilmiyya wa Ijtima'iyya* (Lebanon: Social and Scientific Studies). Beirut: Majmu'a mina al-Udaba', 1918.

Harik, Iliya. "Nushu' Nizam al-Dawla fi al-Watan al-'Arabi" (The Formation of the State System in the Arab World). *Al-Mustaqbal al-'Arabi* 99 (1987): 77-–93.

Ibrahim, Emily Faris. *Adibat Lubnaniyyat* (Lebanese Women Writers). Beirut: Dar al-Rihani, 1964.

Ibrahim, Isma'il. *Al-Sahafa al-Nisa'iyya fil-Watan al-'Arabi* (Women's Journalism in the Arab World). Cairo: Al-Dar al-Dawliyya lil-Nashr wa al-Tawzi', 1996.

Ibrahim, Kamal. "Utruha Yasariyya fi al-'Amal al-Naqabi fi Lubnan" (A Leftist Thesis on the Trade Union's Activities in Lebanon). *Dirasat 'Arabiyya* 8 (Nov. 1971): 52–59.

"Ila Hakim Biladi wa Ibn Biladi" (To the Governor of My Country and My Countryman). *Al-Mar'a al-Jadida* 7, no. 9 (Sept. 1925): 351–53.

"Ila Ibnat Biladi: La Huquq Jadida Natlubuha" (To the Daughter of My Country: We Are Not Demanding New Rights). *Al-Mar'a al-Jadida* 4, no. 6 (June 1924): 229–32.

Isma'il, Munir, and 'Adil Isma'il. *Tarikh Lubnan al-Hadith: Al-Watha'iq al-Dublumasiyya* (The History of Modern Lebanon: Diplomatic Documents). Beirut: Dar al-Nashr lil-Siyasa wa al-Tarikh, 1990.

Al-Jammal, Faruq. *Shushu: "Akh Ya Baladna"* (Shushu: "Alas, Our Country"). Beirut: Dar al-Afaq al-Jadida, 1981.

Al-Jisr, Basim. *Fouad Chihab: Dhalika al-Majhul* (Fouad Chihab: The Unknown). Beirut: Sharikat al-Matbu'at lil-Tawzi' wa al-Nashr, 1988.

Al-Jurdi, 'Issam. *Nissan 24 1997: Mahattat al-Inqisam fi al-Ittihad al-'Ummali al-'Am, Apr. 24 1997* (April 24 1997: The Turning Point in the General Workers Syndicate). Beirut: Al-Markaz al-Lubnani lil-Dirasat, 1998.

———. "Tahmish al-Yad al-'Amila al-Lubnaniyya" (Professional Associations and Trade Unions in Lebanon). In *Al-Naqabat wal-Hay'at al-Mihaniyya fi Lubnan* (The Marginalization of Lebanese Workers), 69–71. Beirut: Al-Mu'asasa al-Lubnanyyi lil-Silm al-'Ahli al-Da'im, 1999.

Kahlawi, 'Abla. *Al-'Amal fi al-Islam wa Hukm 'Amal al-Mar'a. wa al-Ahdath* (Labor in Islam and the Rulings on Women and Child Labor). Cairo: Markaz Dirasat al-Mar'a wal-Tanmiyya, 1979.

Kallas, George. *Al-Haraka al-Fikriyya al-Nasawiyya fi 'Asr al-Nahda, 1849–1928* (Women's Intellectual Movement during the Renaissance, 1849–1928). Beirut: Dar al-Jil, 1996.

Kamal Al-Din, Rafiq. "Muqaraba Naqdiyya li-utruhat Hawla al-Haraka Al-'Ummaliyya fi Lubnan" (A Critical Assessment of the Theses on the Labor Movement in Lebanon). Master's thesis, Lebanese Univ., Beirut, 1987.

Khalifa, Nabil. *Al-Shi'a fi Lubnan: Thawrat al-Dimughrafiyya wa al-Hirman* (The Shi'ites in Lebanon: The Revolution of Demography and Deprivation). Beirut: Markaz Byblus lil-Dirasat wa al-Abhath, 1984.

Khatib, Hanifa. *Tarikh Tatuwwur al-Haraka al-Nisa'iyya fi Lubnan wa Irtibatiha bi-al-'Alam al-'Arabi, 1800–1975* (The History of the Lebanese Women's Movement and Its Links to the Arab World, 1800–1975). Beirut: Dar al-Hadatha, 1984.

Khayr Al-Din, 'Issam As'ad. "Sina'at al-Tabigh wa al-Tanbak fi Lubnan" (The Industry of Tobacco and Tombac in Lebanon). Master's thesis, Lebanese Univ., Beirut, 1994.

Kila, Salami. "Mulahazat 'Ama Hawl Ma'zaq al-Dawla al-Qutriyya fi al-Watan al-'Arabi" (General Remarks on the Crisis of the Regional State in the Arab World). *Dirasat 'Arabiyya* 25 (Aug. 1989): 3–16.

Labaki, Joseph Antoine. *Mutasarrifiyat Jabal Lubnan: Masa'il wa Qadaya, 1861–1915* (Self-Rule of Mount Lebanon: Issues and Matters, 1861–1915). Beirut: Dar al-Karma, 1995.

Labib, Sa'id. *Dirasa Islamiyya fil-'Amal wa al-'Ummal* (An Islamic Study on Work and Workers). Cairo: Al-Hay'a al-Misriyya al-'Amma lil-Kitab, 1985.

Al-Lajna al-Wataniyya li-Shu'un al-Mar'a al-Lubnaniyya. *Waqi' al-Mar'a al-Lubnaniyya 1970–1995, Arqam wa Ma'ani* (The Real Conditions of Lebanese Women 1970–1995: Figures and Findings). Vol. 1. Beirut: Al-Lajna al-Wataniyya li-Shu'un al-Mar'a al-Lubnaniyya, 1997.

Lorfing, Irene, and Julinda Abu al-Nasr. *Dirasa Istitla'iyya Hawla al-'Amilat fi al-Masani' fi Dawahi Bayrut, 1979* (A Survey of Workingwomen in the Factories of Beirut's Suburbs, 1979). Beirut: Institute of Women's Studies in the Arab World, Beirut Univ. College, 1979.

Lortet, Louis. *Ard al-Dhikrayat: 300 Lawha Ra'i'a min al-Qarn al-Madi* (The Land of Memories: 300 Spectacular Paintings from the Past Century). Translated by Hamid Shalaq. Beirut: Sharikat al-Matbu'at, 1993.

Mahmud, Ibrahim Afaf. "Wad' al-Mar'a al-'Amila fi al-Tanzim al-Ijtima'i" (The Condition of Women Workers in the Social Structure of the Factory). *Al-Majalla al-Ijtima'iyya* 14 (1977): 3–32.

Mansur, Ilham. *Nahwa Tahrir al-Mar'a fi Lubnan* (Toward the Liberation of Woman in Lebanon). Beirut: Mukhtarat, 1996.

Al-Mar'a al-'Arabiyya: Bayna Thuql al-Waqi' wa Tatalu'at al-Taharrur (Arab Women: Between Reality and Emancipation). Beirut: Markaz Dirasat al-Wahda al-'Arabiyya, 1999.

Al-Mar'a al-'Arabiyya fil-'Ilm wa al-'Amal (Arab Women in Education and Work). Beirut: Institute of Women's Studies in the Arab World, Beirut Univ. College, 1985.

Al-Mar'a al-Lubnaniyya Shahida 'Ala al-Harb (The Lebanese Woman as a Witness of War). Beirut: League of Arab Nations, Paris, 1989.

Al-Mar'a wa al-'Amal fi Lubnan (Women and Labor in Lebanon). Beirut: Institute of Women's Studies in the Arab World, Beirut Univ. College, 1980.

Al-Mar'a wa al-Harb fi Lubnan, 1990 (Women and War in Lebanon). Beirut: Lebanon Family Planning Association, 1990.

"Al-Mar'a wa al-Shaja'a" (Women and Courage). *Al-Hasna'* 3, no. 3 (Dec. 1911): 124–27.

Massarra, Antun, and Toni Atallah, eds. *Nisf Qarn Difa'an 'an Huquq al-Mar'a fi Lubnan: Watha'iq min al-Tarikh: Arshif Lur Mughayzil, 1947–1997* (A Half-Century Defending Women Rights in Lebanon: Documents from History, the Archives of Lur Mughayzil). Beirut: Mu'assasat Joseph and Lur Mughayzil, 1999.

Mawaqif Hawla Qadaya al-Mar'a fi Lubnan (Debates on Women's Issues in Lebanon). Beirut: Lebanon Family Planning Association, 1996.

Milhim, Mikha'il Afandi. "Zira'at al-Tabigh" (Tobacco Planting). *Al-Muqtataf* 6 (June 1881): 31–32.

Misri, 'Abd Assami'i. *Muqawwimat al-'Amal fil-Islam* (The Foundations of Work in Islam). Cairo: Maktabat Wahba, 1982.

Misri, Sana. *Al-Ikhwan al-Muslimun wa al-Tabaqa al-'Amila al-Misriyya* (The Muslim Brothers and the Egyptian Working Class). Cairo: Matba'at Sharikat al-Amal, 1992.

Muroeh, 'Adnan. "Tanzim al-Usra wa al-Mar'a al-'Amila fi Lubnan" (Family Planning and the Workingwoman in Lebanon). In *Al-Mar'a wa al-'Amal fi Lubnan* (Women and Labor in Lebanon), 39–51. Beirut: Institute of Women's Studies in the Arab World, Beirut Univ. College, 1980.

Muroeh, Husayn, *Al-Naza'at al-Madiyya fi al-Falsafa al-'Arabiyya al-Islamiyya* (Material Trends in Arab Islamic Philosophy). 2 vols. Beirut: Dar al-Farabi, 1985.

Muroeh, Karim. *Al-Muqawama* (The Resistance). Beirut: Dar al-Farabi, 1985.

Murqus, Michael. *Zira'at al-Tibgh fi Lubnan* (The Planting of Tobacco in Lebanon). Beirut: Ma'had al-'Ulum al-Ijtima'iyya al-Lubnaniyya, 1974.

Mustafa, Ahmad Sayid. "Al-'Amala al-Nisa'iyya fi Misr" (Females' Employment in Egypt). *Al-Majalla al-Qawmiyya al-Ijtima'iyya* 14 (1977): 283–308.

Mustafa, Ibrahim. "Tatawwurat Bunyawiyya Hamma" (Important Structural Developments). *Al-Tariq* 40, no. 1 (Feb. 1981): 95–106.

"Nazra fi al-Mar'a wa Ta'thir al-'Adat" (A Glance at Women and the Influence of Customs). *Al-Hasna'* 7 (Jan. 1911): 270–71.

Ni'ma, Ibrahim. *Al-'Amal wa al-'Ummal fil-Fikr al-Islami* (Work and Workers in Islamic Thought). Jeddah, Saudi Arabia: Al-Dar al-Sa'udiyya lil-Nashr wal-Tawzi', 1985.

Nur-al-Din, Suad. "Al-Nuzuh al-Sukkani mina al-Janub: Nazif Mustammir Munzu ma Qabla al-Istiqlal" (The Displacement of the Population from the South: A Movement That Started before Independence). *Al-Safir,* May 12, 2008, 8.

Nuwayhid, Nadia al-Jurdi. *Nisa' min Biladi* (Women from My Homeland). Beirut: Al-Mu'assasa al-'Arabiyya lil-Dirasat wa al-Nashr, 1987.

Qabbanji, Jacques, and As'ad al-Atat. *Al-Mar'a al-'Amila fi Lubnan* (Workingwomen in Lebanon). Beirut: Sharikat al-Matbu'at lil-Tawzi' wa al-Nashr, 1997.

Al-Qadiri, Nahawand. "Nash'at al-Sahafa al-Nisa'iyya al-Lubnaniyya, 1892–1920" (The Rise of Lebanese Women's Journalism: 1892–1920). *Al-Fikr al-'Arabi* 10, no. 58 (1989): 146–68.

Al-Qadiyya al-Zira'iyya fi Lubnan fi Daw' al-Mariksiyya (The Agrarian Question in Lebanon from a Marxist Perspective). Beirut: Manshurat al-Hizb al-Shuyu'i al-Lubnani, ca. 1973–74.

Qanduli, Suhayla S. "Al-Tabaqa al-'Amila al-Lubnaniyya wa al-Harb, 1975–1980" (The Lebanese Working Class and the Civil War, 1975–1980) Master's thesis, Lebanese Univ., Beirut, 1985.

Al-Qarashi, Baqir Sharif. *Huquq al-'Amil fil-Islam* (The Rights of Workers in Islam). Beirut: Dar al-Ta'aruf lil-Matbu'at, 1992.

Al-Qasimi, Said Muhammad. *Qamus al-Sina'at al-Dimashqiyya* (Dictionary of Damascene Industries). Paris: Mouton, 1960.

Al-Qawanin Allati Tahkum al-Sukkan fi Lubnan (The Laws That Govern the Population in Lebanon). Beirut: Lebanon Family Planning Association, 1977.

Qazan, Fu'ad. "Al-Wadi' al-Iqtisadi wa Tatwwur al-Burjuwaziyya al-Mushawwaha wa Ghazu al-Intaj al-Urubbi li-Lubnan wa Suriyya Khilal al-Qarn al-Tasi' 'Ashar" (The Economic Situation and Development of a Deformed Bourgoisie and the Invasion of European Products in Lebanon and Syria during the Nineteenth Century). *Al-Tariq* 31 (1972): 41–53.

Qindlaft, Mitri. "Al-Mar'a wa al-Ma'mal" (Women and the Factory). *Al-Muqtataf* 43 (Dec. 1913): 537–43.

Rahbani, Ziad. *Nazil al-Surur; Bil'nisbi la Bukra Shu? Filim Amiriki Tawil and Shi Fashil* (Inn of Happiness; So, What about Tomorrow? Long American Film; and What a Failure). Beirut: Mukhtarat, 1994.

Rahbani Brothers. *Mawsim al-'Izz*. Beirut, 1960.

Al-Rayyis, Shafiq. *Al-Tahaddi al-Kabir: 1975–1976* (The Big Challenge). Beirut: Dar al-Masira, 1978.

Richards, Evelyn. "Al-Mar'a wa al-'Amal fi Lubnan" (Women and Work in Lebanon). In *Adwa''ala al-Haraka al Nisa'iyya al-Mu'asira* (Highlighting the Modern Women's Movement: Studies and Essays), edited by Rose Ghurayyib, 334–37. Beirut: Institute of Women's Studies in the Arab World, Beirut Univ. College, 1988.

Al-Saghir, Al-Zi'inni. *Umar al-Zi'inni Moliere al-Sharq* (Umar al-Zi'inni, the Moliere of the Orient). Beirut: Mu'asasat Jawad lil-Tiba'a wa al-Taswir, 1980.

Sahhab, Ilyas. "'Asi al-Rahbani: Al-Khalfiyya al-Tarikhiyya wa al-Mukawwinat al-Shakh-siyya wa al-Bidayat" ('Asi al-Rahbani: The Historical and Personal Background and the Beginnings). *Al-Tariq* 45, no. 6 (Dec. 1986): 216–24.

Sa'id, Abdallah. *Tatawwur al-Mulkiyya al-'Iqariyya fi Jabal Lubnan fi 'Ahd al-Mutasarri-fiya* (The Development of Real Estate Property in Mount Lebanon during the Mutassarifate Period). Beirut: Dar al-Mada lil-Tiba'a wa al-Nashr, 1986.

Al-Sa'id, Sadiq Mahdi. *Al-'Amal wa al-Daman al-Ijtima'i fil-Islam* (Work and Social Security in Islam). Baghdad: Matba'at al-Ma'arif, 1965.

Salami, Ghassan. *Al-Mujtama' wa al-Dawla fil-Mashriq al-'Arabi* (Society and State in the Arab East). Beirut: Markaz Dirasat al-Wihda al-'Arabiyya, 1987.

Saliba, 'Aziz Fadlallah. *Tarikh al-Haraka al-Naqabiyya fi al-Biqa': Bayn al-'Ummal wa a'l-Muzari'in wa al-'Ummal al-Zira'iyyin, 1908–1998* (The History of the Syndicate Movement in the Biqa': Between Workers, Farmers and Agricultural Workers, 1908–1998). Beirut: Dar al-Farabi, 1999.

Salman, Ghassan. "Hawla Mushkiliyat Dirasat al-Idrabat fi Lubnan" (The Problem of Studying Strikes in Lebanon). *Al-Tariq* 39 (May 1980): 29–34.

Al-Sawda, Yusuf. *Fi Sabil Lubnan* (For the Sake of Lebanon). Beirut: Manshurat Lahd Khatir, 1988.

Shafiq, Amina. *Al-Tabaqa al-'Amila al-Misriyya: Al-Nash'a, al-Tatawwur, al-Nidalat* (The Egyptian Working Class: The Origin, Development, and Struggles). Cairo: Hizb al-Tajammu' al-Watani al-Taqaddumi al-Wahdawi, Amanat al-Tathqif, 1986.

Al-Shahabi, Muhammad Fuad Bayk. *Al-Rawd al-Nadir fi Tarbiyat Dud al-Harir* (The Flourishing Meadow of Silkworm Cultivation). Beirut: Maktabat Bulus, 1907.

Al-Shami, 'Ali. *Tatawwur al-Tabaqa al-'Amila fi al-Ra'ismaliyya al-Lubnaniyya al-Mu'asira* (The Development of the Working Class within Modern Lebanese Capitalism). Beirut: Dar al-Farabi, 1981.

Sharara, Waddah. *Dawlat Hizbullah: Lubnan Mujtama'an Islamiyyan* (The State of Hizbullah: Lebanon Made into an Islamic Society). Beirut: Dar al-Nahar, 1996.

———. *Fi Usul Lubnan al-Ta'ifi: Khatt al-Yamin al-Jamahiri* (The Roots of Sectarian Lebanon: The Rightwing Populist Line). Beirut: Dar al-Tali'a, 1975.

———. *Al-Silm al-Ahli al-Barid: Lubnan, al-Mujtama' wa al-Dawla, 1964–1967* (The Cold Civil War: Lebanese Society and State, 1964–1967). 2 vols. Beirut: Ma'had al-Inma' al-'Arabi, 1980.

Al-Shawi, Nuqula. *Kitabat wa Dirasat* (Studies and Writings). Beirut: Dar al-Farabi, n.d.

Shawul, Pual. *Al-Masrah al-'Arabi al-Hadith, 1976–1989* (The Modern Arab Theater, 1976–1989). London: Riad el-Rayyes Books, 1989.

Shu'ayb, 'Abd al-Salam. "Al-Mar'a al-'Amila fil-Qanun al-Lubnani" (The Workingwoman in Lebanese Law). In *Al-Mar'a wa al-'Amal fi Lubnan* (Women and Labor in Lebanon). Beirut: Institute of Women's Studies in the Arab World, Beirut Univ. College, 1980.

Shu'ayb, 'Ali 'Abd al-Mun'im. *Tarikh Lubnan: Mina al-Ihtilal ila al-Jala', 1918–1946* (The History of Lebanon: From Occupation to Departure, 1918–1946). Beirut: Dar al-Farabi, 1994.

Al-Shuyu'iyyun al-Lubnaniyyun wa Muhimmat al-Marhala al-Muqbila (The Lebanese Communists and the Missions of the Coming Period). Beirut: Manshurat al-Hizb al-Shuyu'i al-Lubnani, ca. 1969.

Al-Siba'i, Badr al-Din. *Adwa' 'ala al-Ra'ismal al-Ajnabi fi Suriyya: 1850–1958* (Highlighting the Foreign Capital in Syria). Damascus: Dar al-Jamahir, n.d.

S. M. "Ila al-Sayyida al-'Amiriyya" (To the 'Amiriyya Lady). *Al-Mar'a al-Jadida* 7 (Apr. 1925): 141–42.

Smilianskaia, Irina. *Al-Harakat al-Fallahiyya fi Lubnan fi Nisf al-Qarn al-Tasi' 'Ashar* (Peasants Movements in Lebanon during the Mid–Nineteenth Century). Translated by Adnan Jamus. Beirut: Dar al-Farabi, 1972.

Suwayd, Yasin. *Faransa wa al-Mawarina fi Lubnan: Taqarir wa Murasalat al-Hamla al-'Askariyya al-Faransiyya 'ala Suriyya, 1860–1861* (France and the Maronites in Lebanon: The Reports and Correspondences of the French Military Campaign in Syria, 1860–1861). Beirut: Sharikat al-Matbu'at lil-Tawzi' wa al-Nashr, 1992.

Tabrani, Gabi. "Al-Naqbat Lam Ta'ud lil-Rijal . . . Al-Mar'a Aydan Asbahat Naqabiyya" (Trade Unions Are Not Only for Men . . . Women Became Unionists Also). *Al-Hawadith* (Sept. 27, 1974): 73–74.

Taraboulsi, Fawwaz. *In Kan Baddak Ti'shaq: Kitabat fi al-Thaqafa al-Sha'biyya* (If You Wanted to Love: Writings in Popular Culture). Beirut: Dar al-Kunuz, 2005.

Tuwayni, Ghassan. "Hiwar ma' al-Dawla" (A Dialogue with the Government). *Al-Nahar*, Mar. 28, 1965, 1.

———. "Zawaj Julia Tu'ma Dimashqiyya wa Majallatuha Namuzajan" (The Marriage of Julia Tu'ma Dimashiqyya and Her Magazine Are a Good Model). *Al-Nahar*, Feb. 5, 2001, 5

Waqi' al-Mar'a al-Lubnaniyya (The Real Conditions of Lebanese Woman 1970–1995). Beirut: Advisory Center for Studies and Documentation, 1996.

"Ya Alf Sawm wa Sala 'Ala al-Riji," (We Offer a Thousand Prayers and Fasting to Return to the Days of the Régie). *Lisan al-Haal,* May 23, 1930, 1.

Yazbek, Yusif Ibrahim. *Al-Judhur al-Tarikhiyya lil-Harb al-Lubnaniyya* (The Historical Roots of the Lebanese Civil War). Beirut: Dar Nawfal, 1993.

Yunis, Sadir. "Al-Tabaqa al-'Amila al-Lubnaniyya" (The Lebanese Working Class). *Al-Tariq* 39 (Feb. 1980): 13–27, and 40 (Aug. 1981): 11–24.

Zabbal, Salim. "Lubnan fi Maydan al-Sina'a" (Lebanon in the Field of Industry). *Al-'Arabi* 131 (Oct. 1969): 74–91.

Zaydan, 'Abd al-Baqi. *Al-'Amal wa al-'Ummal wa al-Mihan fil-Islam* (Work, Workers, and Professions in Islam). Cairo: Maktabat Wahba, 1978.

Zayn al-Din, Amira. "Nazra fil-Mar'a wa Ta'thir al-'Adat" (A Glance at Women and the Influence of Customs). *Al-Hasna'* 7, no. 3 (Jan. 1911): 270–71.

———. "Nazra 'Umumiyya" (A General Glance). *Al-Hasna'* 2, no. 2 (Aug. 1910): 65–67.

———. *Al-Sufur wal-Hijab* (Veiling and Unveiling). Beirut: Dar al-Mada lil-Thaqafa wa al-Nashr, 1928.

Zoghaib, Henri. *'Asi Rahbani, Mansur Rahbani: Al-A'mal al-Masrahiyya al-Kamila* (The Anthology of the Musicals of the Rahbani Brothers). Vol. 13. Juniya, Lebanon: Dinamik Ghrafik lil-Tiba'a wa al-Nashir, 2003.

Zurayk, Huda. "Dawr al-Mar'a fi al-Tanmiyya al-Ijtima'iyya al-Iqtisadiyya fi al-Buldan al-'Arabiyya" (Women's Role in Social-Economic Growth in Arab Countries). In *Al-Mar'a al-'Arabiyya: Bayn Thuqul al-Waqi' wa Tatallu'at al-Taharrur* (Arab Women: Between Reality and Emancipation), 83–117. Beirut: Markaz Dirasat al-Wihda al-'Arabiyya, 1999).

Western-Language Sources

Abisaab, Malek. "Syrian-Lebanese Communism and the National Question, 1924–1968." Master's thesis, City College, City Univ. of New York, 1992.

Abou Chadid, Eugenie. *Thirty Years of Syria and Lebanon, 1917–1947.* Beirut: Sader-Rihani, 1948.

Abou-El-Haj, Rifa'at Ali. "An Agenda for Research in History: The History of Libya Between the Sixteenth and Nineteenth Centuries." *International Journal of Middle Eastern Studies* 15 (1983): 305–19.

———. *The Formation of the Modern State.* Albany: State Univ. of New York Press, 1991.

———. "The Social Uses of the Past: Recent Arab Historiography of Ottoman Rule." *International Journal of Middle Eastern Studies* 14 (1982): 185–201.

Abou-Zeid, Ahmed. "Shame among the Bedouins of Egypt." In *Honour and Shame: The Values of Mediterranean Society,* edited by John G. Peristiany, 243–60. London: Univ. of Chicago Press, 1966.

Abrahamian, Ervand. *Iran Between Two Revolutions.* Princeton, N.J.: Princeton Univ. Press, 1982.

———. "The Strength and Weaknesses of the Labor Movement in Iran, 1941–1953." In *Modern Iran: The Dialectics of Continuity and Change,* edited by Michael E. Bonine and Nikki R. Keddie, 211–32. Albany: State Univ. of New York Press, 1981.

Abu-Izziddin, Fouad, and George Hakim. "A Contribution to the Study of Labor Conditions in the Lebanon." *International Labour Review* 28 (Nov. 1933): 673–82.

Abu-Lughod, Janet. "Migrant Adjustment to City Life: The Egyptian Case." *American Journal of Sociology* 67 (July 1961): 22–32.

———. *Problems and Policy Implications of Middle Eastern Urbanization.* Beirut: United Nations Economic and Social Office, 1972.

Abu-Lughod, Leila. *Writing Women's Worlds: Bedouin Stories*. Berkeley and Los Angeles: Univ. of California Press, 1993.

Afary, Janet. "The War Against Feminism in the Name of the Almighty: Making Sense of Gender and Muslim Fundamentalism." *New Left Review* 224 (July–Aug. 1997): 89–110.

Afshar, Haleh, ed. *Women, Work, and Ideology in the Third World*. London: Tavistock, 1985.

Ahdab-Yehia, May. "Women, Employment, and Fertility Trends in the Arab Middle East and North Africa." In *The Fertility of Working Women*, edited by Stanley Kupinsky, 172–87. New York: Praeger, 1977.

Ahmad, Eqbal. "Trade Unionism." In *State and Society in Independent North Africa*, edited by Leon Carl Brown, 146–91. Washington, D.C.: Middle East Institute, 1966.

Ahmed, Leila. *Women and Gender in Islam*. New Haven, Conn.: Yale Univ. Press, 1992.

Akarli, Engin Deniz. *The Long Peace: Ottoman Lebanon, 1861–1920*. Berkeley and Los Angeles: Univ. of California Press, 1993.

Akl George, Abdo Ouadat, and Edouard Hunein, eds. *The Black Book of the Lebanese Elections of May 25, 1947*. New York: Phoenicia Press, 1947.

Amin, Samir. *Eurocentrism*. New York: Monthly Review Press, 1989.

Anderson, Benedict. *Imagined Communities: Reflections on the Origin and the Spread of Nationalism*. London: Verso, 1986.

Andree, Michel. "Needs and Aspirations of Married Women Workers in France." *International Labour Review* 94 (1966): 39–53.

Anker, Richard, and Martha Anker. "Measuring the Female Labour Force in Egypt." *International Labour Review* 128 (1989): 511–20.

Al-ʿAqiqi, Antun Dahir. *Lebanon in the Last Years of Feudalism, 1840–1868: A Contemporary Account*. Translated by Malcolm H. Kerr. Beirut: American Univ. of Beirut, 1959.

Asad, Talal, ed. *Anthropology and the Colonial Encounter*. New York: Atlantic Highlands, 1985.

———. "Multiculturalism and British Identity in the Wake of the Rushdie Affair." *Politics and Society* 18 (1990): 455–80.

Asfour, Edmund Y. "Industrial Development in Lebanon." *Middle East Economic Papers* (1955): 1–16.

Aumont, Michele. "Women in the Factory: A Record of Personal Experience." *International Labour Review* 74 (1956): 345–62.

ʿAzzam, Henry, and Diana Shaib. *The Women Left Behind: A Study of the Wives of Lebanese Migrant Workers in the Oil Rich Countries of the Region*. Beirut: Work Employment Program Research, International Labor Organization, 1980.

Badre, Albert. "Economic Development of Lebanon." In *Economic Development and Population Growth in the Middle East,* edited by Charles A. Cooper and Sidney S. Alexander, 160–207. New York: American Elsevier, 1972.

Baer, Gabriel. "Guilds in Middle Eastern History." In *Studies in the Economic History of the Middle East,* edited by M. A. Cook, 11–30. New York: Oxford Univ. Press, 1970.

———. "Ottoman Guilds: A Reassessment." In *The Social and Economic History of Turkey, 1071–1920,* edited by Osman Okyar and Halil Inalcik, 95–102. Ankara, Turkey: Meteksan Limited Sirketi, 1980.

———. *Population and Society in the Arab East.* Westport, Conn.: Greenwood Press, 1976.

Bahl, Vinay. "Class Consciousness and Primordial Values in the Shaping of the Indian Working Class." *South Asia Bulletin* 13 (1993): 152–72.

———. "Cultural Imperialism and Women's Movements: Thinking Globally." *Gender and History* 9 (Apr. 1997): 1–14.

———. *The Making of the Indian Working Class: The Case of the Tata Iron and Steel Co., 1880–1946.* New Delhi: Sage, 1995.

———. "Reflections on the Recent Work of Sheila Rowbotham: Women's Movements and Building Bridges." *Monthly Review* 43 (Nov. 1996): 31–42.

———. "Women in the Third World: Problems in Proletarianization and Class Consciousness." *Sage Race Relations Abstracts* 14 (May 1989): 3–27.

Balibar, Etienne, and Immanuel Wallerstein. *Race, Nation, Class: Ambiguous Identities.* New York: Verso, 1991.

Bani Sadr, Abul Hasan. *Work and the Worker in Islam.* Translated by Hasan Mashadi. Edited by Jala Anderson. Tehran: Hamdami Foundation, 1980.

Baron, Ava. "Gender and Labor History: Learning from the Past, Looking to the Future." In *Work Engendered: Toward a New History of American Labor,* edited by Ava Baron, 1–46. Ithaca, N.Y.: Cornell Univ. Press, 1991.

Baron, Beth. *Egypt as a Woman: Nationalism, Gender, and Politics.* Berkeley and Los Angeles: Univ. of California Press, 2005.

———. "The Making and Breaking of Marital Bonds in Modern Egypt." In *Women in Middle Eastern History: Shifting Boundaries in Sex and Gender,* edited by Nikki R. Keddie and Beth Baron, 275–91. New Haven, Conn.: Yale Univ. Press, 1991.

———. "Nationalist Iconography: Egypt as a Woman." In *Rethinking Nationalism in the Arab Middle East,* edited by James Jankowski and Israel Gershoni, 105–24. New York: Columbia Univ. Press, 1997.

———. *The Women's Awakening in Egypt: Culture, Society, and the Press.* New Haven, Conn.: Yale Univ. Press, 1994.

Batatu, Hanna. *The Old Social Classes and the Revolutionary Movements of Iraq.* Princeton, N.J.: Princeton Univ. Press, 1978.

————. *Syria's Peasantry, the Descendants of Its Lesser Rural Notables, and Their Politics.* Princeton, N.J.: Princeton Univ. Press, 1999.

Bauman, Zygmund. *Modernity and the Holocaust.* Ithaca, N.Y.: Cornell Univ. Press, 1989.

Bawarshi, Tawfiq. "The Lebanese Labour Scene." *Middle East Forum* 39 (1936): 21–24.

Bayat, Assef. "Historiography, Class, and Iranian Workers." In *Workers and Working Class in the Middle East: Struggles, Histories, Historiographies,* edited by Zachary Lockman, 165–210. Albany: State Univ. of New York Press, 1994.

————. *Workers and Revolution in Iran: A Third World Experience of Workers' Control.* London: Zed, 1987.

Bean, Lee L. "Utilisation of Human Resources: The Case of Women in Pakistan." *International Labour Review* 97 (Apr. 1968): 391–410.

Beck, Lois, and Nikki Keddie. *Women in the Muslim World.* Cambridge, Mass.: Harvard Univ. Press, 1978.

Behhabib, Seyla. *Feminist Contentions: A Philosophical Exchange.* New York: Routledge 1995.

Beinin, Joel. "Formation of the Egyptian Working Class." *MERIP Reports* 94 (Feb. 1981): 14–23.

————. "Islam, Marxism, and the Shubra al-Khayma Textile Workers: Muslim Brothers and Communists in the Egyptian Trade Union Movement." In *Islam, Politics, and Social Movements,* edited by Edmund Burke III and Ira M. Lapidus, 207–27. Berkeley and Los Angeles: Univ. of California Press, 1988.

————. "Will the Real Egyptian Working Class Please Stand Up?" In *Workers and Working Classes in the Middle East: Struggles, Histories, Historiographies,* edited by Zachary Lockman, 247–70. Albany: State Univ. of New York Press, 1994.

Beinin, Joel, and Zackary Lockman. *Workers on the Nile: Nationalism, Communism, Islam, and the Egyptian Working Class, 1882–1954.* Princeton, N.J.: Princeton Univ. Press, 1987.

Beling, A. Willard. *Pan Arabism and Labor.* Cambridge, Mass.: Harvard Univ. Press, 1960.

Beneria, Lourdes, ed. *Unequal Burden: Economic Crises, Persistence, Poverty, and Women's Work.* Boulder, Colo.: Westview Press, 1993.

Berent, Jerzy. "Some Demographic Aspects of Female Employment in Eastern Europe and the USSR." *International Labour Review* 101 (Feb. 1970): 175–92.

Bergquist, Charles. "Labor History and Its Challenges: Confessions of a Latin Americanist." *American Historical Review* (June 1993): 757–64.

Berik, Gunseli. *Women Carpet Weavers in Rural Turkey: Patterns of Employment, Earnings, and Status.* Geneva: International Labour Office, 1987.

Berouti, Lucien. *La crise de l'emploi au Liban.* Beirut: Univ. Libanaise, Centre de Recherches, 1973.

———. "Employment Promotion Problems in Arab Countries." *International Labour Review* 114 (Sept.-Oct. 1976): 169–85.

———. *Premiere approche de l'ouvrier d'industrie au Liban.* Beirut: Univ. Libanaise, Centre de Recherches, 1969.

Beydoun, Ahmad. *Identité confessionelle et temps social chez les historiens libanais contemporains.* Beirut: Manshurat al-Jami'a al-Lubnaniyya, 1984.

Bienen, Henry. "Urbanization and Third World Stability." *World Development* 12 (July 1984): 661–91.

Binder, Leonard, ed. *Politics in Lebanon.* New York: Wiley, 1966.

Bisilliat, Jeanne. *Women of the Third World: Work and Daily Life.* Madison, N.J.: Fairleigh Dickinson Univ. Press, 1987.

Blewett, Mary H. *The Last Generation: Work and Life in the Textile Mills of Lowell, Massachusetts, 1910-1960.* Amherst: Univ. of Massachusetts Press, 1990.

Boahen, Adu A. *African Perspectives on Colonialism.* Baltimore: Johns Hopkins Univ. Press, 1989.

———. *Africa under Colonial Domination, 1880-1935.* Berkeley and Los Angeles: Univ. of California Press, 1985.

Bonnel, Victoria E. *Roots of Rebellion: Workers' Politics and Organizations in St. Petersburg and Moscow, 1900-1914.* Berkeley and Los Angeles: Univ. of California Press, 1983.

———. *The Russian Worker: Life and Labor under the Tsarist Regime.* Berkeley and Los Angeles: Univ. of California Press, 1983.

Boserup, Ester. "Employment of Women in Developing Countries." In *Population Growth and Economic Development in the Third World,* edited by Leon Tabah, 79–107. Dolhain, Belgium: Ordina, 1975.

Bottomore, Tom, Laurence Harris, G. V. Kieman, and Ralph Miliband, eds. *A Dictionary of Marxist Thought.* Cambridge, U.K.: Blackwell Reference, 1991.

Bouatta, Cherifa. "Feminine Militancy: *Moudjahidates* during and after the Algerian War." In *Gender and National Identity: Women and Politics in Muslim Societies,* edited by Valentine M. Moghadam, 18–35. London: Oxford Univ. Press and Zed Books, 1994.

Boulding, Elise. "Measure of Women's Work in the Third World: Problems and Suggestions." In *Women and Poverty in the Third World,* edited by Marya Buvinic, Margaret

A. Lycette, and William Paul McGreevy, 286–99. Baltimore: Johns Hopkins Univ. Press, 1983.

Browne, Walter, ed. *The Political History of Lebanon: 1920–1950. Documents on Politics and Political Parties under French Mandate, 1920–1936.* Salisbury, U.K.: Documentary Publications, 1976.

Buheiry, Marwan R. "The Rise of the City of Beirut." In *The Formation and Perception of the Modern Arab World: Studies by Marwan R. Buheiry,* edited by Lawrence I. Conard, 483–87. Princeton, N.J.: Darwin Press, 1989.

Bulloch, John. *Final Conflict: The War in Lebanon.* London: Century, 1983.

Burke, Edmund, III, and Ira M. Lapidus, eds. *Islam, Politics, and Social Movements.* Berkeley and Los Angeles: Univ. of California Press, 1988.

Cameron, Ardis. *Radicals of the Worst Sort: Laboring Women in Lawrence, Massachusetts, 1860–1912.* Champaign: Univ. of Illinois Press, 1993.

Canning, Kathleen. "Gender and the Politics of Class Formation: Rethinking German Labor History." *American Historical Review* 97 (June 1992): 736–68.

Caulfield, Mina Davis. "Imperialism, the Family, and Cultures of Resistance." *Socialist Revolution* 4 (Oct. 1974): 67–85.

Chakrabarty, Dipesh. "Class Consciousness and the Indian Working Class: Dilemmas of Marxist Historiography." *Journal of Asian and African Studies* 23, nos. 1–2 (1988): 21–31.

———. "Labor History and the Politics of Theory: An Indian Angle on the Middle East." In *Workers and Working Classes in the Middle East: Struggles, Histories, Historiographies,* edited by Zachary Lockman, 321–34. Albany: State Univ. of New York Press, 1994.

———. *Rethinking Working Class History.* Princeton, N.J.: Princeton Univ. Press, 1988.

Chamie, Joseph. *Religion and Fertility: Arab Christian-Muslim Differentials.* Cambridge, U.K.: Cambridge Univ. Press, 1981.

Chamie, Mary. "Labour Force Participation of Lebanese Women." In *Women, Employment, and Development in the Arab World,* edited by Julinda Abu Nasr, Nabil F. Khoury, and Henry T. Azzam, 71–102. New York: Mouton, 1985.

———. *Women of the World: Near East and North Africa.* Washington, D.C.: Bureau of the Census, U.S. Department of Commerce, 1985.

Chatterjee, Partha. *Nationalist Thought and the Colonial World: A Derivative Discourse.* Minneapolis: Univ. of Minnesota Press, 1993.

Chevallier, Dominique. "Western Development and Eastern Crisis in the Mid–Nineteenth Century: Syria Confronted with the European Economy." In *Beginnings of Modernization in the Middle East,* edited by William R. Polk and Richard L. Chambers, 205–22. Chicago: Univ. of Chicago Press, 1968.

Chiha, Michel. *Lebanon at Home and Abroad*. Beirut: Dar al-Nahar, 1966.

———. *Politique intérieure*. Beirut: Éditions du Trident, 1964.

———. *Propos d'économie libanaise*. Beirut: Éditions du Trident, 1965.

Choueiri, Youssef. *Arab History and the Nation-State: A Study in Modern Arab Historiography, 1820–1980*. New York: Routledge, 1989.

———, ed. *State and Society in Syria and Lebanon*. New York: St. Martin's Press, 1994.

Churchill, Charles W. *The City of Beirut: A Socio-economic Survey*. Beirut: Dar El-Kitab, 1954.

———. "Village Life of the Central Beqaʿ Valley of Lebanon." *Middle East Economic Papers* (1968): 1–48.

Clark, Janet Hyde, and Irene Lorfing. *Tasks of Women in Industry*. Beirut: Institute of Women's Studies in the Arab World, Beirut Univ. College, 1987.

Cleveland, William L. *A History of the Modern Middle East*. Boulder, Colo.: Westview Press, 2000.

Cobban, Helena. *The Making of Modern Lebanon*. London: Hutchinson, 1985.

Cohen, Lizabeth. *Making A New Deal: Industrial Workers in Chicago, 1919–1939*. New York: Cambridge Univ. Press, 1990.

Cole, Juan R. I. *Colonialism and Revolution in the Middle East: Social and Cultural Origins of Egypt's 'Urabi Movement*. Princeton, N.J.: Princeton Univ. Press, 1993.

———. "Feminism, Class, and Islam in Turn-of-the-Century Egypt." *International Journal of Middle East Studies* 13 (1981): 387–407.

———. "Gender, Tradition, and History." In *Reconstructing Gender in the Middle East: Tradition, Identity, and Power*, edited by Fatma Muge Gocek and Shiva Balaghi, 23–29. New York: Cambridge Univ. Press, 1994.

"Conditions of Work in Syria and the Lebanon under French Mandate." *International Labour Review* 39 (Apr. 1939): 513–25.

Connor, Walker. *Ethnonationalism: The Quest for Understanding*. Princeton, N.J.: Princeton Univ. Press, 1994.

Cooper, Patricia. *Once a Cigar Maker: Men, Women, and Work Culture in American Cigar Factories, 1900–1919*. Chicago: Univ. of Illinois Press, 1992.

Cordova, Efren. "Strikes in the Public Service: Some Determinants and Trends." *International Labour Review* 124 (Apr. 1985): 163–78.

Cuno, Kenneth. *The Pasha's Peasants: Land, Society, and Economy in Lower Egypt, 1740–1858*. Cambridge, U.K.: Cambridge Univ. Press, 1992.

Davis, John. *People of the Mediterranean: An Essay in Comparative Social Anthropology*. London: Routledge, 1977.

Dawley, Alan. *Class and Community: The Industrial Revolution in Lynn.* Cambridge, Mass.: Harvard Univ. Press, 2000.

———. "E. P. Thompson and the Peculiarities of the Americans." *Radical History Review* 19 (winter 1978–79): 33–59.

———. "Workers, Capital, and the State in the Twentieth Century." In *Perspectives on American Labor History: The Problems of Synthesis,* edited by Carroll Moody and Alice Kessler-Harris, 152–202. Dekalb: Northern Illinois Univ. Press, 1990.

De Groot, Gertjan, and Marlou Schrover. "Between Men and Machines: Women Workers in New Industries, 1870–1940." *Social History* 20 (Oct. 1995): 279–96.

De Jesus, Ed C. *The Tobacco Monopoly in the Philippines: Bureaucratic Enterprise and Social Change, 1766–1880.* Manila: Ateno de Manila Univ. Press, 1980.

Denoeux, Guilain. *Urban Unrest in the Middle East: A Comparative Study of Informal Networks in Egypt, Iran, and Lebanon.* Albany: State Univ. of New York Press, 1993.

Denti, Ettore. "Sex-Age Patterns of Labour Force Participation by Urban and Rural Populations." *International Labour Review* 98 (Dec. 1968): 525–50.

Des Villettes, Jacqueline. *La vie des femmes dans un village Maronite libanais ain el Kharoube.* Tunis: Imprimerie N. Bascone and S. Muscat, 1964.

Deyrup, J. Felicia. "Organized Labor and Government in Underdeveloped Countries: Sources of Conflict." *Industrial and Labor Relations Review* 12 (Oct. 1958): 107–31.

Dirlik, Arif. "The Postcolonial Aura: Third World Criticism in the Age of Global Capitalism." *Critical Inquiry* 20 (winter 1994): 328–56.

Dirlik, Arif, Vinay Bahl, and Peter Gran. *History after the Three Worlds: Post-Eurocentric Historiographies.* New York: Rowman and Littlefield, 2000.

Donato, Joseph. "Lebanon and Its Labor Legislation." *International Labour Review* 65, no. 1 (Jan. 1952): 64–92.

Doumani, Alexander. "The Tobacco Growers of Southern Lebanon: Politics and Economics of Change." Ph.D. diss., Univ. of California, Berkeley, 1974.

Dowd Hall, Jacquelyn. "Disorderly Women: Gender and Labor Militancy in the Appalachian South." *Journal of American History* 73 (1986): 354–82.

Dubetsky, Alan. "Kinship, Primordial Ties, and Factory Organization in Turkey." *International Journal of Middle Eastern Studies* 7 (1976): 433–51.

Dublin, Thomas. *When the Mines Closed: Stories of Struggles in Hard Times.* Ithaca, N.Y.: Cornell Univ. Press, 1998.

———. *Women at Work: The Transformation of Work and Community in Lowell, Massachusetts, 1826–1860.* New York: Columbia Univ. Press, 1979.

Dubofsky, Melvyn. *We Shall Be All: A History of the Industrial Workers of the World.* Urbana: Univ. of Illinois Press, 1988.

Economic and Social Commission for Western Asia (ESCWA). *Arab Women in ESCWA Member States.* New York: United Nations, 1994.

Eisenstadt, N. S., and Louis Roniger. "Patron-Client Relations as a Model of Structuring Social Exchange." *Comparative Studies in Society and History* 22 (Jan. 1980): 412–77.

Eley, Geoff. "Labor History, Social History, Alltagsgeschichte: Experience, Culture, and the Politics of the Everyday—A New Direction for German Social History?" *Journal of Modern History* 61 (June 1989): 297–343.

Elizaga, C. Juan. "The Participation of Women in the Labour Force of Latin America: Fertility and Other Factors." *International Labour Review* 109 (May–June 1974): 519–38.

Elkan, Walter. *An African Labour Force: Two Case Studies in East African Factory Employment.* Kampala, Uganda: East African Institute of Social Research, 1956.

"Employment Prospects of Children and Young People in the Near and Middle East." *International Labour Review* 87 (Jan. 1963): 51–66.

Entelis, John P. *Pluralism and Party Transformation in Lebanon, Al- Kata'ib, 1936-1970.* Leiden: E. J. Brill, 1974.

Esman, Milton J., and Itamar Rabinovich, eds. *Ethnicity, Pluralism, and the State in the Middle East.* Ithaca, N.Y.: Cornell Univ. Press, 1988.

Evans, Peter B., Dietrich Rueschemeyer, and Theda Skocpol, eds. *Bringing the State Back In.* Cambridge, U.K.: Cambridge Univ. Press, 1985.

"Facilities for Women Workers with Home Responsibilities." *International Labour Review* 63 (Mar. 1951): 287–301.

Fanon, Franz. *The Wretched of the Earth.* New York: Grove Weidenfeld, 1991.

Farah, Caesar E. *Decision Making and Change in the Ottoman Empire.* Kirksville, Mo.: Thomas Jefferson Univ. Press, 1993.

Faroqhi, Suraiya. "The Fieldglass and the Magnifying Lens: Studies of Ottoman Crafts and Craftsmen." *Journal of European Economic History* 20 (spring 1991): 29–57.

———. "Labor Recruitment and Control in the Ottoman Empire (Sixteenth and Seventeenth Centuries)." In *Manufacturing in the Ottoman Empire and Turkey, 1500-1950,* edited by Donald Quataert, 13–58. Albany: State Univ. of New York Press, 1994.

Farsoun, Samih. *"Student Protests and the Coming Crisis in Lebanon." MERIP Reports* 19 (1973): 3–14.

Farsoun, Samih, and Karen Farsoun. "Class and Patterns of Association among Kinsmen in Contemporary Lebanon." *Anthropological Quarterly* 47 (1974): 93–111.

Farsoun, Samih, and Lisa Hajjar. "The Contemporary Sociology of the Middle East: An Assessment." In *Theory, Politics, and the Arab World,* edited by Hisham Sharabi, 160–97. New York: Routledge, 1990.

Faue, Elizabeth. *Community of Suffering & Struggle: Women, Men, and the Labor Movement in Minneapolis, 1915–1945.* Chapel Hill: Univ. of North Carolina Press, 1991.

Ferguson, Ann, and Nancy Folbre. "The Unhappy Marriage of Patriarchy and Capitalism." In *Women and Revolution: A Discussion of the Unhappy Marriage of Marxism and Feminism,* edited by Lydia Sargent, 313–38. Boston: South End Press, 1981.

Fernea, Elizabeth, and Richard Lobban. *Middle Eastern Women and the Invisible Economy.* Gainesville: Univ. of Florida Press, 1998.

Fernea Warnock, Elizabeth, and Basima Bezirgan, eds. *Middle Eastern Women Speak.* Austin: Univ. of Texas Press, 1977.

Fink, Leon. *Workingmen's Democracy: The Knights of Labor and American Politics.* Urbana: Univ. of Illinois Press, 1985.

Firro, Kais. "Silk and Socio-economic Changes in Lebanon, 1860–1919." In *Essays on the Economic History of the Middle East,* edited by Elie Kedourie and Sylvia G. Haim, 20–50. London: F. Cass, 1988.

Flores, Alexander. "The Early History of Lebanese Communism Reconsidered." *Khamsin* 7 (1980): 7–20.

Forget, Nelly. "Attitudes toward Work by Women in Morocco." *International Social Science Journal* 14 (1962): 92–123.

Fraser, Nancy, and Linda J. Nicholson. "Social Criticism Without Philosophy: An Encounter Between Feminism and Postmodernism." In *Feminist/Postmodernism,* edited by Linda J. Nicholson, 19–38. New York: Routledge, 1990.

Galenson, Walter, ed. *Comparative Labor Movements.* New York: Prentice-Hall, 1952.

———. *Labor in Developing Economies.* Berkeley and Los Angeles: Univ. of California Press, 1962.

Gannage, Elias. *L'imposition des tabacs au Liban.* Paris: Librairie Generale de Droit et de Jurisprudence, 1956.

Gates, Carolyn. *The Historical Role of Political Economy in the Development of Modern Lebanon.* Oxford, U.K.: Centre for Lebanese Studies, 1989.

———. *The Merchant Republic of Lebanon: Rise of an Open Economy.* New York: St. Martin's Press, 1998.

———. "Laissez-faire, Outward-Orientation, and Regional Economic Disintegration: A Case Study of the Dissolution of the Syro-Lebanese Customs Unions." In *State and Society in Syria and Lebanon,* edited by Youssef Choueiri, 74–83. New York: St. Martin's Press, 1994.

Gellner, Ernest, and John Waterbury, eds. *Patrons and Clients in Mediterranean Societies.* London: Duckworth, 1977.

Gerstle, Gary. *Working-Class Americanism: The Politics of Labor in a Textile City, 1914–1960.* Cambridge, U.K.: Cambridge Univ. Press, 1989.

Ghorayshi, Parvin. *Women and Work in Developing Countries.* Westport, Conn.: Greenwood Press, 1994.

Ghoussoub, Mai. "Feminism—or the Eternal Masculine—in the Arab World." *New Left Review* 161 (Jan.–Feb. 1987): 3–18.

———. "A Reply to Hammami and Rieker." *New Left Review* 170 (July–Aug. 1988): 107–9.

Gibb, Alexander R., and Partners. *The Economic Development of Lebanon.* London: Sir Alexander Gibb and Partners, 1948.

———. *The Economic Development of Syria.* London: Knapp Dewett and Sons, 1947.

———. *Islamic Society and the West: A Study of the Impact of Western Civilization on Moslem Culture in the Middle East.* London: Oxford Univ. Press, 1950.

Glickman, Rose. *Russian Factory Women: Workplace and Society, 1880–1914.* Berkeley and Los Angeles: Univ. of California Press, 1984.

Goldberg, Ellis. "Muslim Union Politics in Egypt: Two Cases." In *Islam, Politics, and Social Movements,* edited by Edmund Burke III and Ira M. Lapidus, 228–43. Berkeley and Los Angeles: Univ. of California Press, 1988.

———, ed. *The Social History of Labor in the Middle East.* Boulder, Colo.: Westview Press, 1996.

———. *Tinker, Tailor, and Textile Worker: Class and Politics in Egypt, 1930–1952.* Berkeley and Los Angeles: Univ. of California Press, 1986.

Goode, William J. *World Revolution and Family Patterns.* New York: Free Press, 1970.

Gordon, Marshall. "Some Remarks on the Study of Working Class Consciousness." *Politics and Society* 12 (1983): 263–301.

Goria, Wade R. *Sovereignty and Leadership in Lebanon, 1943–1976.* London: Ithaca Press, 1985.

Gramwald, Kurt, and O. Joachim Ronall. *Industrialization in the Middle East.* Westport, Conn.: Greenwood Press, 1970.

Gran, Judith. "Impact of the World Market on Egyptian Woman." *MERIP Reports* 58 (June 1977): 3–7.

Gran, Peter. *Beyond Eurocentrism: A New View of Modern World History.* Syracuse, N.Y.: Syracuse Univ. Press, 1996.

———. "The Failure of Social Theory to Keep Up with Our Times: The Study of Women and Structural Adjustment Programs in the Middle East as an Example." Paper presented at the Thirty-fourth Annual Meeting of the Association of Muslim Social Scientists, Sept. 30, 2005, Philadelphia.

————. *Islamic Roots of Capitalism: Egypt, 1760–1840.* Syracuse, N.Y.: Syracuse Univ. Press, 1979.

————. "Organization of Culture and the Construction of the Family in the Modern Middle East." In *Women, the Family, and Divorce Laws in Islamic History,* edited by Amira El Azhary Sonbol, 64–80. Syracuse, N.Y.: Syracuse Univ. Press, 1996.

————. "Political Economy as a Paradigm for the Study of *Islamic History.*" *International Journal of Middle East Studies* 11 (1980): 511–26.

————. *The Rise of the Rich: A New View of Modern World History.* Syracuse, N.Y.: Syracuse Univ. Press, 2008.

————. "Studies of Anglo-American Political Economy: Democracy, Orientalism, and the Left." In *Theory, Politics, and the Arab World: Critical Responses,* edited by Hisham Sharabi, 228—-54. New York: Routledge, 1990.

————. "Subaltern Studies, Racism, and Class Struggle: Examples from India and the United States." In *The Working Papers Series in Cultural Studies, Ethnicity, and Race Relations,* 1–20. Pullman: Department of Comparative American Cultures, Washington State Univ., 1999.

Greenstreet, Miranda. "Employment of Women in Ghana." *International Labour Review* 103 (Feb. 1971): 117–29.

Guha, Sunil. "The Contribution of Non-farm Activities to Rural Employment Promotion: Experience in Iran, India, Syria." *International Labour Review* 109 (Mar. 1974): 235–50.

Gupta, Nirmal K., and Falendra Sudan. *Women at Work in Developing Economy.* New Delhi: Anmol, 1990.

Gunseli, Berik. *Women Carpet Weavers in Rural Turkey: Patterns of Employment, Earnings, and Status.* Geneva: International Labour Office, 1987.

Haimson, Leopold, and Charles Tilly, eds. *Strikes, Wars, and Revolutions in an International Perspectives.* Cambridge, U.K.: Cambridge Univ. Press, 1989.

Hajjar, Lisa. "Gender, Ethnocentrism, and Middle East Studies." *News from Within* (May 1993): 7–15.

Hakim, George. "The Economic Basis of Lebanese Polity." In *Politics in Lebanon,* edited by Leonard Binder, 57–68. New York: Wiley, 1966.

————. "The Fiscal System." In *Economic Organization of Syria,* edited by Sa'id Himadeh, 333–402. Beirut: American Univ. of Beirut, 1973.

————. "Industry." In *Economic Organization of Syria,* edited by Sa'id Himadeh, 119–73. Beirut: American Univ. of Beirut, 1973.

Halim, Fatimah. "Workers' Resistance and Management Control: A Comparative Case Study of Male and Female Workers in West Malaysia." *Journal of Contemporary Asia* 13 (1983): 131–50.

Hallsworth, J. A. "Freedom of Association and Industrial Relations in the Countries of the Near and Middle East. I." *International Labour Review* 70 (Nov. 1954): 363–84, 526–41.

———. "Freedom of Association and Industrial Relations in the Countries of the Near and Middle East. II." *International Labour Review* 70 (Dec. 1954): 526–41.

Hammam, Mona. "Labor Migration and the Sexual Division of Labor." *MERIP Reports* 95 (Mar.–Apr. 1981): 5–11.

———. "Women and Industrial Work in Egypt: The Chubra el-Kheima Case." *Arab Studies Quarterly* 2, no. 1 (winter 1980): 50–69.

Hammami, Reza, and Martina Rieker. "Feminist Orientalism and Orientalist Marxism." *New Left Review* 170 (July–Aug. 1988): 93–106.

Hanagan, Michael P. *The Logic of Solidarity: Artisans and Industrial Workers in Three French Towns, 1871–1890.* Urbana: Univ. of Illinois Press, 1980.

———. *Proletarians and Protest: The Roots of Class Formation in an Industrializing World.* Westport, Conn.: Greenwood Press, 1986.

———. "Response to Sean Wilentz, 'Against Exceptionalism: Class Consciousness and the American Labor Movement, 1790–1920.'" *International Labor and Working Class History* 26 (fall 1984): 31–36.

Hanagan, Michael P., and Charles Stephenson, eds. *Confrontation, Class Consciousness, and the Labor Process: Studies in Proletarian Class Formation.* Westport, Conn.: Greenwood Press, 1986.

Hanf, Theodor. *Coexistence in Wartime Lebanon: Decline of a State and Rise of a Nation.* London: Center for Lebanese Studies, 1993.

———. "*Homo oeconomicus–Homo communaitaris:* Crosscutting Loyalties in a Deeply Divided Society: The Case of Trade Unions in Lebanon." In *Ethnicity, Pluralism, and the State in the Middle East,* edited by Milton J. Esman and Itmar Rabinovich, 173–84. Ithaca, N.Y.: Cornell Univ. Press, 1988.

Hann, Chris. "Culture and Anti-culture: The Specter of Orientalism in New Anthropological Writing on Turkey." *Journal of the Anthropological Society of Oxford* 24 (1993): 223–43.

Haraven, Tamara K. *Family Time and Industrial Time: The Relationship Between the Family and Work in a New England Industrial Community.* New York: Cambridge Univ. Press, 1982.

Hartman, Heidi. "The Unhappy Marriage of Marxism and Feminism: Towards a More Progressive Union." In *Women and Revolution: A Discussion of the Unhappy Marriage of Marxism,* edited by Lydia Sargent, 1–41. Boston: South End Press, 1981.

Hartman, Michelle, and Alessandro Olsaretti. "The First Boat and the First Oar: Inventions of Lebanon in the Writings of Michel Chiha." *Radical History Review* 86, no. 1 (2003): 37–65.

Hatem, Mervat. "Class and Patriarchy as Competing Paradigms for the Study of Middle Eastern Women." *Comparative Study of Society and History* (1987): 811–18.

———. "Toward a Critique of Modernization: Narrative in Middle East Women Studies." *Arab Studies Quarterly* 15 (spring 1993): 117–22.

Hijab, Nadia. *Womanpower: The Arab Debate on Women at Work.* New York: Cambridge Univ. Press, 1988.

Himadeh, Saʻid. "Economic Factors Underlying Social Problems in the Arab Middle East." *Middle East Journal* 5 (summer 1951): 168–93.

———, ed. *Economic Organization of Syria.* Beirut: American Univ. of Beirut, 1973.

Hobsbawm, Eric. "Class Consciousness in History." In *Aspects of History and Class Consciousness,* edited by Istvan Meszaros, 5—-22. New York: Herder and Herder, 1973.

———. "Farewell to the Classic Labour Movement?" *New Left Review* 173 (Jan. 1989): 69–74.

———. *Labouring Men: Studies in the History of Labour.* London: Weidenfeld and Nicolson, 1964.

———. *Nations and Nationalism since 1780: Programme, Myth, Reality.* Cambridge, U.K.: Cambridge Univ. Press, 1990.

———. "Peasants and Politics." *Journal of Peasant Studies* 1 (Oct. 1973): 3–22.

———. "The Social Function of the Past." *Past and Present* 55 (May 1972): 3–17.

———. *Workers: World of Labor.* New York: Pantheon Books, 1984.

Holloway, John, and Sol Piccioto, eds. *State and Capital: A Marxist Debate.* Austin: Univ. of Texas Press, 1978.

Honig, Emily. *Sisters and Strangers: Women in the Shanghai Cotton Mills, 1919–1949.* Stanford, Calif.: Stanford Univ. Press, 1986.

Hooglund, Eric, ed. *Crossing the Waters: Arab-Speaking Immigrants to the US before 1940.* Washington, D.C.: Smithsonian Institution Press, 1987.

Hourani, Albert H. *Arabic Thought in the Liberal Age: 1798–1939.* Cambridge, U.K.: Cambridge Univ. Press, 1983.

———. "Historians of Lebanon." In *Historians of the Middle East,* edited by Bernard Lewis and P. M. Holt, 226–46. Oxford: Oxford Univ. Press, 1962.

———. *A History of the Arab Peoples.* Cambridge, Mass.: Belknap Press of Harvard Univ. Press, 1991.

———. "Ideologies of the Mountain and the City." In *Essays on the Crises in Lebanon,* edited by Roger Owen, 33–41. London: Ithaca Press, 1976.

———. "Lebanon: The Development of a Political Society." In *Politics in Lebanon,* edited by Leonard Binder, 13–30. New York: Wiley, 1966.

————. *Minorities of the Arab World*. London: Oxford Univ. Press, 1947.

————. "Race, Religion, and Nation-State in the Near East." In *A Vision of History*, edited by Albert Hourani, 71–105. Beirut: Khayats, 1961.

————. *Syria and Lebanon: A Political Essay*. Beirut: Lebanon Bookshop, 1968.

Hourani, Albert H., and Nadim Shehadi, eds. *The Lebanese in the World: A Century of Emigration*. London: Center for Lebanese Studies, 1992.

Hourani, Benjamin T. "Unionism in the Lebanese Labor Code of 1946." Master's thesis, American Univ. of Beirut, 1959.

Hudson, Michael. *The Precarious Republic: Political Modernization in Lebanon*. Boulder, Colo.: Westview Press, 1985.

Humphries, Jane. "The Working Class Family, Women's Liberation, and Class Struggle: The Case of Nineteenth Century British History." *Review of Radical Political Economics* 9 (fall 1977): 25–41.

Inalcik, Halil, and Donald Quataert, eds. *An Economic and Social History of the Ottoman Empire*. Cambridge, U.K.: Cambridge Univ. Press, 1994.

Isambert-Jamati, Viviane. "Absenteeism among Women Workers in Industry." *International Labour eview* 85 (Mar. 1962): 248–61.

Iskandar, Marwan, and Elias Baroudi. "Industry." In *The Lebanese Economy in 1981–82*, edited by Marwan Iskandar and Elias Baroudi, 11–25. Beirut: Middle East Economic Consultants, 1982.

————, eds. *The Lebanese Economy in 1981–1982*. Beirut: Middle East Economic Consultants, 1982.

Ismael, Tareq. *The Communist Movement in Syria and Lebanon*. Gainesville: Univ. of Florida Press, 1998.

Ismael, Tareq, and Rifaʿat El-Saʿid. *The Communist Movement in Egypt: 1920–1988*. Syracuse, N.Y.: Syracuse Univ. Press, 1990.

Issawi, Charles. "Economic Development and Liberalism in Lebanon." *Middle East Journal* 18 (summer 1964): 279–92.

————, ed. *The Economic History of the Middle East, 1800–1914: A Book of Readings*. Chicago: Univ. of Chicago Press, 1966.

————. *Egypt: An Economic and Social Analysis*. London: Oxford Univ. Press, 1947.

————. *The Fertile Crescent, 1800–1914: A Documentary Economic History*. New York: Oxford Univ. Press, 1988.

————. *The Middle East Economy: Decline and Recovery*. Princeton, N.J.: Markus Wiener, 1995.

Jameson, Fredric. *Postmodernism, or, the Cultural Logic of Late Capitalism*. Durham, N.C.: Duke Univ. Press, 1991.

Janiewski, Dolores E. *Sisterhood Denied: Race, Gender, and Class in a New South Community.* Philadelphia: Temple Univ. Press, 1985.

Janjic, Marion. "Women's Employment and Conditions of Work in Switzerland." *International Labour Review* 96 (Sept. 1967): 292–317.

Jauregui, Bereciatu Gurutz. *Decline of the Nation State.* Reno: Univ. of Nevada Press, 1994.

Jazani, Bizhan. *Capitalism and Revolution in Iran.* New Delhi and London: Vikas and Zed Press, 1982.

Jenson, Jane, Elizabeth Hagen, and Reddy Ceallagh, eds. *Feminization of the Labor Force: Paradoxes and Promises.* New York: Oxford Univ. Press, 1988.

Johnson, Michael. *Class and Client in Beirut: The Sunni Muslim Community and the Lebanese State, 1840–1985.* London: Atlantic Highlands, 1986.

Johnson, Paul R. *The Economics of the Tobacco Industry.* New York: Praeger, 1984.

Joseph, Suad. "Family as Security and Bondage: A Political Strategy of the Lebanese Urban Working Class." In *Toward a Political Economy of Urbanization in Third World Countries,* edited by Helen I. Safa, 151–71. Oxford, U.K.: Oxford Univ. Press, 1982.

———. "Gender and Citizenship in Middle Eastern States." *MERIP Reports* 26 (Jan.– Mar. 1996): 4–10.

———. "Gender and Civil Society." *MERIP Reports* 23 (July–Aug. 1993): 22–26.

———. "The Politicization of Religious Sects in Borj Hammoud, Lebanon." Ph.D. diss., Univ. of Michigan, Ann Arbor, 1975.

———. "Women and Political Movements in the Middle East: Agenda for Research." *Middle East Reports* 16 (1986): 3–7.

———. "Working-Class Women's Networks in a Sectarian State: A Political Paradox." *American Ethnologist* 10 (Feb. 1983): 1–22.

———. "Zaynab: An Urban Working-Class Lebanese Woman." In *Middle Eastern Muslim Women Speak,* edited by Elizabeth Warnock Fernea and Basima Bezirgan, 359–72. Austin: Univ. of Texas Press, 1977.

Kandiyoti, Deniz. "Contemporary Feminist Scholarship and Middle Eastern Studies." In *Gendering the Middle East: Emerging Perspectives,* edited by Deniz Kandiyoti, 1–27. Syracuse, N.Y.: Syracuse Univ. Press, 1996.

———, ed. *Gendering the Middle East: Emerging Perspectives.* Syracuse, N.Y.: Syracuse Univ. Press, 1996.

———. "Islam and Patriarchy: A Comparative Perspective." In *Women in Middle Eastern History: Shifting Boundaries in Sex and Gender,* edited by Nikki R. Keddie and Beth Baron, 23–42. New Haven, Conn.: Yale Univ. Press, 1991.

————, ed. *Women, Islam, and the State*. Philadelphia: Temple Univ. Press, 1991.

Kaplan, Temma. "Female Consciousness and Collective Action: The Case of Barcelona, 1910–18." *Signs* 11 (1982): 545–66.

Karakïşla, Yavuz Selim. "The Emergence of the Ottoman Industrial Working Class, 1836–1823." In *Workers and the Working Class in the Ottoman Empire and the Turkish Republic: 1839–1950*, edited by Donald Quataert and Erik Jan Zurcher, 19–34. New York: Tauris Academic Studies, 1995.

Karyergatian, Yahe. "Monopoly in the Lebanese Tobacco Industry." Master's thesis, American Univ. of Beirut, 1965.

Kasir, Samir. *Histoire de Beyrouth*. Paris: Fayard, 2003.

Keddie, Nikki R. "Introduction." In *Religion and Politics in Iran: Shi'ism from Quietism to Revolution*, edited by Nikki R. Keddie, 1–18. New Haven, Conn.: Yale Univ. Press, 1983.

————. "Problems in the Study of Middle Eastern Women." *International Journal of Middle East Studies* 10 (1979): 225–40.

————, ed. *Religion and Politics in Iran: Shi'ism from Quietism to Revolution*. New Haven, Conn.: Yale Univ. Press, 1983.

Kedourie, Elie. *Nationalism*. London: Hutchinson Univ. Library, 1971.

Kerr, Malcolm. *America's Middle East Policy: Kissinger, Carter, and the Future*. Beirut: Institute for Palestine Studies, 1980.

————. *The Arab Cold War, 1958–1964: A Study of Ideology in Politics*. New York: Oxford Univ. Press, 1965.

————. *Egypt under Nasser*. New York: Foreign Policy Association, 1963.

————. "Lebanese Views on the 1958 Crisis." *Middle East Journal* 15 (spring 1969): 211–17.

Kessler-Harris, Alice. "A New Agenda for American Labor History: A Gendered Analysis and the Question of Class." In *Perspectives on American Labor History: The Problems of Synthesis*, edited by Alice Kessler-Harris, 217–34. Dekalb: Northern Illinois Univ. Press, 1989.

————. *Out to Work: A History of Wage-Earning Women in the United States*. New York: Oxford Univ. Press, 1982.

————. "Where Are the Organized Women Workers?" *Feminist Studies* 3 (fall 1975): 92–110.

Khalaf, Nadim G., and Gaston V. Rimlinger. "The Response of the Lebanese Labour Force to Economic Dislocation." *Middle Eastern Studies* 18 (July 1982): 300–310.

Khalaf, Samir. *Civil and Uncivil Violence in Lebanon: A History of Internationalization of Communal Conflict*. New York: Columbia Univ. Press, 2002.

————. "Industrial Conflict in Lebanon." *Human Organization* 24 (spring 1965): 25–33.

————. "Lebanese Labour Unions: Some Comparative Structural Features." *Middle East Economic Papers* (1968): 111–38.

————. *Lebanon's Predicament.* New York: Columbia Univ. Press, 1987.

————. *Persistence and Change in Nineteenth Century Lebanon.* Beirut: American Univ. of Beirut, 1979.

————. "Primordial Ties and Politics in Lebanon." *Middle Eastern Studies* 3 (Apr. 1968): 243–69.

————. "Social Structure and Urban Planning in Lebanon." In *Property, Social Structure, and Law in the Modern Middle East,* edited by Elizabeth Mayer, 213–36. Albany: State Univ. of New York Press, 1985.

Khalifa, Ahmad. *Status of Women in Relation to Fertility and Family Planning in Egypt.* Cairo: National Center for Social and Criminological Research, 1973.

Khater, Akram Fouad. "'House' to 'Goddess of the House': Gender, Class, and Silk in 19th-Century Mount Lebanon." *International Journal of Middle East Studies* 28 (Aug. 1996): 325–48.

————. *Inventing Home: Emigration, Gender, and the Middle Class in Lebanon, 1870–1920.* Berkeley and Los Angeles: Univ. of California Press, 2001.

————. *Sources in the History of the Modern Middle East.* Boston: Houghton Mifflin, 2004.

El Khazen, Farid. *The Breakdown of the State in Lebanon, 1967–1976.* Cambridge, Mass.: Harvard Univ. Press, 2000.

Khodja, Souad. "Women's Work as Viewed in Present-Day Algerian Society." *International Labour Review* 121 (July–Aug. 1982): 481–87.

Khoury, Enver M. *The Crisis in the Lebanese System: Confessionalism and Chaos.* Washington, D.C.: American Enterprise Institute for Public Research, 1976.

Khoury, Philip S. *Syria and the French Mandate: The Politics of Arab Nationalism, 1920–1945.* Princeton, N.J.: Princeton Univ. Press, 1987.

Khoury, Philip S., and Joseph Kostiner, eds. *Tribes and State Formation in the Middle East.* Berkeley and Los Angeles: Univ. of California Press, 1990.

Khoury Rizk, Dina. *State and Provincial Society in the Ottoman Empire: Mosul, 1540–1834.* New York: Cambridge Univ. Press, 1997.

Khuri, Fuad. "The Changing Class Structure in Lebanon." *Middle East Journal* 23 (1969): 29–44.

————. *From Village to Suburb: Order and Change in Greater Beirut.* Chicago: Univ. of Chicago Press, 1975.

———. "Sectarian Loyalty among Rural Migrants in Two Lebanese Suburbs: A Stage Between Family and National Allegiance." In *Rural Politics and Social Change in the Middle East,* edited by Richard Antoun and Iliya Harik, 198–213. Bloomington: Indiana Univ. Press, 1972.

Klat, Paul. "Labor Legislation in Lebanon." *Middle East Economic Papers* (1959): 69–82.

Labaki, Boutros. "The Commercial Network of Beirut in the Last Twenty Five Years of Ottoman Rule." In *Decision Making and Change in the Ottoman Empire,* edited by Caesar Farah, 243–62. Kirksville, Mo.: Thomas Jefferson Univ. Press, 1993.

———. *Introduction a l'histoire économique du Liban.* Beirut: Univ. Libanaise, 1984.

Ladjevardi, Habib. *Labor Unions and Autocracy in Iran.* Syracuse, N.Y.: Syracuse Univ. Press, 1985.

Lampman, J. Robert. "The Lebanese Labor Code of 1946." *Labor Law Journal* (July 1954): 491–503.

Laroque, Pierre. "Women's Rights and Widows' Pensions." *International Labour Review* 106 (July 1972): 1–10.

Layne, Linda. "Women in Jordan's Workforce." *MERIP Reports* 9 (Mar.–Apr. 1981): 19–23.

Lazreg, Marnia. *The Eloquence of Silence: Algerian Women in Question.* New York: Routledge, 1994.

———. "Feminism and Difference: The Perils of Writing as a Woman on Women in Algeria." *Feminist Studies* 14 (1988): 95–112.

———. *Women's Experience and Feminist Epistemology: A Critical Neo-rationalist Approach.* New York: Routledge, 1994.

Leacock, Eleanor, and Helen I. Safa. *Women's Work: Development and Division of Labor by Gender.* South Hadley, Mass.: Begin and Garvey, 1986.

Leijon, Anna-Greta. "Sexual Equality in the Labour Market: Some Experiences and Views of the Nordic Countries." *International Labour Review* 112 (Aug.–Sept. 1975): 109–23.

Lewis, Jane. "Gender, the Family, and Women's Agency in the Building of 'Welfare States': The British Case." *Social History* 19 (Jan. 1994): 37–66.

Lichtenstein, Nelson. *Labor's War at Home: The ICO in World War II.* New York: Cambridge Univ. Press, 1982.

Lloyd, Peter. *A Third World Proletariat.* London: G. Allen and Unwin, 1982.

Lockman, Zachary. "Arab Workers and Arab Nationalism in Palestine: A View from Below." In *Rethinking Nationalism in the Arab Middle East,* edited by James Jankowski and Israel Gershoni, 249–72. New York: Columbia Univ. Press, 1997.

———, ed. *Workers and Working Classes in the Middle East: Struggles, Histories, Historiography*. Albany: State Univ. of New York Press, 1994.

Longrigg, Stephen H. *Syria and Lebanon under French Mandate*. London: Oxford Univ. Press, 1958.

Longuenesse, Elizabeth. "The Syrian Working Class Today." *MERIP Reports* 134 (July–Aug. 1985): 17–24.

Lorfing, Irene. "Women Workers in Lebanese Industry." In *Women Work in the Third World: The Impact of Industrialization and Global Economic Interdependence*, edited by Nagat M. El-Sanabary, 183–92. Berkeley: Center for the Study, Education, and Advancement of Women, Univ. of California, 1983.

Lubeck, Paul M. *Islam and Urban Labor in Northern Nigeria: The Making of a Muslim Working Class*. New York: Columbia Univ. Press, 1986.

Lukacs, Georg. *History and Class Consciousness*. Cambridge, Mass.: MIT Press, 1971.

Macleod, Arlene. *Accommodating Protest: Working Women, the New Veiling, and Change in Cairo*. New York: Columbia Univ. Press, 1993.

Makdisi, Usama. "After 1860: Debating Religion, Reform, and Nationalism in the Ottoman Empire." *International Journal of Middle East Studies* 34, no. 3 (2002): 601–17.

———. *The Culture of Sectarianism: Community, History, and Violence in Nineteenth-Century Ottoman Lebanon*. Berkeley and Los Angeles: Univ. of California Press, 2000.

Mann, Michael. *The Rise and Decline of the Nation-State*. Cambridge, U.K.: Blackwell, 1990.

Marcus, Abraham. *The Middle East on the Eve of Modernity: Aleppo in the Eighteenth Century*. New York: Columbia Univ. Press, 1989.

Mardin, Serif. *Religion and Social Change in Modern Turkey*. Albany: State Univ. of New York Press, 1989.

Marshall, Gordon. "Some Remarks on the Studying of Working Class Consciousness." *Politics and Society* 12 (1983): 274–75.

Marsot, Afaf. *Women and Men in Late Eighteenth Century Egypt*. Austin: Univ. of Texas Press, 1995.

Mernissi, Fatima. *Beyond the Veil: Male-Female Dynamics in a Modern Muslim Society*. Bloomington: Indiana Univ. Press, 1987.

Meyer, Stephen, III. *The Five Dollar Day: Labor Management and Social Control in the Ford Motor Company, 1906–1921*. Albany: State Univ. of New York Press, 1981.

Michel, Andree. "Needs and Aspirations of Married Women Workers in France." *International Labour Review* 94 (July 1966): 39–53.

Mitter, Sawsti, and Sheila Rowbotham, eds. *Women Encounter Technology: Changing Patterns of Employment in the Third World*. London: Routledge, 1995.

Moghadam, Fatmeh. "Commoditization of Sexuality and Female Labor Participation in Islam: Implications for Iran." In *The Eye of the Storm: Women in Post-revolutionary Iran*, edited by Mahnaz Afkhami and Erika Friedle, 80–97. Syracuse, N.Y.: Syracuse Univ. Press, 1994.

Moghadam, Valentine M., ed. *Gender and National Identity: Women and Politics in Muslim Societies*. London: Zed Books, 1994.

———. *Modernizing Women: Gender and Social Change in the Middle East*. Boulder, Colo.: Lynne Rienner, 1993.

Mohanty, Chandra. *Feminism Without Borders: Decolonization Theory, Practicing Solidarity*. Durham, N.C.: Duke Univ. Press, 2003.

———, ed. *Third World Women and the Politics of Feminism*. Bloomington: Indiana Univ. Press, 1991.

Molyneux, Maxine. *State Policies and the Position of Women Workers in the People's Democratic Republic of Yemen: 1967–1977*. Geneva: International Labour Organization, 1982.

Mongardini, Carlo. "The Ideology of Postmodernity." *Theory, Culture, and Society* 9 (1992): 55–65.

Moore, Henrietta. *Feminism and Anthropology*. Minneapolis: Univ. of Minnesota Press, 1988.

Morgenstern, Felice. "Women Workers and the Courts." *International Labour Review* 112 (July 1975): 15–27.

Moss, Bernard. *The Origins of the French Labor Movement, 1830–1914: The Socialism of Skilled Workers*. Berkeley and Los Angeles: Univ. of California Press, 1976.

Mukherjee, Ramkrishna. "Illusion and Reality: A Review of Ranjit Guha." *Sociological Bulletin* 37, nos. 1–2 (Mar.–Sept. 1988): 127–39.

———. *The Quality of Life: Valuation in Social Research*. New Delhi: Sage, 1989.

———. "Social and Cultural Components of Society and Appraisal of Social Reality." *Economic and Political Weekly* 26 (Jan. 26, 1991): 21–36.

———. *Society, Culture, Development*. New Delhi: Sage, 1991.

Nandy, Ashis. *The Intimate Enemy: Loss and Recovery of Self under Colonialism*. Delhi: Oxford Univ. Press, 1983.

Nemer, Barbara. "An Industrial Solution for Bekaa's Burley Tobacco." Master's thesis, Holy Spirit Univ.–Kaslik, Beirut, 1997.

Nicholson, Linda J. "Feminism and Marx: Integrating Kinship with Economics." In *Feminism as Critique: On the Politics of Gender,* edited by Seyal Behabib and Drucilla Cornell, 16–30. Minneapolis: Univ. of Minnesota Press, 1987.

———, ed. *Feminism/Postmodernism*. New York: Routledge, 1990.

Nickie, Charles. *Gender Division and Social Change.* Lanham, Md.: Barnes and Noble Books, 1993.

Northrup, Herbert Roof. *The Negro in the Tobacco Industry.* Philadelphia: Univ. of Pennsylvania Press, 1970.

Norton, Richard Augustus. *Hezbollah.* Princeton, N.J.: Princeton Univ. Press, 2007.

Owen, Roger. *The Middle East in the World Economy: 1800–1914.* London: Methuen, 1981.

———. *Migrant Workers in the Gulf.* London: Minority Rights Group, 1992.

———. "The Political Economy of Grand Liban: 1920–1970." In *Essays on the Crisis in Lebanon,* edited by Roger Owen, 23–32. London: Ithaca Press, 1976.

Ozveren, Yasar Eyup. "The Making and Unmaking of an Ottoman Port-City: Nineteenth-Century Beirut, Its Hinterland, and the World Economy." Ph.D. diss., State Univ. of New York, Binghamton, 1990.

Palmer, Ingrid. "Rural Women and the Basic-Needs Approach to Development." *International Labour Review* 115 (Jan.–Feb. 1977): 97–107.

Paoli, Chantal. "Women Workers and Maternity: Some Examples from Western Europe." *International Labour Review* 121 (Jan.–Feb. 1982): 1–16.

Papps, Ivy. "Attitudes to Female Employment in Four Middle Eastern Countries." In *Women in the Middle East: Perceptions, Realities, and Struggles for Liberation,* edited by Haleh Afshar, 94–117. New York: St. Martin's Press, 1993.

Pashukains, Evgeny B. *Law and Marxism: A General Theory.* London: Ink Links, 1978.

Peek, Peter. "Female Employment and Fertility: A Study Based on Children Data." *International Labor Review* 112 (Aug.–Sept. 1975): 207–16.

Peristiany, John, ed. *Honor and Shame: The Values of Mediterranean Society.* London: Weidenfeld and Nicolson, 1966.

Perlin, Frank. "Proto-industrialization and Pre-colonial South Asia." *Past and Present* (1983): 30–95.

———. *The Invisible City: Monetary, Administrative, and Popular Infrastructure in Asia and Europe, 1500–1900.* Brookfield, Vt.: Ashgate, 1993.

———. *Unbroken Landscape: Commodity, Category, Sign, and Identity: Their Production as Myth and Knowledge from 1500.* Brookfield, Vt.: Ashgate, 1994.

Perrot, Michelle. "On the Formation of the French Working Class." In *Working Class Formation: Nineteenth-Century Patterns in Western Europe and the United States,* edited by Ira Katznelson and Aristide R. Zolberg, 71–110. Princeton, N.J.: Princeton Univ. Press, 1986.

———. *Workers on Strike: France 1871–1890.* New Haven, Conn.: Yale Univ. Press, 1987.

Persen, William. "Lebanese Economic Development since 1950." *Middle East Journal* 12 (1958): 277–94.

Peteet, Julie M. *Gender in Crisis: Women and the Palestinian Resistance Movement.* New York: Columbia Univ. Press, 1992.

Plank, Thomas A. "An Appraisal of the Labor Movement in Lebanon." Master's thesis, American Univ. of Beirut, 1968.

Polk, William. *The Opening of South Lebanon, 1788-1840: A Study of the Impact of the West on the Middle East.* Cambridge, Mass.: Harvard Univ. Press, 1963.

Pollert, Anna. *Girls, Wives, Factory Lives.* London: Macmillan, 1981.

"The Population and Labour Force of Asia: 1950-80." *International Labour Review* 86 (Oct. 1962): 348-68.

Pott-Buter, Hettie. *Facts and Fairy Tales about Female Labor, Family, and Fertility: A Seven-Country Comparison, 1850-1990.* Amsterdam: Amsterdam Univ. Press, 1993.

Poulantzas, Nicos. *Classes in Contemporary Capitalism.* London: NLB, 1975.

——. *Political Power and Social Class.* London: Sheed and Ward, 1973.

Posusney, Marsha Pripstein. *Labor and the State in Egypt: Workers, Unions, and Economic Restructuring.* New York: Columbia Univ. Press, 1997.

Poya, Maryam. *Women, Work, and Islamism: Ideology and Resistance in Iran.* London: Zed Books, 1999.

Protho, Edwin Terry, and Lutfy Najib Diab. *Changing Family Patterns in the Arab East.* Beirut: American Univ. of Beirut, 1974.

Provence, Michael. *The Great Syrian Revolt and the Rise of Arab Nationalism.* Austin: Univ. of Texas Press, 2005.

Quataert, Donald. "Introduction." In *Workers and the Working Class in the Ottoman Empire and the Turkish Republic: 1839-1950,* edited by Donald Quataert and Erik Jan Zurcher, 11-18. New York: Tauris Academic Studies, 1995.

——. "Labor and the State in the Ottoman Empire during the Nineteenth Century." Unpublished paper, n.d.

——. "Machine Breaking and the Changing Carpet Industry of Western Anatolia, 1860-1908." *Journal of Social History* 16 (spring 1986): 473-89.

——, ed. *Manufacturing in the Ottoman Empire and Turkey, 1500-1950.* Albany: State Univ. of New York Press, 1994.

——. *Ottoman Manufacturing in the Age of the Industrial Revolution.* Cambridge, U.K.: Cambridge Univ. Press, 1993.

——. "Ottoman Manufacturing in the Nineteenth Century." In *Manufacturing in the Ottoman Empire and Turkey, 1500-1950,* edited by Donald Quataert, 87-122. Albany: State Univ. of New York Press, 1994.

——. "Ottoman Women, Households, and Textile Manufacturing: 1800-1914." In *Women in Middle Eastern History: Shifting Boundaries in Sex and Gender,* edited by Nikki R. Keddie and Beth Baron, 161–76. New Haven, Conn.: Yale Univ. Press, 1991.

———. "Ottoman Workers and the State, 1826–1914." In *Workers and Working Classes in the Middle East: Struggles, Histories, Historiography*, edited by Zachary Lockman, 21–40. Albany: State Univ. of New York Press, 1994.

———. *Social Disintegration and Popular Resistance in the Ottoman Empire, 1882–1908: Reaction to European Economic Penetration*. New York: New York Univ. Press, 1983.

———. "Social History of Labor in the Ottoman Empire, c. 1800–1914." Unpublished paper, n.d.

Quataert, Donald, and Erik Jan Zurcher, eds. *Workers and the Working Class in the Ottoman Empire and the Turkish Republic: 1839–1950*. New York: Tauris Academic Studies, 1995.

Quataert, Jean. "An Approach to Modern Labor: Worker Peasantries in Historic Saxony and the Friuli Region over Three Centuries." *Comparative Study of Society and History* 28 (1986): 191–216.

———. "Combining Agrarian and Industrial Livelihood: Rural Households in the Saxon Oberlausitz in the Nineteenth Century." *Journal of Family History* 10 (summer 1985): 145–61.

———. "A New Look at Working-Class Formation: Reflections on the Historical Perspective." *International Labor and Working Class History* 27 (spring 1985): 72–76.

———. "A New View of Industrialization: 'Protoindustry' or the Role of Small-Scale, Labor-Intensive Manufacture in the Capitalist Environment." *International Labor and Working Class History* 33 (spring 1988): 3–22.

———. "The Shaping of Women's Work in Manufacturing: Guilds, Households, and the State in Central Europe, 1648–1870." *American Historical Review* 90 (Dec. 1985): 1122–48.

Qubain, Fahim. *Crisis in Lebanon*. Washington, D.C.: Middle East Institute, 1961.

Randal, Jonathan. *The Tragedy of Lebanon: Christian Warlords, Israeli Adventurers, and American Bunglers*. London: Hogarth Press, 1983.

Rassam, Amal, ed. *Social Science Research and Women in the Arab World*. Paris: United Nations Educational, Scientific, and Cultural Organization, 1984.

Reid, Elizabeth. "Women at a Standstill: The Need for Radical Change." *International Labour Review* 111 (June 1975): 459–68.

Richard, Nelly. "Postmodernism and Periphery." *Third Text* 11 (1987–88): 24–49.

Richards, Alan, and John Waterbury. *A Political Economy of the Middle East: State, Class, and Economic Development*. Boulder, Colo.: Westview Press, 1990.

Rihani, May. "Women and Work in Morocco." In *Women and Work in the Third World: The Impact of Industrialization and Global Economic Interdependence,* edited by Nagat M. El-Sanabary, 193–98. Berkeley: Center for the Study, Education, and Advancement of Women, Univ. of California, 1983.

Rizkallah-Boulad, Magda. "La Régie des Tabacs et son syndicat." *Travaux et Jours* 44 (July–Sept. 1972): 47–73.

Rosaldo, Michelle Z., and Louis Lamphere, eds. *Women, Culture, and Society.* Stanford, Calif.: Stanford Univ. Press, 1974.

Rossillion, C. "Cultural Pluralism, Equality of Treatment, and Equality of Opportunity in the Lebanon." *International Labour Review* 98, no. 3 (Sept. 1968): 225–44.

Rothstein, Frances Abrahmer, and Michael L. Blim, eds. *Anthropology and the Global Factory: Studies in the New Industrialization in the Late Twentieth Century.* New York: Bergin and Garvey, 1992.

Rowbotham, Sheila, and Sawsti Mitter, eds. *Dignity and Daily Bread: New Forms of Economic Organizing among Poor Women in the Third World.* London: Routledge, 1994.

Saba, Paul. "The Creation of the Lebanese Economy: Economic Growth in the Nineteenth and Twentieth Centuries." In *Essays on the Crisis in Lebanon,* edited by Roger Owen, 1–22. London: Ithaca Press, 1976.

Said, Edward W. *Culture and Imperialism.* London: A. A. Knopf, 1991.

———. *Orientalism.* New York: Vintage Books, 1978.

Said, Hakim Mohammad, ed. *The Employer and the Employee: Islamic Concept.* Karachi, Pakistan: Dar al-Fikr al-Islami, 1972.

Salaff, Janet, and Aline Wong. "Women's Work: Factory, Family, and Social Class in an Industrializing Order." In *Women and Work in the Third World: The Impact of Industrialization and Global Economic Interdependence,* edited by Nagat M. El-Sanabary, 215–34. Berkeley: Center for the Study, Education, and Advancement of Women, Univ. of California, 1983.

Salem, Elie Adib. *Modernization Without a Revolution: Lebanon's Experience.* Bloomington: Indiana Univ. Press, 1973.

Salem, Elise. "Imagining Lebanon Through Rahbani Musicals." *Al-Jadid* 5, no. 29 (fall 1999): 4–6.

Salibi, Kamal. *Crossroads to Civil War: Lebanon 1958–1976.* New York: Caravan Books, 1976.

———. *A House of Many Mansions: The History of Lebanon Reconsidered.* Berkeley and Los Angeles: Univ. of California Press, 1988.

————. "The Lebanese Crisis in Perspective." *Third World Today* 9 (1958): 214–49.

————. *The Modern History of Lebanon.* New York: Praeger, 1965.

Salih, Mohammed. "The Lebanese Regie of Tobaccos and Tambacs: Current Problems and Recommended Solutions." Master's thesis, American Univ. of Beirut, 1990.

Salim, Salim. "Political Significance of Labor Conditions in Iraq, Egypt, and Lebanon," Ph.D. diss., Univ. of Southern California, Los Angeles, 1958.

Salvatore, Nick. *Eugene V. Debs: Citizen and Socialist.* Urbana: Univ. of Illinois, 1982.

————. "Response to Sean Wilentz, 'Against Exceptionalism: Class Consciousness and the American Labor Movement, 1790–1920.'" *International Labor and Working Class History* (fall 1984): 25.

Samuell, Edward W., Jr. "A Contribution to the Study of Lebanese Labor Syndicates." Master's thesis, American Univ. of Beirut, 1952.

El-Sanabary, Nagat M. "Introduction." In *Women and Work in the Third World: The Impact of Industrialization and Global Economic Interdependence,* edited by Nagat M. El-Sanabary, viii–xvi. Berkeley: Center for the Study, Education, and Advancement of Women, Univ. of California, 1983.

————, ed. *Women and Work in the Third World: The Impact of Industrialization and Global Economic Independence.* Berkeley: Center for the Study, Education, and Advancement of Women, Univ. of California, 1983.

Sapolsky, Steven. "Response to Sean Wilentz's 'Against Exceptionalism.'" *International Labor and Working-Class History* 27 (spring 1985): 35–37.

Sayigh, Rosemary. "Roles and Functions of Arab Women: A Reappraisal." *Arab Studies Quarterly* 111 (autumn 1981): 102–24.

Sayigh, Yusif. *Entrepreneurs of Lebanon.* Cambridge, Mass.: Harvard Univ. Press, 1962.

————. "Lebanon: Special Economic Problems Arising from a Special Structure." *Middle East Economic Papers* (1957): 60–88.

————. "Management-Labor Relations in Selected Arab Countries: Major Aspects and Determinants." *International Labour Review* 77 (Jan.–June 1958): 519–37.

Schneider de Villegas, Gisela. "Home Work: A Case for Social Protection." *International Labour Review* 129 (1990): 423–39.

Scott, Alison. "Informal Sector or Female Sector: Male Bias in Urban Labor Market Models." In *Male Bias in Development Process,* edited by Diane Elson, 105–32. New York: Manchester Univ. Press, 1991.

Scott, James. *Weapons of the Weak: Everyday Forms of Peasant Resistance.* New Haven, Conn.: Yale Univ. Press, 1985.

Scott, Joan W. "Gender: A Useful Category of Historical Analysis." *American Historical Review* 91 (Dec. 1986): 1053–75.

————. "On Language, Gender, and Working-Class History." *International Labor and Working-Class History* 31 (spring 1987): 1–13.

Scott, Joan W., and Louise A. Tilly. "Women's Work and the Family in Nineteenth-Century Europe." *Comparative Studies in Society and History* 17, no. 1 (Jan. 1975): 36–64.

Seguert, Marie-Claire. "Women and Working Conditions: Prospects for Improvement." *International Labour Review* 122 (May–June 1982): 295–311.

Sewell, William H., Jr. "Artisans, Factory Workers, and the Formation of the French Working Class, 1789–1848." In *Working Class Formation: Nineteenth-Century Patterns in Western Europe and the United States,* edited by Ira Katznelson and Aristide Zolberg, 45–70. Princeton, N.J.: Princeton Univ. Press, 1986.

————. *Work and Revolution in France: The Language of Labor from the Old Regime to 1848.* New York: Cambridge Univ. Press, 1980.

Shalaq, Al-Fadl. "Concepts of Nation and State with Special Reference to the Sunnis in Lebanon." In *State and Society in Syria and Lebanon,* edited by Youssef M. Choueiri, 120–29. New York: St. Martin's Press, 1994.

Shararah, Yolla. "Women and Politics in Lebanon." *Khamsin* 6 (1978): 6–15.

Skocpol, Theda, ed. *Vision and Method in Historical Sociology.* New York: Cambridge Univ. Press, 1984.

Smilianskaia, Irina M. "From Subsistence to Market Economy, 1850s: Razlozhenie feodalnikh otnoshenii v Sirii i Livane v seredine XIX v" (The Disintegration of Feudal Relations in Syria and Lebanon in the Middle of the Nineteenth Century). In *The Economic History of the Middle East, 1800–1914: A Book of Readings,* edited by Charles Issawi, 226–47. Chicago: Univ. of Chicago Press, 1966.

Smith, Anthony. *Theories of Nationalism.* London: Duckworth, 1971.

Smith, Steve. "Class and Gender: Women's Strikes in St. Petersburg, 1895–1917, and in Shanghai, 1895–1927." *Social History* 19, no. 2 (May 1994): 141–68.

————. "Workers and Supervisors in St. Petersburg, 1906–Oct. 1917, and Shanghai, 1895–Mar. 1927." *Past and Present* (1993): 159–65.

Smitka, Michael, ed. *The Textile Industry and the Rise of the Japanese Economy.* New York: Garland, 1998.

Standing, Guy. "Education and Female Participation in the Labour Force." *International Labour Review* 114 (1976): 281–97.

Stauffer, Thomas B. "The Industrial Worker." In *Social Forces in the Middle East,* edited by Sydney Nettleton Fisher, 83–98. New York: Cornell Univ. Press, 1955.

Stowasser, Barbara Freyer. "Liberated Equal or Protected Dependent? Contemporary Religious Paradigms on Women's Status in Islam." *Arab Studies Quarterly* 9 (summer 1987): 260–83.

Strickland, Susan. "Feminism, Postmodernism, and Difference." In *Knowing the Difference: Feminist Perspective in Epistemology*, edited by Kathleen Lennon and Margaret Whitford, 265–74. New York: Routledge, 1994.

Stubbs, Jean. *Tobacco on the Periphery: A Case Study in Cuban Labour History, 1860–1958*. Cambridge, U.K.: Cambridge Univ. Press, 1985.

Stycos, Mayone J. *Human Fertility in Latin America: Sociological Perspective*. Ithaca, N.Y.: Cornell Univ. Press, 1968.

Suleiman, Michael W. "Crisis and Revolution in Lebanon." *Middle East Journal* 26 (winter 1972): 11–24.

———. "The Lebanese Communist Party." *Middle Eastern Studies* 3 (Jan. 1967): 134–59.

———. *Political Parties in Lebanon*. Ithaca, N.Y.: Cornell Univ. Press, 1967.

Tannous, Afif. "Social Change in an Arab Village." *American Sociological Review* 6 (1941): 650–62.

Taraboulsi, Fawwaz. *A History of Modern Lebanon*. London: Pluto Press, 2007.

Tarazi Fawaz, Leila. *Merchants and Migrants in Nineteenth Century Beirut*. Cambridge, Mass.: Harvard Univ. Press, 1983.

———. *An Occasion for War: Civil Conflict in Lebanon and Damascus in 1860*. London: Center for Lebanese Studies, 1994.

Terrell, Katherine. "Female-Male Earnings Differentials and Occupational Structure." *International Labour Review* 129 (1992): 387–404.

Thobie, Jacques. *Intérêts et impérialisme français dans l'Empire Ottoman, 1895–1914*. Paris: Impérial Nationale, 1977.

Thompson, Edward P. *The Making of the English Working Class*. New York: Vintage Books, 1966.

Thompson, Elizabeth. *Colonial Citizens: Republican Rights, Paternal Privilege, and Gender in French Syria and Lebanon*. New York: Columbia Univ. Press, 2000.

Tilley, Nannie M. *The Bright Tobacco Industry, 1860–1929*. Chapel Hill: Univ. of North Carolina Press, 1948.

Tilly, Charles. *Big Structures, Large Processes, Huge Comparisons*. New York: Russell Sage Foundation, 1985.

Tilly, Louise, and Joan W. Scott. *Women, Work, and Family*. New York: Holt, Rinehart and Winston, 1978.

Tucker, Judith E. "Egyptian Women in the Work Force: A Historical Survey." *MERIP Reports* 50 (Aug. 1976): 3–9, 26–28.

———. "Problems in the Historiography of Women in the Middle East: The Case of Nineteenth-Century Egypt." *International Journal of Middle East Studies* 15 (Aug. 1983): 320–36.

Tucker, Robert, ed. *The Lenin Anthology.* New York: Norton, 1975.

Tueni, Ghassan. *Une guerre pour les autres.* Paris: J. C. Lattes, 1985.

United Nations Educational, Scientific, and Cultural Organization (UNESCO). *Social Science Research and Women in the Arab World.* Paris: UNESCO, 1984.

Van Dusen, Roxanne A. "Changing Women's Role and Family Planning in Lebanon." In *Culture, Natality, and Family Planning,* edited by John F. Marshall and Steven Polgar, 79–97. Chapel Hill, N.C.: Carolina Population Center, 1976.

Van Horn, Susan Householder. *Women, Work, and Fertility, 1900–1986.* New York: New York Univ. Press, 1988.

Van Leeuwen, Richard. *Notables and Clergy in Mount Lebanon: The Khazin Sheiks and the Maronite Church.* Leiden: E. J. Brill, 1994.

Vatter, Sherry. "Journeymen Textile Weavers' Lives in Nineteenth Century Damascus: A Collective Biography." In *Struggle and Survival in Modern Middle East,* edited by Edmund Burke III, 64–79. Berkeley and Los Angeles: Univ. of California Press, 1993.

———. "Militant Textile Weavers in Damascus: Waged Artisans and the Ottoman Labor Movement, 1850–1914." In *Workers and the Working Class in the Ottoman Empire and the Turkish Republic: 1839–1950,* edited by Donald Quataert and Erik Jan Zurcher, 35–58. New York: Tauris Academic Studies, 1995.

Wallerstein, Immanuel. *Historical Capitalism.* London: Verso, 1987.

———, ed. *Labor in the World Social Structure.* Beverly Hills, Calif.: Sage, 1983.

———. *Unthinking Social Science: The Limits of Nineteenth-Century Paradigms.* Cambridge, U.K.: Polity Press, 1991.

Weiss, Anita M. "Women and Factory Work in Punjab, Pakistan." In *Women and Work in the Third World: The Impact of Industrialization and Global Economic Interdependence,* edited by Nagat M. El-Sanabary, 207–14. Berkeley: Center for the Study, Education, and Advancement of Women, Univ. of California, 1983.

Werneke, Diane. "The Economic Slowdown and Women's Employment Opportunities." *International Labour Review* 117 (1978): 37–52.

White, Mary C. "Improving the Welfare of Women Factory Workers: Lessons from Indonesia." *International Labour Review* 129 (1990): 121–33.

White, Jenny B. *Money Makes Us Relatives: Women's Labor in Urban Turkey.* Austin: Univ. of Texas Press, 1994.

Wilentz, Sean. "Against Exceptionalism: Class Consciousness and the American Labor Movement." *International Labor and Working Class History* 26 (fall 1984): 1–24.

Wolfgang, Mommsen F. "The Varieties of the Nation State in Modern History: Liberal, Imperialist, Fascist, and Contemporary Notions of Nation and Nationality." In *The*

Rise and Decline of the Nation-State, edited by Michael Mann, 210–26. Cambridge, U.K.: Blackwell, 1990.

"Women's Work in the Lebanon." *International Labour Review* 58 (Sept. 1948): 395.

Woodsmall, Ruth F. *Study of the Role of Women: Their Activities and Organizations in Lebanon, Egypt, Iraq, Jordan, and Syria.* New York: International Federation of Business and Professional Women, 1956.

"Working Conditions in Handicrafts and Modern Industry in Syria." *International Labour Review* 29 (Mar. 1934): 407–11.

Wright, Erik O. *Class Structure and Income Determination.* New York: Academic Press, 1979.

———. "Varieties of Marxist Conceptions of Class Structure." *Politics and Society* 9 (1980): 333–70.

Wrobel, David M. *The End of American Exceptionalism: Frontier Anxiety from the Old West to the New Deal.* Lawrence: Univ. Press of Kansas, 1993.

Yacoub, George T. "The Régie Libanaise des Tabacs et Tombacs: An Economic and Organizational Appraisal." Master's thesis, American Univ. of Beirut, 1972.

Yamazawa, Ippei. "Raw-Silk Exports and Japanese Economic Development." In *The Textile Industry and the Rise of the Japanese Economy,* edited by Michael Smitka, 301–18. New York: Garland, 1998.

Yaukey, David. *Fertility Differences in a Modernizing Country: A Survey of Lebanese Couples.* Princeton, N.J.: Princeton Univ. Press, 1961.

———. *Marriage Reduction and Fertility.* Lanham, Md.: Lexington Books, 1973.

Youssef, Nadia Haggag. *Women and Work in Developing Societies.* Berkeley, Calif.: Institute of International Studies, 1974.

Ziadeh, Nicola. "The Lebanese Elections, 1960." *Middle East Journal* 24 (1960): 367–81.

Zurayk, Huda. "A Two Stage Analysis of the Determinants of Fertility in Rural South Lebanon." *Population Studies* 33 (Nov. 1979): 489–504.

Zurayk, Huda, and Haroutune K. Armenian, eds. *Beirut 1984: A Population and Health Profile.* Beirut: American Univ. of Beirut, 1985.

Zurcher, Erik Jan. "Preface." In *Workers and the Working Class in the Ottoman Empire and the Turkish Republic, 1839–1950,* edited by Donald Quataert and Erik Jan Zurcher, 7–10. New York: Tauris Academic Studies, 1995.

Index

Page numbers in italics indicate illustrations and tables.

106, 218n46; rural, 47–48, 90, 99–101,
123, 142
Eden, Anthony, 214n92
education, 38–40, 101
Egypt, 11, 14, 194n42, 195n46, 199n57
Eid, Joseph, 23
elections (Lebanon, 1943), 73
electricity company strike (1946), 69, 211n43,
212n48
elite women. *See* upper-class women
emigration, 101–2, 122
employees' law (Nizam al-Muwazaffin, 1959),
119, 120
employment discrimination, xxix, 192n23.
See also gender inequality
Entelis, John, 158
Entra Bank, 159
ethnic groups, 222n77
Europe, waged labor in, 50–51, 52, 53
European society. *See* Western society
evening jobs, 118, 222nn6–7
executive power, 219n56

factory girl (*shirkawiyya*), 11
factory work. *See* industrial labor; waged
labor
Fahs, 'Adnan, 216n19, 217n26
Fahs, Hani, 7
fair compensation, 19–20
family: Bayhum on, 38; opposition to
industrial labor, 117, 134, 135–36, 139,
183; waged labor and, 38, 52–53, 208n62;
women writers on, 40. *See also* households; kinship systems
family-based economic activities. *See* domestic labor
family clusters, 111–14, 136–40, 183, 225n62;
strike of 1965 and, 173–74, 232–33n136;
workforce statistics (1954–69), 227n19;

workforce statistics (1954–81), *112;* workingwomen and, 149, 177
family grants, 120
family size, 52–53, 208n62
Faris, Edmund, 214n93
farmers. *See* agricultural workers
al-farz department. *See* sorting (*al-farz*)
department
fasting, 160–61, 163–64, 166, 168, 173,
230nn–70, 230n72
Fatima N., 174
female radicalism. *See* radicalization
female workers. *See* workingwomen
feminism: activism, 41, 45; cultural distinctiveness of, 38; identity of, 45; solidarity
of, 54; upper- vs. working-class, 36, 55,
180; on waged labor, 41, 52, 54. *See also*
Arab Feminist Union
financial sector, 106, 218n50
Food and Agricultural Organization, 89
food production, 4, 6–7, 123, 127, 196n5
forced migration (*muhajjar*), 103, 104, 115,
218n42
foreign companies. *See* concessionary
companies
foreign workers, 122–23, 143, 184
France, 38
Franco, Francisco, 158
Free France, 59–60
Free Nationalists Party, 184
free professions, 47, 207n43
French colonial period: activism against,
xxviii, 36, 44–45, 73, 87, 180; Communist
Party and, 73; concessionary companies
and, xix, 64, 66, 69, 210n20; economic system of, xv; experiences of, 35–36; Grand
Liban formed, 4; industrialization and, 19;
industrial labor, 118; labor law and, 59–60,
62, 91, 118; labor movement in, 146;
mechanization and, 17; Mutasarrifiyya

French colonial period (*cont.*)
and, xvii, 4, 195n2; nationalism and, 55;
nationalist uprising against, 55, 66; peasant revolts against, 18, 200n81; tobacco
monopoly and, xix, 20–22, 200–201n97;
tobacco tariffs in, xviii; transition to
Lebanese nationhood, xvi, 69, 86, 91–92,
180, 211n42; UN resolution on, 67; women
writers on, 35. *See also* independence
French Communist Party, 73

GCFUWE. *See* General Confederation of the
Unions of Workers and Employees
Gemayel, Joseph, 25
Gemayyel, Pierre, 158–59, 166
gender differences, xxiii, 125
gender discrimination. *See* gender inequality
gendered consciousness, 178, 185–86
gender equality: conservative voices on, 168;
demand for, 145; economic liberalism and,
xxiii, xxiv; middle-class men on, 39; sectarianism and, 178; working class and, 164
gender identity, xxii, 186
gender inequality: of administrative employees,
94; Communists and, xxvi, 74–75, 182,
213n65; in division of labor, 36; hiring practices and, 121–24; in households, 43–44; in
industrial labor, 124–25, 143; job permanency and, 85, 87; labor law and, 119–20;
in Lebanese society, 166–67; mechanization
and, 117, 123, 126, 184; militancy against,
xvi; silk industry and, 10; strike of 1965
and, 166–70; tobacco workers and, 133–36,
224n56; in wages, 147, 155–56, 163–64,
166–68, 217n26; in workforce representation, 93–95, 114–15, 215nn8–9
gender roles: in agrarian society, 195n3;
case studies of women workers and, 134;
Lebanese Civil War and, 116; Lebanese

government and, 167; in nineteenth
century, 179–80; in Rahbani Brothers
musicals, 111; tribal-ethnic states and, 78.
See also women's role
General Confederation of the Unions of
Workers and Employees (GCFUWE, Al-
Ittihad al-'Am li-Naqabat al-'Ummal wa
al-Mustakhdamin fi Lubnan): Communist Party and, 73–74; demands of, 87–88;
formation of, 64; al-Khouri case and,
83–84; Labor Front and, 79, 213n84; labor
law and, 64–68; militancy and, 72
general strikes, 67, 79–80, 214n86
General Trade Union of Tobacco Workers
(GTUTW, Al-Naqaba al-'Amma li 'Ummal
al-Tabigh fi Lubnan), 17, 200n80, 209n2
Georgette H., 65, 139
Georgette N., 139
Ghanim family, 113
al-Gharib, Antun, 233n147
al-Ghassani family, 113
Ghaziyya plant, *93*, 93–94, 107
Ghurayyib, Rose, 52
girls. *See* child labor
"Goddess of the House" status, 10–11
Gran, Peter, xxi, xxiii, xxiv, 78
Grand Liban, xvi, 4, 23, 24, 92
Great Britain, 59–60, 81, 214n92
Greater Syria, 1
Greek Orthodox, 95, *95*, 112
GTUTW (General Trade Union of Tobacco
Workers; Al-Naqaba al-'Amma li 'Ummal
al-Tabigh fi Lubnan), 17, 200n80, 209n2

Hadath plant, *149, 154, 155, 181*; activism, 90–91; administrative employees,
226n1; Khunaysir/Zalzal encounter,
160–61, 230n70, 230n72; Lebanese army
deployment, 169–70; Lebanese Civil

War and, 130; sectarian and regional representation, 89–90; sorting department, *157*; strike of 1963 incident, 153–55, 165, 228n41; strike of 1965 and, 160–61, 169–70, 175; strikes and protests, 90–91, 96–98; transfers to, 147–48; workforce age stratification, 96–97, *97*; workforce family clusters and kinship, 111–14, *112*, 183; workforce regional representation, *103*, 103–4, 114–15; workforce sectarian and gender characteristics, 93–94, 114–15

Haffar, Ikram, 119–20

Hama, West Syria, 42

Hamid, Hasan, 172

Hammam, Mona, 132

handicraft production. *See* cottage industry

Haniya A., 139

Hanna Chikhani plant, 203n128

Hannih D., 196n5

Harfush, 'Abdul 'Aziz, 171, 172, 174, 232n124

harvest days, 7

Al-Hasna' (The Beauty) (magazine), 37

Hawi, George, 172

Al-Hayat (newspaper), 158, 171

Haydar family, 112

Hayik, Sa'id, 132, 230n69

Haykal, Joseph, 14

health insurance, 119, 120, 130–31

health issues: industrial labor and, 39; labor law on, 120, 222n13; in rural areas, 101, 216n14; for tobacco workers, 31–32, *32*

Helou, Charles, 107, 156, 159, 168–69

Hilu family, 112

hiring practices, 121–24, 138, 139

Hobsbawm, Eric, xxix, 195n46, 226n1

holidays, religious, 169

"homeland, mothers of the," 40

Homs, West Syria, 42, 43

honor, 41

Hourani, Albert, 68, 211n38

households: destruction by Western society, 39; domestic economy, 5–7, 9, 53, 104, 133; gender inequality in, 43–44; primacy of women in, 38–39. *See also* domestic labor

"House" status, 10–11

Hubayqa, George, 224n49

Hubayqa, Najim, 76

Hunayn, Edward, 173, 232n134

Huriya I, 139

Husayn (imam), 196n5

al-Husayni, 'Ali Nasir, 214n93

Hyde, Janet, 127

Ibrahim, Emily, 206n17

Ibrahim, Warda Butrus, *76*, 76–77, 78–79, 80, 213n71, 214n88

identification papers, 128, 141

identity: citizenship and, 181; class, xxii, 180; feminist, 45; gender, xxii, 186; industrial labor and, 180; national, 110, 221n68; proto-nationalist, 1; working class, 113, 145, 180

ideology, political, 90, 105–7

illegal workers, 218n47

illiteracy, 100–101

'illiyi, 111

iltizam (broker) system, 130

imprisoned workers, 174

In'am A., 50, 141–42

income. *See* wages

income taxes, 65

independence: British-French relations and, 59–60; Communist Party and, 73; declaration of, 60, 211n42; historical texts on, 60, 209n5; labor unrest and, xxviii, 57; transition to, xvi, 69, 86, 91–92, 180, 211n42

India, 222n77

individualism, 38

industrialization, xxiv, 19, 160. *See also* mechanization

waged labor: by Algerian women, 101;
'Azzam on, 54; class variations in,
36; cultural meaning of, 126–27; in
Europe, 50–51, 52; family and, 38,
52–53; family size and, 52–53, 208n62;
labor statistics and, 123; Lebanese Civil
War and, 116–17; lower-class women
and, 36, 55; *Al-Mar'a al-Jadida* on, 41,
205–6n17, 205n17; in Ottoman Empire,
6, 196–97n15; Ottoman women and, 6;
by peasant women, 49–54; in Rahbani
Brothers' musicals, 111; social factors
and, 51–52, 53–54, 142; statistics on
(1950s–1970), 46, 47–49; to supplement
agricultural labor, 50–52; traditional
roles and, 124–25; Western society on,
56; women's participation in, 196–97n15;
women's role in, 36; women writers on,
40. *See also* industrial labor
wages: of agricultural workers, 99–101;
domestic economy and, 5; gender
inequality in, 147, 155–56, 163–64,
166–68, 217n26; for industrial labor, 99,
100, 104; for men, 10, 16, 100, 198n39,
217n26; minimum, 163–64, 166–68, 173,
176, 184; Shi'i Muslims, 100–101; silk
industry, 10, 198n39; tobacco industry
(1930s), 16; tobacco industry (1970s),
217n26; weaving industry, *16*
watan, 40
weaving industry, *16*
welfare system, 158
Western society, 37, 39, 41, 42, 56
Whaiba W., 140
What a Failure (*Shi Fashil*) (play), 109–10
white-collar workers. *See* administrative
employees
wildcat strikes, 148, 156, 229n52
Woman's Chamber, A (*Al-Khidr*) (magazine), 37

women: biographical sketches of, 206n17;
education for, 38–40; food production by,
6–7, 196n5; as "Goddess of the House,"
10–11; as "House," 10–11; illiteracy of,
101; perception of skills, 121–24, 143;
population of (1925), 205n16; subordination of, 39, 133
women's history, 36–37
women's liberation, 168
women's role: in domestic economy, 5–7,
133; male thinkers on, 38–39; in market
economy, 36; traditional, 124–25; in
waged labor, 36; women writers on, 39–40
women writers, 35, 37–42, 55; biographical
sketches of, 206n17; magazines by, 37,
40–42, 204n4, 205–6n17; on male protests, 39–40; on modernization, 38, 40; on
nationalism, 38; workingwomen and, 180
wood, 198n42
Woodsmall, Ruth F., 209n68
workforce (national): age of, 127–28, *128;*
census (1970), 48–49, *49;* distribution by
economic activity, 105–6, *106;* foreign
workers and, 122–23; history (1950s–
1970), 47–49; Lebanese Civil War and,
122; by occupation, 49, *49,* 121; percentage of women in Arab countries, 123–24,
223n31; statistics on (1950s–1970), 46;
statistics on (1970–85), 121–23. *See also*
silk industry; tobacco workers
work hours, 62, 81
working class: anticolonialism and, xxviii;
Communist Party and, 73; gender equality and, 164; identity, 113, 145, 180; informal networks and, 137–38; militancy, 186;
nationalism and, 60; political ideology
and, 105; radicalization of, 195n46; in
urban areas, 117; waged labor and, 142
working conditions, 3–4, 61–62, 119, 125,
210n5